CORPOREALITY IN EARLY CINEMA

EARLY CINEMA IN REVIEW:
PROCEEDINGS OF DOMITOR

CORPOREALITY IN EARLY CINEMA

Viscera, Skin, and Physical Form

Edited by Marina Dahlquist, Doron Galili,
Jan Olsson, and Valentine Robert

Indiana University Press

This book is a publication of

Indiana University Press
Office of Scholarly Publishing
Herman B Wells Library 350
1320 East 10th Street
Bloomington, Indiana 47405 USA

iupress.indiana.edu

© 2018 by Domitor

All rights reserved
No part of this book may be reproduced or utilized in any form or by any means, electronic or mechanical, including photocopying and recording, or by any information storage and retrieval system, without permission in writing from the publisher. The paper used in this publication meets the minimum requirements of the American National Standard for Information Sciences—Permanence of Paper for Printed Library Materials, ANSI Z39.48-1992.

Manufactured in the United States of America

Cataloging information is available from the Library of Congress.

ISBN 978-0-253-03365-9 (pbk.)
ISBN 978-0-253-03366-6 (web PDF)

1 2 3 4 5   23 22 21 20 19 18

Contents

General Introduction   *1*
Marina Dahlquist, Doron Galili, Jan Olsson, and Valentine Robert

Part I: Impossible Bodies   *11*

   Introduction   *11*

  1 The Impossible Body of Early Film   *13*
     Tom Gunning

  2 Ovidian Violence: George Méliès's Explosive Screen Bodies   *25*
     Vito Adriaensens

  3 The Body under the Scalpel in the Illustrated Press and the Cinema   *35*
     Jérémy Houillère, Translated by Timothy Barnard

  4 Ghosts and Their Nationality in the Fin de Siècle Machinery   *46*
     Ian Christie

Part II: Inventories of the Body   *59*

   Introduction   *59*

  5 Field Trip to Insanity: Bodies and Minds in the Dr. Maestre Film Collection (Spain, 1915)   *61*
     Luis Alonso García, Daniel Sánchez-Salas, and Begoña Soto-Vázquez

  6 The Celluloid Specimens: Animal Origins for the Moving Image   *74*
     Benjamin Schultz-Figueroa

  7 Death by a Thousand Cuts: On-Screen Executions in Early American Cinema   *85*
     Gary D. Rhodes

8   Staged Bodies, Caged Bodies: Early Cinema in the Age
    of Human Zoos   94
    Rodolphe Gahéry, Translated by Timothy Barnard

9   "Stills from a Film That Is Missing": Indigenous Images
    and the Photographic Interval in Early Cinema   103
    Joanna Hearne

Part III: Performing Bodies   117

    Introduction   117

10 Risky Business: The Early Film Actor and Discourses of Danger   119
    Charlie Keil and Denise McKenna

11 Bodies in Motion: Dancing and Boxing in Early
    Norwegian Cinema   134
    Gunnar Iversen

12 The Beauty of the *Forzuti*: Irresistible Male Bodies
    On- and Offscreen   146
    Ivo Blom

13 Nudity in Early Cinema; or, the Pictorial Transgression   156
    Valentine Robert

14 Paul Capellani: The Body Put to the Test by Cinema   167
    Sébastien Dupont-Bloch, Translated by Timothy Barnard

Part IV: Bodily Features   173

    Introduction   173

15 Hair and Hairiness in Early Cinema   175
    Jean-Claude Seguin, Translated by Timothy Barnard

16 Lumière Agents in Mexico: The "Body" of Film as a
    Late-Nineteenth-Century Discourse   181
    John Fullerton

17 Breathing Faces, Twinkling Eyes: On the Cinematic Visage in
    Russian Films of the 1910s   191
    Oksana Chefranova

| 18 | Making Faces: Character and Makeup in Early Cinema | 206 |
| | Alice Maurice | |

Part V: Embodied Audiences — 219

Introduction — 219

| 19 | "Keep It Dark": The Fatale Attraction of the Female Viewer's Body | 221 |
| | Mireille Berton | |

| 20 | "The Best Synonym of Youth": G. Stanley Hall, Mimetic Play, and Early Cinema's Embodied Youth Spectator | 231 |
| | Christina Petersen | |

| 21 | Perils of Cinema? The German Cinema Debate and the "Nerve-Racking" Medium | 240 |
| | Stephanie Werder | |

| 22 | "The Taste of the Moment Seems All for 'Pictures'": Irish Historical Bodies before the Early Cinema Screen | 249 |
| | Denis Condon | |

Part VI: Bodies in Exhibition Spaces — 261

Introduction — 261

| 23 | The Viewer's Body in Motion: Physical and Virtual Effects of Three-Dimensional Spectacles | 263 |
| | Martin Barnier, Translated by Timothy Barnard | |

| 24 | Moving the Spectator, Dancing with the Screen: Early Dance Instruction Films and Reconfigurations of Film Spectatorship in the 1910s | 275 |
| | Kristina Köhler | |

| 25 | A Rational and Entertaining Species of Amusement to Bipeds of All Ages: The Splendid Camera Obscura | 289 |
| | Alison Reiko Loader | |

Appendix: Original French Texts — 301

| 26 | Le corps sous le scalpel de la presse illustrée et du cinéma | 303 |
| | Jérémy Houillère | |

27 Corps mis en scène, corps mis en cage: Le cinématographe
   au temps des zoos humains 314
   Rodolphe Gahéry

28 Paul Capellani: Le corps à l'épreuve du cinéma 323
   Sébastien Dupont-Bloch

29 Poils et pilosités dans le cinéma des origines 329
   Jean-Claude Seguin

30 Le corps du spectateur en mouvement: Effets réels et virtuels
   des spectacles tridimensionnels 336
   Martin Barnier

   Index 349

CORPOREALITY IN EARLY CINEMA

General Introduction

Marina Dahlquist, Doron Galili, Jan Olsson, and Valentine Robert

SCREENED BODIES ARE at the crosshairs of all cinemas—whether glorious or grotesque, mundane or majestic, dressed or disrobed; impossible, improbable, or imperiled; "deviant," "normal," or spectral; and across the panoramas of ethnicities, skin colors, sexualities, and ages. Mediated bodies and the bodies watching them provide the focal point for this collection, its explorative punctum. Films and film cultures have been studied from an array of productive vantage points. Within the framework of modernity, such studies situate cinema as a key strand of modern life and its convoluted hardships, bounteous pleasures, displacements of space, temporal multiplicities, and everyday lives. Historiographic models for studying cinema rarely offer an explicit attention to the meanings that screen bodies and bodies in attendance convey—and their interdependencies and manners of intersecting. The collection of essays presented here interrogates mediated corporeality within the larger sphere of screen practices and visual technologies, as well as their theories—and mainly during a time frame before 1915.

Clearly, film and media scholarship have often been bodily inclined, but predominantly in indirect ways. Why, then, does the body merit attention as a prime and explicit critical notion for early cinema at this particular moment in historiography and theory? The need for a body-focused collection can be gauged by the absence of this keyword in two recent volumes: *Keywords for Media Studies* and *Keywords for American Cultural Studies*.[1] No "body" can be found among the lists of entry terms; instead, we find related notions such as affect, audience, gaze, gender, identity, intersectionality, mass, othering, personalization, queer, race, and many more. As the following group of essays evidences, an explicit awareness of the body as punctum and connectivity helps us better understand the many attractions of early cinema as a productive domain for studying modernity and its intertwined historiographies and theories. More generally, early cinema in its many varieties can, of course, be read as an encyclopedic archive for bodies in motion across all aspects of everyday life and its fictions.

This volume, hence, aims at inspiring a heightened awareness of film culture, and screen practices overall, as inherently embodied as well as inherently intermedial. Here the body is a bundle of flesh and nerves on- and offscreen (and in "affiliated" media and technological constellations), not an abstract spectator, not a mere statistical audience entity. At the same time, the studies included here are mindful of early cinema's place alongside multiple screen practices and medial configurations, taking into account how the films work within and in relation to media and technologies that altered the embodied experience, and indeed existence, in the modern era. In the process, the theoretical approaches and case studies of these essays offer models for stimulating new historical research along this many-pronged line of corporeal inquiry.

The contributions, with their different accents, thus interrogate the vital matrix of bodies on-screen and their connections to the bodies in front of the screen. Alignments, detachments, identifications, disgust, arousal, contemplation, and many other reactions and responses are unpacked in the twenty-five essays. The essays are grouped in six registers, with some partial overlaps: "Impossible Bodies" deals with the unique configurations and fabrications made possible in the cinema; "Inventories of the Body" concerns how early cinema was a means not only for representing bodies in action but also for cataloging and scrutinizing the human body; "Performing Bodies" explores the risks, sensations, and transgressions connected to actors' and actresses' physical performances; "Bodily Features" follows how cinematic fragmentation of the represented body allows for insights on both mediation and conceptualization of the body in history; and the two final sections, "Embodied Audiences" and "Bodies in Exhibition Spaces" turn our attention to the embodied functions, pleasures, and cultural meanings of the film audiences themselves, first as viewers and then as active bodies vis-à-vis the screen. As the individual introductory passages to each section show, the essays engage with rare archive resources, deploy innovative methodologies, make productive interventions in theoretical debates, and/ or draw new insights from well-chosen pairs of specific examples. And many of the essays are preoccupied with what audiences discerned at the cinema, be it a propensity for mimetic behavior emulating screen events or a productive, albeit temporary, regression into playful feelings of freedom bracketing modernity's taxing everyday life.

For decades, the analyses framed around the immensely productive concept "cinema of attractions" have put a premium on early film's use of direct address that at times acknowledges the audience, to mention just one aspect of bodily tinged connections invoking shock and astonishment.[2] This approach was, in a way, a theoretical spin-off from and summation of the now-legendary conference in Brighton in 1978, hosted by Fédération Internationale des Archives du Film (FIAF), that opened up the archival vaults for films produced up until 1906. Gradually, the aftermath of this moment unleashed an unprecedented research interest in silent cinema at large due to the opportunities for close analyses of film style and narrative. Much of this body of research coalesced around the seminal notion of the cinema of attractions and the segue to prefeatures and features, as analyzed by Richard Abel in a French context.[3] These research endeavors were further fanned by film festivals working in tandem with archives, especially the one that turned the Verdi Theater in Pordenone into a beacon for several generations of scholars. Domitor, the organization for scholarship on early film, was founded and gained momentum in this milieu.

Outside the trick genre and its body plasticity, which was a key strand in the screenings at Brighton, many forms of nonfiction films display body registers: think about the customary playing up to the camera in street scenes, shyly or brashly, not to mention the prevalent phantom rides and their vertiginous manner of virtually transporting the bodies in the seats. Add to this the heightened emphases on the rainbow of sexualities in recent criticisms, which have generated new, exciting works promising a stronger awareness of the diverse body-coding in early cinema, as well as dress and masquerading practices on-screen and among bodies in attendance.[4]

The flaunting of naked skin and genitalia in early smokers and stag films were obviously designed for visceral purposes, and they offered hidden, and sometimes open, lines of steady production in the early years. Linda Williams's notion of body genres covers not only brazen sexual practices, but also films that put skin color at the forefront in a wide variety of genres in films such as *The Watermelon Patch* (Edison, 1905), *The Birth of a Nation* (Epoch, 1915), and *The Cheat* (Lasky, 1915); a panoply of films featuring depictions of Native Americans as "savages"; and teary melodramas.[5] This is just a small sample of skin-and-viscera-focused elements of film culture on which the collection's essays offer deeper, broader, and innovative perspectives.

Two of the essays in particular—the contributions by Tom Gunning and Alison Reiko Loader—highlight the collection's ethos: to engage with theoretical models for embodied cinema and visual mediation through research attuned to historical materials, films, and the discourses that negotiated screen practices overall. Positioned to open and close the volume, respectively, the two texts frame the range and richness of perspectives that the collection's ensemble of contributors brings to the fore in manners further made clear in the section introductions.

The attractions of the camera obscura and its embodiments, as Loader discusses from a discursive perspective rather than as a theoretical regime, provide a salient case in point. In Jonathan Crary's influential analysis, the camera obscura offers a disembodied model for watching bodies in the world, and the world at large, from inside a dark or semidark space.[6] In his account, the obscura regime, if you will, represents an allegory for pre-Kantian (or classical) epistemology's posited detachment of a removed observer from the world. From a classical vantage point along such lines, minimal weight was put on the human physiology;

the world picture was independent from the observer's perceptions of it, and not shaped by her or his sensual makeup. Crary's study additionally argues that the human sensorium in a post-Kantian world of modernity, in contrast, is integral for fabricating our embodied epistemological inferences from the world.

In this context, Loader's contribution shows that corporeal aspects of actual camera obscura spectatorship were also important to the viewing pleasures between the bodies in attendance inside the camera. Furthermore, the separation between the model observer and the world was not absolute. Spectators enjoyed far-from-bodiless—and shared—engagements with the apparatus and its operator, and they could move about and shift positions and vantage points. Loader's essay thus moves away from the camera obscura as an abstract model for viewing and provides a discursively thick account of embodied obscura practices across several centuries. This blurs the camera obscura's boundaries between subject and object in precisely the sense that Crary's analysis posits for modernity's embodied perceptual network and its subjectivities and observational fallibilities. Blurred boundaries and liminality are, hence, recurrent features of obscura viewing as well—and a reverberating theme for the collection's overall engagements with embodied visual cultures and screen practices at large.

Tom Gunning's essay discusses what he labels "impossible bodies" in perspectives that have critical implications, precisely for notions of liminality. Screen bodies, in pointed contrast to our own bodily experiences, can be briskly dismantled and instantly reassembled by way of tricks. In the absence of such magic in our world, flesh cannot heal in the blink of an eye if run over or otherwise manhandled. And our limbs, if severed, cannot take on an agency of their own, as in *Le Rêve des marmitons* (Pathé, 1908), where cut-off hands busily perform kitchen chores in a dream sequence. The uncanny capabilities and agencies of screen bodies—even a prosthetic arm has a life of its own in *The Thieving Hand* (Vitagraph, 1908)—have repercussions for how we understand embodied spectatorship and its liminalities.

If the spectatorial mind teeters at the brink of the screen world, the bodies watching are clued in and included across virtually all senses—but still with an awareness of a somewhat safe distance when challenged, even shocked, for instance, by shots symbolically running over the on-screen camera and "us." Phenomenological approaches to cinema dissolve the duality between the flow of life on the screen and real-life audiences perceived to be in touch and haptic immersion with what Vivian Sobchack calls the film's body and its consciousness. She has explored this carnal intersection in ingenious ways in many texts, and so has Laura U. Marks in a discussion of what she calls intercultural cinema, which she analyzes in terms of haptic visuality in a broad theoretical perspective moving from art historian Aloïs Riegl to Gilles Deleuze's film philosophy.[7]

If haptic proximity is a default for cinematic experiences at large, certain genres foreground the screen's bodily realm in ways that charge the spectators' physical engagement a few extra amps, not least in body genres—pornography being one of several. Similarly, to incur the shocks Gunning highlights within attraction-based films, and especially bearing on the trick films' crafting of impossible bodies, there is a dialectics informing our viewing between the seen and unseen, the on-screen and offscreen, and the bodily interiors and exteriors. This liminality, partly setting us apart, comes with impediments that ensure that the film world's "embodiedness" does not engulf or swallow us. Gunning's approach challenges in productive ways a too-literal notion of the film body by insisting on distances and differences, but still from within an embodied understanding of spectatorship. Even if sympathetic to the phenomenological analysis, he emphasizes the problems of fully teasing out distinctions between the "film body" and the body in attendance. Instead, he suggests an audience awareness of being outside and then pulled in by the machinery's operations, which then throw us out again as we acknowledge our differences from the technological devices of the "film body." Gunning, in his reading of a group of trick films, claims that we experience an extension of the body, rather than an incorporation of the "film body" into our body in attendance. These impossible screen bodies are machined, separated, and assembled by the cinematic apparatus's tricky fecundity, which alone can bring them to life, as it were. The cinema of Georges Méliès features prominently in Gunning's reading, as well as in several essays discussing trickality's roster of transformative powers. The notion of the impossible body is at the heart of the collection's corpus of texts.

Notions of media seriality offered filmmakers familiar elements for orchestrating both the framing of the earliest films and their often intermedial program presentations.[8] The collection's essays share ideas concerning embodied spectatorship's grounding in an intermedial frame of reference, albeit with some distinct specificities that should not be obliterated in the process. As research in media archaeology has vividly demonstrated, media and technologies across history are highly intertwined in their shifting manners of connecting the human body and its sensorium to media machines with spatiotemporal capacities.[9]

In today's world of the media uncanny, we may, for example, wonder if there is a real body behind a Facebook post, or a bot, or some other type of masquerading predator. This is not unlike sound film's uncanniness from around 1910, often featuring a performer on-screen mimicking a more famous singer on the synchronized phonograph cylinder or gramophone record. In this wider sense, for technological hookups across interfaces, projected moving pictures offered no radical departure from previous practices on stages and screens.[10] Instead, their differences fit into a series of intermedial technologies and communication devices with related powers of connectivity. Such *dispositifs* provided sets of conditions for the imbrication of our embodied interaction with the screen's worlds and their figures and intermedial figurations.[11]

Screen bodies cannot avoid exciting, educating, inspiring, and offering ideas and blueprints for emulations and negotiations. Why waste a nickel if there was nothing to take away from the theaters' offerings, no lessons to learn, no insights to pick up, no inspirations to gain? Distractions are never mere distractions; entertainments are never devoid of significance beyond themselves. Experiences have impact, however difficult it is to put them into a convincing causal pattern. Many of the debates calling for censorship and policing of film culture centered on notions of cinema's putative negative education. The overvisibility of bodies and their activities on-screen in depictions of crime, cruelty, and sexuality were presumed to inspire imitation in excitable audiences and stamp imprints on youngsters' impressionable minds—imprints that later turned into models for behavior.[12] A particular danger was perceived to stem from actions highlighted by way of close shots, at times labeled "enlargements." Scores of debates in such terms analyzed the screens' onslaught of impressions in relation to audiences' bodies and "nerves."

Many of the essays here deal with nonfilmic screen practices, neglected film genres, and imagery with nontheatrical designs that emerge from spaces far removed from film studios. Such imageries were often produced with classificatory purposes as a form of document making, be it the before-and-after images of racialized photography evidencing the effects of transformative schooling in the interval between photographs, or films from inside mental institutions depicting patients. The latter type of footage "cataloged" symptoms and was shot for the purposes of illustrating medical lectures. Several essays discuss films that feature the animal sphere—for example, in the lab environment where a vivisectionist increasingly turned to the film camera in lieu of endlessly cutting up living specimens. In addition, several essays demonstrate the merits of drawing on nonfilmic historical material for the exploration of cinematic embodiments, as they offer interpretations of advertisements, architectural plans, popular debates in the press, and pictorial materials ranging from the fine arts to postcards.

Movie theaters are real physical spaces that merit inquiry as such, and for the interactions, sexual or otherwise, that took place between audience members. During the nickelodeon era, the storefront theaters' unsanitary hazards were repeatedly foregrounded in comprehensive regulations and license requirements. An evident attraction in the auditoriums was the spectacle of the eroticized bodies of female audience members. Desires were by no means restricted to the screen, but also enveloped the women in the theaters and the fantasies they inspired. Furthermore, in the movie theater couples could avoid inquisitive eyes in the dark. Darkness—contributing to the erotic atmosphere of cinema and its illicit opportunities, encompassing consensual interactions as well as unwelcome touching and groping—was a much-contested issue concerning American movie theaters. These concerns resulted in ordinances in several cities and states with light regulations aiming to curb and disinvite sexual practices.[13]

In such debates, the female spectator emerged as a disruptive spectacle and exciting distraction in her own right. Many of the worries centered on the heterosocial commingling of men and women of many ethnicities in the presence of children. Movie theaters were, of course, just one of the many versions of the public sphere accessible to twentieth-century women during a time when gender roles and social interaction at large were being redefined. Besides women's bodies, their dress codes were a frequent discursive feature from inside film theaters, their hats in particular. Women's alleged chattiness was another oft-reported form of disruption.[14]

Minds and bodies were positioned within a web of attractions both in the theater space and in relation to screen bodies, with an awareness of potential risks in front of the screens, from germs to flames. Work "behind" the screens posed other forms of risks and accidents during shooting. Film labor in the studios and on location was fraught with dangers. Actors' bodies encountered enormous vicissitudes and perils in body genres that offered vicarious attractions, from thrills to comedic abuse. Such risks were not restricted to American serial films branded by franchise terms like "perils" and "hazards." Among the stars who died on set was the Savoia studio's Adriana Costamagna, tragically killed by leopards during a shoot in 1913.

Screen bodies were an endless source of fascination and offered launchpads for fantasies of many kinds—irrespective of whether the films displayed virtual female nudity in *tableaux vivants*, spectacles of near-death experiences, or the exceptional body à la Edison's strongman, Sandow, in the very first films, and his subsequent muscular screen brethren. From the earliest of cinemas onward, corporeality was especially poignant as audiences sought terms for their emotional responses and intellectual processing of the enframed world, with its embodied movements and bustling energies. Storytelling gradually turned into a privileged feature of programming, albeit with capacities for harboring a swath of visceral elements in its unraveling of tales.

The screen bodies were at times explicitly mobilized not only to be looked at, as in the genre of *tableaux vivants*, but to be physically mimicked by spectators in an educational exchange. Of late, scholars have increasingly turned their attention to such previously neglected genres, partly inspired by the orphan film movement and its symposia and research endeavors. In this spirit, cinema's educational might has recently been analyzed in several important anthologies.[15] Overall, the early cinemas generated a vast amount of debate regarding the interplay between their entertainment and educational practices and purposes.

Research efforts devoted to genres outside the scholarly mainstream of feature films are a result of increasingly accessible archival collections, be it within or outside the traditional film archives. The ongoing shift toward a world driven by digital fuel has sped up the access. Measuring access, or "use," has turned into a convenient performance concept favored by the archive's funding bodies, be it governments or agencies.[16] And, as important, the availability of big data of many kinds provides paper trails and contexts, not least the historical newspapers and the digital collections of trade papers. Such databases critically partake in opening up new avenues of inquiry for innovative engagements with historical materials on a scale that reframes the humanities and our historiographies. Most of the essays here have benefitted from initiatives such as the Media History Digital Library and its spinoffs.[17]

In our current moment in media history, more than ever, it is imperative that we benefit from novel opportunities to study historical screen practices and their on-screen and in-theater bodies, as well as the hermeneutics of skin, faces, human hair, the eyes, and the physical form in toto, including animal bodies put under the camera's scrutiny. This collection provides historically inspired forays into media's embodiments in essays that discuss body destruction and instruction on the screen, as well as films and media preoccupied with the pleasures and horrors of mediated corporeality.

MARINA DAHLQUIST is Associate Professor of Cinema Studies at Stockholm University. She is editor of *Exporting Perilous Pauline: Pearl White and the Serial Film Craze*.

DORON GALILI is Research Fellow in the Department of Media Studies at Stockholm University.

JAN OLSSON is Professor of Cinema Studies and former Head of Department at Stockholm University. He is author of *Hitchcock à la Carte*.

VALENTINE ROBERT is Lecturer in Film Studies at the University of Lausanne. She is editor with Laurent Le Forestier and François Albera of *Le Film sur l'art. Entre histoire de l'art et documentaire de creation*.

Notes

1. Laurie Ouellette and Jonathan Gray, eds., *Keywords for Media Studies* (New York: New York University Press, 2017); Bruce Burgett and Glenn Hendler, eds., *Keywords for American Cultural Studies* (New York: New York University Press, 2014).

2. For a reappraisal of the notion of "the cinema of attraction," originally introduced by André Gaudreault and Tom Gunning, see Wanda Strauwen, ed., *The Cinema of Attractions Reloaded* (Amsterdam: Amsterdam University Press, 2006).

3. Richard Abel, *The Ciné Goes to Town: French Cinema, 1896–1914* (Berkeley: University of California Press, 1994).

4. An indication of the heightened focus on the body in recent criticism is the novel journal *Screen Bodies*, which commenced publication in 2016. See also Laura Horak, *Girls Will Be Boys: Cross-Dressed Women, Lesbians, and American Cinema, 1908–1934* (New Brunswick, NJ: Rutgers University Press, 2016).

5. Linda Williams, *Playing the Race Card: Melodramas of Black and White from Uncle Tom to O. J. Simpson* (Princeton, NJ: Princeton University Press, 2001), and *Screening Sex* (Durham, NC: Duke University Press, 2008).

6. Jonathan Crary, *The Techniques of the Observer: On Vision and Modernity in the Nineteenth Century* (Cambridge, MA: MIT Press, 1990).

7. For example, see Vivian Sobchack, *Carnal Thoughts: Embodiment and Moving Image Culture* (Berkeley: University of California Press, 2006); Laura U. Marks, *The Skin of the Film: Intercultural Cinema, Embodiment, and the Senses* (Durham, NC: Duke University Press, 2000).

8. André Gaudreault and Philippe Marion, "A Medium Is Always Born Twice," *Early Popular Visual Culture* 3, no. 1 (May 2005): 3–15.

9. Erkki Huhtamo and Jussi Parikka, eds. *Media Archaeology: Approaches, Applications, and Implications* (Berkeley: University of California Press, 2011).

10. For an account of the history of screen practice, see Charles Musser, *The Emergence of Cinema: The American Cinema to 1907* (Berkeley: University of California Press, 1994 [1990]), esp. 15–54.

11. Santiago Hidalgo, ed., *Technology and Film Scholarship: Experience, Study, Theory* (Amsterdam: Amsterdam University Press, 2017).

12. Lee Grieveson, *Policing Cinema: Movies and Censorship in Early-Twenty-Century America* (Berkeley: University of California Press, 2004).

13. Jan Olsson, *Los Angeles before Hollywood: Journalism and American Film Culture, 1905 to 1915* (Stockholm: National Library of Sweden, 2008), 230–51; Noam M. Elcott, *Artificial Darkness: An Obscure History of Modern Art and Media* (Chicago: University of Chicago Press, 2016).

14. Shelly Stamp, *Movie-Struck Girls: Women and Motion Picture Culture after the Nickelodeon* (Princeton, NJ: Princeton University Press, 2000); Maggie Hennefeld, "Women's Hats and Silent Film Spectatorship: Between Ostrich Plume and Moving Image," *Film History: An International Journal* 28, no. 3 (2016): 24–53.

15. Charles R. Ackland and Haidee Wasson, eds., *Useful Cinema* (Durham, NC: Duke University Press, 2011); Devin Oregon, Marsha Oregon, and Dan Streible, eds., *Learning with the Lights Off: Educational Film in the United States* (New York: Oxford University Press, 2012).

16. See Nico de Klerk, *Showing and Telling: Film Heritage Institutes and Their Performance of Public Accountability* (Wilmington, DE: Vernon, 2017).

17. Thanks to the financial support of Domitor, the Media History Digital Library was able to add many important early cinema publications to its collection. See domitor.org/collaborations/.

Part I
Impossible Bodies

Introduction

The kinematographic machinery and its illusory realism plays up marvelous worlds and on-screen bodies with potential for instantaneous changes, transformations, and mutations. The corporeal limitations and stabilities of our day-to-day world dissolve in the interstices between real-world physicality and its cinematic reproduction. This play with photographic images, still or moving, is enabled by the apparatus's trick capacity, and most obviously so when the technology's presumable restrictions were presented as a film's, or a scene's, main focus. The playfulness with what is possible or not, realistic or not, presupposes a flexible contract with the spectators as the integrity of the indexical images is questioned and negotiated. This rift between fantasy and reproductive realism italicizes early cinema's fascination with the construction and metamorphosis of the image, which often delivered depictions of impossible bodies.

The open-ended logic of dreams and the fantastic in early cinema is most recognizable in the work of Georges Méliès. Here the "cinémagicien," to use Vito Adriaensens's pertinent designation for characterizing Méliès's play with the new medium, creates a chaotic film world where the body is never safe from violations, assaults, or improvements. The portrayal of impossible bodies took many forms and variations, as the visual reproductions of bodies in motion by Eadweard Muybridge and Étienne-Jules Marey became propelling forces for film practices, not least within comedies and trick films. Explorations of the photographic image and its limitations and possibilities were driven by a never-ending curiosity of the medium's wherewithal. The actors' physical competence, together with machinery's propensities for playing with character stability, offered pinnacle moments of plasticity.

This section presents some of the ways impossible bodies were portrayed on-screen. The texts represent a crossfertilization of popular precinema stage performances, such as *tableau vivant*, vaudeville, and stage illusions, but also the illustrated press and spirit photography; all contributed intermedially to the magic of cinema. One example of this fruitful media transposition is the composite image of ghostly bodies, via the multiple-exposure technique, that Ian Christie discusses in his contribution. Jérémy Houillère, in contrast, explores impossible bodies in early cinema from a tradition of caricaturing doctors and the medical world. Such visualizations highlight the fear of surgical methods and new inventions being practiced on bodies under the knife.

As Tom Gunning argues in his contribution to this volume, even though the film medium appropriated older precinema traditions, a specifically cinematic body was created in the process. *The Big Swallow*, James Williamson's ingenious 1901 film, serves up a quintessential impossible film body. In his interaction with the cinematic technology, the cameraman is swallowed by a man who is irritated by his presence. Early cinema inventively explored the existence of such impossible bodies in an unrealistic and malleable cinematic space by way of techniques, plot, and narrative structure. Highly popular among the audience back in the days, this play with cinematographic possibilities still inspires filmmakers.

1 The Impossible Body of Early Film

Tom Gunning

Fascination with the Body Invented the Cinema

Cinema was invented at the end of the nineteenth century to record the moving bodies of humans and animals. Most obviously, the chronophotography of Eadweard Muybridge and Étienne-Jules Marey was designed to study bodies in motion. Although both Muybridge and Marey promoted the use of their images by artists portraying humans and animals in motion, chronophotography existed primarily to serve physiology. The scientific study of the body through motion pictures soon branched off into a nontheatrical, nonentertainment practice destined for the laboratory and the lecture hall. Yet even entertainment cinema remained preoccupied with the body. Thomas Edison and his kinetoscope, with its films of dancers, acrobats, and knockabout comedians, exploited the entertainment aspect of cinema that Marey had scorned in particular. But the visual presentation of Edison's *Black Maria* films of the 1890s, with their dark, undefined backgrounds and accent on physical performance, revealed that the attraction of early cinema remained rooted in the observation of skilled, beautiful, unusual bodies in motion as much as creating a fictional world.

While I do not simply intend to resurrect the traditional distinction between the Lumières and Méliès, with its too-simple dichotomy between cinematic realism and fantasy, portrayals of the body in early cinema do show sharply differing approaches. As a scientist, Marey forced photography beyond the visual surfaces of the world in order to reveal its invisible laws and regularities. Marey processed the body into information, generating graphs and numbers as well as presenting an image of motion. However, the trick film, exemplified by the work of Georges Méliès, treated the body in a radically defamiliarized manner that drew on fantasy and traditions of the grotesque rather than scientific investigation. These fantastical bodies drew on a long tradition of iconography of monsters and demons and undoubtedly mined the resources of unconscious fantasy. Méliès also derived many tricks and imagery from the modern optical magic of the turn-of-the-century theater of illusions. The trick film not only appropriated these traditions but also reinvented them in cinematic terms and thereby created a new cinematically conceived body, endowing the new medium with its own technological, fantastic physiology. This body and its implications for the new medium form the topic of this essay.

Hard to Swallow

> I am born in a beam of light
> I move continuously, yet I am still
> I am larger than life, but do not breathe
> Only in the darkness am I visible
> You can see me, but never touch me
> I speak to you, but can never listen
> You know me intimately, and I know you not at all
> We are strangers, and yet you take me inside of you
> What am I?
> —Sally Potter in *The Gold Diggers*

James Williamson's 1901 film, *The Big Swallow*, exemplifies the cinematic body of the trick film. It also offers a satire on the new media of photography and motion pictures and their relation to the body. Although its action and gag are immediately comprehensible, at least within a certain absurd logic, Williamson's original catalog description details an almost forgotten context: the craze for snapping photographs of passersby without their permission. Kodak's portable hand camera, with its brief exposure time and ease of handling, released a horde of "camera fiends" on an unsuspecting public, often arousing their ire.[1] Williamson's description of his film clearly refers to this context: "'I won't! I won't! I'll eat the camera first.' Gentleman reading, finds a camera fiend with his head under a cloth, focusing him up. He orders him off, approaching nearer and nearer, gesticulating and ordering the photographer off, until his head fills the picture, and finally his mouth only occupies the screen. He opens it, and first the camera, and then the operator disappear inside. He retires munching him up and expressing his great satisfaction."[2]

The Big Swallow is deceptively simple, seeming to consist of a single shot (and employing an almost seamless continuity editing to convey the action of swallowing). The irate gentleman approaches the camera, coming into looming close-up, opens his greatly enlarged mouth, and seems to engulf a photographer, who topples into the dark, gaping mouth. The gentleman closes his mouth, withdraws a bit, and laughs heartily. The nearly invisible splices join, within a matrix of artificial darkness, a bodily exterior and its imagined interior in the act of swallowing. With this early example of elegant trick editing, Williamson sutures interior and exterior by constructing a truly impossible body that also ingests the very means of imaging itself, the camera.

While the film continues to evoke immediate laughter, even in undergraduates unused to silent cinema, it also sows some confusion among contemporary viewers. A recent account of the film by Michael Brooke on a British Film Institute (BFI) website reflects this uncertainty as a criticism: "The film might have been still more effective if Williamson had omitted the second and third shots altogether, since they detract from the logical purity of the first, ending on a completely blank screen as the swallowed camera is no longer able to function as a surrogate for the audience's point of view."[3] While I am not exactly sure what "logical purity" means for an overtly absurdist comedy, the shot of the camera and its fiend disappearing into a dark, undefined space (admittedly with a suspiciously shrouded barrier inadvertently peeking out of the bottom of the frame) does introduce certain confusions. The large-format camera we see swallowed is not the Kodak-style hand camera that camera fiends used, but that may pose an unimportant inconsistency within a good joke. More complexly, many viewers (and quite a few commentators) have mistaken this still camera for a movie camera, and therefore miss the reference to camera fiends snapping pictures of unwary bystanders. But the paradox Brooke pointed out is more interesting than the type of camera. If the camera has been swallowed, how is the act of swallowing and its aftermath filmed?

This rift in rationally constructed space exemplifies early cinema's fascination with the construction and destruction of impossible bodies, imaginable only through the technology of cinema. Early film not only plays with human anatomy but also, as in *The Big Swallow*, uses this irrational physiology to display the new possibilities of cinema, especially its play with the seen and the unseen, offscreen spaces, and the ambiguities of the interior and exterior. The plague of camera fiends snapping pictures without permission sets up a metaphor that Williamson's joke literalizes and comically reverses. The black box of the camera arrogantly "swallows" its subjects whether they are willing or not. Refusing to suffer this fate passively, the protagonist of *The Big Swallow* reclaims his image by swallowing the apparatus—and the fiend to boot. Photography as swallowing the world was a common simile. (To quote only one example, the cameraman Serafino Gubbio in Pirandello's 1916 novel *Shoot!* describes his camera as a machine made "to swallow up our soul, to devour our life.")[4] Williamson not only produced an original gag but also transformed an act of vision into the more grossly physical act of swallowing, chewing, and presumably ingesting. Swallowing appears as a carnivalesque version of picture-snatching.

Moving away from the film's original historical context of late-nineteenth-century outrage over amateur photographers to more contemporary theoretical debates, film theorist Jennifer Barker has proposed Williamson's film as offering insight into the experience of cinema spectatorship. This big swallow, for Barker, literally takes in the spectator as well: "The film appears to engulf not only the cinematographer and the apparatus but also, by extension, the viewer."[5] She explains, "We initially view the filmed gentleman from the same position that the cinematographer does. Thus when the cinematographer is swallowed so must we be."[6] Barker acknowledges the paradoxical aspect of this swallowing, collapsing the world depicted in the film into the realm of the audience and theater. Williamson's film (with its lack of "logical purity") boldly breaches the barrier between filmic fictional space and the offscreen space of production with its eponymous swallow. This paradox provides the punch line of the joke, based in the film's irrational approach to the cinematic construction of both space and the human body.

How exactly does the film accomplish this undermining of both bodily and spatial integrity? The use of what Noam Elcott calls "artificial darkness" plays a key role.[7] As Elcott shows, at the turn of the twentieth century, stage magicians, photographers, and trick filmmakers (all professions Williamson had mastered) used darkness as an optical device that allowed both spectacular transformations and a new relation to the spectator. The multiple associations of the black maw into which the camera fiend vanishes enable a fusion between bodily and other spaces. This darkness fuses the "black coffer of the body" (as Foucault describes it),[8] the black box of the camera, and the darkened auditorium in which spectators sit. Artificial darkness becomes the space of metamorphosis, an uncharted and ambiguous space that defies traditional categories—the space that cinema creates.

Technology Swallows the Cinematic Body: A Detour through Theory

For Barker, *The Big Swallow* turns on this obscure melding of exterior to interior and back again. As she nicely puts it, "The film turns inside and outside itself and back again, swallows itself up and spits itself back out, in the space of a few seconds."[9] Barker interprets this interchange between interior and exterior as emblematic of the relation that cinema generally sets up between film and viewer, a relation she describes (as does Vivian Sobchack) in terms of "the film's body."[10] This somewhat slippery concept serves these theorists to describe the chiastic relation between a film viewer and a film. I will use this discussion of the cinema's relation to the body to explore both what it tells us about early cinema and what early cinema can tell us about it.

Sobchack uses the term "the film's body" to describe the way a film, through its stylistic devices, opens onto a world. This is not a passive portrayal or recording of a world but an active penetration, as the cinematic apparatus mimes the "intentions" (the phenomenological principle that consciousness is always directed at something) of human consciousness. Through this immersion in intentions, the film is "perceived not only as an *object for vision* but also as a *subject of vision*."[11] In other words, films are not only seen by a spectator; they offer her a mode of seeing. In watching a film we see a world through a series of framings that express intentions, which we also discern and participate in. For instance, camera movements target specific objects or trace trajectories through space, endowing the cinematic image with a sense of an intentional consciousness. For Sobchack, the "film's body" names the vehicle of this sense of an active consciousness, its embodiment in the film's images and sounds. She describes this "objective (if generally invisible) body" as "an instrumentality through which the *visible behavior* of an intending consciousness is expressed."[12] Barker's understanding of the term seems similar: "For me, the 'film's body' is a concrete but distinctly cinematic lived-body, neither equated in nor encompassing the viewer's or filmmaker's body, but engages with both of these even as it takes up its own intentional projects in the world."[13]

Neither Barker nor Sobchack forgets that the spectator's experience of a projected film cannot be identical with a direct perception of the world.[14] A film is perceived through its technology. Film's technological processes, Sobchack claims, "substantially embody the film," but in way that "exceeds their characterization as merely mechanical instruments and discrete pieces of apparatus."[15] In other words, the camera and projector (and I would add all the technological processes of editing, printing, etc.) make perceptible the intentional processes through which the spectator is given access to a world. Thus, Sobchack claims, a film "is lived as a visual kinetic and gestural discourse, as the immediate and direct enunciation of its own present engagement with a world enabled by a bodily presence in it."[16]

While I have some problems with Sobchack's discussion of the film's body (especially her discussion of its role in film history), I think her description of the way films address a viewer through an openness toward and an exploration of the world is rich and valuable. Rather than simply reproducing visual surfaces and aural phenomena, a film mimes the way an embodied consciousness encounters and interacts with a world. But what does it mean to describe this encounter as involving the film's *body*? A film expresses curiosity or expectations simultaneously with its presentation of the world. In this way a film recalls an embodied being making its way through the world. The primary gestures of movement and navigation through this fictive world have a physical quality, certainly. But aren't there as many things about the way a film opens up a world that are *not* at all like a body, at least the lived body we humans experience?

The tangible qualities of fleshly being, its sense of mortality and vulnerability, its material limitation in terms of gravity or speed, all seem at odds with the way we experience a film. Now, neither Barker nor Sobchack is naïve in her descriptions. Sobchack stresses "the material incongruence between the film's body and the human body," and this disparity is essential as well to Barker's description of *The Big Swallow*.[17] Both theorists not only acknowledge this incongruence but also derive some important observations about how films work from this difference.

Hoping to break down previous understandings of film viewing as an inert, passive confrontation between a viewing subject and a film object, this image of the mutual engulfing of film and viewer offers a figure more like the chiasmus that Maurice Merleau-Ponty proposed for the relation between human perception and the world, a relation based in mutual imbrication. Barker asserts, "We are certainly not *in* the film, but we are not entirely *outside* it either."[18] This chiasmus of mutual exchange of "inside and outside turning about one another" defines the relation of the spectator and film that Barker calls "the film's body."[19] Thus the figure of *swallowing*, more than simply observing visually or understanding cognitively, may serve as a particularly powerful image for our relation to the cinema as viewers (and the cinema's relation to us). This is especially true when the figure of swallowing is understood as both involving technology (the camera swallows us and we swallow the camera) and the *impossible* body this paradoxical action assumes (or creates).

Therefore, I find the figure of the film's body useful in conveying the way a film viewer does not merely observe the world but also dwells within it. But I am also concerned about the naturalization that the term "body" invites, absorbing the complex processes of film narration and spectatorship into the organic unity of the human body. Since both Barker and Sobchack acknowledge this basic disparity between the film and the human body, my critique of the term may be more a matter of stress than definition. Sobchack states, "The machine is incorporated into the human intentional act of perceiving the world, even as the machine enables a patently 'impossible' human perception, that is, one otherwise unrealizable without the machine's incorporation."[20] But rather than anchoring our sense of the cinematic in the familiarity of the lived body, "incorporating" it as it were, I would stress the radical transformative potential of cinematic technology, not opposed to the human body but providing its extension and transformation. It seems to me, in fact, that the disparities between a film and a human body become as important as the similarities. This is a lesson that the trick film of early cinema teaches us.

Stressing the impossible nature of this filmic body—one that can turn inside out, multiply, or come to pieces is able to swallow the world or be swallowed by it—becomes necessary. This filmic body evokes less a familiar and grounded entry to the world than a process of defamiliarization, discovery, and recreation. Comparisons, such as those that Barker and Sobchack offer, to the phenomenology of the lived body as described by Merleau-Ponty and others may open up our understanding of the way the devices of cinema operate. But I believe this comparison must be completed with a thorough understanding of what I will call film's technological body, the body that has been extended through its immersion in a technological system, such as the one cinema offers.

I do not think the chiasmus Merleau-Ponty described between human and world, in which each implies the other, really describes a body. Similarly, I believe that early cinema confronted its magical technical possibilities and imagined creating something different from the organic human body: a flexible, polymorphic body that could turn itself inside out, engulfing the world, even as it projected its gaze beyond itself. The impossible body sketched by a number of early trick films understands inside and outside not as opposites but as a process of continuous exchange, so that the inside becomes outside and vice versa.

The genre of the early trick film (like much of contemporary special effects cinema) fundamentally reimagines the human body. Recent film theorists (including Sobchack and Steven Shaviro)[21] have stressed the embodied nature of the cinema, highlighting the manner in which the cinema viewer is addressed not simply through the eye and cognitive processes, but viscerally, affected by the perception of motion, space, and tempo and virtually participating in the physical process portrayed on the screen—whether sexual activity, pain, or mobile actions such as running, leaping, or even flying. But the relation of the body to the processes of cinema goes beyond stimulation and representation. The cinematic body not only draws on our ordinary bodily experience but exceeds it, drawing on fantasies of impossible bodies that could be experienced through technology. The unique cinematic manipulations of space and the image of the body demand that we think in terms of cinema's *technological* body.

Media theory needs to think about the relation of the body to technology broadly. The discussion of technology found in Andre Leroi-Gourhan's, Gilbert Simondon's, and Bernard Stiegler's work describes a relation between the body and technology that I believe founds the impossible body of the early trick films.[22] This technological body exceeds existing physiology, extending the physical body through technological prostheses. Stiegler uses the myth of Epimetheus to show that technology and the human body become inseparable. According to Plato, the titan Prometheus, after creating all the mortal creatures, animals as well as human, left the final distribution of abilities to his none-too-bright brother, Epimetheus, who distributed these gifts (speed, fur, hooves, claws, sharp fangs, etc.) among the animals, maintaining a balance between the various species. However, when he came to humans, he found he had exhausted his store of powers, so the human was presented to Prometheus "naked, unshod, unbedded and unarmed."[23] To compensate for his brother's lack of foresight, Prometheus stole fire and skill in the arts of civilization from the gods. Stiegler reads this myth as presenting technology as a compensation for a human body that remains vulnerable in relation to other animals, serving as a sort of prosthesis. But within technological thinking (and here I am perhaps closer to Simondon than to Stiegler), the prosthesis needs to be seen as more than a *faute de mieux*, a barely adequate substitute. Technology offers an extension, a reinvention of the human body, stretching its possibilities and horizons, redefining what it is to be human. As both Martin Heidegger and Stiegler claim, the technological is fundamentally defamiliarizing, *unheimlich*, uncanny.[24] It takes us someplace we otherwise could not reach.

Projecting the Inside Outside: The Body of Méliès's Magic Lantern

In 1902 Georges Méliès produced the film *Up-to-Date Surgery* (also known as *Sure Cure for Indigestion*), which we could consider a sequel to *The Big Swallow*. The Méliès Catalog described the film this way:

> A patient enters, and judging from the expression on his face, he is in great pain. The doctor tells him that he is troubled with acute indigestion, and immediately places him upon the operating table. He begins his treatment by cutting off the patient's arms and legs with a huge saw. After removing these members, he takes a large knife and makes an incision in the unfortunate's stomach large enough to put his arm in. He then removes such things as bottles, knives and forks, lamps and other articles of furniture from the patient's body. The patient evidently complains of the great pain he is suffering, and to relieve this, the doctor cuts off his head and places it upon a near-by chair. Next a large water pump is brought into play, and after pumping about two gallons of water from the stomach of the patient the doctor sews up the wound, which heals immediately, then places the head back in its place. He next attempts to adjust the man's legs and arms in their proper places, but in his hurry a leg is placed where an arm should be, and vice versa. After discovering his mistake he corrects it, and the man, entirely cured of his trouble, rises from the table and after paying the doctor his fee departs from the office in great glee.[25]

The theme of the disassembled and reassembled body was not only common in the films of Méliès but a standard motif of early trick films internationally (see Alice Guy's *Chirurgie fin de siècle* [1901], Cecil Hepworth's *Explosion of a Motor Car* [1900], or J. Stuart Blackton's *The Thieving Hand* [1908]). *Up-to-Date Surgery* deals not only with this magical motif (derived ultimately from shamanism) of bodies being hacked to pieces and then put back together but with the mysterious interior space of the body opened up in *The Big Swallow*. Presumably the indigestion of Méliès's patient was caused by indiscriminately swallowing diverse objects, which the surgeon/magician extricates with a flourish. The disproportionate and random series of things that emerge during surgery seem to literalize Lautréamont's phrase "beautiful as the chance meeting upon an operating table of a sewing machine and an umbrella." After the removal of the most detachable body part, the head, a huge pumping machine finishes draining the patient's interior. Linda Williams, in her pioneering 1981 essay on the body in early cinema, comments on the various machines in Méliès's films that served as magical wombs (following Lucy Fischer's classic analysis of trick films as indicating an envy of woman's procreative power)[26] from which people, things, and animals emerge. Williams identifies such machines with the cinematic apparatus and its ability to not only produce but also multiply images: "The proliferation of the machines themselves—the many fantastic vehicles, futuristic laboratories . . . are obvious ways in which Méliès celebrates and makes visible, the primary invisible machinery of the cinema itself."[27]

Filmic references to the cinematic apparatus, whether literal or metaphorical, were often valorized by critics in the 1970s and 1980s for their anti-illusionist, or modernist, effects. Reminding the viewer of the means by which cinema is produced supposedly jolted spectators out of their dreamlike complicity with the cinematic image. I find this description as limited as the theory that underlies it but would like to reclaim the practice of self-reference in cinema, an impulse more often baroque than modernist. Fundamental to both the realist aspiration to the transparency of the medium and the modernist pursuit of self-reflective opacity, is the assumption that technology is something to hide, or at least forget—unless one wants to cause the image to self-destruct. But the machines of Méliès, the elaborate technology of the tricks of early cinema, and indeed the fascination with the cinema that I see as essential to the cinema of attractions—not to mention the role of special effects in contemporary digital cinema—all reveal the delight that viewers take in cinema's ability to generate, proliferate, and manipulate images: objects and especially bodies. They celebrate and make cinema visible as an aspect of modern technology.

Williams's essay also describes Méliès's 1903 film *The Magic Lantern* in detail. As the first medium of the projected image, with a strong symbiosis with the cinema, the magic lantern clearly provides, as she claims, "a metaphor for the cinematic apparatus."[28] Williams's description of the film is basically accurate, although I want to modify some aspects. The setting, as she says, is a child's playroom, and the figures of Pierrot and Polichinelle, as well as the lantern, are supposed to be understood as toys. Once we realize the scale of these animated figures, the apparatus Williams describes as "a giant magic lantern" actually becomes rather small, matching the size of the doll characters who put it together. The film enacts, then, a scenario of animation, the childhood dream of toys coming to life. The process that Williams describes as "building" the lantern systematically assembles and thereby demonstrates the different technical elements of the device, especially displaying the construction of the casing and chimney and the placing of the lamp.

After the projected images they have been enjoying suddenly disappear from the screen, Pierrot and Polichinelle open the casing of the magic lantern as if searching inside for them. The lantern casing now become one of those magic boxes Méliès so loved, from which living figures appear seemingly endlessly. As the lantern casing opens, then closes, it reveals successively a chorus line of skirt dancers, two servings of ballerinas in tutus, a harlequin, and a columbine. Finally, the Pierrot and Polichinelle figures take refuge inside the lantern from a phalanx of toy soldiers that arrive, apparently to restore order. When the box opens one last time, the dolls have been transformed into a single, grotesque Punch figure whose body extends and collapses impossibly and performs the contortion of looking through its own legs. Without denying Williams's psychoanalytic reading, I would stress the film's dynamic exchange of inside and outside, the seen and the unseen, the projected image and the living figures, and the transforming and impossible body of Punch—an inventory of the bodily transformations of the trick film. The film seems to celebrate and demonstrate the capacity of the machinery of projected images to multiply and transform images into bodies climaxing in a grotesque phallic puppet, twisting and transforming.

Conclusion: Turning Inside Out, New Bodies, New Images

> For what is inside of you is what is outside of you,
> and the one who fashions you on the outside
> is the one who shaped the inside of you.
> And what you see outside of you, you see inside of you;
> it is visible and it is your garment.
> —"Thunder, Perfect Mind," Nag Hammadi Library, circa 300 CE

The value of the concept of the film's body lies in the dynamic model of film viewing it offers, in which we are no longer a distanced, disembodied eye contemplating pictures representing a story or a reality but rather a prowling consciousness impelled by cinema into a series of encounters that evoke both our sensory and cognitive reactions. The film's body, as Sobchack and Barker describe it, does not remain outside the film but becomes swallowed up in a world, and thereby swallows us as viewers. But at the same time, our immersion in a film remains in some sense disembodied: we do not encounter actual physical resistance, pain, or pleasure. This difference is an aspect that we must acknowledge to fully understand the complex nature of our bodily experience of the cinema. In cinema it is always an impossible body we encounter, and its paradoxes provide its pleasures. Cinema technology creates a body we could never have, but one that, like technological prostheses, extends and transforms the affordances of our natural body. Stiegler claims (somewhat convolutedly) that the nature of bodily experience is to project itself outward: "A pro-thesis is what is placed in front, that is, what is outside, outside what it is placed in front of. However if what is outside constitutes the very being of what it lies in front of, then this being is *outside itself*. The being of humankind is to be outside itself."[29]

As Heidegger also claims, *Dasein*, human being, is always outside itself, projected into a future and a world. This dynamic displacement defines—but also defies—the situation of the embodied human. Embodiment does not define the human in the sense of confining it. Rather, the body is a horizon beyond which the imagination always projects itself. Almost immediately the cinema recognized the affinity between the new medium and the human body. But the affinity was paradoxical: it projected an impossible body; as Barker says, it "turns inside and outside itself and back again, swallows itself up and spits itself back out."[30] Fundamental to the impossible body of early cinema is this interchange between the inside and the outside, between what can be swallowed and what can be projected outward.

Merleau-Ponty quoted an axiom of Goethe's, "What is inside is also outside," as a good description of the cinema.[31] I want to stress that the technology of the cinema makes us rethink the boundaries of the human body, rather than simply miming it. The cinema provides a means of both swallowing the world and regurgitating it. But this process exceeds the mechanical process of filming and projection. It is, as Méliès's *Up-to-Date Surgery* seems to hint, also a process of digestion in which things become transformed and oddly juxtaposed within. Nor does this process remain outside the viewer, simply on the screen; its images also enter her, while they simultaneously transport her beyond herself.

TOM GUNNING is Edwin A. and Betty L. Bergman Distinguished Service Professor in the Departments of Art History, Cinema and Media Studies, and the College at the University of Chicago. He is author of *D. W. Griffith and the Origins of American Narrative Film*, *The Films of Fritz Lang; Allegories of Vision and Modernity*, and author with Giovanna Fossati, Joshua Yumibe, and Jonathon Rosen of *Fantasia of Color in Early Cinema*.

Notes

1. For the camera-fiend phenomenon see Bill Jay, "The Camera Fiend," *FotoView Wales* (Autumn 1982).

2. James Williamson, *The Big Swallow* catalog description, cited in Rachel Low and Roger Manvell, *The History of the British Film*, vol. I, 1896–1906 (London: Allen and Unwin, 1973), 75.

3. BFI Screen Online, *The Big Swallow*, http://www.screenonline.org.uk/film/id/444628/index.html.

4. Luigi Pirandello, *Shoot! The Notebooks of Serafino Gubbio* (Chicago: University of Chicago Press, 2005), 9.

5. Jennifer Barker, *The Tactile Eye: Touch and the Cinematic Experience* (Berkeley: University of California Press, 2009), 157.

6. Ibid., 158.
7. Noam Elcott, *Artificial Darkness: An Obscure History of Modern Art and Media* (Chicago: University of Chicago Press, 2016).
8. Michel Foucault, *The Birth of the Clinic* (London: Routledge, 1976), 166.
9. Barker, *The Tactile Eye*, 158.
10. Vivian Sobchack, *The Address of the Eye: A Phenomenology of Film Experience* (Princeton, NJ: Princeton University Press, 1991).
11. Ibid., 62–63.
12. Ibid., 167.
13. Barker, *The Tactile Eye*, 8.
14. Sobchack, *The Address of the Eye*, 178.
15. Ibid., 205.
16. Ibid., 216.
17. Barker, *The Tactile Eye*, 244.
18. Ibid., 13.
19. Ibid., 158.
20. Sobchack, *The Address of the Eye*, 184.
21. Vivian Sobchack, *Carnal Thoughts: Embodiment and Moving Image Culture* (Berkeley: University of California Press, 2004); Steven Shaviro, *The Cinematic Body* (Minneapolis: University of Minnesota Press, 1993). See also Scott C. Richmond, *Cinema's Bodily Illusions: Flying, Floating, and Hallucinating* (Minneapolis: University of Minnesota Press, 2016).
22. Andre Leroi-Gourhan, *Gesture and Speech* (Cambridge, MA: MIT Press, 1993); Gilbert Simondon, *Du mode d'existence des objets techniques* (Paris: Editions Aubier, 2012); Bernard Stiegler, *Technics and Time, Vol. I: The Fault of Epimetheus* (Stanford, CA: Stanford University Press, 1998).
23. Plato, *Protagoras* (320–21d), in *Plato in 12 Volumes*, trans. W.R.M. Lamb (Cambridge, MA: Harvard University Press, 1967).
24. Martin Heidegger, *Holderlin's Hymn "Der Ister"* (Bloomington: Indiana University Press, 1996).
25. *Complete Catalogue of Genuine and Original "Star" Films (Motion Pictures) Manufactured by Geo. Méliès of Paris* (Paris: Star Films, 1905), 20.
26. Lucy Fischer, "The Lady Vanishes: Women, Magic and the Movies," *Film Quarterly* 33, no. 1 (Autumn 1979), 30–40.
27. Linda Williams, "Film Body: An Implantation of Perversions," *Cine-Tracts 12* 2, no. 4 (Winter 1981).
28. Ibid., 32.
29. Stiegler, *Technics and Time*, 193.
30. Barker, *The Tactile Eye*, 158.
31. Maurice Merleau-Ponty, "Film and the New Psychology," in *Sense and Nonsense* (Evanston, IL: Northwestern University Press, 1964), 59.

2 Ovidian Violence

Georges Méliès's Explosive Screen Bodies

Vito Adriaensens

FROM LARGE-SCALE MEDIEVAL passion plays to Goethe's vivid descriptions of the singular Lady Hamilton's posed "attitudes" in *Die Wahlverwandtschaften* (Elective Affinities, 1809), or the explosion of bodies standing motionless on nineteenth-century stages, the *tableau vivant* or "living painting" was a popular mode of performance that saw many different applications and variations depending on the scale and cultural validity of its performative context. In its most literal translation, a *tableau vivant* can be a metaphorical freezing of bodies into the re-creation of a well-known painting, whether it be in an outdoor passion play or to end a high-brow operetta, but in the nineteenth century, the mode exploded in popularity along with the exchangeability of many new and old terms that were applied to it, and this meant that the *tableau vivant* was seldom an actual re-creation of a painting. Bodies were whitewashed, marbled, coppered, or veiled, and they ranged from fully dressed to entirely nude. They performed solo and in large ensemble companies, and the term "*tableau vivant*" was often used synonymously with living pictures, living statues, attitudes, *poses plastiques, statues vivants,* Venetian statues, Grecian statues, living statuary, *tableaux,* or *marbres vivants.* The same was true in early cinema, where both *tableaux vivants* and living statues debuted early on in many different guises, in a medium whose very essence revolved around bringing motion to static bodies. This chapter will delve into early cinema's exploration and transfiguration of this popular mode, relating it to its Ovidian essence of grotesque physicality and explosive bodily transformation in the work of Georges Méliès.

An Ovidian Renaissance

It can be convincingly argued that cinema is defined by a Pygmalion complex, as it magically brings to life static figures from Eadweard Muybridge's experiments in chronophotography onward.[1] The myth of Pygmalion not only serves as an apt metaphor, however; it was also a highly popular trope in nineteenth- and early-twentieth-century performance culture, from its literal transfiguration of marble into flesh to George Bernard Shaw's 1912 update of the myth as a class commentary. Shaw's play, *Pygmalion*, was remade numerous times over the span of the following decades—most notably as the stage musical *My Fair Lady* (Alan Jay Lerner and Frederick Loewe, 1956).

The original Ovidian account of Pygmalion in *The Metamorphoses* (ca. AD 8) tells of a Cypriot sculptor who, frustrated with the vices of the immoral local women known as the Propoetides (i.e., Cypriot women who were turned into the first prostitutes by a vengeful Venus, whom they dared deny the title of goddess), decided to create his own perfect female out of ivory. The beauty of the virtuous statue was so breathtaking that the sculptor fell in love with his own creation and beseeched Venus to bestow it with life. The artist's wish was granted and the cold ivory turned to warm flesh at his touch.[2] Whereas the popular retelling of Ovid's myth leaves Pygmalion with a subservient spouse, statues coming to life in cinema almost always signal death and destruction. This trope becomes most apparent in horror films from the 1930s onward, as well as in a number of films of the 1960s and 1970s that take place in an ancient Greco-Roman or more generalized historical setting—these films are also known as peplum films, referring to the tunics worn by the actors, or sword-and-sandal films, for more obvious reasons.

The myth's popularity in the nineteenth century was solidly anchored in a more general artistic revival of classicism that saw ancient Greek culture—or more precisely, the *idea* of ancient Greek culture—as its pinnacle.[3] The second half of the nineteenth century was especially marked by an overwhelming theatrical proliferation of *tableaux vivants* due to the efforts of stage producers such as Edward Kilanyi.[4] His methods proved to be highly precinematic in their execution; not only did Kilanyi use illusionary matte techniques and lighting to perform his "Venus de Milo" act (making his model's arms disappear against a black backdrop), he also took out a patent on an "Apparatus for Displaying Tableaux Vivant" [sic], which was a turntable platform that allowed for an uninterrupted series of *tableaux*, or "Kilanyi's Living Pictures."[5] The "Famous Rahl & Bradley" duo were also, for instance, part of this classicist revival, as the two performers put on a neoclassicist living-statue act at the turn of the century, covered entirely in bronze paint—an alternative to the more prevalent whitewash—to imitate mythical figures such as Orpheus and Eurydice.[6] In the early twentieth century, vaudeville performers like the famous "La Milo," the Australian Pansy Montague, continued in the same vein. La Milo gave evidence of the period's fascination with the "perfect female body"—that of the Venus de Milo—with whom she identified herself, posing in alabaster whiting to achieve a marble effect as she performed statues of goddesses that walked the line between art and voyeurism.[7]

It comes as no surprise, then, that film producers and directors picked up the idea of the statue coming to life early on. I argue that the silver-screen iterations did the most justice to the violence and viscerality that is inherent in the Ovidian transformation myths from *Metamorphoses*. As classicist Charles Segal has noted, Ovid's depiction of the body is marked by "his representation of a world in which reason and order decompose into frightening confusion and chaos," and this "grotesque physicality of the body" returns throughout Western literature to comment on the "darker, less organized, perhaps more primordial . . . visions of the self."[8] If there is one cinematic universe that corresponds to this description it is surely the chaotic world of Georges Méliès, where the body is never safe from violation, violent transformation, or sheer disintegration. Taking an Ovidian stance, this chapter focuses on Méliès's many adaptations and transfigurations of the Pygmalion myth.

Celluloid Pygmalion

The success of *tableaux vivants* coincided with the birth of film, and recent scholarship in early cinema has started paying more attention to the phenomenon on screen.[9] In the late 1890s, for instance, the American Mutoscope and Biograph Company produced numerous film versions of living pictures, joining the craze for living pictures that dominated the American popular stage in the mid-1890s, when stage directors and impresarios such as Kilanyi and Oscar Hammerstein had become popular with their *tableaux vivants* based on European paintings and sculptures. Such films were intended for vaudeville houses, where spectators could compare living pictures on film either to living pictures as performed on stage or to the artwork that was evoked (or more likely a reproduction of it). According to Charles Musser, both living pictures and Edison's motion pictures "offered their respective spectators similar kinds of pleasure as each produced a cultural work (painting, sculpture or performance) in another medium, encouraging comparison between the 'original' and its reproduction."[10]

Early cinema's fascination for *tableaux vivants* and the effect of stasis goes hand in hand with a penchant for its opposite—the picture or statue coming to life. Trick or transformation films such as *The Devil in the Studio* (Paul's Animatograph Works, 1901), *An Artist's Dream* (Edison Manufacturing Company, 1900), *The Artist's Dilemma* (Edison Manufacturing Company, 1901), *The Artist's Studio* (American Mutoscope and Biograph Company, 1903), *Animated Picture Studio* (American Mutoscope and Biograph Company, 1903), and *Animated Painting* (Edison Manufacturing Company, 1904) showcase remarkable scenes in which enchanted paintings come to life.[11] These also pervade early cinema in *La Statue* (Gaumont, 1905), *L'Homme de Marbre* (Gaumont, 1908), *Mephisto's Affinity* (Lubin, 1908), *The Sculptor's Nightmare* (American Mutoscope and Biograph Company/Wallace McCutcheon, 1908), *Amour d'Esclave* (Pathé Frères, 1907), the artistic ensemble *tableau vivant* demonstration film *Meissner Porzellan! Lebende Skulpturen der Diodattis im Berliner Wintergarten* (Gaumont, ca. 1912–1914), and *Il Fauno* (Ambrosio, 1917), among others.

These films usually have similar tricks, effects, and narratives to those that feature animated paintings, but there are also some crucial differences. In contrast to two-dimensional paintings, which evoke another world within the limits of their frames, three-dimensional sculptures are part of the same world as the film's characters. In addition, within the context of the film medium, which precisely animates or mobilizes static objects, the different associations evoked by the arts of painting and sculpture regarding life and death are highly relevant. Cinema, after all, originated at a time when painting itself attempted to evoke life and movement. With its fascination for the contingencies of the everyday and its preference for movement and the play of light, modernist painting, for instance, has often been associated with "filmic" qualities. While the pictorial innovations of impressionism were often explained by referring to the vividness and flux of cinema, sculpture was often associated with history, the past, eternity, and death. The tableau's inherent oscillation between movement and stillness is therefore often used as a metaphor for the tension between life and death. *Tableaux vivants* invert the age-old fascination for the inanimate statue, like Pygmalion's Galatea, magically coming to life. It is no coincidence that the Pygmalion motif first became important in the arts of the eighteenth century, which also saw the rise of *tableaux vivants* as a popular art form. Early cinema continued this "Pygmalionism" that marked the legitimate and popular stage throughout the nineteenth century.

Méliès's Screen Bodies

One of the first extant instances of the cinematic living statue can be found in a short and frenetic presentation of the photographic talents of Georges Méliès. In 1898 Méliès produced his first (extant) living-statue shorts, *Le Magicien* and *Pygmalion et Galathée*. Méliès embodied the figure of the mythical sculptor Pygmalion like no other, willing life into the lifeless, but by virtue of his magical apparatus he takes on the additional role of the deity. In what he has dubbed the "Pygmalion effect," Victor Stoichita sees the blurring of boundaries between model and sculpture—or between original and copy, if you will—operating within the connected realm of aesthetics, magic, and technical skill.[12]

For his feverish expression of Pygmalionism in *Le Magicien*, Méliès chose a decidedly nonnarrative approach that let cinematographic trickery mesh with his own brand of performance against a cardboard stage backdrop resembling a medieval wizard's lair and featuring a very large matted-out "entrance," indicative of the superimposition effects that follow. At a certain moment in the film, a nobleman grabs a Pierrot character by the shoulder. Thanks to the simple but effective stop-camera technique, the setting suddenly changes, with the Pierrot disappearing and the nobleman turning into what appears to be a bearded ancient Greek or Roman sculptor in a toga. He picks up a marble-looking bust of a woman, places it on a sculpting stand, and goes to work with a hammer and chisel. The bust comes to life, however, and throws away the sculptor's tools with newly sprouted arms. The sculptor cries out in disbelief, while the woman's bust changes into a fully fledged statue on a pedestal before his eyes—though we are actually looking at a motionless woman, performing a *pose plastique*. She is clad in a long tunic, seems slightly whitewashed, and is holding a harp at arm's length. Utterly delighted, the sculptor tries to grab the statue, but it vanishes and reappears behind his back in a different pose, hands now held skyward. The same thing happens again, and the statue is now in a seated position on a stool with its legs crossed, holding a pitcher above its head and a cup in the other hand. When the sculptor tries to go for it again, the statue vanishes into smoke and the nobleman reappears, kicking him in the behind. It is immediately apparent from *Le Magicien* that the magician's stage tradition was assimilated in the new film medium, with Méliès actively playing the part of the newly formed *cinémagicien*, who brought to life a multitude of imagery such as paintings, posters, and playing cards, and often also working with typical stage types such as the Chinese conjurer, the drunk clown, the medieval jester, and the Pierrot figure.

The living-statue trope was, however, particularly prevalent in Méliès's work, appearing in no less than seventeen of his (extant) films between 1898 and 1911, when one compiles a "statuography."[13] Twelve of these are mostly nonnarrative acts,[14] often with the conjurer character as protagonist, while five of the films provide a more plot-driven context for the living statue,[15] with two out of those five placing it in a(n) (even more) fantastical or dreamlike setting.[16] A common thread in all of these films is the period setting, with a prevalence of the medieval setting and the "Antique" backdrop—referring to either a general Greco-Roman style or an eighteenth-century revival version of it. A wide variety of transformations occurred in Méliès's work, often within the same film, but in most cases the statues themselves were represented by (wax) mannequins or women in togas posing as living statues. In spite of the stage traditions, however, these women did not seem to be whitewashed in any way; a possible explanation for this might be the time frame Méliès was working in, as the length of most of his (statue) films was limited.

The longer narrative films did not set out to show a single living-statue act unfurling slowly, as it would on the stage, but rather to display Méliès's craft with regard to the creation of fantastical imagery through special effects, set, and costume design. His shorter trick films were equally jam-packed showreels filled to the brim with special effects and jokes that bombarded the audience at a near murderous pace, thus creating a strong contrast with the immobility and tranquility of statuary. Furthermore, these living statues were certainly not always whitewashed on the stage, and Méliès not only might have thought his live models to be convincing enough for the short period of time that they were on-screen, which sometimes amounted to mere seconds, but also might have found the appearance of "live flesh" preferable, as this revealed certain titillating details such as ankles, partly bared chests and, of course, underarm hair, which was considered highly intimate and sexually suggestive.[17]

The latter was very visible in several statuesque poses in *Le Magicien*, and the scantily dressed woman reappears in the 1903 *La Statue Animée*, in which an eighteenth-century-clad and periwigged gentleman jokester conjures up a living statue in a white dress out of thin air, wearing and holding a veil, to play a joke on a visiting drawing class. The professor of the class marvels at the beauty of the statue, making rather explicit hand gestures with regard to its female contours, and checking on the work of his students vigorously. When he passes the statue, however, it comes to life and takes off his hat, lifting it high into the sky in a new pose that reveals her underarm hair. The class is baffled at the statue's lively gesture, but before they realize what has happened, the living statue has turned into a statuesque fountain with a dragon's head, and the jokester returns to dump the professor into the water.

The use of mannequins brought an even more visceral edge to Méliès's work, as his cinematic magic sees them being taken apart and built up quite violently at times. His living-statue films demonstrate not only the malleability of bodies—be they mannequin, bronze, marble, cardboard, or flesh—but also the strength and violence with which the filmmaker enforces his own Ovidian metamorphoses; as Stoichita so aptly put it, "The myth of Pygmalion challenges the visual in the name of the tactile."[18] We can also draw a parallel between Ovid and Méliès following Philip Hardie's conception of what he dubs Ovid's "illusionist aesthetics." As Hardie sees it, Ovid's writing is illusionistic in that it has the power to summon "vivid visions" for its readership, inspiring a sense of reality in spite of the often fantastic and visceral content; with this aesthetic approach, Hardie states, Ovid shares a challenge similar to painters or sculptors, who often strive to evoke reality just enough to "elide the boundary between art and nature."[19] Georges Méliès's use of mannequins similarly plays on the idea of presenting the viewer with an "illusionist aesthetic." The mannequin is per definition an imitation of human life that holds in itself both an outspoken artificiality and the innate possibility of life. In this way, the mannequins further the elision of the boundary between art and nature, and Méliès's special effects push them far over that edge. The mannequins made their appearance almost exclusively in Méliès's nonnarrative films such as *Guillaume Tell et le Clown* (1898), *L'Illusionniste Fin de Siècle* (1899), and the 1903 *Illusions Funambulesques* and *Tom Tight et Dum Dum*, among others.[20]

A more conventional interpretation of the living-statue trope can be found in Méliès's narrative films, where we see that the living statue is employed as a religious or mythological occurrence. In *La Tentation de Saint Antoine* (1898), for instance, the French filmmaker explores the famous literary and art-historical motif of the temptation of Saint Anthony the Great, who was said to have experienced supernatural temptations during his pilgrimage into the desert.[21] The motif is widely known via sixteenth-century paintings by Hieronymus Bosch, who depicted the saint as an old man in a monk's habit sporting a large beard, surrounded by demons. Méliès presents him in the same way, taking inspiration from an episode in the life of Saint Anthony, where he hides from demons in a cave. The film shows the hermit in a cave before a large crucifix holding a life-sized statue of Christ on a pedestal, but before long scantily clad women seem to appear out of thin air to bother. When he prays to his crucifix, the statue of Jesus transforms into a real woman, stepping down from the cross to taunt him. Anthony is finally released from his misery when an angel appears to rid him of the women and make Jesus reappear on the cross.

A divine intervention similarly ends a medieval couple's plight in *Le Diable Géant ou le Miracle de la Madone* (1901), when a wax Madonna statue comes to life to banish a hyperactive devil and reunite the lovers. Méliès tackles the same trope from a mythological angle in *L'Oracle de Delphes* (1903), but although Delphi and its Oracle were very much part of Greek culture, the setting is nevertheless an Egyptian one. We see a small temple in the foreground, guarded by two stone male sphinxes on pedestals, while the background shows a large pyramid and another temple featuring an Egyptian mural. A thief attempts to steal the shrine in the temple but stops in dread when a priestlike apparition summons him to give back the shrine. The thief begs for mercy, but the priest then transforms his two male sphinxes into two female helpers who turn the thief's head into that of a donkey, before returning to their pedestals and turning back into sphinxes.[22]

Conclusion

Not to be overlooked in this discourse is the comic potential of the statue. Most, if not all, of the Méliès films were comedies that played on the possibilities that the living-statue trope offered: people mistaken for statues; people pretending to be statues; statues striking back; statues surprising visitors who are violating the taboo against touching a statue of a human; statues ridiculing their maker; or statues just running off. As Matthew Solomon has already proven at length, Georges Méliès's films represent a cross-fertilization of popular vaudevillian entertainment and the magic of cinema,[23] and they foreshadow marked instances of slapstick statues in films such as *The Goat* (Buster Keaton and Malcolm St. Clair, 1921), *Roaming Romeo* (Lupino Lane, 1928), *Animal Crackers* (Victor Heerman, 1930), and *City Lights* (Charles Chaplin, 1931). Méliès employs a satirical take on the figure of the sculptor, sticking to stagey backdrops and caricature, and banking on his explosive and erratic stage presence for most of his trick work. The switch from inert, dead matter to living flesh and back was a key component of his act, as it demonstrated his skill and strengthened the illusionary aspect of his oeuvre, infusing it with the mythos of cinema.

His films also exemplify the conflation of media (theater, painting, and sculpture) that defined the *tableau vivant*, while also showing the early twentieth century's fascination with classicism and illusionism; Méliès's camera made for the ultimate illusionary machine. Furthermore, the three-dimensionality of the statues forms a sharp contrast with the two-dimensional cardboard backdrops in Méliès's work. Interestingly, however, the presence of a (living) statue did not halt the narrative but rather accelerated or started it. We can see that in these films, Méliès takes a fluid approach to notions of life and death—one that sees statues come to life and revert back, and has characters pulled apart and put back together again, all with great ease, in what can be called bloodless Ovidian violence. This connects with Kenneth Gross's view that the statue is a transitional form—retaining the idea of both past and future life.[24] This view is, of course, prompted by the particularity of the medium, as sculpture has been imbued with both magic vivification and mortification from the earliest mythological texts onward, with the trope of Pygmalion being one of the foremost examples. In this tradition, sculpture is easily equated with magic, witchcraft, or alchemy, not coincidentally in the same vein as cinema. Thus, we can state that the living-statue trope was surely one of the most interesting dialectical forms of its time, combining highbrow and lowbrow art in popular entertainment and living on in the newest of media. The living statue in early cinema was thus comic and erotic, explosive and visceral, often *unheimlich*, and inherently intermedial.

VITO ADRIAENSENS is Visiting Scholar and Adjunct Assistant Professor at Columbia University. He is author with Steven Jacobs, Susan Felleman, and Lisa Colpaert of *Screening Statues: Sculpture and Cinema*.

Notes

1. In Ovid studies, this comparison was recently elaborated in Martin M. Winkler, "Ovid and the Cinema: An Introduction," in *A Handbook to the Reception of Ovid*, ed. John F. Miller and Carole E. Newlands (Oxford, UK: Wiley, 2014), 469–83.
2. Paula James, *Ovid's Myth of Pygmalion on Screen: In Pursuit of the Perfect Woman* (London: Continuum, 2011), 12.
3. Jack W. McCullough, *Living Pictures on the New York Stage* (Ann Arbor, MI: UMI Research Press, 1983), 16.
4. Ibid., 101.

5. Ibid., 104.

6. See "The Famous Rahl & Bradley Living Bronze Statues" (ca. 1895), photograph in the Library of Congress Prints and Photographs Division, LOT 11805 (F) [P&P].

7. See Andrew L. Erdman, *Blue Vaudeville: Sex, Morals and the Mass Marketing of Amusement, 1895–1915* (Jefferson, NC: McFarland, 2004), 106; and David Huxley, "Music Hall Art: La Milo, Nudity and the Pose Plastique 1905–1915," *Early Popular Visual Culture* 11, no. 3 (2013): 218–36.

8. Charles Segal, "Ovid's Metamorphic Bodies: Art, Gender, and Violence in the 'Metamorphoses,'" *Arion: A Journal of Humanities and the Classics* 5, no. 3 (1998): 10–11.

9. See Ivo Blom, "Quo Vadis? From Painting to Cinema and Everything in Between," in *La decima musa. Il cinema e le altre arti/The Tenth Muse. Cinema and other arts*, ed. Leonardo Quaresima and Laura Vichi (Udine, Italy: Forum, 2001), 281–96; Valentine Robert, "La pose au cinéma: film et tableau en corps-à-corps," in *Entre code et corps. Tableau vivant et photographie mise en scène*, ed. Christine Buignet and Arnaud Rykner (Pau, France: Presses Universitaires de Pau et des Pays de l'Adour, 2012), 73–89; and Daniel Wiegand, "'Performed Live and Talking. No kinematograph': Amateur Performances of Tableaux Vivants and Local Film Exhibition in Germany around 1900," in *Performing New Media, 1890–1915*, ed. Kaveh Askari, Scott Curtis, Frank Gray, Louis Pelletier, Tami Williams, and Joshua Yumibe (New Barnet, UK: John Libbey Publishing, 2014), 373–87.

10. Charles Musser, "A Cornucopia of Images: Comparison and Judgment across Theater, Film, and the Visual Arts during the Late Nineteenth Century," in *Moving Pictures: American Art and Early Film 1880–1910*, ed. Nancy Mowll Mathews and Charles Musser (Manchester, VT: Hudson Hills Press, 2005), 8.

11. Since the 2016 Domitor conference, this and the previous paragraph have been appropriated in Vito Adriaensens and Steven Jacobs, "The Sculptor's Dream: Living Statues in Early Cinema," in *Screening Statues: Sculpture and Cinema*, eds. Steven Jacobs, Susan Felleman, Vito Adriaensens, and Lisa Colpaert (Edinburgh, UK: Edinburgh University Press, 2017), 29–45. See also Steven Jacobs, *Framing Pictures: Film and the Visual Arts* (Edinburgh, UK: Edinburgh University Press, 2011), 91.

12. Victor Stoichita, *The Pygmalion Effect: From Ovid to Hitchcock* (Chicago: University of Chicago Press, 2008), 5.

13. Georges Méliès's statuography: *Le Magicien* (1898); *Pygmalion et Galathée* (1898); *Guillaume Tell et le Clown* (1898); *La Tentation de Saint Antoine* (1898); *L'Illusionniste fin de siècle* (1899); *Le Diable géant ou le Miracle de la madone* (1901); *La Statue animée* (1903); *L'Oracle de Delphes* (1903); *Tom Tight et Dum Dum* (1903); *Illusions funambulesques* (1903); *Le Baquet de Mesmer* (1904); *La Chaise à porteurs enchantée* (1905); *Les Bulles de savon vivantes* (1906); *Le Tambourin fantastique* (1908); *La Bonne Bergère et la Mauvaise Princesse* (1908); *Les Illusions fantaisistes* (1909); and *Les Hallucinations du baron de Münchhausen* (1911). All films were produced by Méliès's own Star Films.

14. Respectively: *Le Magicien* (1898); *Pygmalion et Galathée* (1898); *Guillaume Tell et le Clown* (1898); *L'Illusionniste fin de siècle* (1899); *La statue animée* (1903); *Tom Tight et Dum Dum* (1903); *Illusions funambulesques* (1903); *Le Baquet de Mesmer* (1904); *La Chaise à porteurs enchantée* (1905); *Les Bulles de savon vivantes* (1906); *Le Tambourin fantastique* (1908); and *Les Illusions fantaisistes* (1909).

15. *La Tentation de Saint Antoine* (1898); *Le diable géant ou le miracle de la madone* (1901); *L'oracle de Delphes* (1903); *La Bonne Bergère et La Mauvaise Princesse* (1908); and *Les Hallucinations de Baron de Munchausen* (1911).

16. *La Bonne Bergère et la Mauvaise Princesse* (1908) and *Les Hallucinations du baron de Münchhausen* (1911).

17. Francesca Berry, "Bedrooms: Corporeality and Subjectivity," in *Domestic Interiors: Representing Homes from the Victorians to the Moderns*, ed. Georgina Downey (London: Bloomsbury Academic, 2013), 132–33.

18. Stoichita, *The Pygmalion Effect*, 203.

19. Philip Hardie, *Ovid's Poetics of Illusion* (Cambridge, UK: Cambridge University Press, 2002), 7.

20. Mannequins were used in *Guillaume Tell et le Clown* (1898); *L'Illusionniste fin de siècle* (1899); *Le diable géant ou le miracle de la madone* (1901); *Tom Tight et Dum Dum* (1903); *Illusions funambulesques* (1903); *La chaise à porteurs enchantée* (1905); and *Les Illusions fantaisistes* (1909).

21. David M. Gwynn, *Athanasius of Alexandria: Bishop, Theologian, Ascetic, Father* (Oxford, UK: Oxford University Press, 2012).

22. Almut-Barbara Renger, *Oedipus and the Sphinx: The Threshold Myth from Sophocles through Freud to Cocteau* (Chicago: University of Chicago Press, 2013), 33. Méliès's choice to turn male sphinxes into rather scantily clad females is not surprising, but it is interesting to note that the Egyptian sphinxes were indeed mostly male, whereas the Greek sphinx was predominantly female.

23. Matthew Solomon, *Disappearing Tricks: Silent Film, Houdini, and the New Magic of the Twentieth Century* (Urbana: University of Illinois Press, 2011).

24. Kenneth Gross, *The Dream of the Moving Statue* (Philadelphia: Pennsylvania State University Press, 2006), 130.

3 The Body under the Scalpel in the Illustrated Press and the Cinema

Jérémy Houillère

Translated by Timothy Barnard

IN THE LATTER half of the nineteenth century, people sought to reclaim their bodies. Sports and clothing fashions were popular ways to modify one's physical appearance during this period. Engravings and drawings of a variety of athletes (wrestlers, jockeys, boxers) began to circulate widely in the popular press. Advertising, too, was full of all kinds of body-care products, to both improve one's appearance and prevent improbable illnesses (a pill to add inches to your chest, a lotion to make your hair grow, a syrup to cure all ailments). In the private sphere, the use of the bath became more diversified and was now employed to clean and care for one's body. This largely European hygiene movement intensified the image of a sound, healthy, and young body.[1] Scientific progress would play a part in this trend, particularly in the fields of medicine and anatomy. Health became a major social issue at the same time as knowledge about the human body was growing. Microbiology and, in particular, the discovery of X-rays in 1895 radically changed people's perception of the body, which seemed to no longer hold any secrets.[2] With X-rays, it became possible for the first time to contemplate one's own living skeleton, providing individuals with their "inner portrait." And yet, as David Le Breton remarks, this shift did not take place without an upheaval in people's way of thinking. The X-ray experience did not leave one unscathed; being confronted with the "satanic" image of one's own skeleton was especially traumatic.[3] The magazine *Life* caricatured the procedure with a mocking skull captioned, "Look pleasant, please."[4]

This illustration, at once cynical and morbid, drew on the tradition of caricaturing doctors. In the nineteenth-century satirical press, it was common for doctors' examining rooms to be pictured as littered with human skulls or skeletons. Not intended as an anatomy lesson, these skeletons reminded readers that doctors more often caused their patients' death than they succeeded in healing them. Constantly made fun of by illustrators for their lack of empathy toward the sick and the obvious ineffectiveness of their interventions, doctors (or surgeons—both terms were used to describe the same scourge) were regularly compared to butchers. Despite the progress that had been made in numerous scientific fields, the suspicions that took root in popular culture were a good indication of people's reluctance to entrust their body to medical science. The case of anesthesia, which developed rapidly in the latter half of the nineteenth century, is a good example of this ambivalence. While anesthesia made it possible for the sick to avoid horrible pain, it was seen most of all as a Machiavellian means to deprive patients of control over their body and give the surgeon, that omnipotent demiurge, complete power over it.

The cinema, whose invention contributed to this scientific effervescence late in the century, immediately took hold of the satirical image of the doctor. In the illustrated press and the earliest films, several narratives circulated featuring a doctor and his patient; for example, that of the surgeon who, after an operation, realizes he has left a number of personal effects inside the patient. Georges Méliès reproduced this subject in *Une indigestion* (*Sure Cure for Indigestion*) in 1902, before Gaumont seized on it in 1909 with *Un chirurgien distrait* (*The Absent-Minded Surgeon*). In this film, after his operation the patient prepares to leave, but the surgeon realizes he has lost his pince-nez. He finds it—in the patient's stomach! And so he opens the patient up again, recovers his pince-nez, sews the patient's belly back up, and then realizes that he also left his newspaper there, and then his toothpick, his hat, and his wallet. In the newspaper *Le Rire*, also in the year 1909, this gag took the form of a short text titled "Une opération," in which three surgeons operate on and lose an object somewhere in the patient's body: a snuff box in his stomach, forceps in the small intestine, eyeglasses in the rectum.[5]

The patient's body is at the heart of this narrative formula. The doctor's negligence leads him to cut the patient open in various places, which in another context could be seen as a form of torture (we will see shortly the extent to which doctors were seen as similar to torturers). The mistreated, manhandled, and abused body can also be seen from the perspective of intermediality. When the illustrated press and the cinema met, the satirical figure of the doctor was consistently related to the body in ways this essay will explore. I will begin with a discussion of the doctor himself and the various caricatures that circulated from one medium to another. I will then examine in greater detail the patient's body, and in particular the way in which the cinema seized hold of it to create an invulnerable body that could stand up to any ordeal, far from the suffering and battered body of the illustrated papers.

Images of Surgeons

By the late nineteenth century, the tradition of satirizing doctors was well established in the illustrated press.[6] Surgeons and doctors were depicted as paragons of indifference toward their patients. Whereas eighteenth-century engravers showed prestigious surgeons operating with elegant gestures in lace sleeves,[7] the poor reputation of doctors in the nineteenth century largely transformed this kind of depiction.[8] In humorous newspapers it was common to see caricatures of distracted surgeons amputating the wrong member. The patient, stretched out and held in place when he was not put to sleep, often had no part in the operation taking place. Most often he was merely an extra. In a drawing published in 1901 in the newspaper *Le Pêle-Mêle*, two surgeons "haggle over" their patient's legs.[9] One thinks it is necessary to cut off one leg, the other two. Finally, they agree on a leg and a half. This compromise, naturally, comes at the expense of the health of the patient, who watches the scene in the background with a scowl, confined to his bed. We see only his head. His body is supposed to be the principal thing at stake in this discussion, but it is practically absent from the picture, while the smiling doctors appear in the foreground. Even the drawing's title—"Entre chirurgiens" ("Between Surgeons")—underscores the patient's effacement.

Dialogue has a very small role in the relations between doctor and patient. And when there is dialogue, it is often tinged with cynicism. In another drawing in *Le Pêle-Mêle* (figure 3.1), the surgeon tells his patient, whose leg has been amputated, that his socks will now last a year rather than six months.[10] In the upper right-hand corner of the picture, the doctor's intern stifles a laugh with one hand, a knife in the other. This attitude could be attributed to the legendary "irreverence" of medical students, who were depicted as reproducing or extending some of the behavior of their predecessors: a "dehumanized vocabulary, black humor, grotesque or comic use of pieces of corpses, [and] hurling bits of human flesh in 'scrap meat battles.'"[11] It is thus not surprising to see several drawings flirt with a kind of cruelty, which the authors depict ironically, as if the surgeon was taking pleasure in cutting up his patient. There were many cases, moreover, of drawings in the press showing a patient who does not necessarily require an amputation losing a member only because of his doctor's zeal.

Above all, these drawings target an entire profession, making little distinction between the country doctor and the hospital surgeon. The caricaturists of the most "politicized" publications, however, took aim directly at public figures, such as Dr. Doyen. A special issue of *L'Assiette au beurre*, titled "Les Écorcheurs" ("The Flayers"), depicts on its cover a full-length portrait of Doyen, whose name is written on the desk behind which he is standing.[12] In *Chanteclair*, he prepares to anesthetize a decomposed mummy;[13] several bloody knives and a pincer call to mind the title of the issue of *L'Assiette au beurre* just mentioned. The symbolic figure of death, in the form of a winged skeleton, overlooks the scene with a horrified gaze, a scythe in its hand. When even death appears to fear Dr. Doyen, that's saying something. The cinema did not lag behind when it came to this kind of caricature. In this respect, Thierry Lefebvre discusses the Méliès films *Une*

CONSOLATION
— Eh bien vous avez tout de même de la chance ; maintenant une paire de chaussettes va vous faire un an au lieu de six mois.

Figure 3.1. A surgeon's "consolation," cartoon published in *Le Pêle-Mêle*, July 8, 1900, 12 (Bibliothèque nationale de France, Gallica).

indigestion (1902), mentioned earlier, and his *Le Malade hydrophobe* (*The Man with Wheels in His Head*, 1900), in which a doctor uses the same instruments that made Dr. Doyen famous: a punch, a mortiser, a mallet, and bone shears.[14] But the most famous film, and the one most cited, is certainly *Opération chirurgicale* (*Surgical Operation*), produced by Pathé in 1905. According to Lefebvre, this film was made to get revenge on Doyen after he brought suit against Pathé a few months earlier.[15] In the film, a surgeon (played by Alphonse Émile Dieudonné) and his interns operate on a patient, from whom they extract all sorts of improbable objects: a pipe, a hat, a piece of rope, a fan, and so on. The surgeon carries out the operation with disconcerting levity, rummaging in the belly of his patient as it were a toy chest. Beside him, his interns are jovial and play with the objects as they are removed from the patient's stomach. The last object to emerge is a pocket watch, which the patient tries to recover. The presence of this watch, the only object of value removed by the surgeon, which the patient does not want to let him have, is most certainly an allusion to the greediness of which doctors were regularly accused.

Doyen was thus not an exception. Like his colleagues, he is depicted as greedy. Indeed, a large majority of satirical drawings show doctors as being very concerned about their fees, even if it meant the patient's health was secondary to their money. In some cases, the artist would go so far as to compare surgeons explicitly to merchants and even bankers. In a drawing in Le Pêle-Mêle, for example, it was suggested that practice operations be carried out on living models.[16] The surgeon, like a dressmaker, demonstrates a sample of his knowledge to a potential customer—to the detriment of the patient-model, of course, who is truly operated on. Every operation has its price, which quite often can be very high indeed. It must be earned. It is quite clear from another drawing in Le Pêle-Mêle prophesying what a surgical office would look like in the 1920s, that surgery was not available to everyone.[17] On the ground floor, patients are pictured as divided up according to their social class. For the less well-off (government employees, members of the military, clergymen), obtaining care is difficult: they have to present themselves at a different counter. If you are a worker, you simply go on your way. In the operating room, operations are done as if on an automobile assembly line. Everything is in place to rationalize the work and speed up the treatment, with the goal, of course, of increasing profits. This system, which puts performance ahead of quality, treats the body as common merchandise, a consumer good.

The Body in Pieces

This overt disdain for the ill body is a recurring motif in the illustrated press, to the point of taking a morbid turn. As in the drawing about Doyen, death is almost always present, whether in an explicit and brutal manner or in a more diffuse fashion, lurking in the background. In one Le Pêle-Mêle drawing (figure 3.2), a surgeon addresses the reader in the following terms: "I had barely begun when I saw that the patient was dead. Nevertheless, I continued the operation with all my usual care and zeal."[18] Some illustrators even appear to have made a game of this, with winks to the reader; for example, in a drawing for Le Rire, Manfredini placed a revolver among the doctor's instruments in the background.[19]

Figure 3.2. A "conscientious" surgeon, strip published in *Le Pêle-Mêle*, May 26, 1907, 12 (Bibliothèque nationale de France, Gallica).

We have to assume that this appeal of the macabre was specific to the illustrated press, because the cinema offered a somewhat more optimistic view of the patient's lot. There, while surgeons were zealous, they nevertheless succeeded—under sometimes fantastic circumstances—to care for the sick. Alice Guy's film *Chirurgie fin de siècle* (*Turn-of-the-Century Surgery*, Gaumont, 1900) describes a surgical operation from beginning to end. The first half of the film is devoted entirely to the surgeon's choice of instruments. First, on the left-hand edge of the frame, he hesitates for a long while as his interns anesthetize the patient. He begins by choosing a hand saw, then quickly falls back on a bow saw, the kind most often used for amputations, before taking hold of a large pair of shears. Surgical instruments are given special treatment in the films and drawings of this period. Most often, they are disproportionately large, and sometimes even stained with blood. They are not there to reassure the patient, the reader, or the viewer; on the contrary, through metonymy, they represent the savagery with which the surgeon carries out the operation. In this case, precisely, after choosing his instruments the surgeon gets down to work, alternating several times between his three instruments before succeeding, finally, in amputating the arm and leg of his patient.

All the barbarity associated with surgery in the public's imagination is crystallized in the first half of this film. The surgeon, caricatured to the utmost, makes a dozen attempts before managing to amputate the patient's members. This film appears to want to remind us that surgery was originally practiced in torture chambers. During their interrogations, torturers would ask questions and then treat the victim by reducing their dislocations or fractures or by amputating their battered members.[20] It is not by chance that we find depictions in this body of work that explicitly compare surgeons with torturers.[21] The image of the surgeon thus remained associated with that of the torturer, and his tools likened to those of torture.

In the second half of the film, the surgeon leaves the room and lets his interns carry on. Their task is to graft new members onto the patient. They have with them a selection of "spare parts" that they attach to the amputated patient with animal glue, commonly used to mend broken bones. After a brief drying time, the patient gets out of bed and moves around as good as new; he is healed. The damaged members have been replaced by new ones in good condition.

When Alice Guy made this film in 1908, surgical grafting was not yet done on humans. It was still a fantasy. The first tests by French surgeons took place in 1906, and on animals. Moreover, the illustrated press made very little mention of this kind of miraculous reconstitution. There were many amputees, but they appeared destined to remain so. Amputation was irremediable and was one of the cruelties doctors were guilty of. And yet in theaters, circuses, and music halls, pantomimes and magic shows were full of dismembered bodies put back together. Méliès cut up bodies and put them back together in his theater, the Robert-Houdin, for a long time before doing so in front of a moving-picture camera. Patrick Désile's research has convincingly demonstrated the importance of the comic decapitation motif in Belle Époque live entertainment and its circulation in early cinema.[22] Heads rolled and bodies ran after them in the hopes of putting them back in their place. It was more in this context, I believe, that films such as *Chirurgie fin de siècle* and *Chirurgie esthétique* (*Cosmetic Surgery* [Lux], 1907 [?]) should be seen. In the latter film, a mad surgeon removes his patient's head in order to give her a new one more in keeping with the beauty standards of the day. The detached head continues to move about on its stand, its facial features stretching and contracting to make all kinds of grimaces, exactly like the decapitated astrologer in *Zazezizozu* (1835), whose head pops up throughout the play.[23]

The Spectacle of the Machine

In early cinema, the body cut into pieces and put back together was thus, above all, a spectacular body, an attraction. This attraction, developed in stage entertainment, was seized on by the cinema, which lost no time in "machine treating" it. In the same way that early cinema "machined the world," in François Albera's expression,[24] we might say that it began to "machine the body." The body was deconstructed and reconstructed over and over again. In the Lumière film *Chirurgie mécanique* (*Mechanical Surgery*, 1903) the surgeon, like a blacksmith, uses an anvil and a hammer to straighten the leg of a patient who limps. Once the leg is repaired, he puts it back on the patient, who immediately begins to walk. He repeats the operation on a patient with a hunchback by striking his back with a sledgehammer, miraculously straightening him out.

This *mechanical* model, which can be traced back to Descartes and La Mettrie,[25] is part of what François Albera and Maria Tortajada call the "*clock*

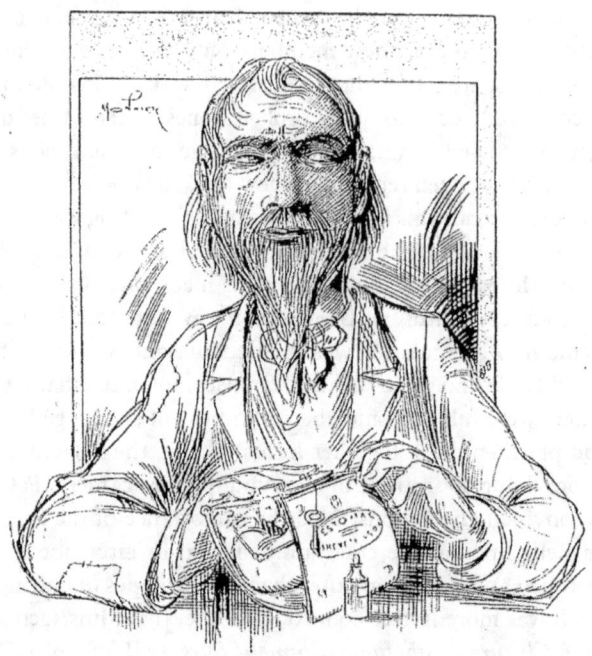

UNE TROUVAILLE

Le docteur Lesuc-Gastrique, inventeur d'un estomac mécanique à réglage variable, échappement à ancre, broyeur, concasseur, tritureur automatiques. Cet instrument remplace avantageusement les vieux estomacs délabrés et hors d'usage.

Figure 3.3. "A find" by a mechanically talented surgeon, cartoon published in *Le Pêle-Mêle*, March 10, 1901, 3 (Bibliothèque nationale de France, Gallica).

episteme." Separation, assemblage, articulation, and automatism are recurring forms of this episteme—forms that early cinema explored at length.[26] In the context of "turn-of-the-century medicine," this mechanical conception of the human body found astonishing applications. There was, for example, a "mechanical stomach," developed by Dr. Lesuc-Gastrique (figure 3.3), the advantage of which was its ability to replace a defective stomach without fail.[27] The mechanical body was thought to be impossible to wear out and able to make up for all the deficiencies of the biological body. Every member was interchangeable; defective members were replaced by a "spare part," like the savagely decapitated patient in Alice Guy's film. The logical conclusion of this model, of course, was the automaton, an entirely mechanized machine-body that was very popular at the turn of the century. *Le Pêle-Mêle* asked, precisely, "Where will the progress in automatism stop?" The article discussed the creation in Holland of an "automaton doctor":

This device offers the sight of an old doctor in a wig whose body is pierced with a great many small holes, each of them bearing the name of an illness. If you are afflicted with a particular condition, whether a head cold or tapeworm, you need only insert a ten cent coin in the space "head cold" or "tapeworm" and you will immediately receive the appropriate remedy.[28]

Comic films were full of this kind of character acting like an automaton. There was, for example, the film *Calino a mangé du cheval* (*Lehmann Eats Horse Meat*, Pathé, 1908), in which the title character is suddenly seized by a frenzy that sends him racing into town at top speed. Calino's body is swept along in a sprint that nothing, it seems, is able to stop. His legs carry him along despite himself, "gobbling up impediments" like a Michelin tire. Grabbing a hand cart, he upends everything he finds in his way. Fast-motion photography gives even greater speed to his movements. His body is indefatigable, as if relieved of its biological constraints. Officers finally manage to stop him and take him by force to a doctor who, in a hasty operation, removes a (wooden) horse from Calino's stomach, where it had become lodged. Once this object is removed, his body returns to its original state. The "steam-horse" he literally had inside him gave him phenomenal abilities, equal to an automobile, or better yet a train, symbols par excellence of modernity racing along at top speed. The only way to stop this infernal machine was to remove its engine, no more and no less.

The cinema recognized no limit to the machine-body. Whereas the illustrated press, through the figure of the surgeon, described bodies that were suffering, cut into pieces, deranged, muzzled, and subject to the whims of incompetent and greedy healers, the cinema showed that it was possible to transform and repair bodies, to make them stronger and faster. The techniques it used are well known and unique to it, in particular fast motion to heighten the speed of bodies and trick effects such as the "stop-camera" technique to break down the body and put it back together. Cinema's machinery set the body in motion, put it into action. Unlike the press drawing, which could only depict immobile and lifeless bodies, the cinematic body—we might say the kinematic body—seems destined for perpetual motion, like Calino and his "steam-horse." Or like the characters in optical toys, as André Gaudreault and Nicolas Dulac describe:

> Their figures were seen as Sisyphean, condemned for all time to turn about, jump and dance. In a sense, they were machine-humans, indefatigable and unalterable, "acted-upon subjects" rather than "acting-out subjects." ... Were they eternal and unbreakable machines, worthy of the craziest dreams of modernity?[29]

JÉRÉMY HOUILLÈRE is a doctoral student in film studies at the University of Rennes 2 and the University of Montreal and teaching assistant at the University Rennes 2.

TIMOTHY BARNARD is a translator, author, and book publisher. He has translated and published volumes by André Bazin and Jean-Luc Godard and is author of the short volume *Découpage*.

Notes

1. Jean Poirier, *Histoire des mœurs I*, vol. 1 (Paris: Gallimard, 1990), 642–45.
2. David Le Breton, *La Chair à vif: Usages médicaux et mondains du corps humain* (Paris: Métailié, 1993), 107–8.
3. Ibid., 108.
4. *Life*, February 27, 1896, quoted in Ibid.
5. Gabriel de Lautrec, "Une opération," *Le Rire*, no. 353 November 6, 1909.
6. See Elisabeth Dixmier and Michel Dixmier, *"L'Assiette au beurre": revue satirique illustrée, 1901–1912* (Paris: François Maspero, 1974), 135.
7. Poirier, *Histoire des mœurs*, 789–90.
8. See Sandra Menenteau, "Le corps autopsié à l'épreuve du XIXe siècle," in *Corps saccagés: une histoire des violences corporelles du siècle des Lumières à nos jours*, ed. Frédéric Chauvaud (Rennes, France: Presses Universitaires de Rennes, 2009), 33.
9. *Le Pêle-Mêle*, December 15, 1901, 5.
10. *Le Pêle-Mêle*, July 8, 1900, 12.
11. Menenteau, "Le corps autopsié," 35.
12. *L'Assiette au beurre* 187, October 29, 1904, cover page.
13. *Chanteclair* 92, December 1, 1911, 3.
14. Thierry Lefebvre, "Cinéma et discours hygiéniste (1890–1930)," PhD diss., Université Paris 3, 1996, p. 42.
15. Thierry Lefebvre, *"Les Joyeux Microbes*: un film sous influence?," *1895* 53 (December 2007): 178.
16. *Le Pêle-Mêle*, March 25, 1906, 8.
17. *Le Pêle-Mêle*, January 22, 1905, 8.
18. *Le Pêle-Mêle*, May 26, 1907, 12.
19. *Le Rire*, April 25, 1914, n.p.
20. Poirier, *Histoire des mœurs*, 794–95.
21. *Le Pêle-Mêle*, September 23, 1906, 8.
22. See in particular Patrick Désile, "Une 'atmosphère de nursery du diable': Pantomime de cirque et premier cinéma comique," *1895* 61 (September 2010): 115–27.
23. Théodore Baudouin d'Aubigny et al., *Zazezizozu*, fairy play-vaudeville in five acts (Paris: Marchant, 1835). My thanks to Patrick Désile for drawing this work to my attention.
24. François Albera, "'L'école comique française,' une avant-garde posthume?," *1895* 61 (September 2010): 81.
25. Bruno Jacomy, "Automates et hommes-machines, de la Renaissance à nos jours," in *L'homme artificiel*, ed. Jean-Pierre Changeux (Paris: Odile Jacob, 2007), 32.
26. François Albera and Maria Tortajada, "L'Epistémé 1900" in *Le Cinématographe, nouvelle technologie du XXe siècle*, ed. André Gaudreault, Catherine Russel, and Pierre Véronneau (Lausanne, Switzerland: Payot, 2004), 45.

27. *Le Pêle-Mêle*, March 10, 1901, 3.

28. Robert Trinquet, "L'automatisme," *Le Pêle-Mêle*, January 11, 1903, 11.

29. André Gaudreault and Nicolas Dulac, "La circularité et la répétitivité au cœur de l'attraction: les jouets optiques et l'émergence d'une nouvelle série culturelle," *1895* 50 (December 2006): 37.

4   Ghosts and Their Nationality in the Fin de Siècle Machinery

Ian Christie

THERE IS NO question that spectrality and screen ghosts have become a major focus for film and new media studies in recent years. If we take Tom Gunning's seminal 1995 article, "Phantom Images and Modern Manifestations: Spirit Photography, Magic Theater, Trick Films and Photography's Uncanny," as a starting point for the new scholarship that links nineteenth-century cultural studies with early film and associated modern media, clearly there is a continuing fascination among younger scholars with aspects of this conjunction.[1] Whether this is seen through the prism of Laura Mulvey's "technological uncanny," associating it with the eeriness of new media experiences, or as the continuation by novel means of well-established cultural preoccupations such as spiritualism and spirit photography—as Gunning assumed, and both Murray Leeder and Simone Natale debate in recent works—it would appear that a significant number of films made between approximately 1897 and 1907 do center on visible ghosts.

This contribution to the continuing discussion of "ghostly bodies" proposes a comparative approach, based on sampling the extensive catalogs of major producers, in order to counteract a merely impressionistic view that may result from the randomness of early film survival, or indeed from our own latter-day interest in diagnosing this fascination. Here, it may be useful to recall Gunning's later survey in "To Scan a Ghost," in which he drew a line in the history of the ghostly at the point where the Enlightenment made this essentially a matter of psychology or optics.[2] Despite the rise of the scientific method, it would be hard to deny that a theological undertow has persisted, which, as Gunning observed, "was partly cued by the Reformation." Put crudely, disproving the existence of ghosts became a trait in Protestant cultures, initially linked to anti-Catholic assertions that, for instance, the Jesuits were active in faking ghostly apparitions to influence the gullible.[3] By the later nineteenth century, when "exposing fake spiritualists" had become a standard trope in magic theater, such confessional tensions may have receded, or been replaced by the challenge of Spiritualism itself as a new religious movement, alongside Theosophy, Swedenborgianism, and others.[4] Yet it would appear from contemporary discourse that fin de siècle screen ghosts

Figure 4.1. English ghosts in R. W. Paul's *The Magic Sword* (1901).

did retain distinct national characteristics, reflecting the traditions from which they emerged.

Evidence of this occurs in Robert Paul's presentation of his elaborate fantasy, *The Magic Sword*, subtitled *A Medieval Mystery*, in 1901.[5] In an unusually extended catalog text, Paul claimed that the use of "Old English" figures and costumes "cannot fail to please English-speaking audiences, who have become weary of foreign pictures of this class."[6] Whether or not there was any contemporary evidence of this, Paul seems likely to have been referring to the popularity of Georges Méliès's trick-based fantasies. *The Prince of Magicians* (*Excelsior!*), *The Brahmin and the Butterfly*, and many other titles had appeared in that same year, as had *Bluebeard*, Méliès's longest narrative to date, based on the classic Perrault fairy tale. As if to emphasize the "national" distinction, almost simultaneously Paul released his own longest film, *Scrooge, or Marley's Ghost*, based on Charles Dickens's popular *A Christmas Carol*.[7] In doing so, he was continuing and "remediating" what had become one of the great secular traditions of the "British Christmas."[8] First published in 1843, Dickens's "ghost story for Christmas" had been widely republished and adapted for the stage and for lantern shows.[9] In this process, its illustration effectively created a new iconography of the supernatural. As John Sutherland has noted, "The ghosts are imported from

Figure 4.2. Ghosts were already a feature of Méliès's theater repertoire before he produced *Le Manoir du diable* in 1896.

folklore and legend, not the Christian gospels. The famous spirit of Christmas designed by the artist John Leech for the first edition of *A Christmas Carol* clearly draws on classic pagan iconography."[10] Paul had already released *Chinese Magic* a year earlier.[11] But he seems to have realized that Englishness was a potential asset, quickly following *The Magic Sword* and *Scrooge* with *Mr Pickwick's Christmas at Wardle's*, drawn from the most popular work of England's most genuinely popular author.

Since *Scrooge* largely survives, we know that it used the latest techniques of multiple exposure and differential scale to create Scrooge's dreams and his ghostly guide. In doing so, it built on two innovations of the previous fifty years. One was the genre of "spirit photography," whereby the image of a dead person was added to that of a living subject, which had achieved extraordinary popularity by the 1870s, making objectively and permanently visible the numinous or transient.[12] The other new form of ghostly visibility was a stage illusion, in which a large, angled mirror allows an illuminated figure below or beside the stage to be seen as a spectral accompaniment to the visible figures. This was popularly known as Pepper's Ghost, after the flamboyant curator of the Royal Polytechnic

Institution in London, John Henry Pepper, who had revived it as a modern presentation in 1862.[13] Although cumbersome to use on the commercial stage, this offered a viable alternative to the elaborate trapdoor mechanisms used in mid-century melodramas, such as Dion Boucicault's *The Corsican Brothers* (1852), to present performing ghostly figures.

Moving pictures could effectively use the multiple-exposure technique involved in spirit photography to produce a simplified version of the mobile reflection image of Pepper's Ghost, making possible increasingly complex images of ghostly bodies. Interestingly, this effect appears to have been launched with at least six films from three different producers from 1896 to 1898. Two were by the accomplished magician Méliès and two by the Brighton-based G. A. Smith, who had previously been involved with the Society for Psychical Research (SPR) as a "hypnotizer," while two more are assumed to be by Georges Hatot for Lumière. Of these, Smith's *The Haunted Castle* (1897) and *Photographing a Ghost* (1898) are lost, though Méliès's *Le Château hanté* and *Le Manoir du diable* are both now accessible.[14] And in 1898, two versions of *Pierrot et le fantôme* appeared in the Lumière catalog.[15] By the early 1900s, ghostly bodies were clearly a recurrent, presumably fashionable item in the output of all the main producers, boosted by imitations and usually unacknowledged borrowing. But before sampling a selection of catalogs, it is necessary to consider the different cultural traditions that maintained the currency of ghostly bodies.

Even a cursory study of the catalog entries reveals a wide range of different conceptions of what an "immaterial body" or "presence" might be. Fundamentally, these all derived from the Christian cultural tradition that the major producing countries shared, even if representing Christ on screen, by means of an actor with or without supernatural effects, posed an immediate theological challenge.[16] At least three kinds of supernatural figures were recognized. One of these is the disembodied spirit of a dead person, which may appear to "haunt" the living for a wide range of reasons. Another is the figure of the angel, common to all Abrahamic religions, defined as a kind of intermediary between the divine and the human. The third is technically, or theologically, a form of the angelic, originally termed "fallen angel," resulting from a "war in heaven" that created a band of rebel angels led by Satan, or simply "the devil."

By the era of the Renaissance, there was an emerging secular culture based on the opposition of two spheres of the supernatural: good and evil, or the angelic and the demonic. Two of its major sources were Dante's *Divine Comedy*, which literalized the medieval Church's conception of the afterlife, and the German *Faust* chapbooks, which introduced the enduring trickster figure of Mephistopheles, a servant of Lucifer. Building on these, major and minor authors, and folk cultures, would all incorporate ghostly appearances, while the new pictorial arts of the Renaissance and the print era would give them visible form. In the eighteenth

Figure 4.3. *Pierrot et le fantôme (bougies)*, vue n°897 (Lumière, 1897).

century, the new literary genre of the Gothic would rely heavily on supernatural manifestations, while in the later nineteenth century "ghost stories" became an increasingly popular new fictional genre, overlapping with beginnings of moving pictures.

These cultural traditions and their national inflections produced a corpus of stories invoking the supernatural with varying degrees of seriousness, which would furnish early moving pictures with a repertoire of tales involving evil spirits, witches, magicians, tricksters, and, of course, mere "revenant" ghosts. But what produced an additional frisson, and arguably made the supernatural a matter of both everyday concern and controversy, was the rise of a new, more serious belief in the possibility of communication with the spirits of the dead, generally known as Spiritualism. Philosophers, scientists, and public figures came together in the late nineteenth century to pursue a modern program of research into what many considered to be evidence of some kind of existence beyond death—the "survival of human personality," as the title of a book by one of its leading figures maintained.[17] In Britain, the formation of the SPR in 1882, with the Cambridge University Professor of Moral Philosophy as its president, gave what had previously been considered mere superstition a new status within Victorian science.

Yet despite the SPR's determination to expose fakery and humbug, the popular culture of séances, with their table-rapping and dubious mediumship, continued. And exposing the fraudulent methods of professional mediums itself became a part of fin de siècle culture. After skeptically witnessing a performance by Daniel Dunglas Home, the Scottish-born medium, Robert Browning published his dramatic monologue, "Mr Sludge, The 'Medium,'" in 1864, in which a fraudulent operator admits his subterfuges. Thirty years later, George and Weedon Grossmith's popular satire on middle-class mores, *Diary of a Nobody*, would record regular séances.[18] And at the Egyptian Hall, styled as "London's home of mystery," the leading theatrical magician J. N. Maskelyne presented a show titled *Arcana*, which promised "an ingenious interweaving of refined fun and profound mystery." Exposing the techniques of professional mediums would soon become a staple of Maskelyne's repertoire, and the distinctive tone of skepticism surrounding claims about the supernatural would translate most immediately into early film's fascination with the ghostly.

So how prevalent were such spirit figurations in fin de siècle film? The short answer would be that only one producer, Méliès, made these a specialty. Yet even their infrequent appearance in other producers' catalogs points to a peak of interest around 1901–1903. In order to overcome any bias due to films that have survived, I offer here a preliminary survey of four of the main producers active from the late 1890s—Edison, Lumière, Paul, and Méliès—by word-searching their catalogs.

The Edison catalog, consisting of some two thousand subjects up to 1905, appears at first sight to include hardly any supernatural subjects, and few that lay claim to any originality. Those that did were mainly "borrowed" from other manufacturers. The allegorical *A Chinese Mystery* (1902) strikes an explicitly topical note after the Boxer Rebellion, with a "Chinese hobgoblin" split open by "an American traveller," to disgorge "three small Chinamen, who dance about in a fantastic manner" before being replaced by a group of "allied soldiers," representing England, France, Russia, America and Germany" and giving way to "a beautiful woman representing the Goddess of Liberty."[19] Another example of elaborate chinoiserie, *Extraordinary Chinese Magic* (1902), was in fact Paul's 1900 production *Chinese Magic*, with a Chinese magician whose head expands before he "flies directly at the audience." However, there are other pockets of the supernatural in the Edison catalog, such as the three "Devil" subjects of 1902 (set in Kitchen, Prison, and Theatre), characterized as "mystical," along with other groups of "mysterious" and "mystical" subjects in this same year. There are also several "Uncle Josh" films from 1900 involving nocturnal visitors, and a fully fledged *Visit to the Spiritualist* (Blackton and Smith, 1899), in which a "ghost of enormous proportions" terrifies the countryman who has paid his fee and is finally chased by "numerous ghosts and hobgoblins." The key to this genre finding a place among Edison's otherwise steady diet of public events and knockabout comedies seems to have been the familiarity of both "Spiritualist" practices and Uncle Josh as an everyman figure.

The extensive Lumière catalog, like Edison's, consisted largely of objective "views" of the natural world, interspersed with knockabout comedies. However, during two phases of the Lumières' ten-year career in moving pictures, they experimented by hiring filmmakers with very different skills and interests. The first was Georges Hatot, who made a *Haunted Pierrot* in 1897, the same year as his *Vie et Passion de Jésus-Christ* and series of historic "death tableaux." Then in 1902–1903, Gaston Velle made another thirteen films that were very different from the familiar Lumière output. These *vues fantasmagoriques* included at least seven in which demonic or magical figures are central, with one a "haunted Pierrot" and another featuring Mephistopheles. A typical subject from this group is *The Haunted Castle*, which is summarized as follows:

> A Wizard raises the apparition of an old witch whom he sends to look for a young girl; he orders the latter to attract a young traveler in the castle. On arrival, he is exposed to all sorts of unpleasant surprises: seats that give way under him, a ghost he tries to fight which then disappears, etc. Finally the ghost turns into a girl whom the young man woos, but when he approaches her, he finds a skeleton instead. Furious, he grabs a stick to hit the skeleton, who then turns into the Wizard, and captures the traveller, making him disappear in a cloud of smoke.[20]

This highly condensed sequence of shape- or identity-changing upsets is quite typical of much production around this time, including Paul's *Magic Sword*, with its bewildering changes of location and transformations, and of course Méliès, whose work has often been confused with Velle's.[21] In fact, Velle would go on to become a leading trick-film specialist for Pathé, and later Cines in Italy. Like Segundo de Chomón, he was part of a highly mobile fraternity of "artificers of fantasy" who were in great demand during this phase of production, before some of them went on to become the pioneers of special effects.[22]

In Britain, although the earliest exponent of the ghostly was G. A. Smith, it would be Paul who produced a number of "supernatural" subjects between 1899 and 1908 that run a gamut from the lighthearted comic Spiritualism of *Upside Down, or the Human Flies* (1899) to the more mordant *The Medium Exposed*, subtitled *Is Spiritualism a Fraud?* (1905). Paul's catalog amounted to some 660 titles by 1905, and he had close business connections with a number of stage magicians, including Maskelyne, David Devant, and Carl Hertz, even before employing Walter Booth around 1899. By 1901, magic and the spectral were becoming important features of his output, presumably reflecting his new employee's skills and interests. Booth appears in *The Waif and the Wizard* (1901) as a stage magician visiting a young admirer's bedridden mother. This appeared during the later months of 1901, accompanied by *The Devil in the Studio*, *The Haunted Curiosity Shop*, *The Drunkard's Conversion* (featuring *The Spirit of Temperance*), and *Ora Pro Nobis* (with angels), before *The Magic Sword* and *Scrooge* were offered as major Christmas attractions.[23] Thereafter, ghostly subjects are rare from Paul, other than *The Medium Exposed* (1906), which shows the preparation of a fake séance and the subsequent punishment of the fraudulent medium.

Méliès would earn his reputation as the supreme creator of early phantasmagoric fantasy films. Without a doubt, the popularity of some of these films has created the impression that early cinema was largely devoted to this genre. However, there is an important distinction to be made. The many supernatural or magical figures in Méliès's work are rarely, if ever, shown as "ghostly," even if they are sometimes skeletal or of exaggerated scale. Whatever marvels his devils, ghosts, Fausts, and fairies perform, they do so on essentially the same terms as "natural" bodies. These are highly performative, protean figures made capable of "impossible" feats through multiple exposure and sheer gymnastic energy, and often played by Méliès himself.

A preliminary word search of some four hundred Méliès titles yields over 12 percent having supernatural or occult themes: 8 *diable* [devil]; 7 *rêve* [dream]; 6 *fantastique*; 5 *enchanté/e*; 4 Faust; 3 *cauchemar* [nightmare]; 3 *sorcier* [sorcerer]; 3 infernal; 2 *fantôme* [phantom]; 2 *mysterieuse*; 2 damnation; 2 *terrible*; and 2 *spirite*. The reason why Méliès preferred such subjects seems obvious, since they gave him maximum scope for the "transformations" that were his stock-in-trade. They can also be related to a distinctively French cultural tradition, which Timothy Chesters has traced back to its sixteenth-century roots, describing the intellectual climate of that period as being "one of the most haunted in European history."[24] Chesters suggests that during this period, "we also begin to see emerge characteristics recognisable from modern ghost tales: the setting of the 'haunted house,' the eroticised ghost, and the embodied revenant."[25] They were also typical of the popular magic-theater culture that Méliès had first witnessed at Maskelyne's Egyptian Hall show, before he reopened the Théâtre Robert-Houdin in 1888. But as Dan North has observed, "Magic theatre was designed to remove any fearful elements from the stagecraft, the illusions took on an anti-realistic quality which would enable spectators to appreciate the artistry and the science behind a trick without ever being completely deceived."[26] North goes on to suggest that there were "technologically literate audiences" for the films that drew upon this tradition of magic theater.

What has perhaps been missing from the recent attention paid to spectral images is that for the audiences of 1897–1907, magic and its concomitant "ghostly" genre had a number of distinctive national variations. These included French *diablerie*;[27] Mephisthophelean cunning rooted in the modern retelling of Faust by Goethe, and its French and Italian adaptations; "Chinese magic" as an exotic addition to the international repertoire; and Dickensian "English" ghosts. In film, however, many of these became effectively cross-cultural, passed from one producer to another, like the "bewitched inn" that Méliès first filmed in 1897, which is thought to have originated in an English music-hall stage act of the 1850s, and eventually became the "spooky" or "haunted hotel" of later American films.[28] Indeed, the internationalism of the film industry may well have played a significant role in creating a syncretic or global occult in the early twentieth century, familiarizing widely separated audiences with what had previously been national or local versions of the supernatural.[29]

The cross-cultural mapping of this terrain sketched here is no more than a first step toward what could be a study in the "cultural semiotics" of the supernatural in early film.[30] Provisional conclusions indicate that France was certainly perceived as the center of supernatural phantasmagoria, with both Lumière and Pathé drawn into the tradition that Méliès had largely created in film. And further afield, both Edison and Paul were encouraged by the obvious success of Méliès to experiment with local variations in this genre, even if they felt their audiences' main interests lay elsewhere. For Booth/Paul and Porter/Edison, Chinese magic seemed to hold a special attraction, no doubt inspired by the popularity of the Chinese magician Ching Ling Foo and his American imitator, Ching Ling Soo,[31] although Paul attempted to exploit an English vein of the supernatural with his version of Dickens's *Christmas Carol*, and *The Magic Sword*. But none of these screen ventures was taking place in a vacuum. The longstanding traditions of conjuring and pantomime, and of *féerie* and fairy tales, were interacting with the new popularity of spiritualism and its debunking, creating audiences that were exceptionally well prepared for the supernatural on screen.

In his survey of "the haunted minds of modernity," Murray Leeder adduces Terry Castle's verdict: "By the end of the nineteenth century, ghosts had disappeared from everyday life, but as the poets intimated, human experience had become more ghost-ridden than ever. Through a strange process of rhetorical displacement, thought itself had become phantasmagorical."[32] The initial upsurge of ghostly performance on early screens was hardly calculated to frighten or disturb and seems to have been more concerned to re-mediate aspects of the previous century's popular entertainment culture. Trying to understand the prevailing mind-set, we might add to North's technological literacy a degree of cultural literacy among viewers, many of whom were also the readers of Arthur Conan Doyle's Sherlock Holmes stories. Holmes famously rejects any belief in the supernatural. In a late story, "The Adventure of the Sussex Vampire," he says, "This Agency stands flat-footed upon the ground and there it must remain. The world is big enough for us. No ghost need apply."[33] Yet his creator, Conan Doyle, was a leading devotee of Spiritualism, open to "fairy photographs" and other pseudoscientific proofs of the reality of the supernatural.[34] His case is striking proof that a capacity to entertain both the supernatural and its rejection would become one of the hallmarks of modernity. In his "Ontology of Mediated Vision," Gunning quotes a Russian writer observing in 1899 that the modern city's "multiple reflections" provide "the natural medium of haunting."[35] If cinema would eventually become that "natural medium," with its elaborate theologies of the occult in vampirism, zombies, and the like, then early film's ghosts, although hardly numerous, might be considered an important rehearsal zone for the modernization of the supernatural.

IAN CHRISTIE is Professor of Film and Media History at Birkbeck, University of London. He was writer and co-producer of the BBC TV series *The Last Machine*. His recent books include *The Art of Film: John Box and Production Design* and *Audiences*.

Notes

1. My book and television series, *The Last Machine* (BBC, 1994), devoted its final part to the "spectral" quality of early film and its immediate cultural resonance. And at the 1998 Domitor conference in Washington, both Tom Gunning and I found that we had converged on Jules Verne's novel *The Carpathian Castle* as a prime instance of the fin de siècle mediated phantasmatic. In recent scholarship, see especially Murray Leeder's collection, *Cinematic Ghosts: Haunting and Spectrality from Silent Cinema to the Digital Era* (New York: Bloomsbury Academic, 2015), which includes a reprint of Gunning's 1995 chapter, and articles by Simone Natale, culminating in his book *Supernatural Entertainments: Victorian Spiritualism and the Rise of Modern Media Culture* (University Park: Pennsylvania State University Press, 2016). Gunning's article "Phantom Images and Modern Manifestations: Spirit Photography, Magic Theater, Trick Films and Photography's Uncanny" originally appeared in Patrice Petro, ed., *Fugitive Images from Photography to Video* (Bloomington: Indiana University Press, 1995).

2. Tom Gunning, "To Scan a Ghost: The Ontology of Mediated Vision," *Grey Room* 26 (Winter 2007): 107.

3. Ibid. Gunning draws here on Roy Thomas's classic study *Religion and the Decline of Magic* (Oxford, UK: Oxford University Press, 1971).

4. From the 1860s onward, the growth of the Spiritualist movement was accompanied by a succession of exposés, and even trials, alleging deliberate deception. Robert Browning's dramatic monologue "Mr Sludge, 'The Medium'" (*Dramatis Personae*, 1864) was an early example of a medium supposedly confessing fakery, while Maskelyne would later build his reputation as an impresario of magic theater at the Egyptian Hall in London on demonstrating the techniques used by the spiritualist performers and brothers Ira and William Davenport. However, honest doubt and belief persisted. The great French astronomer Camille Flammarion published a defense of the Davenports in 1865, and the pioneer spirit photographer William Mumler was acquitted by a New York judge in 1869. See, inter alia, Cristia Cloutier, "Mumler's Ghosts," and Denis Canguilhem, "Flammarion

and Eusapia Palladino," both in Clément Chéroux, Andreas Fischer, Pierre Apraxine, Denis Canguilhem, and Sophie Schmit, eds., *The Perfect Medium: Photography and the Occult* (New Haven, CT: Yale University Press, 2005), 22, 235.

5. On this film's cultural roots in nineteenth-century pantomime and magic theater, see Ian Christie, "*The Magic Sword*: Genealogy of an English Trick Film," *Film History: An International Journal* 16, no. 2 (2004): 163–71.

6. Entry for *The Magic Sword*, R. W. Paul Animatograph Films, 1901 catalog.

7. The film survives in truncated form. It was originally 620 feet and in three titled, separate scenes, following Dickens's own division into "three spirits," in what he called his "Christmas ghost story."

8. For the general theory of remediation, see Jay Bolter and Richard Grusin, *Remediation: Understanding New Media* (Cambridge, MA: MIT Press, 1998).

9. Ann Hecht suggested that Scrooge's visions in *A Christmas Carol* may have been inspired by Dickens's own experience of the "surprising transformations" created by magic-lantern dissolving views. "Magic Lantern References in Literature," in *Encyclopaedia of the Magic Lantern*, ed. David Robinson, Stephen Herbert, and Richard Crangle (London: Magic Lantern Society, 2001), 175–76.

10. John Sutherland, "The Origins of *A Christmas Carol*," British Library, May 15, 2014, https://www.bl.uk/romantics-and-victorians/articles/the-origins-of-a-christmas-carol.

11. *Chinese Magic* would become *Extraordinary Chinese Magic* when listed in Edison's catalog in 1902, with a detailed synopsis: "The climax of this great scene is reached when the magician spreads his arms and the long sleeves of his costume become gigantic bat's wings, while his head grows larger and larger and his body smaller and smaller and he flies directly at the audience." The film, however, is not known to exist.

12. See, for instance, William Mumler's 1872 portrait of Mary Todd Lincoln with the "spirit" of Abraham Lincoln cradling her. Lincoln Financial Foundation Collection, Allen County Public Library, Fort Wayne, Indiana, accessed March 27, 2018, http://contentdm.acpl.lib.in.us/cdm/singleitem/collection/p15155coll1/id/56. See also Kate Scott, "Phantoms and Frauds: The History of Spirit Photography," OUP Blog, October 29, 2013, http://blog.oup.com/2013/10/history-spirit-photography/. Simone Natale has argued for "a more solid insertion of spiritualism's visual culture into the pre-history of film practice," based on its growing use in stage magic, in "A Short History of Superimposition: From Spirit Photography to Early Film," *Early Popular Visual Culture* 10, no. 2 (2012): 125–45.

13. For a detailed account of Pepper and the sources and exploitation of his illusion, see Jeremy Brooker, *The Temple of Minerva: Magic and the Magic Lantern at the Royal Polytechnic Institution, London, 1837–1901* (London: Magic Lantern Society, 2013). The first account of this illusion is attributed to Giambattista della Porta, who described in his *Magia Naturalis* (Natural Magic, 1558), "How we may see in a Chamber things that are not." This was the title of chapter XII, Book XVII, "Of Strange Glasses," *Natural Magick*, (English translation of *Magia Naturalis*, 1658, online at http://www.faculty.umb.edu/gary_zabel/Courses/Phil%20281b/Philosophy%20of%20Magic/Natural_Magic/jportac17.html#bk17XII.

14. Confusion continues to surround Smith's and Méliès's "ghost" films of this period. A Wikipedia entry for Smith's *Photographing a Ghost* is illustrated with Méliès's 1896 *Le Château hanté*, his second film in this genre after the previous year's *Le Manoir du diable* (1897), which was rediscovered in 1988.

15. Nos. 896 and 897 are titled "bougies" and "table" to distinguish them. See photograms in Catalogue Lumière: l'œuvre cinématographique des frères Lumière (https://catalogue-lumiere.com), the database created from Michelle Aubert and Jean-Claude

Seguin, eds., *La production cinématographique des Frères Lumière* (Paris: Mémoire du Cinéma, 1996).

16. See discussion of this in *The Last Machine*; also in various contributions to Roland Cosandey, Andre Gaudreault, and Tom Gunning, eds., *Une invention du diable? Cinéma des premiers temps et religion* (Sainte-Foy, Québec/Lausanne, Switzerland: Presses de l'Université Laval/Payot, 1992). Georges Hatot's first engagement with Lumière, in 1898, was to film *La Vie et la Passion de Jésus-Christ*, a thirteen-part passion play, which was followed by increasingly elaborate passion series, predominantly produced in Catholic countries.

17. Frederic Myers's *Human Personality and Its Survival of Bodily Death* was published posthumously in 1903.

18. George and Weedon Grossmith's *Diary of a Nobody* was first serialized in *Punch*, then published in book form in 1892, and subsequently appeared in many editions. Charles Pooter disapproves of séances but records that his wife, "Carrie, at our old house, used to have séances every night with poor Mrs Fussters (who is now dead)." The *Diary* is widely regarded as an accurate satire on lower-middle-class London life.

19. Josephine Lee et al., *Re/collecting Early Asian America: Essays in Cultural History* (Philadelphia, PA: Temple University Press, 2012), 108.

20. "Vue n°2001" in Catalogue Lumière: l'œuvre cinématographique des frères Lumière, https://catalogue-lumiere.com/le-chateau-hante/.

21. Paul Hammond discusses this confusion and points to the differences between the films of Méliès and Velle in "Georges, This Is Charles," *Afterimage* 8–9 (Spring 1981): 39–48.

22. See Ian Christie, "The Visible and the Invisible: From 'Tricks' to 'Effects,'" *Early Popular Visual Culture* 13, no. 2 (2016): 106–12.

23. *The Devil in the Studio*, which does not survive, is one of six films in Paul's 1901–1902 catalog that all use stop-motion, and especially multiple exposure, to create "magical" effects.

24. Timothy Chesters, *Ghost Stories in Late Renaissance France: Walking by Night* (Oxford, UK: Oxford University Press, 2011).

25. Ibid., Introduction, 13.

26. Dan North, "Magic and Illusion in Early Cinema," *Studies in French Cinema* 1, no. 2 (2001): 70–79.

27. See the series of grotesque tableaux modeled and photographed for stereographs in France by Pierre Adolphe Hennetier and Louis Alfred Habier, and illustrated in Brian May, Denis Pellerin, and Paula Fleming, *Diableries: Stereoscopic Adventures in Hell* (London: London Stereoscopic Company, 2013), also on the London Stereoscopic Company website, http://londonstereo.com/diableries/index.html.

28. *The Haunted Hotel* (Blackton, 1907) for Vitagraph is probably the best known of this series. See also Mark Cosdon, "A Chronological Outline of the Hanlon Brothers, 1833–1931," accessed March 27, 2018, http://docplayer.net/4059524-A-chronological-outline-of-the-hanlon-brothers-1833-1931-mark-cosdon-allegheny-college.html.

29. Leeder's wide-ranging collection, *Cinematic Ghosts*, points to this globalization of the occult in its third part, "Millennial Ghosts."

30. I borrow this concept from Lotman and Uspensky, as outlined in Y. M. Lotman, B. A. Uspensky, and George Mihaychuk, "On the Semiotic Mechanism of Culture," *New Literary History* 9, no. 2 (Winter 1978): 211–32, and elsewhere.

31. Ching Ling Foo was praised in the *New York Dramatic Mirror* in 1899; see "A Wonderful Conjuror: Ching Ling Foo," *Magical-Past Times*, accessed March 27, 2018, https://web.archive.org/web/20110323050347/http://www.miraclefactory.net/mpt/view.php?id=73&type=articles. Christopher Nolan's film *The Prestige* (2006) was partly inspired by Ching Ling Foo.

32. In his chapter in *Cinematic Ghosts*, "Visualizing the Phantoms of the Imagination: Projecting the Haunted Minds of Modernity," Leeder quotes Terry Castle, *The Female Thermometer: 18th-Century Culture and the Invention of the Uncanny* (New York: Oxford University Press, 1995), 144.

33. "The Adventure of the Sussex Vampire" first appeared in the *Strand Magazine* in January 1924 and in the collection *The Case-Book of Sherlock Holmes* (London: John Murray, 1927).

34. Conan Doyle joined the Society for Psychical Research in 1893 and wrote twenty books supporting Spiritualism, including a two-volume history of the movement, which appeared in the same year as "The Adventure of the Sussex Vampire." For a discussion of his Spiritualist beliefs and bibliography, see Andrzej Diniejko, "Sir Arthur Conan Doyle and Victorian Spiritualism," *Victorian Web*, last modified November 14, 2013, http://www.victorianweb.org/authors/doyle/spiritualism.html.

35. Gunning, referring to M. V. Pogorelsky writing in a Russian occult journal, in "To Scan a Ghost," 114.

Part II
Inventories of the Body

Introduction

Early cinema opened new representational avenues for the nineteenth-century preoccupation with exploring, exploiting, and cataloging the human body and its functions. Alphonse Bertillon's famous mug shots are but one example of an urge to formalize bodily features, in his case for purposes of identification, but the overall trend also included mapping ethnicity and even intelligence. The film medium offered new possibilities for outlining and recording bodies in movement: changes of movements, outbursts of symptoms, clinical procedures, and abstruse bodily changes. The moment of death, for example, could now be recorded for the "benefit" of both academic and regular theater audiences. Many of these were later deemed to be unscientific and highly problematic recordings of human beings and animals alike. For these reasons, many of the films were left to oblivion, forgotten in labs, universities, and private archives.

The collective contribution of Luis Alonso García, Daniel Sánchez Salas, and Begoña Soto Vázquez analyzes an attempt at empirical observation through the example of Dr. Maestre's filming of patients at the Manicomio de Ciempozuelos, a mental asylum in Spain. This is an intriguing case study in which the patients' bodies become protagonists. The films display an effort to show the patients' bodies as objects of control, more or less successfully, by demonstrating and cataloging their symptoms in front of the camera.

Benjamin Schultz-Figueroa, on the other hand, discusses methods for rearranging animal bodies for the purpose of cinematic research, especially when it comes to the use of film as a substitute for vivisection. By way of reproducibility and repetition, the moving image emerges as a promising tool for experimental medicine and a more "humane" alternative practice that spares animal lives.

One of the most sensational and startling phenomena when it comes to the temporality of bodily changes is the moving image that captures moments of death, which Gary D. Rhodes discusses in his contribution. Displays of executions and lynching were, for a few years, a recurring topic in films produced by several companies, both fictional dramatizations and authentic ones, that drew on the tradition of public executions in the United States. Condemnations of the practice of public executions, as well as the films showing them, grew intensely by 1910, causing the film industry to worry about what such imagery would do to its reputation.

Rodolphe Gahéry discusses a disturbing example of the corporeality and imagery of otherness in his contribution concerning two series of Lumière films that depict "human zoos" and "black villages" in turn-of-the-twentieth-century France. The phenomenon of exhibiting exotic human "specimens" developed in European societies from the early voyages of discovery and encouraged the exhibition of "human zoos" encompassing entire villages in colonized areas. According to Gahéry, the black body in these media representations became not only the principal object of exhibition—the spectacle—but also an "object" of exploitation: a racialized scientific object and a colonized body. These imaginaries enabled, according to Gahéry, the rise of an imaginary of the black body that could be described as "zoological."

The ability of moving pictures to record movement and progression was also used to depict cultural differences and social change, as Joanna Hearne discusses in her essay. Before-and-after photographs, with a special focus on the US government's program of institutional education for Native American children, provides a poignant case study for this type of comparative imagery and its overall role in photography and early cinema. The colonial rescue narrative that Hearne discusses is, similar to the other practices analyzed in this section, extremely offensive to the general audience today. The ideologies behind much of the filming of bodily inventories are beyond the pale of humanity and modern enlightenment but still imperative to study as one aspect of early cinema's bodily engagements.

5 Field Trip to Insanity

Bodies and Minds in the Dr. Maestre Film Collection (Spain, 1915)

Luis Alonso García, Daniel Sánchez-Salas, and Begoña Soto-Vázquez

Introduction

According to the most recent research, the earliest scientific footage shot in Spain dates from 1909 or 1910.[1] In the following years an activity developed that, beyond some exceptional cases,[2] fell into oblivion and has barely been studied since. This is the case with the material we will discuss here, a short 28mm film deposited with the Filmoteca Española in 2006: *Excursión Escolar con el Dr. Maestre al Manicomio de Ciempozuelos* (*Educational Field Trip with Dr. Maestre to the Ciempozuelos Insane Asylum*) (1915).[3]

When we started our research we knew practically nothing about this film, namely due to an almost complete lack of information on the materials and its creator. This was somewhat surprising, given the social stature of the person apparently responsible for them: Tomás Maestre Pérez (1857–1936), forensic surgeon, university professor, writer, and member of parliament.[4] It was even more astonishing, however, that the aforementioned film is part of a broad and complex collection of sources grouped at the Filmoteca Española since 1987 under two general titles: *Microscopias de la Sangre* (*Microscopy of the Blood*) and *Manicomio de Ciempozuelos* (*Ciempozuelos Insane Asylum*). We have not examined the materials in the first group, because both its title and what we know of its content lets us deduce that it has nothing to do with our research objective. While those in the second—which we examined manually because they cannot be projected or watched on a moviola[5]—have always been seen as dispensable elements of the recuperated version of *Excursión Escolar con el Dr. Maestre*.[6]

Two attributes stand out when viewing *Excursión Escolar*, especially when considered as part of a wider collection. The first is its technical and expressive qualities. In the first part, a fixed frame in medium close-up shows nine cases of the mentally ill, with students and colleagues standing in a semicircle around the doctor and patient. In the second part, shot with either a fixed frame or pans, a number of patients are running, falling, and stopping on the patio of the asylum. In both parts, the body, especially of the patient, becomes a compelling protagonist. As we will discuss shortly, the patients' bodies were objects of control: care had to be taken so they remained inside the frame and demonstrated the symptoms of their illness in front of the camera. Nevertheless, the result is strikingly marked by the contingent—unavoidable when filming the human body—and by what we presume was a lack of a scientific plan for which patients to film and how. Thus we will see how improvisation and the unexpected came together to create some disturbing images, quite different from the more aseptic neurological films that scientists such as Camillo Negro made during this period.

Second, the film stands out precisely for its fragmentary, inconclusive, evanescent, nonfilmlike quality. For example, nothing explains the connection between the two parts we have described: the patients are not the same and there are no students in the second part. Although the film has an initial title card—"Universidad de Madrid, Instituto de Medicina Legal Toxicología y Psiquiatría. Facultad de Medicina. Director profesor, T. Maestre" ("University of Madrid, Institute of Legal Medicine, Toxicology, and Psychiatry. Faculty of Medicine. Director Professor, T. Maestre")—it is general and does not unify the two distinct parts.

The first of these qualities is what made us choose *Excursión Escolar* for a discussion of the body in early cinema. But as our work progressed, the second quality led us to another inescapable research objective.

Elements of the Maestre Collection

The Maestre Collection, as we refer to it, made up of mostly 28mm positives and negatives, is an exceptional case by virtue of being, without a doubt, the oldest preserved medical and scientific footage in Spanish film.[7] There are also 35mm positive and negative materials,[8] but because it is quite varied (some is very similar to the 28mm material, but some is quite different) we will not discuss it here.[9] The 28mm positive material is composed of three series of different cases: two with the institute's initial title card and the third without, but with the same technical qualities.[10] The subjects in the three series are different (they include men, women, and children), and we can identify at least two of the insane asylums (Toledo and Ciempozuelos). One of these is what has been known, since 2006, as Excursión Escolar. In all, the three series total approximately 489 meters, or approximately 30 minutes and 45 seconds. We believe they represent special cases that were compiled for the lecture, class, or talk they accompanied, which we can infer from work carried out on similar collections, like those of Camillo Negro and Vincenzo Neri.[11] This is how we interpret the splices from different dates, the lack of explanatory intertitles, and the fact that the negatives and positives were stored in the same place before they were housed at the Filmoteca Española.

Figure 5.1. "Educational Field Trip with Dr. Maestre to the Ciempozuelos Insane Asylum," 1915. Original initial title card and first frame join with a type of splice probably made after 1915. Demonstration of an example of mental patient by Dr Maestre. 28mm copy. Filmoteca Española.

Press reports tell us that scientific excursions to different insane asylums were some of the primary activities of the Instituto de Medicina Legal, which Maestre founded in 1915. A brief description in the press explained the structure and content of the practical lessons provided by such excursions, as seen in the first part of *Excursión Escolar*.

> In front of the residents' pavilion, and in one of the gardens of the spacious building, the learned Doctor Maestre, Director of the Institute, gave one of the finest and most significant lectures we have heard. In the midst of a large number of his students, the distinguished professor demonstrated typical examples of mental patients shut up in this hospitable mansion. We saw notable cases of elated agitated mania, melancholic manic depressive disorder, progressive general paralysis, highly expansive elated mania, catatonia, agitated paralysis, chorea, and melancholy. He also demonstrated for his listeners the use of the instruments necessary to determine the size of the skull and the degree of patients' sensitivity. The lesson lasted an hour and a half, and was listened to with great attention.[12]

This detailed description tells us that the film thus contains two texts with two different purposes: a practical lesson featuring patients for students and colleagues, and a scientific register of clinical cases of patients in a state of paroxysm or walking around.

In both cases, it seems certain that Dr. Maestre never intended for his filmed material to be anything but strictly academic, whether used for research or education or for making scientific knowledge available—hence the complementary nature of the material (having no intertitles or explanatory text) as an illustration accompanying the specialist's lecture. To describe *Excursión Escolar* as a non-film is not to say that it is not finished but rather to assume that its inconclusive or open quality is intentional. We hypothesize that during the years 1915–1918, new cases were added and others dropped according to whether they changed or broadened the research carried out by the institute and its director. And here is where we must account for the very strange and eventful lives of the films before they completely faded from view around 1918.

Dr. Maestre and the Cinema

Shooting and projecting film were part of Maestre's educational field trips from the beginning. The doctor had at least a passing familiarity with what Simone Venturini, Lorenzo Lorusso, and Federico Vanone call the neurological network: a group of researchers across Europe who placed great value on chronographical and cinematic recordings of neurological and psychiatric pathologies.[13] Thus, throughout 1915, references to Maestre's films in the press were fairly numerous—first, because of the excursions to the insane asylums, and second, for the various screenings that took place in university lecture halls and at public talks. Maestre gave two lectures, accompanied by projections of fixed and moving images, at the Congreso por el Progreso de la Ciencias (Congress for the Advancement of the Sciences) in Valladolid in October 1915, which also drew the attention of the press. Subsequently, there were only a few indirect mentions of Sunday visits to Ciempozuelos, and always in relation with the work being done on ultramicroscopic cinematography. After 1918, there was nothing.

An initial explanation for the strange, gradual disappearance of such original and interesting material may have to do with the fierce controversy over the disastrous conditions of Spanish insane asylums, sparked by an article written by well-known psychiatrist Gonzalo Rodríguez Lafora in the magazine *España* in October 1916—to which we must add the protests around the commercial exhibition of the film *Oftalmología* (Francesc Puigvert, 1917), which shows the internationally famous Dr. Barraquer performing ocular surgery. But we believe that the invisibility of this material up to the present day has to do with Dr. Maestre's feeble academic and scientific ideas, with respect to his theory of both the degeneration of humanity and the structure of blood, and its role in various pathologies such as cancer or madness.

In a sense, 1918 was a key date in Dr. Tomás Maestre Pérez's biography. He seems to have realized that he would never achieve the recognition enjoyed by figures he admired, such as Santiago Ramón y Cajal, the 1906 Nobel Prize winner in medicine, or the neurologist Luis Simarro Lacabra. Maestre, who was sixty years old at the time, seems to have given up on the idea of obtaining a place in the pantheon of Spanish science. In actuality, and this is what is of interest here, the real prejudice against Dr. Maestre in this respect was the film production itself. The institution's films and materials, damaged by the academic weaknesses of its director, appear to have no scientific merit whatsoever within their discipline. Instead, this footage evidences how scientific knowledge advances through trial and error.

The Body in the Maestre Collection

In the footage, we see Professor Tomás Maestre, his students, members of the San Juan de Dios religious order, which managed several Spanish insane asylums, and health care workers. But above all, we see the insane—not only men and women but also boys and girls—a living pathological museum, to use Jean-Martin Charcot's description of his inmates in the Salpêtrière, as Georges Didi-Huberman reminds us in his denunciation of Charcot's procedures and methods.[14] From the outset, we could say that these bodies are subject to a logic that affects their behavior entirely: they had to submit to being filmed. For everyone, the sane and the insane, the cinematic apparatus interrupted their lives and forced them to submit to a particular spatial order that is not so easy to adhere to in the context of mental illness. The subjects were filmed outside the asylums, where the walls or façades of the buildings form a backdrop. The camera never ventures inside, possibly because of insufficient lighting or the condition of the facilities. It is not a coincidence that in 1916, soon after at least some of this footage was shot, the aforementioned fierce national debate erupted around the deplorable conditions of many insane asylums in Spain.

Whatever the case, the lunatics, as they would have been called in the English of the day,[15] were filmed outside in the daylight, almost always in a medium-long shot that recorded the movements of their entire body. This may have been for lack of time, or because wide-angle shots were thought to be the best way to film these cases, given their symptoms. For this reason, the potentially uncontrollable bodies needed to be controlled so that they appeared properly in the frame. To this end, both on-screen and surely offscreen as well, the devoted San Juan de Dios monks, the nuns who looked after the women and children, the health care workers, Tomás Maestre himself, and even his students participated. Their mission was to manipulate the patients' bodies so that they would show in the shot. In some cases it appears that this must have been easy, given the patient's natural stillness and docility. But in others, even the operator had to struggle while filming to keep the patient from exiting the frame. Thus, the viewer witnesses the struggle to control the contingent and unpredictable circumstances in which the camera is recording—a struggle that, as Mary Ann Doane remarks, has been connected since cinema's earliest beginnings precisely with the presence of the body in film images and with "[film's] ability to capture a moment, to register and repeat 'that which happens.'"[16]

But there is another logic underlying the images of the bodies in the Maestre Collection. We refer to the way in which the footage serves a precise objective: explaining these bodies. Maestre himself appears, explaining different clinical cases to his supposed students, who occupy the background of the shot and, judging from the professor's gaze, are also located behind the camera. Maestre speaks and behaves as if he were conducting a class. His gestures are professorial, while his body attempts to dominate not just the frame but also the center of the scene. This footage reveals an expository mechanism that presides over both the images in which Maestre appears and those in which he does not, or only fleetingly: the patients must behave in front of the camera in a manner that displays the symptoms of their illness. We see Maestre employ various methods to achieve this, including instructing or coaxing a patient to carry out an action.[17] But these images do not succeed in becoming a mechanical demonstration of an isolated case study, as in a laboratory—above all, because of the role the asylum grounds play in the footage and because of the human interaction we see in these images. On the one hand, we see students, monks, and other patients in the background, along with natural elements such as light, the ground, and trees. On the other hand, Maestre speaks with some of the patients,

Figure 5.2. Frames of original copy of the series dedicated to female mental patients [1915]. Demonstration of an example of mental patient by a nun. 28mm copy without initial title. Filmoteca Española.

68 | *Corporeality in Early Cinema*

Figure 5.3. "Educational Field Trip with Dr. Maestre to the Ciempozuelos Insane Asylum," 1915. Two frames of the same shot join with a type of an original splice. Demonstration of an example of mental patient by Dr. Maestre. 28mm copy. Filmoteca Española.

Field Trip to Insanity | 69

Figure 5.4. "Educational Field Trip with Dr. Maestre to the Ciempozuelos Insane Asylum," 1915. Three frames of the same shot with a broken original splice. Demonstration of an example of mental patient. 28mm copy. Filmoteca Española.

or physically manipulates their bodies alone or with the help of others, or tries to control those who suddenly act unpredictably. All these postures and presences spill beyond the exclusively scientific objective of these images and open the door once again to the contingent.[18] The specialized audience for which this footage was originally intended would need ancillary materials to interpret these symptoms, such as an accompanying lecture to help the viewer understand the different cases and fully grasp what he or she was seeing. This is how the explanatory model of the footage was rounded out.

We do not know the content of the distinguished professor's lectures, neither for the images in which he appears nor apart from them. The newspaper article we quoted earlier on Maestre's first educational field trips, however, gives us a clue. This news report mentions cases with pathologies that may match some of the images in the professor's practical lesson: melancholic bipolar disorder, progressive general paralysis, highly expansive elated mania, catatonia, and so on.[19] At the same time, we can also formulate a thesis around the medical point of view that Maestre may have employed to explain his cases. When at least some of this footage was shot, in 1915, he had completely rejected the concept of neuropathology in ailments associated with hysteria. Instead, Maestre championed the older concept of degeneration, in keeping with Cesare Lombroso, whom he admired.[20] According to Maestre's interpretation, degeneration was a hereditary illness made up of four stages: hysteria, epilepsy, moral idiocy, and imbecility. From his writings we can deduce that he appeared to believe that the two final stages of the ailment would manifest through striking physical inclinations. The images under discussion here demonstrate this precisely.

Conclusion

Whether or not Maestre wanted to film the bodies of different kinds of patients, it appears that neither he nor the others involved in these shoots carried them out with a scientific plan in mind. The footage gives the impression that the patients who were filmed were simply those they had found there, and that no particular selection was made with respect to their bodies or symptoms. We believe that this quality renders the Maestre Collection unique among similar footage from the same era. Among the copious circulation of images and ideas that united science and popular culture at the turn of the century—essential to what Mark Micale calls the "culture of hysteria" that developed in the nineteenth and twentieth centuries—we must not forget the neurological films that were made shortly after the invention of moving images.[21] The materials we have discussed here belong to the context established by the body of films that European neurologists made in the first decades of the twentieth century.

If there is a film from this period that truly stands out in this field it is undoubtedly *La neuropatología* (*Neuropathology*, 1906–1918), by Camillo Negro and Roberto Omegna, which offers a clear counterpoint to the Maestre Collection. Negro, an Italian doctor, also filmed cases for use in his classes. He also appears, surrounded by his students, observing some of the patients. But he can be distinguished from Maestre in that some of the cases he filmed with Omegna were clearly made with specific goals in mind: to identify concrete symptoms or specific stages in psychiatric illnesses. Indeed, Negro not only sought out and selected certain behaviors, such as epileptic fits, but also went so far as to orchestrate their performance. Significantly, there is not a single fit or seizure in the Maestre Collection footage, surely because none took place when Maestre and his team happened to be filming the patients. This indicates the distinction in scientific stature between Camillo Negro and Dr. Maestre, with his anachronistic theory. But it also leads us once again to argue that the images of the bodies of the patients who appear in this collection are less controlled. In this nonfilm there is room for the unexpected with respect to the bodies, which are part of an organic whole, a fragment of life, haphazard and brutal, far from the antiseptic realm of the clinical.

LUIS ALONSO GARCÍA is Professor in the Communication Department at the Universidad Rey Juan Carlos, Madrid. He is author of *Lenguaje del Cine, Praxis del Filme* and *Historia y Praxis de los Media*.

DANIEL SÁNCHEZ-SALAS is Assistant Professor of Communication and Sociology Studies at the Universidad Rey Juan Carlos, Madrid. He is author of *Historias de luz y papel. El cine español de los años veinte, a través de su adaptación de narrativa literaria española*. He is editor with Laura Gómez Vaquero of *El espíritu del caos. Recepción y representación de las imágenes durante el franquismo*.

BEGOÑA SOTO-VÁZQUEZ is Professor in Cinema and Media History at the Universidad Rey Juan Carlos, Madrid, and the creator and director of the Andalusian Film Archive.

Notes

1. Fernando Camarero Rioja, "Primeros Años del Cine Médico en España," in *De Cimientos y Contrafuertes: XIV Congreso Internacional de la Asociación Española de Historiadores del Cine, AEHC*, ed. Julio Pérez Perucha and Agustín Rubio Alcover (Bilbao, Spain: Universidad del País Vasco, 2013), 25–35.

2. Specifically, the title *Oftalmología* (Ophthalmology, 1917), in which the camera operator, Francesc Puigvert, films a series of eye operations by the famous Dr. Ignasi Barraquer i Barraquer; see Juan Antonio Cabero, *Historia de la Cinematografía Española: Once Jornadas 1896–1946* (Madrid: Gráficas Cinema, 1949), 109–11. Gaumont distributed

the film internationally. Paradoxically, it owes its place in film history to, as Joan Minguet argues, being one of the sources of inspiration for the famous first scene of *Un chien andalou* (Luis Buñuel and Salvador Dalí, 1929). Joan M. Minguet Batllori, *Paisaje(s) del Cine Mudo en España* (Valencia, Spain: Filmoteca de Valencia, 2008), 77–78. A fragment of *Oftalmología* can be viewed at http://vimeo.com/album/1705991/video/28940255.

3. The film can be viewed at http://www.cienciatk.csic.es/Videos/EXCURSION +ESCOLAR+CON+EL+DR+MAESTRE+AL+MANICOMIO+DE+CIEMPOZUELOS%2C +1915_24963.html.

4. Eduardo Bonet, *Vida y Obra del Dr. Tomás Maestre* (Alicante, Spain: Museo de Artes y Oficios de Monovar, 1983); Jose Antonio Lorenzo Solano, *Biografía del Doctor Tomás Maestre Pérez (1857–1936)* (Murcia, Spain: Caja de Ahorros del Mediterráneo, 1992).

5. Most of the footage has not been preserved, meaning that only the elements on nitrate stock exist.

6. The notes on how the deposits were made, by whom, and the initial identification of all the footage were done by José Manuel Valés (who kindly supplied us with all his notes on the elements) and Alfonso del Amo. Both worked at the Filmoteca Española in 2006. Records for all the titles deposited to date have not been found in the Filmoteca Española.

7. There is very little material in the Spanish archives in this format, leading us to believe that it must have been unusual in Spain at the time.

8. The 35mm material probably dates from a later time, in or around the 1920s.

9. We examine here only the 28mm material, given that the 35mm material would require a study of greater depth to reach any kind of conclusion.

10. Technical qualities such as the aperture, the kind of physical splices, and the kind of film stock used.

11. Adriano Chiò, Claudia Gianetto, and Stella Dagna, "Professor Camillo Negro's Neuropathological Films," *Journal of the History of the Neurosciences* 25, no. 1 (2016): 39–50; Simone Venturini, Lorenzo Lorusso, and Federico Vanone, "L'Archivio e le sue Tracce: la collezione Vincenzo Neri," *Immagine* 6 (2012): 32–54.

12. "Excursión universitaria a Ciempozuelos," *El Heraldo de Madrid*, February 2, 2015, 4. The original text in Spanish can be found at http://hemerotecadigital.bne.es/issue .vm?id=0000668040&page=1&search=&lang=es.

13. Venturini et al., "L'Archivio e le sue Tracce," 32–33.

14. Georges Didi-Huberman, *Invention of Hysteria: Charcot and the Photographic Iconography of the Salpêtrière*, trans. Alisa Hartz (Cambridge, MA: MIT Press, 2003).

15. In the Spanish of the day they would have been called *alienados*.

16. Mary Ann Doane, *The Emergence of Cinematic Time: Modernity, Contingency, the Archive* (Cambridge, MA: Harvard University Press, 2002), 22.

17. Pasi Väliaho, "Biopolitics of Gesture: Cinema and the Neurological Body," in *Cinema and Agamben: Ethics, Biopolitics and the Moving Image*, ed. Henrik Gustafsson and Asbjørn Grønstad (London: Bloomsbury Academy, 2014), 112–16.

18. To a large extent, the Maestre Collection takes part in cinema as an apparatus of modernity, one that, as Väliaho remarks by way of a direct quotation of Giorgio Agamben, can "capture, orient, determine, intercept, model, control, or secure the gestures, behaviors, opinions, or discourses of living beings" (Väliaho, "Biopolitics of Gesture," 112). Väliaho uses the films of the Italian neurologist Vincenzo Neri to argue this point, seeing in them the "neurological gaze" of which Michel Foucault spoke. This gaze, Väliaho claims, "tracks down

the corporeal surface, disinterested of the depths of the flesh or of the psyche" (116). The images in the Maestre Collection do not fit with this lack of interest, precisely because of the postures and presences mentioned.

19. "Excursión universitaria a Ciempozuelos."
20. Neither should we discount the possible influence of Dr. Max Nordau, whose famous cultural treatise on hysteria, *Degeneration*, published in 1894, was translated into Spanish in 1902 under the title *Degeneración*. Max Nordau, *Degeneración* (Madrid, Spain: Marzo, 1902).
21. Mark S. Micale, "Discourses of Hysteria in Fin-de-Siècle France," in *The Mind of Modernism: Medicine, Psychology, and the Cultural Arts in Europe and America, 1880–1940*, ed. Mark S. Micale (Stanford, CA: Stanford University Press, 2004), 85–86.

6 The Celluloid Specimens
Animal Origins for the Moving Image
Benjamin Schultz-Figueroa

IF YOU LOOK through the index cards of the Yerkes National Primate Research Center archives you will find traces of Mona, a chimpanzee from the Yerkes lab who died on September 24, 1942.[1] Mona was preserved as a specimen within this archive in a variety of ways. Her cadaver, head with brain, placentas and umbilical cords from two births, uterus, fallopian tubes, and ovaries all exist as different item cards in the laboratory filing system. But she is also present in four separate cards representing films that document her behavior with her children and her performance on intelligence tests. Within this filing system, and that of many other labs, film reels are itemized on par with anatomical portions, both existing as scientific documents of animal life to be preserved and stored for future use. Here André Bazin's famous adage on the ontological status of film might best be rephrased as "change in formaldehyde."[2]

The history of such cinematic specimens has yet to be written, despite the centrality of animal testing for many scientific disciplines and the abundance of films produced on the subject. Both materially and analytically, these films have been forgotten, left to languish unseen in the vaults of labs, universities, and archives. Film historians have largely ignored the genealogies and methodologies of rearranging animal bodies for the purposes of cinematic research, and many of the central films that make up this history have not been widely seen or preserved. From the laboratory films of Yerkes to the educational films of Neal E. Miller to the filmed presentations of B. F. Skinner, both film scholars and scientific communities alike often leave these vital works unattended. I explore this history in a larger research project titled *The Celluloid Specimen: Moving Image Research of Animal Life*.

This essay begins to write the story of celluloid specimens by looking at two early moments in the history of physiology: first, exploring Claude Bernard's advocacy for vivisection as an experimental procedure in the 1860s, and then turning to the debate over the use of film as a replacement for vivisection in the first quarter of the twentieth century. Tracing the threads of reproducibility and repetition that connect both of these moments, I contend that physiologists' use of animal bodies provided the epistemological groundwork for the reproducible cinematic body that would later make the technology of the moving image such a promising innovation for experimental medicine. As Scott Curtis and others have shown, the ability to reobserve films of risky and invasive medical experiments offered scientists a possibly ground-shifting solution to ethical, political, and practical concerns about repeating such potentially deadly procedures.[3] Repeated (cinematic) observations of a single procedure—exactingly recorded—could stand in for the multiple repetitions that would otherwise be required, thus offering a less morally and emotionally fraught alternative to human and animal testing by expanding the scientific vision of the Victorian vivisectionists. However, I argue that the legacy of the debate over animal experiments ultimately curtailed film's use in physiology and medicine, specifically as a substitute for vivisection. Despite attempts to distance film from the stakes of live vivisections by emphasizing its status as simply an image, the moral and the corporeal could never be totally left behind, which made the medium a volatile subject in arguments over scientific ethics.

Claude Bernard's groundbreaking book published in 1865, *An Introduction to Experimental Medicine*, is widely credited with the ascendance of physiology as an experimental science in the mid-nineteenth century.[4] His influence over early scientific filmmaking is also well documented. Bernard's concept of the interior environment and his precise breakdown of the use of both empirical observation and experimental intervention are recognized as guiding structural theories in the early physiological pursuit of movement that would eventually produce the technology of film. Marta Braun's historical investigation of Étienne-Jules Marey's career demonstrates how Bernard initially inspired and subsequently acted as a foil for Marey's graphing method.[5] Lisa Cartwright also demonstrates how Bernard continues to condition scientific filmmaking practices in the form of radiological imagining through the application of his model mapping dynamic systems through surveillance and control.[6] While these works demonstrate Bernard's persisting influence over medical and scientific film, I will focus on a lesser-known aspect of his work by detailing his role in tackling the primary methodological problem of repetition in living bodies, and how this work is linked to later filmmaking practices.

Bernard needed to create repetition in living bodies for physiology to be considered a full-fledged science.[7] For him, this transformation of medicine and physiology into properly scientific pursuits fundamentally required the use of animals as test subjects. He wrote, "Without such comparative study of animals, practical medicine can never acquire a scientific character."[8] During the early days of physiology, the singular qualities of living beings seemed to prohibit any easy systematic repetition of physiological experiments, which scientists in other disciplines such as physics and chemistry could produce rather easily. At this

Figure 6.1. Claude Bernard and his pupils. Oil painting by Léon Augustin Lhermitte, 1889.

time physiology's primary tool of vivisection—the practice of operating on living animals—was so rudimentary that the dependable reproduction of one's findings in living systems was nearly impossible to achieve.[9] Compounding this problem, the invasive experiments of physiology—what Bernard titled his "experiments by destruction"—tended to damage or destroy the bodies of their test subjects, thus prohibiting multiple experimental repetitions on the same living thing.[10] Finally, this deadly component to the experiments invariably sparked debates around ethics and morality, creating a perennial question for physiologists (whether they liked it or not) as to whether it was legally, theologically, and/or humanely acceptable to cause extreme suffering or to take a life in the pursuit of knowledge. A unique set of prerequisites existed for the laboratory subjects of experimental life science. In order to produce the repetition necessary to be methodologically acceptable, experimental bodies needed to be morally neutral, disposable, and reproducible. Bernard used the bodies of living animals to build this form of experimental life.

This transformation required that the animal body be tamed for the purposes of experimentation. Bernard outlined a set of procedures whereby animals could be made to satisfy the prerequisites of being reproducible, disposable, and morally neutral.[11] Reproducibility was probably the most technically difficult to generate, but Bernard resolved it through replacement, in which one animal became the surrogate body for another. The general tendency to erase distinctions between animals, which Jacques Derrida details in *The Animal That Therefore I Am*, would seem to allow one to stand in for another, creating a fundamental equivalency between animals of all types.[12] But enacting such an equivalency, making the *animot* a manifest reality within the laboratory setting, was no small feat, since experiments with animals often produced frustratingly aberrant results. Bernard's intervention was a call for a massive recalibration of both the subject and the setting of physiological research in order to allow one animal's body to stand in for another's. He advocated an approach in which vivisections were performed repeatedly by the same scientist, in the same lab, with multiple animals of the same species, age, and type.[13] Unlike the broad blurring between species that Derrida identifies in works of philosophy from Aristotle to Heidegger, Bernard built his equivalence based on a fine understanding of the details of difference. Only by delicately calibrating for the variances between species and individual animal bodies could underlying comparisons be made and a single body of knowledge produced from the diversity of animal test subjects.[14]

While theoretically, Bernard acknowledged that no absolute comparisons could be made between different individual animals (or even with a single animal at different moments in its life span), he felt comparisons could and should be made as long as the proper precautions were taken. There were, of course, other practical concerns as well. Expense and availability largely prescribed which animals qualified as disposable enough for vivisection.[15] Readily accessible bodies of dogs, rabbits, and frogs provided the bulk numbers of replacements necessary for experimentation. The economic disposability of overabundance also generally aligned with a moral disposability—allowing physiologists to harness the cultural standings of crawlers, vermin, strays, and game of all sorts to justify their use in experiments. These were animals that were systematically killed for food, cleanliness, or sport, to which the addition of human welfare seemed of little concern.

Nonetheless, the killing of animals, including pests, was never completely uncontroversial. Even in the early days of Bernard's writing—when vivisection was hardly in the public's eye—he felt the need to defend his experiments against the moral and humanitarian outrage of his critics.[16] His defense, like his procedures for producing comparable results, was predicated on a fine calibration of both the experimenter and the experimental subject. Fundamental to this position was the *attitude* of the physiologist while performing the vivisection. As Bernard infamously wrote, "A physiologist . . . no longer hears the cry of animals, he no longer sees the blood that flows, he sees only his idea and perceives only organisms concealing problems which he intends to solve."[17] What distinguishes the physiologist here from, say, the murderer was ultimately the way they *perceived* their material—with the eyes of the professional scientist. Through this act of specialized perception, the morality of the vivisection as an encounter was lifted from the scene of an individual killing and placed in the broader arena of sacrifice in the name of a greater good. The scientist did not see what would horrify the lay person or thrill the sadist but rather elevated vivisection by viewing it as a conceptual puzzle.

This attitude required an active effort to produce. Just as physiologists needed to tame the bodies of animals in order to conduct experiments, they also needed to tame their own feelings and senses in order to perform vivisections. These efforts were not always successful. One of Bernard's own students wrote a passionate exposé for the London *Morning Post* detailing a dog's attempts to elicit sympathy in the moments leading up to its death by vivisection, which included facial expressions, tail wagging, and hand licking.[18] As Susan Hamilton and others have shown, physiology constructed a visual culture of vivisection to refuse these emotional triggers—from woodcuts that depicted animals as passive conveyers of anatomical information, to restraints and drugs that prohibited animals from actively relaying signals of fear and pain.[19] Both during the procedure and in the images that represented it, the animal body was conditioned to be mute and restrained—almost lifeless except for the movements of its organs and circulatory system that were under observation. The limiting of animal bodies to abstract problems fundamentally required a dispassionate disposition and setting for the experiment to be conducted at all.

The cohesion of physiology's experimental practice was thus wrapped up in the identity of its practitioners. Enforcing this analytical vision often relied on prevailing gender scripts, in which the detached male scientist was contrasted with the imagined figure of the female antivivisectionist, whose supposed emotional responses to the blood and cries of the vivisection procedure made her blind to the greater moral good that the physiologists were pursuing.[20] Pairing emotion and gender created a strong disciplinary weapon for vivisection's defenders to disqualify humanitarian critiques as misguidedly sentimental. The perception of vivisection as an affectively intense scene was denigrated as that of a hypothetical female amateur, while physiologists used all the tools at their disposal to rinse the experience of vivisection clean of the sights and sounds that might pull them toward emotionally engaging with the animal specimen.

Therefore, in the constant cycle of calibrating scientists, experimental apparatuses, and animal test subjects, the transformation of the animal into an experimental body required not only the precise selection of the animal itself and control over the settings of the experiment but also the production of a proper attitude or posture for the experimenter—an act of viewing that rested in the (masculine) realm of abstract ideas rather than (feminized) carnal stimulation.

It is into this controversial ecosystem of methodologies, technologies, and inflamed moral debate that film enters as a tool for experimental medicine. The trade press for educational and scientific filmmaking often raised the issue of film's capacity to largely supplant vivisection.[21] Through the act of substituting a single film for numerous living bodies, they argued, film created its own reproducible, disposable, and morally neutral experimental body, which could potentially replace the experimental body of animals. Now comparisons could be made between screenings rather than between multiple individual animals, a much simpler procedure. At times a single specimen was literally transformed into a roll of celluloid. Through a process called "serial sectioning," which was practiced from the turn of the century into the 1950s, micromillimeter slivers of animal specimens—which were thin enough to allow light to pass through—were attached to film strips and projected.[22] Based on the fundamental similarities between a paraffin ribbon and the frames of a film, such experiments literally reconfigured the animal body as an abstract moving image, which could be repeatedly replayed. As one scientist commented in 1903, viewing these films was "extremely interesting and curious," as the organs and body parts of the animal were transformed into shifting geometric shapes.[23] Whether literally attaching animal sections to strips of film or simply recording vivisection procedures, the corporeality of the animal test subject—with all of its affectively troubling signals of pain and the overwhelming variability of its bodily responses—could finally be replaced with a rigorously detailed cinematic body that would not require the same extreme measures to control.

The potential for film to solve the ongoing problems that had persistently plagued physiology long after Bernard's writing was the subject of continued debate within the popular press and specialized medical journals at the turn of the century.[24] In "The Progress of Science: Cinematographs and Vivisectors: How Pain can be Saved," a 1922 article published in the London-based newspaper *The Times*, an anonymous correspondent ticks off a series of arguments for replacing the majority of vivisections with filmed recordings of individual experiments.[25] They argue that these films could be replayed over and over to answer new questions as different lines of inquiry emerged, with the added benefits of frame-by-frame analysis and the manipulation of projection speeds. Film would also mitigate the need for multiple repetitions of the same experiment to verify the fleeting observations of the initial experimenter, or to teach well-known procedures to incoming students. Finally, the author reiterated the by-then popular line that the fact that these reproductions simply *replay* the images of suffering meant that they offered a morally neutral reproduction of the experiment that did not require the actual reenactment of its pain.

Framing "The Progress of Science" as a set of helpful suggestions for the Society for the Defense of Medical Research (a vivisection advocacy group), its

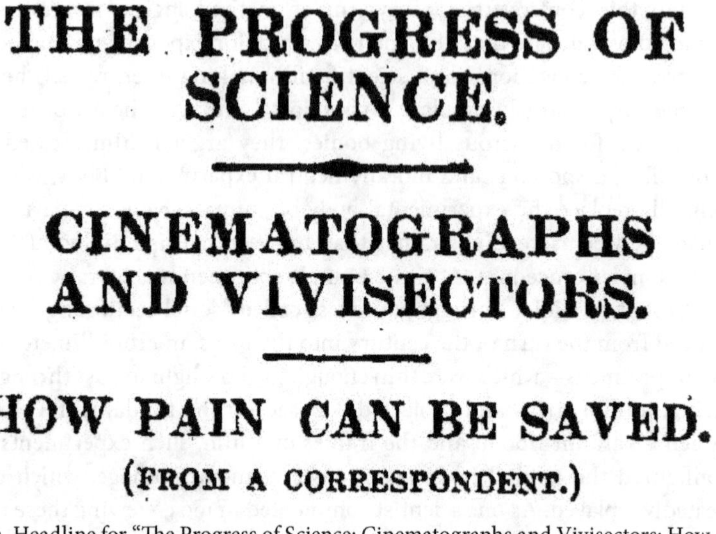

THE PROGRESS OF SCIENCE.

CINEMATOGRAPHS AND VIVISECTORS.

HOW PAIN CAN BE SAVED.

(FROM A CORRESPONDENT.)

Figure 6.2. Headline for "The Progress of Science: Cinematographs and Vivisectors: How Pain can be Saved," *The Times*, March 28, 1922, 10.

author was probably surprised by the extremely negative response it received in the pages of the *British Medical Journal*.[26] This rebuke, titled "'Cinematographs and Vivisectors': A Flank Attack," also written anonymously, attacked the assertion that vivisection caused any unnecessary pain that needed to be reduced. It marshaled the passing of the Cruelty to Animals Act of 1876—which required the use of painkilling drugs when conducting animal experiments—as proof that such pain was no longer a part of the vivisection procedure. This legislation, along with the professionalization of physiology, and its subsequent movement into the laboratory setting and out of the public's view, had largely succeeded in averting attention away from vivisection itself.[27] By 1922, this debate was no longer the hot-button issue it had been during the 1880s and 1890s, which had included heated rhetoric on all sides and even a series of antivivisectionist riots.[28] In this context, *The Times*'s "Progress of Science" article was seen by physiologists as a hostile attempt to reintroduce the subject of animal pain into public discourse, despite the fact that the author sought to fundamentally preserve the practice of vivisection while also avoiding unnecessary animal suffering. The claim that films could reduce the pain felt by animals during vivisection threatened to reopen an argument that a majority of physiologists were happy to leave forgotten or marginalized.

"'Cinematographs and Vivisectors': A Flank Attack" admits that film has an important future in medical and physiological science but also insists that "it is not true that humanitarian grounds are involved."[29] Film ultimately played a divisive role in the debate over vivisection for reasons precisely rooted in previous concerns over experimental bodies. Even while discounting the humanitarian goals propagated in "The Progress of Science," physiologists acknowledged the potential power of film to reproduce vivisections for their peers as an aid to comprehension and measurement. Periodic accounts appear in the *British Medical Journal* throughout the early twentieth century, extolling the value of this experimental tool—especially as a means of convincing other professionals of a study's validity.[30]

However, concerns persisted among physiologists that other, less sympathetic, viewers might get a chance to watch films of animal vivisections. Within the pages of the *British Medical Journal*, authors fretted over antivivisectionists' calls for using film to disseminate the visceral documentation of vivisection to a general public.[31] Physiologists attempted to discredit the antivivisectionists' use of film as morbid and exploitative, labeling this appropriation of the medium a "carnal means of information."[32] Indeed, antivivisectionists were intent on making films of vivisection as troubling and upsetting as possible. As early as 1909, antivivisectionists advocated pairing phonographs with film to reproduce both the sounds and the images of the dying animals.[33] Even the suggestion of such presentations stood in stark contrast to the abstract geometric forms of projected serial section. Antivivisectionists persistently threatened to illustrate their public lectures with filmed examples of animal experiments, taking the sights and sounds of the lab out of the rarefied space of scientific discourse. It seemed that film could be just as corporeal as the living body, including all the unpredictable emotional reactions that it elicited. An experiment performed by specialists in the lab could become damning material when viewed by the broader population. Mirroring the debates of the late nineteenth century—when antivivisectionists used physiologists' own imagery and language as evidence of the horrors of vivisection—physiologists of the early twentieth century attacked nonsanctioned uses of film to distribute the images of vivisection as prurient and salacious. Physiologists derided the emotions elicited by such films as fundamentally unscientific, comparing viewers to spiritualists being taken in by an excess of emotion.[34] Just as in Bernard's writing, vivisectionists at the time sought to distinguish between moral and immoral visual material based on the attitude of a film's viewers, not its content—a film could be either "carnal" propaganda or compelling proof, depending on its audience.

To conclude, film was portrayed as an unstable element in the debates over animal testing. It offered an incredible potential to repeat experiments with an indexical exactness that was otherwise impossible. Film made experimental life replicable with a hitherto unseen accuracy, allowing physiologists to break away from the demanding process of reproducing earlier experiments—the labor of replicating the laboratory, the scientist, and the animal could all be erased. Additionally, the filmed vivisection was thought to be an experimental scene without the emotional and moral stakes of a live procedure, a long-sought-after goal. But at the same time, a preference for "repeating" vivisections through film involved a tacit acknowledgment that the live procedure was itself cruel, and there was an uncontrollable risk in how these films might be viewed. The act of dissecting a living being could mutate from knowledge production to sadistic violence if seen by the wrong eyes. The easy replay of filmed vivisections revealed the procedure beyond the walls of the lab, where viewers might respond more strongly to the onscreen blood and cries of the animal than to the questions pursued by the experimenter. By the 1920s, the audiovisual reproduction of animal experiments threatened to explode what had become a carefully contained conversation, whose ruling logic for decades had been "out of sight, out of mind." These celluloid specimens, like the live animals before them, had a wild capacity to misbehave, to send mixed messages, to produce different findings in different circumstances, and thus required a similar technical, disciplinary, and moral framework to contain.

Like other body genres, animal-research films have the potential to elicit intense affective responses from nonspecialized audience members. As the recent spate of ag-gag laws attest to, moving images of animal research still have this disruptive capacity.[35] In many laboratories there are decaying film reels that document animal experiments, which are often concealed over concerns of public outrage. Whether produced by physiology or behavioral psychology, genetics, zoology, and so on, these films played and continue to play a central role in defining animal life for experimental and cultural purposes. Only by focusing on this history can we begin to analyze the effects of celluloid specimens, in which the feelings, bodies, and lives of nonhuman animals are forcibly transformed into the knowledge, techniques, and images of scientific power.

BENJAMIN SCHULTZ-FIGUEROA is a doctoral candidate in Film and Digital Media at the University of California, Santa Cruz.

Notes

1. Box 66, Folder 2, Yerkes National Primate Research Center records, Emory University Archives, Manuscript, Archives, and Rare Book Library, Emory University.
2. André Bazin, "The Ontology of the Photographic Image," trans. Hugh Gray, *Film Quarterly* 13, no. 4 (1960): 6. The original phrasing is "change mummified."
3. Scott Curtis, *The Shape of Spectatorship: Art, Science, and Early Cinema in Germany* (New York: Columbia University Press, 2015), 100.

4. Claude Bernard, *An Introduction to the Study of Experimental Medicine* (Mineola, NY: Courier Dover, 1957). Originally published in 1865.

5. Marta Braun, *Picturing Time: The Work of Étienne-Jules Marey (1830–1904)* (Chicago: University of Chicago Press, 1994), 9–10.

6. Lisa Cartwright, "'Experiments of Destruction': Cinematic Inscriptions of Physiology," *Representations* 40 (October 1, 1992): 131.

7. Bernard, *An Introduction to the Study of Experimental Medicine*, 68. As Bernard wrote, "Once the conditions of a phenomenon are known and fulfilled, the phenomenon must always and necessarily be reproduced at the will of the experimenter. Negation of this proposition would be nothing less than negation of science itself."

8. Ibid.

9. Karl E. Rothschuh, *History of Physiology: Transl. and Ed. with a New English Bibliography by Guenter B. Risse* (Huntington, NY: Krieger, 1973), 269.

10. Bernard, *An Introduction to the Study of Experimental Medicine*, 8.

11. This transformation is still required, a process that Michael Lynch outlines in a more contemporary laboratory setting: Michael E. Lynch, "Sacrifice and the Transformation of the Animal Body into a Scientific Object: Laboratory Culture and Ritual Practice in the Neurosciences," *Social Studies of Science* 18, no. 2 (May 1, 1988): 265–89.

12. Jacques Derrida, *The Animal That Therefore I Am* (New York: Fordham University Press, 2008), 34.

13. The issue of diversity among individual animals would be greatly reduced by major innovations in inbreeding, which would eventually produce the albino laboratory rat. This animal promised to be remarkably consistent in the physiology and behavior across individuals, providing a control animal for experiments. S. A. Barnett, *The Rat: A Study in Behavior* (New Brunswick, NJ: Aldine Transaction, 2007), 3.

14. Lorraine Daston and Peter Galison, *Objectivity* (New York: Zone, 2007). Bernard's use of these techniques position him as part of a general shift in nineteenth-century science toward findings that were built on the indexing of detailed differences rather than the intuiting of ideal forms.

15. Bernard, *An Introduction to the Study of Experimental Medicine*, 115.

16. Mary Midgley, *Animals and Why They Matter*, reissue edition (Athens: University of Georgia Press, 1998). This was an outrage Bernard would have known quite intimately: his wife, who was disgusted to find him experimenting on rabbits and dogs in their kitchen, would eventually divorce him and become an outspoken critic of vivisection.

17. Bernard, *An Introduction to the Study of Experimental Medicine*, 103.

18. George Hoggan, "Vivisection: (To the Editor of the 'Morning Post')," London *Morning Post*, 1875, 177–78.

19. Hilda Kean, "The 'Smooth Cool Men of Science': The Feminist and Socialist Response to Vivisection," *History Workshop Journal* 40 (October 1, 1995): 16–38; Susan Hamilton, "'Still Lives': Gender and the Literature of the Victorian Vivisection Controversy," *Victorian Review* 17, no. 2 (December 1, 1991): 21–34; Chris Danta, "The Metaphysical Cut: Darwin and Stevenson on Vivisection," *Victorian Review* 36, no. 2 (2010): 51–65.

20. One example among many is the satirical article "How These Antivivisectors Love One Another," which features the absurd description of a female antivivisectionist crying sorrowfully over a swatted mosquito. "How These Antivivisectors Love One Another," *British Medical Journal* 1, no. 1991 (February 25, 1899): 493–94.

21. For a partial list of proponents for replacing vivisections with film, read Frank Benford, J. I. Crabtree, C. E. Egeler, and K. C. D. Hickman. "Progress in the Motion Picture Industry: September 1928—Report of the Progress Committee," *Transactions of the Society of Motion Picture Engineers* 12, no. 35 (1928): 588–96; G. d. F., "The Cinema and the School," *International Review of Educational Cinematography*, no. 8 (August 1931): 769–82; Charles Francis Jenkins, *Handbook for Motion Picture and Stereopticon Operators* (Washington, DC: Knega Company, 1908); "Great University Makes New Use of Movie," *Educational Screen*, February 1925; and Charles Urban, "The Cinematograph in Science and Education," *Moving Picture World* 1, no. 26 (August 1907): 372–73.

22. Anthony R. Michaelis, *Research Films in Biology, Anthropology, Psychology, and Medicine* (New York: Academic, 1955), 91–93.

23. Robert E. Kelly, "Preliminary Note on the Application of the Cinematograph Principle to the Study of Serial Sections," *British Medical Journal* 2, no. 2223 (1903): 312–13.

24. For an account of the heated battles over vivisection, see Coral Lansbury, *The Old Brown Dog: Women, Workers, and Vivisection in Edwardian England* (Madison: University of Wisconsin Press, 1985).

25. "The Progress of Science: Cinematographs and Vivisectors: How Pain can be Saved," *The Times*, March 28, 1922, 10.

26. "'Cinematographs and Vivisectors': A Flank Attack," *British Medical Journal* 1, no. 3197 (1922): 569–70.

27. Susan Hamilton, "Reading and the Popular Critique of Science in the Victorian Anti-Vivisection Press: Frances Power Cobbe's Writing for the Victoria Street Society," *Victorian Review* 36, no. 2 (2010):, 72.

28. Lansbury, *The Old Brown Dog.*

29. "'Cinematographs And Vivisectors': A Flank Attack," 570.

30. For instance, see Chalmers Watson, "Cinematograph and Lantern Demonstration upon Nervous Diseases in the Lower Animals," *British Medical Journal* 2, no. 2178 (1902): 929; "The International Congress Of Physiologists," *British Medical Journal* 2, no. 2751 (1913): 750–52.

31. "Antivivisection and the Protection of Animals," *British Medical Journal* 2, no. 2533 (1909): 169–70; "Another Antivivisection Congress," *British Medical Journal* 2, no. 2535 (1909): 272–74.

32. "Antivivisection and the Protection of Animals."

33. Ibid., 170.

34. Ibid.

35. Between 2009 and 2013, a series of restrictions were passed on filming animal abuse in industrial settings, called ag-gag laws. For a full description, read Jessalee Landfried, "Bound & Gagged: Potential First Amendment Challenges to 'Ag-Gag' Laws," *Duke Environmental Law and Policy Forum* 23, no. 2 (March 22, 2013): 377.

7   Death by a Thousand Cuts
On-Screen Executions in Early American Cinema

Gary D. Rhodes

Even before the age of American film projection began in 1896, the Edison Manufacturing Company manufactured death for the kinetoscope. In August 1895, Alfred Clark and William Heise created *The Execution of Mary, Queen of Scots*, which used "stop-motion substitution" to depict the decapitation of its title character by the single blow of an ax, and, as a result, an executioner holding up the severed head.[1] Without moving the camera, the filmmakers replaced the actor portraying Mary with a dummy immediately prior to shooting the beheading. The two images were spliced together, thus making the execution appear to take place in a single, continuous shot.[2] According to an 1895 newspaper advertisement, *The Execution of Mary, Queen of Scots* represented the very first "Chamber of Horrors" moving picture to be "seen on the kinetoscope," adding that it was "blood-curdling in the extreme."[3]

Though based on the infamous British execution of 1587, *The Execution of Mary, Queen of Scots* also drew on America's lengthy and evolving relationship with public executions, a history that would be reexplored in the age of early cinema. In the nineteenth century, many enlightened people fought to end all public executions, believing it was the duty of those in positions of authority to protect American citizens from such grisly displays, as well as—in some, or even many cases—the bloodthirsty desire of the citizenry to see such displays. The result meant a transition from public hangings to private electrocutions, as well as regular, if largely ineffectual, pleas to end public lynching.

In 1913, *Moving Picture World* editorialized on this issue: "Pictures showing the harrowing details of an execution by hanging ought never to be passed by a board of censorship. It has cost years of agitation to abolish public executions. Are they to be revived by the motion pictures?"[4] The question was apt, though it was nearly twenty years late, as the very films that worried *Moving Picture World* had been in production since 1895.

Indeed, the first ten years of the American cinema saw a number of films that followed in the style of *The Execution of Mary, Queen of Scots* but did not even possess the aura of being a simulated, historical reenactment. Produced by major film-manufacturing companies, these moving pictures glorified the violence of executions and lynchings, not only acting against the efforts of nineteenth-century reformers but also presenting such images to the whole of America, rather than being limited by the geography that in many cases restricted such acts to certain regions of the country.

Public executions and lynchings had long attracted both the attention and condemnation of members of the entertainment industry. In 1880, for example, the *National Police Gazette* reported on a lynching in Colorado, telling readers that after the victim had been dead for an hour, the "committee" sent for a photographer. "In the foreground the committee could be seen and every face recognized—while just behind them was the dangling dead man, his diamonds and jewelry shining in the early morning sun, and above him sat the assistant hangman, evidently proud of his station."[5]

In the precinema era, photographs and stereographs of these events were sometimes taken and distributed, but usually by small companies that sold them to regional audiences. But the national media and entertainment press usually condemned the practice. For example, in 1888, Harry Rouclere, of the Steen-Rouclere Show, told the *New York Clipper* that his traveling company attended a lynching party near Asheville, North Carolina. In an act of ghoulish commercialism, the victim promised that he would mention their show in his closing speech on the scaffold, but he "weakened at the last moment." The *Clipper* decried Rouclere, declaring, "For an original advertising scheme this is indeed appalling."[6]

Such condemnations grew more intense in the years that followed. In 1914, *Moving Picture World* discussed the "forbidden theme" of the "killing of a man or woman in public":

> It was admitted that the spectacle was hideous, offensive and gruesome, but the claim was made in all sincerity, no doubt, that the supposed moral effects [of deterrence] outweighed the obvious horrors of the spectacle. The public whipping post and all its brutalizing influences were ardently defended on the same unsounded theory. To-day no man in his senses would dream of advocating a return to public executions. Even the portrayal of such horrible affairs upon the screen has been justly forbidden by law in some countries and rejected by public taste and decency in every part of the Christian world.[7]

Once again, *Moving Picture World* worried about rogue filmmakers and films that might do damage to the industry's reputation but ignored the fact that the founding companies of the American industry had initiated such moving pictures. For example, *Execution of a Murderess* (American Mutoscope and Biograph, 1905, aka *Execution by Hanging*) featured an actress portraying Mary Rogers, who

Figure 7.1. *Execution of a Murderess* (aka *Execution by Hanging*, American Mutoscope and Biograph, 1905). Courtesy of Robert J. Kiss.

murdered her husband in Vermont in 1902. Similar to how the effect was created in *The Execution of Mary, Queen of Scots*, the filmmaker replaced the actor with a dummy to depict the execution.[8]

More famously, Edison had released Edwin S. Porter's "imitation" of the *Execution of Czolgosz* in 1901, only two weeks after President McKinley's assassin was put to death.[9] The superintendent of Auburn State Prison, where Leon Czolgosz was put to death, had already refused an offer of $2,000 that the "owner of a kinetoscope" had made him to "take a moving picture" of the assassin "entering the death chamber."[10] In Porter's docudrama, the first two shots are authentic images of the exterior of Auburn State Prison. The third shot begins the fictional footage, with the warden removing Czolgosz from his cell. The fourth shot shows the electric chair being tested and then Czolgosz being put to death in the same.[11] Here was a new addition to the cinematic "Chamber of Horrors," an on-screen representation of an execution that was not open to the public. Here was special access to the "forbidden scene." It was a reenactment, but a reenactment that Edison's publicity rightly described as "realistic."

At times film companies implied that their execution films were authentic, even when they were not, as in *Execution of a Spy* (American Mutoscope and

Biograph, ca. 1900), which depicted a firing squad killing the title character. This film may or may not be the same as *Execution of the Spanish Spy*, which Prescott offered for sale in 1899.[12] In any event, the footage was apparently fictional. The same was definitely true of *A Career of Crime, No. 5: The Death Chair* (American Mutoscope and Biograph, 1900), which—in the carefully worded language of a catalog description—was an "accurate and thrilling representation" of its topic.[13] A surviving copy depicts an actor providing anguished expressions and squirming at the time of his on-screen death.[14]

For some early audience members, reenactments did not go far enough. In 1897, *The Phonoscope* reported that a man in Philadelphia suggested the "grewsome" [sic] proposition that a real execution be filmed and screened. He claimed that such an actuality would make an "enormous hit" with audiences, a possibility *The Phonoscope* bemoaned.[15] Nevertheless, at least two such moving pictures of this type were produced, one less than six months after the Philadelphian's suggestion.

In late 1897, *The Phonoscope* reported at length on Frank Guth's production of *The Hanging of William Carr*, a cinematic record of Carr's execution for murdering his three-year-old daughter: "It was revolting—four hundred persons crying and shrieking and laughing, surging under the very gallows, shunting against the horrible, swinging body. . . . That is how it will look—the hideous, grewsome [sic] views taken by the vitascope man. . . . It is the masterpiece of the vitascope man."[16] In this instance, *The Phonoscope* blamed the camera's presence for making a travesty of the hanging, that the process of filming the event affected the manner in which it unfolded, adding that, once Carr was pronounced dead and filming ceased, the crowd "became quiet in an instant." The trade added, "The vitascope had all the disgrace and honor and riot [it] wanted. There was no other reason for the frantic conduct of the crowd at the hanging."[17]

A newspaper editorial published in the *Cleveland Leader* pleaded for a state law that would prevent the exhibition of the Carr "vitascope horrors," which could have "brutalizing effects" on those who saw them, far more than any of the boxing films that drew the ire of so many citizens.[18] The *Washington Post* directly responded to the *Leader*, asking, "Is a picture of a murderer on his way to the scaffold and waiting for the hangman to do his work a degrading exhibition?" The *Post* proceeded to draw a comparison between authentic death films and the "mock murders" committed on the stage, including the works of Shakespeare. "We have laws enough for the regulation of public executions," the newspaper advised.[19]

The following year, in 1898, American Mutoscope and Biograph produced *An Execution by Hanging* (aka *Execution of Negro at County Jail, Jacksonville, Fla*), which depicted the authentic execution of an African American in Florida.

Cinematographer Arthur Marvin later recalled that the filming occurred because his party was on their way to cover the Spanish-American War:

> One of our unusual experiences came before the actual beginning of the war, during those weeks of tedious waiting in Tampa. We heard that there was to be an execution by hanging in Jacksonville, and in the interest of science and the camera we decided to obtain views of it if we could. We got permission to set up our machine in the jail yard, and succeeded in photographing the proceeding from the time the death march appeared outside the jail door until the drop was sprung. That is perhaps one of the most unusual subjects ever reproduced in detail by means of photographs.[20]

A catalog description warned that the film was "very ghastly," but that seems to be language intended to excite interest rather than dissuade it.[21] Put another way, here was yet another "Chamber of Horrors" subject in the tradition of *Execution of Mary, Queen of Scots*, a film intended to titillate viewers due to its visceral footage.

Related to these execution films were several moving pictures that depicted public lynchings. According to Amy Louise Wood, "Lynching assumed tremendous symbolic power precisely because it was extraordinary and, by its very nature, public and visually sensational. Those lynchings that hundreds, sometimes thousands, of white spectators gathered and watched as their fellow citizens were tortured, mutilated, and hanged or burned in full view were, for obvious reasons, the most potently haunting."[22] Wood also writes that the "cultural power of lynching" rested on "spectacle: the crowds, the rituals and performances, and their sensational representations in narratives, photographs, and films."[23]

The earliest film to depict a lynching was likely *Lynching Scene at Paris, Texas* (International Film Company, 1897, aka *Lynching Scene*). A description published in *The Phonoscope* promised "the most thrilling and realistic subject ever offered for sale. This scene shows an angry mob overpowering the sheriff, storming the jail, and dragging their prisoner to the nearest telephone pole, from which he is immediately swung into eternity, as bullet after bullet is fired into his writhing body. A most impressive and stirring subject."[24] While the moving picture was a staged re-creation of the events described, International Film's catalog nevertheless touted it as "genuine." The description went so far as to add, "By our contract with the authorities, [the] names of party and place cannot be given."[25]

In 1904, Selig Polyscope released *Tracked by Bloodhounds; or, A Lynching at Cripple Creek*. Ads and catalog descriptions for the film claimed that it was "actually" shot in Colorado when the "exciting events occurred," thus implying it was authentic, even though it, too, was a fictional dramatization.[26] In the film, a tramp murders a woman, whose husband and friends chase him down. The final shot shows the party of men with the culprit. They throw a rope around a tree limb and pull the tramp up, his arms swaying as they do. The climactic moments feature realistic effects and restrained acting.²⁷ It was, according to an ad in the *New York Clipper*, the "most sensational film ever made."²⁸

The other key lynching film of the era was Paley & Streiner's *Avenging a Crime; or Burned at the Stake* (1904, aka *Lynch Law*).²⁹ Its plot is similar to *Tracked by Bloodhounds*, with an African American character (enacted by a Caucasian in blackface) killing a white woman and fleeing, only to be caught by his white pursuers. They tie the African American to a stake, set him ablaze, and then fire bullets at him. The image is depicted in long shot, which—together with the billowing smoke—makes the death scene lacking in detail. In this case, the audience watches the fictional event but is still kept at some remove from it.

As Robert Jackson has noted, films like *Avenging a Crime* "provide a severe but valuable insight into the racial views of mainstream American popular culture in the first years of the cinema," views that would be most famously explored in D. W. Griffith's *The Birth of a Nation* in 1915.³⁰ They also impelled Americans to "bear witness, to take moral and social responsibility for the brutal injustice of lynching."³¹ But such a viewer, one who took moral and social responsibility for lynchings, was clearly only one type of audience member in the era. Consider the following letter to the editor, which was published in the *New York Times* in 1905 and titled "A Suggestion":

> After reading the account of the burning of that "nigger" at Howard, Texas, I am moved to make a suggestion. It was stated that "2,000 persons gathered to see the burning," and that "the roofs of prairie farmhouses and farm buildings for miles around were covered with people." With those facts in mind permit me to say that it would be good business to . . . send a kinetoscope to the next lynching of the kind in order to secure a complete series of photographs of the event. As every one knows, this photographic material can then be used to portray to people elsewhere just how such work is done.³²

The author of the letter, who lived in Northwood, New York, offers an awareness of the brevity of the victims' struggles, noting that they might last only five minutes. As a result, he suggested—for the "interest of public entertainment"—the filmed lynching should use a slow-burning fire, one started with limited wood or without kerosene, in order to prolong the killing and thus prolong the running time of the film.

Researching the author, Jan Olsson has determined that its contents were likely ironic, and that may well have been the case.³³ To this assessment, consideration could also be meaningfully paid to what newspaper readers thought of it, as most of them likely took it to be serious, just as *The Phonoscope* had in 1897 when its editor learned about a viewer's suggestion for an authentic execution film.

Collectively, these early moving pictures—manufactured as they were by reputable companies and distributed nationally—not only ignored or even counteracted the efforts of those in the late nineteenth century to end public

Figure 7.2. *A Neck-Tie Party Given by the Vigilants* (T. W. Ingersoll, 1898).

executions and lynchings but may also have incited interest among some citizens in viewing such scenes as a sadistic form of pleasure, including those living in regions where such actual events were rare or unknown. Moreover, these films may have encouraged other reputable companies to produce and distribute photographs of similar events, even those who had earlier forgone such imagery. Here we can consider *A Neck-Tie Party Given by the Vigilants* (T. W. Ingersoll, 1898) as well as *And "Speedily" the Punishment Fits the Crime* (Universal Photo Art, 1901), both being examples of stereographs manufactured in large quantities with national distribution.

For reasons that are difficult to substantiate, moving pictures depicting executions largely disappeared by the time of the nickelodeon era. The letter writer of 1905 did not receive his wish of seeing the kind of lynching film he described. However, the subject gained renewed discussion in America in 1910, when *Variety* reported that a cinematographer had filmed a death by guillotine in France, only to have his footage confiscated after the event.[34] That same year, *Moving Picture World* deemed that same film—and by extension all films of authentic executions—to be "inadmissible" to the nickelodeon, adding, "In this matter, the public have a right to be protected from the inadmissible in the shape of the brutal, the degrading, the gruesome, the repulsive, or the immoral. And certainly, an execution shown on the screen is brutalizing and repulsive." The trade announced it had a "duty" to "denounce" such films.[35]

As *Moving Picture World* noted in 1914, "Morbid instincts and atavistic cravings grow by what they feed upon. Nothing would draw a crowd more quickly than a public execution, but the growth of humanity and modern enlightenment have banished such hideous spectacles within prison walls."[36] Except perhaps in the case of the cinema. That same year, the trade noted with disdain that an exhibitor in New York "fitted out an imitation of the electric chair in Sing Sing, and placing a man in it he had a 'barker' call attention to the spectacle and urging people to come inside." That exhibitor, *Moving Picture World* happily reported, was arrested for "disorderly conduct."[37]

In 1915, *Moving Picture World* worried about new "pictures exploiting the sensational lynching of a man who had been condemned to death and whose sentence had been commuted."[38] It is difficult to determine whether this footage was authentic or the extent to which it was screened, if at all, but it was the source of major concern—the same kind of concern that industry trades had shown since approximately 1910, by which time production of American execution and lynching films had been largely terminated for five years.

In conclusion, death by mob, or by state decree, or a combination of both, never disappears from the cinematic consciousness, embedded as they are in the larger narratives of such Hollywood films as *Angels with Dirty Faces* (Warner Bros., 1938), *I Want to Live!* (United Artists, 1958), *In Cold Blood* (Columbia, 1967), *Dead Man Walking* (Gramercy, 1995), and *The Green Mile* (Warner Bros., 1999), to name but a few examples, as well as featured on internet sites like YouTube, in which ghastly simulated and real events such as those described in this chapter are viewed by millions. Nevertheless, major American companies eschewed execution spectacles of the type described here after 1905. Their origins remain silent.

GARY D. RHODES is Postgraduate Director for Film Studies at Queen's University, Belfast and a documentary filmmaker and film historian. His latest book is *The Birth of the American Horror Film*.

Notes

1. *The Execution of Mary, Queen of Scots* is available in the DVD boxed set *Edison: The Invention of the Movies* (New York: Kino, 2005).
2. Charles Musser, *The Emergence of Cinema: The American Screen to 1907* (Berkeley: University of California Press), 86–87.
3. Advertisement, *Evening Star* (Washington, DC), October 19, 1895, 8.
4. "Facts and Comments," *Moving Picture World*, February 1, 1913, 440.
5. "An Interesting Picture," *National Police Gazette*, December 18, 1880, 7.
6. Untitled, *New York Clipper*, July 28, 1888, 315.
7. W. Stephen Bush, "Forbidden Themes," *Moving Picture World*, November 14, 1914, 902.
8. A copy of *Execution of a Murderess* under the title *Execution by Hanging* is available at the Library of Congress.
9. A copy of *Execution of Czolgosz* (1901) is available at the Library of Congress.
10. "Czolgosz's Body to Be Destroyed at Auburn," *New York Times*, October 29, 1901, 1.

11. Exhibitors could purchase the film with or without the two opening shots of Auburn State Prison. Musser, *The Emergence of Cinema*, 320.
12. *Catalogue of New Films for Projection and Other Purposes* (New York: Prescott, 1899), 24. Available in *A Guide to Motion Picture Catalogs by American Producers and Distributors, 1894-1908: A Microfilm Edition*, Reel 1 (New Brunswick, NJ: Rutgers University Press, 1985).
13. *Picture Catalogue* (New York: American Mutoscope and Biograph, November 1902), 244. Available in *A Guide to Motion Picture Catalogs by American Producers and Distributors, 1894-1908: A Microfilm Edition*, Reel 2 (New Brunswick, NJ: Rutgers University Press, 1985).
14. A copy of *A Career of Crime, No. 5: The Death Chair* is available at the Library of Congress.
15. "Our Tattler," *The Phonoscope*, June 1897, 7.
16. "Vitascope Mob at the Hanging," *The Phonoscope*, November–December 1897, 8.
17. Ibid.
18. "Another Picture Horror," *Cleveland Leader*, December 21, 1897, 4.
19. "Vitascope Horrors," *Washington Post*, December 25, 1897, 6.
20. "Photography That Is Exceedingly Perilous," *Philadelphia Inquirer*, August 13, 1899, 3.
21. *Picture Catalogue*, 240.
22. Amy Louise Wood, *Lynching and Spectacle: Witnessing Racial Violence in America, 1890-1940* (Chapel Hill: University of North Carolina Press, 2009), 1.
23. Ibid., 3.
24. "New Films for 'Screen' Machines," *The Phonoscope*, November–December 1897, 13.
25. *International Photographic Films for Use on All Projecting Machines Using the Standard Gauge* (New York: International Film, Winter 1897–1898), 18, Reel 1.
26. Advertisement, *New York Clipper*, March 25, 1905, 134.
27. A copy of *Tracked by Bloodhounds; or, A Lynching at Cripple Creek* is available at the Library of Congress.
28. Advertisement, *New York Clipper*, September 24, 1904, 713.
29. Elias Savada, ed., *The American Film Institute Catalog of Motion Pictures Produced in the United States: Film Beginnings, 1893-1910* (Lanham, MD: Scarecrow, 1995), 57–58.
30. Robert Jackson, "The Celluloid War before *The Birth of a Nation*: Race and History in Early American Film," in *American Cinema and the Southern Imaginary*, ed. Deborah Barker and Kathryn McKee (Athens: University of Georgia Press, 2011), 32.
31. Wood, *Lynching and Spectacle*, 5.
32. John R. Spears, "A Suggestion," Letter to the Editor, *New York Times*, October 8, 1905, 6.
33. Jan Olsson, "Modernity Stops at Nothing: The American Chase Film and the Specter of Lynching," in *A Companion to Early Cinema*, ed. André Gaudreault, Nicolas Dulac, and Santiago Hidalgo (West Sussex, UK: Wiley-Blackwell, 2012), 261–65.
34. "Pictures of an Execution," *Variety*, January 22, 1910, 14.
35. "The Inadmissible Subject," *Moving Picture World*, January 22, 1910, 83.
36. "Facts and Comments," *Moving Picture World*, May 9, 1914, 791.
37. "Facts and Comments," *Moving Picture World*, April 18, 1914, 487.
38. Quoted in "Facts and Comments," *Moving Picture World*, September 18, 1915, 1967.

8 Staged Bodies, Caged Bodies
Early Cinema in the Age of Human Zoos

Rodolphe Gahéry

Translated by Timothy Barnard

The Corporeality and Imagery of Otherness

Two series in the Lumière catalog appear to crystallize the question of the body, and in particular the body of the Other—the black body: *Le Village noir au jardin d'acclimatation à Paris* (*The Black Village in the Zoological Gardens in Paris*, a series composed of two films shot in June and July 1896),[1] and *Le Village Achantis à Lyon* (*The Ashanti Village in Lyon*, fourteen films shot in April and May 1897).[2] These series show images of "human zoos" and "black villages" in turn-of-the-century France. There are at least two reasons for including these films in a discussion of otherness through corporeality.

First, the zoo, in its narrowest definition, represents an encounter between two desires—one might even say two impulses: one exhibitionist, the other voyeuristic. In the present instance, the principal object of desire and impulse is, of course, the body, the black body, which is both the center of gravity and the origin, the basis, of this staging. What is shown is, *above all else*, bodies, but also bodies *before all else*. Approaching this issue through corporeality will thus enable us to analyze phenomena of human exhibition as well as their history—to analyze their evolution as apparatuses.

More important, a corporeality approach will then enable us to analyze the images produced by this apparatus—in other words, to apprehend the difficult question of representation. "Human zoos" were indeed forms of representation, first and foremost; they were representations of Western society that, in the nineteenth century, constructed and asserted in hitherto unseen ways its relationship with otherness, whether colonial or not, by constructing and asserting a corollary Western "identity." This representation of otherness came into being out of necessity through corporeality; to represent the Other is, above all, to show its body in images and then to stage it in order to gradually give it the attributes of its otherness—of its varied forms of otherness, as these were plural, evolving, and often contradictory. Bodies are privileged vectors of representations of the Other while being both *representations* and, when exhibited, systematically *represented*. Bodies are thus the objects of what we will call an *imagery of otherness*.

This expression describes the production and reception, on a civilization or at the least "collective" scale, of visual methods for creating media representations of the Other. This includes images of exhibitions and the exhibitions themselves, in that they are already themselves a spectacle, a representation. I will first undertake an archaeology of these imageries, endeavoring to distinguish three types that became, over quite a long period of time, decisive to the advent of a turn-of-the-century imagery of the "zoological" black body. This exercise will culminate with a discussion of film images and their role in these imageries between 1890 and 1910.

Three Imageries of Black Bodies

This archaeology is based on a compilation of studies carried out over the past twenty years and more by a research group called ACHAC, the Association pour la connaissance de l'histoire de l'Afrique contemporaine (Association for the Study of Contemporary African History), on the concept of the "human zoo" and on its history and historiography.[3] More precisely, I will draw on the latest major synthesis of this work, published in 2011.[4] This volume, in particular, has enabled me to draw up a typology of three decisive imageries of the black body, though I do not pretend to do an exhaustive study here.

An Object of Exploitation: The Black Body on Exhibit

When examining practices occurring over a long, and sometimes very long, period of time, we must consider, first of all, the secular practice of exhibiting the body of the Other, of which the black body was just one of many. This was a body of exhibited otherness that, in the modern era, became an exotic body. Thus, as Pascal Blanchard remarks, "Already in ancient Egypt black dwarves from the Sudan were exhibited."[5] In other words, from its beginnings the practice of exhibition was synonymous with domination, and dominant relations are, of course, at the root of the construction of otherness. Across the Western world, this history of the Other has been inseparable from a history of the gradual discovery of the world and the ways it has been dominated.

This is why the modern era and the "Great Discoveries" that began to be made in the late fifteenth century were an important stage. Blanchard and his colleagues also underscore the crucial importance, especially from the eighteenth century onward, of the rise of aristocratic practices such as keeping curiosity cabinets and animal menageries.[6] Three aspects of these phenomena are worth noting here. First, the modern European era reinvented its relations with otherness through exoticism.[7] Second, this fascination with the marvelous and the strange belonged exclusively to the elites, particularly the aristocracy.[8]

Finally, in this context, the exhibition of black individuals is similar to that of other peoples, like the Tahitian individual whom Louis-Antoine de Bougainville "brought back" in 1769 or the "troupe of Africans" Prince Frederick II of Hesse-Cassel relocated to Frankfurt in 1784.[9] However, there is one noteworthy detail that ACHAC's historians have given little consideration: these exhibited black bodies were also exploited black bodies. While I cannot explore this aspect in further detail here, the slave trade played a major role in the history of the construction of Western visions of the black body and was certainly one of the points of departure for projecting a great many fantasies—from "savagery" to "domesticity" and from physical strength to laziness, among others—onto these bodies.[10] And we should not forget that exhibition itself, from its beginnings, was a form of exploitation.

To return to the chronology of the exhibited body, we must note that the nineteenth century was a major turning point in that it democratized practices that had hitherto been reserved for aristocrats and a few scientists. After the French Revolution, the observation of "exotic" life forms (animals or human beings, which sometimes were barely differentiated, or not at all) came to be seen as a kind of educational right, to which the masses could and should aspire as part of the desire to educate the "people." Hence, for example, the rise more or less throughout Europe of zoos with free or low-cost admission.[11]

A Scientific Object: The Racialized Black Body

The second imagery to consider is that of the body as a scientific object. Here, again, the eighteenth-century naturalists were decisive, with figures such as Georges Louis-Leclerc de Buffon and his *Histoire naturelle* (thirty-six volumes published between 1749 and 1789), but the positivist and racist nineteenth century was the real turning point. The first scientist to classify human beings into "races" was Johann Friedrich Blumenbach in 1795, opening the door to a series of works throughout the next century, all of them based on the postulate of a link between certain physical or physiological qualities, and thus corporeal qualities, and certain moral, intellectual, and cultural aptitudes.[12]

The body—a racialized, scientific object—was thus studied, observed, classified, measured, and dissected by scientists, for whom exhibitions were often opportunities to work on living subjects, even if some of these scientists (few in number before the end of the century) were more critical.[13] The racialized body is depicted in the numerous articles produced by racist "science." (Blanchard and his colleagues have identified more than eighty articles in French journals alone dealing with exhibitions at the Zoological Gardens in Paris until 1909.[14]) These representations often took the form of engravings, but the racialized body was also photographed at a very early date, a topic to which I will return shortly.

In this racist vision, the black body was perhaps the most disadvantaged with respect to the criteria around physiognomy and taxonomy in force at the time, such as the colorimetric scale of the skin (which is less and less "auspicious" the darker it becomes), the degree of certain facial angles, and the size of the nose. These harebrained criteria were seen at the time as "defects," making the racialized black body a "defective" body, relegated to the lower reaches of the global "scale of civilization," which, for its part, was legitimized in turn by the authority of scientific discourse.

A Political Object: The Colonized Black Body

The third and final "imagery" of the black body is political in nature. According to ACHAC, there is a connection between the colonial conquests, the policies of the metropolis, and the ways in which they represented and exhibited colonized peoples. This took concrete form, in particular, in an evolution in the way black bodies were presented in "human zoos." As Blanchard points out, "The status of the Other in these exhibitions was transformed [as politics changed over time]. Initially reified as 'savage,' the 'exotic' was gradually 'tamed' as colonial conquests were completed and then 'civilized' in order to make clear the advance of the colonial 'civilizing mission.'"[15] This transformation basically took place through corporeality. The "savage" body was not the same as the "exotic" or, later, the "civilized" body. In a very schematic manner, we could almost say that it involved a reversal of perception on the part of the colonists, from repulsion to attraction, on both the "physical" and "moral" levels, even though the repulsion/attraction pair is inherent to the zoological experience. Where the "savage" body inspired fear and a kind of animal nature, the "civilized" body could be a vector for a degree of sympathy or fascination, when there was not a form of eroticization in play.[16]

The principal colonial conquests that France carried out in black Africa took place in the 1870s and 1880s, culminating in 1895 with the founding of the AOF (Afrique occidentale française, or French West Africa) federation. The first "black villages" were exhibited in metropolitan France in the early 1880s—at the same time, according to ACHAC, as the so-called taming phase of the Other. In their amalgamation, still without canceling each other out, these three imageries seemed to have enabled the rise, beginning in the 1870s, of an imagery of the black body that we could describe as "zoological."

From Imageries to Images, "Villages" to Screens

The Rise of "Black Villages"

Among the wide range of manifestations that could be described as "human zoos," the nineteenth-century "village" appears to be the third stage of a genealogy, following the exhibition and sadly famous fate of the "Hottentot Venus" in London and Paris from 1810 to 1815,[17] and then the rise of so-called ethnographic or (zoo-)anthropological exhibitions from the 1870s onward throughout much of Europe.[18]

In the case of the former two exhibition models, viewers were quite often confined to the role of "voyeur," because the boundary between them and those on exhibit was sharp, often taking the material form of bars. In this sense, "re-created villages" began a new, third stage. Found, for the most part, in state and imperial exhibitions,[19] the villages stood out for their promise of "encountering" the Other. While the boundary between viewers and those on exhibit was quite real, and their encounter quite false, the bars disappeared in favor of the folkloric decor of a fantasized elsewhere. The bodies were dressed in costumes and staged in such a way as to supposedly illustrate an unchanging way of everyday life (meals, garments, school, etc.) or artisanal and artistic skills (music, dance, combat skills, etc.). Within a decade, the phenomenon had spread throughout most of Europe (particularly Germany, France, and Switzerland), as well as to the Americas.[20] While the practice was not homogeneous, estimates indicate that more than half of the troupes or individuals exhibited in these "re-created villages" were black.[21] The years 1890–1900 were thus the zenith of the exhibition of black bodies in this manner, simultaneous with the first moving and projected images.

Images of "Black Villages"

Images of these "black villages" are remarkable above all for the great number of them, the variety of media in which they appeared, and their modes of production and reception. Again, it is impossible to draw up an exhaustive inventory of such practices; instead I will simply identify a few significant categories.

The scientific engravings mentioned earlier formed a direct part of what has been described as a "scientific imagery of black bodies," characterized by the racialization of bodies. They are obsessed on the one hand with taxonomy, and thus with the classification and categorization of all humankind, and on the other hand, with valorizing "defects," deformities, and other physiological "aberrations" that supposedly gave nuance to the great universal positivist schema.

Posters and press illustrations were quite similar to the engravings, with respect to both their modes of representation and their function—at once informative and highly commercial in the form of advertising. Hence there was a marked propensity for sensationalism, a direct outgrowth of the popularization of so-called scientific knowledge. Images such as these illustrated in the most explicit manner "extreme" bodies, in the sense of both their repulsion (related to the animality, savagery, violence, barbarism, strangeness) and their attraction (related to the valorization of "ways and customs," the exoticism, the sensuality, perhaps even the eroticism). In this sense, posters and press drawings appear to be the purest products of the outrageous imagery of popular exhibition, although they became somewhat less caricatured over time.

Postcards were the most common visual medium and attest to the extent and success of these exhibitions.[22] We can distinguish at least two subcategories: on the one hand, drawings and illustrations, quite similar to posters and to the press, and on the other, photographs, which I will discuss shortly. While postcards are interesting as a case study, as a visual medium they are less so, apart from the functions they served, one of which was to create for the viewer a souvenir, a trace, a memory. Before moving images did, and in a quite different manner, postcards prolonged viewers' images of these black bodies. We should note, finally, a specificity of these "re-created villages": postcards were made by the very people on exhibit,[23] to be sold to the public, allowing the viewer to fantasize about being a budding anthropologist (without leaving their home).

While postcards were certainly the most widespread medium, photography was the most widely used technique, appearing in practically all media and in every register. Thus we see photographs of "black villages" with scientific, journalistic, touristic, advertising, and other aims. This inclination to photographic technology can be accounted for not only by the visual novelty it embodied but also by the presumed authenticity of its depictions, fascinating both anonymous viewers and "scholars" such as Roland Bonaparte, who sought to construct a "scientific" imagery of the Other.[24]

Cinematic Ambiguity

While film images of the day supposedly shared the same "reality" as photography, one difference stands out: the limited number of films. Unlike other media, and even taking into account the vagaries of time and archival preservation, it is difficult to find any films other than those in the two Lumière series mentioned earlier that contain images of "black villages" shot in France between 1890 and 1900. A few short films were made of the Wolof people by Félix-Louis Régnault in the Zoological Gardens of Paris in 1895—in a manner very similar to scientific photography[25]—in addition to one film attributed to Eugène Pirou, *Les Plongeurs soudanais* (*The Sudanese Divers*), shot in Paris in 1896.[26]

As for the sixteen Lumière pictures, together they form an ensemble of bathing, dance, combat, mealtime, and school-time scenes, and even breast-feeding and the washing and dressing of children. Unlike the fixed and completely isolated images discussed earlier, all of which had great simplicity and clarity, in other words a univocity, the Lumière films have a fundamental ambiguity. This "cinematic ambiguity" derives from at least two factors.

First of all, there are explicit indications that the action was staged. For example, in the picture *Baignade de nègres* (*Negroes Swimming*),[27] there is a white man at the edge of the ornamental lake giving orders to the young blacks to dive into the water. Is this really an outburst of improvised authority, an exercise in everyday domination on the part of a mere visitor, or is it staging the work in tandem with the camera operator to ensure that the picture turns out as planned? In the same vein, what are we to think of some of the ways in which the subjects look at the camera, particularly in the scenes entitled *Toilette d'un négrillon, I and II* (*Bathing a Piccaninny, I and II*)?[28] Here mothers are shown breast-feeding and washing their children while looking questioningly at the camera operator, as if waiting for instructions. Another example is the children in the picture *Repas des négrillons, I* (*A Piccaninny Meal, I*),[29] who are not really eating. More broadly, is staging that reveals itself in this way still truly staging? Of course, the "human zoo," and even more so the "re-created village," is already and inherently a representation, a spectacle. But everything takes place as if the kinematograph, by revealing its "tricks" and pulling back the curtain from some of its own methods, was at the same time placing an obstacle in the path of the spectacular element, veiling it in such a way as to conceal some of its content from the viewer, who must thereby reckon with a degree of ambiguity.

The second factor we can identify that contributes to the ambiguity of these pictures is the very status of the films. At the time, people occasionally saw these films as "actualities," or at least that was the case in the local press. On May 2, 1897, the newspaper *Le Lyon républicain* spoke of a "new program" that included "a whole series of actualities shot amongst the Ashanti."[30] Thus there emerges if not a paradox at least a tension between a film's rootedness in a relatively proximate present consistent with an "actuality," and its rootedness in a timeless past, almost outside of time—an inherent quality of the staging found in these "re-created villages." This ambiguity is also evident in the practice of projecting their own images for those on exhibit; in this case, as described by *Le Progrès* on May 25, 1897, a screening organized at a hotel in Lyon was attended by some thirty black people from the exhibition, including numerous children.[31] In this instance the ambiguity arises from both the *spectacular* and the *specular* functions of these films.

From "Object Bodies" to "Subject Bodies?"

The forms this cinematic ambiguity takes are numerous and certainly deserve to be explored in greater depth. Not having the space to do so in the present text, I will limit myself to setting out a few concluding hypotheses. This ambivalence in the Lumière pictures compared to other images of "black villages," but also with respect to other film images of black people,[32] may just be the product of an individual's subjectivity, which would be the least interesting possible hypothesis. While it may seem prudent never to elude one's subjectivity, another explanation may pay closer attention to the question of the body, precisely, and in particular to the specificity of the "cinematic body." Indeed, one of the major points in common among the noncinematic images discussed here is the reduction of the black body, fairly systematically, to the status of pure object (a scientific object or an object of amusement, curiosity, fantasy, etc.), hence their clarity and univocity. The Lumière pictures, on the contrary, do not do this. It is almost as if the act of filming itself cannot completely reduce a body to the status of pure object, even when that body is as dominated as those of the people on exhibit. This does not mean that there is less or no desire to do so, or that early cinema was less racist than the press or science of the day. There nevertheless emerges a huge, final question: can a body be something other than a subject when one films it, and, by extension, to what extent can the act of filming reduce it to the status of an object?

RODOLPHE GAHÉRY is a Doctoral Fellow at Université Paris Nanterre. He is presently writing a doctoral dissertation entitled *Les premières actualités filmées (1895–1914): des Cinématographes au Cinéma*.

TIMOTHY BARNARD is a translator, author, and book publisher. He has translated and published volumes by André Bazin and Jean-Luc Godard and is author of the short volume *Découpage*.

Notes

1. Films nos. 12 and 66 (Lumière) and nos. 517 and 518 (Aubert & Seguin). In the case of Lumière films, the numbering differs in the catalogs of the day ("Lumière") and the volume edited by Michelle Aubert and Jean-Claude Seguin, *La production cinématographique des Frères Lumière* (Paris: Mémoire du Cinéma, 1996) ("Aubert & Seguin").
2. Films nos. 441–452 and 464–465 (Lumière); nos. 520–533 (Aubert & Seguin).
3. For more information, consult the association's website at http://achac.com/zoos-humains/.
4. Pascal Blanchard, Nicolas Bancel, Gilles Boëtsch, Éric Deroo, and Sandrine Lemaire, eds., *Zoos humains et exhibitions coloniales. 150 ans d'inventions de l'Autre* (Paris: Découverte, 2011).
5. Ibid., 12.
6. Ibid., 10.
7. Ibid., 40.
8. Ibid., 10.
9. Ibid., 13.
10. On this topic, see the reference volume by Olivier Pétré-Grenouilleau, *Les traites négrières, essai d'histoire globale* (Paris: Gallimard, 2004).
11. Blanchard et al., *Zoos humains et exhibitions coloniales*, 10–11.
12. For a finer-grained discussion of naturalists and racialization, see Jacqueline Duvernay-Bolens, "L'Homme zoologique: race et racisme chez les naturalistes de la première moitié du XIXe siècle," *L'Homme* 35, no. 133 (1995): 9–32.
13. Blanchard et al., *Zoos humains et exhibitions coloniales*, 23.
14. Ibid., 29, note 1.
15. Ibid., 28.

16. Ibid., 35.

17. *Vénus noire* (*Black Venus*, Abdellatif Kechiche, 2010) is one of the most recent symptoms of this "phenomenon" (to quote Pascal Blanchard and Gilles Boëtsch, "La Vénus hottentote ou la naissance d'un 'phénomène,'" in Blanchard et al., *Zoos humains et exhibitions coloniales*, 95–105), and proves cinema's enduring attraction to these historical exhibitions of the black body, now explored in the form of a critical and denunciatory filmic discourse.

18. In particular, through the efforts of two individuals, the German Carl Hagenbeck and the Frenchman Geoffroy de Saint-Hilaire, director of the Zoological Gardens in Paris. See, for example, William H. Schneider, "Les expositions ethnographiques du Jardin zoologique d'acclimatation," in Blanchard et al., *Zoos humains et exhibitions coloniales*, 132–41.

19. In Amsterdam in 1883, London in 1886, and Paris in 1889. See Blanchard et al., *Zoos humains et exhibitions coloniales*, 48.

20. Ibid.

21. Ibid., 42–43.

22. Ibid., 23.

23. See Pascal Blanchard, Gilles Boëtsch, and Jacomijn Snoep Nanette, *Exhibitions. L'invention du sauvage* (Paris: Actes Sud/Musée du Quai Branly, 2011).

24. On Roland Bonaparte, see in particular Elizabeth Edwards, "La photographie ou la construction de l'image de l'Autre," in Blanchard et al., *Zoos humains et exhibitions coloniales*, 484–85; and Gérard Joly, "Bonaparte (Prince Roland)," in *Dictionnaire biographique de géographes français du XXe siècle, aujourd'hui disparus* (Paris: PRODIG, 2013), 39.

25. See Marc-Henri Piault, *Anthropologie et cinéma. Passage à l'image, passage par l'image* (Paris: Nathan, 2000), 13.

26. See Camille Blot-Wellens, "Les plongeurs soudanais," in *El cinematógrafo Joly-Normandin (1896–1897). Dos colecciones: João Anacleto Rodrigues y Antonino Sagarmínaga* (Madrid: Ministerio de Educación, Cultura y Deporte/ICAA/Filmoteca Española, 2014), 163–65. My thanks to Blot-Wellens for bringing this picture to my attention.

27. Film no. 12 (Lumière); no. 517 (Aubert & Seguin).

28. Films nos. 449–450 (Lumière); nos. 529–530 (Aubert & Seguin).

29. Film no. 447 (Lumière); no. 532 (Aubert & Seguin).

30. In an article reproduced in *La production cinématographique des Frères Lumière*, 174ff.

31. Ibid.

32. For example, the Lumière picture *Nègres dansant dans la rue* (*Negro Street Dancers*, 1896) (no. 252 of the catalog of the time), or, by Pathé Frères, *Le Nègre gourmand* (*Gluttonous Negro*, 1905).

9 "Stills from a Film That Is Missing"

Indigenous Images and the Photographic Interval in Early Cinema

Joanna Hearne

BEFORE-AND-AFTER PHOTOGRAPHS, a form of comparative photography, pair images to depict a person or scene across two moments in time, with the earlier image on the left and the later image on the right. While "rephotography" uses a two-image sequence to depict places (repeat photography of the same site "then and now"), before-and-after photographs in their earliest instances more often depicted people. Currently these forms are widely deployed in advertising (especially real estate, cosmetics, and the fitness and diet industries), scientific research (such as NASA satellite images of glacial retreat), medicine, and other fields.

This chapter explores the history of before-and-after pictures and their influence in early cinema.[1] Though comparative photography has multiple origins in medical, penal, and social reform discourses, it entered into US popular visual discourses most dramatically (and most importantly, for early film) through the nineteenth and early-twentieth-century images that promoted the US government's program of institutional education for Native American children. Before-and-after images circulated by the Carlisle Indian Industrial School across the turn of the twentieth century infused photographic sequencing with emphatically colonialist structures of dualism and temporal progression. While the image sequences sold the idea of racial uplift, they were predicated on social control and supported both the ideologies and practices of cultural genocide (as current scholarship has widely acknowledged). By turning to this historical moment of comparative photography's foundation as part of a colonial rescue narrative, just before its broader popularization in mass media advertising, we see how before-and-after pictures teach audiences to read sequential images in a certain way. Most importantly, we see how such images contributed technologically, stylistically, and structurally to early cinema in ways that are distinct from other kinds of photographic sequencing, such as chronophotography, by exploiting the narrative potential of the photographic interval. But far from suggesting that cinema simply replicates a repressive visual regime, I argue that early films create, from the structural interval of photographic sequencing, a field of contestation.

Before-and-after image structures bring together multiple functions of photographic technology, including scientific and legal evidence, commercial product, and aesthetic system. With their sequencing techniques and attendant narrative potentialities, they supported early films as precinematic and extracinematic texts, providing a source of scenarios for early frontier dramas and later westerns. In this chapter I theorize the formal qualities of before-and-after pictures and attend in subsequent sections to their social history, the relationship of this photographic form to early cinema, and its articulation with genre traditions such as the melodrama and the western.

The intermedial relationship of sequential photography to cinema involves both nonfiction and fiction at the discursive intersections of social reform with documents of comparative measurement and stylized racial physicality that were prevalent in fields such as medicine, criminology, and early anthropology. These photographic and cinematic rhetorics combined to form a regime of visibility and disciplinary control over the bodies of Indigenous children. In what follows, I bring together scholarship in Indigenous studies, photography, and early cinema to explore the photographic interval as a visual poetics of ellipsis.

The Structural Space of the Interval

Before-and-after photographs are intended to be evidentiary documents that record the results of a transformation by manufacture, force of nature, change of custodial authority, or other intervention or event. I have argued that "because they are bound up with the production of desire in their promises to transform bodily appearance, the morally freighted progression of before-and-after photographs carries strong evaluative connotations regarding the way the body—and the world—should look."[2] The comparative framework positions the "before" as a problem to be solved, generating desire in viewers for the invisible solution that produces the "after." In this visual iteration of a confidence game (not unlike the obfuscation of agency in market economics), "concealed hands" create the desired "after" effect and evidence "the power of another, un-photographed person or force to transform a passive subject."[3]

Between the "before" and the "after" images is an interval, an event that is unseen but reorders the world. The event that takes place in the interval is only manifest through the indirect evidence of its effects on the body or the landscape, the implication of comparative difference between one state and another. Thus the photographs function as excerpts from a larger story that is missing but implied—a completely different kind of "optical unconscious" than instantaneous photography's illusion of movement, but equally legible. Of these two ways of photographing and closely reading the body in time, each using techniques of temporal deceleration and acceleration, motion studies "move" photographs to cinematic flow by representing movement in a short time, breaking down movements into individual "cells" and putting them back together as motion. Before-and-after photographs are defined by stasis and by ellipsis, the omission of action. If chronophotography narrows the space of the interval, before-and-after photographs widen it.

The stasis of each photograph exists in tension with the narrative the photographic sequence can tell. Before-and-after pictures take up a past-to-future trajectory—offering a story about the past and how things came to be the way they are—while chronophotography operates by parsing the "now" of unfolding action. Before-and-after pictures measure difference; the bigger the difference, the more unseen but implied action has taken place in the interval. Thus before-and-after pictures lend themselves to explanatory, evidentiary, and persuasive projects and to mythmaking. Their usefulness for telling expansive stories about time explains their uptake for various narratives of both colonization and social progress. They are more overtly comparative than chronophotography because rather than immersing viewers in the flow of motion, before-and-after pictures suppress action, emphasizing stillness in order to invite reflection on the contrast between two fixed states. As a result, the "action" that is omitted or goes unseen in the interval requires greater activity on the part of the viewer in the form of critical or imaginative engagement. The efficacy of this tension between the formal strategies of suppression (in the interval) and exhibition (in the posed images) suggest that this form of sequencing hinges not only on absence—the poetics of ellipsis—but also on its opposite, the poetics of excess.

Before-and-After Pictures and the Carlisle Indian Industrial School

Because of their emphasis on temporal progress and the bodily manifestation of virtue, before-and-after pictures were taken up by various social-reform movements in the second half of the nineteenth century—the abolitionist movement in the 1860s, British private charity homes in the 1870s, and US residential schools for Native American children beginning in the 1880s. Photography's appearance of visual empiricism supported didactic messages of transformation, rescue, reform, progress, and moral improvement as before-and-after pictures became teaching texts and persuasive fund-raising tools across these multiple reform movements. Before-and-after photographs also represented a visual rhetoric that was critical to US federal Indian policy at the height of settler land acquisition and consolidation (and before-and-after imagery was engaged to represent Indigenous peoples even before the proliferation of photography, for example in George Catlin's painting *Pigeon's Egg Head (The Light) Going to and Returning from Washington*, 1837–1839). While these examples do not comprise a complete social history of comparative photography or establish its incontrovertible origin point, examining Indigenous images articulated in before-and-after pictures alongside early cinema shows us one way that comparative photography worked as a politicized visual system in North America.

In the United States, the infrastructure powering the circulation of before-and-after images came from the practice, from the 1880s onward, of removing Native American children from their families to be educated at residential schools. The history of these boarding schools has already been extensively documented by scholars such as David Wallace Adams, Brenda Child, Jacqueline Fear-Segal, Amelia Katanski, Tsianina Lomawaima, and Hayes Peter Mauro (among many others). I sketch it briefly here to show how comparative photography was deployed to operationalize what Patrick Wolfe calls the settler colonial logics of Indigenous elimination.[4] Before-and-after pictures were not neutral but rather performed both containment and circulation, functioning additionally as a platform for working through the social contradictions embedded in the settler colonial project—that is, "the Indian problem"—by wielding images of Indigenous youth to form narrative fragments.

The influential founder of the Carlisle Indian Industrial School in Carlisle, Pennsylvania, Captain Richard Henry Pratt, developed his educational system as an experiment during his oversight of the Apache prisoners of war housed at the Fort Marion Prison in St. Augustine, Florida, in the 1870s. He came to advocate total assimilation as a way to, as he said, "kill the Indian in him and save the man," with the goal of eradicating Indigenous languages, religions, and cultures.[5] The school operated from 1879 until 1918 and became part of the blueprint for patterns of institutional intervention in Indigenous families that other settler nations such as Australia, Canada, and nations encompassing the Sápmi (Russia, Finland, Norway, and Sweden) also took up, and that persisted throughout the twentieth century. With its barracks housing, frequent marching and flag drills, military uniforms, and food allocations based on the US Army rationing table, the school piloted an incorporation of students into military systems of institutional discipline and control. The schools punished students for speaking their Indigenous languages and provided all instruction in English. Though students learned basic academics, the primary emphasis was on agriculture and domestic arts and trades, and in practice, students supplied much of the labor to maintain the school. Pratt also developed the "outing system," a form of temporary fostering in which Carlisle students apprenticed at local farms during holidays and summer breaks, where they worked for settler families instead of going home to their reservations and tribal communities. Pratt explained his purpose to the Pennsylvania *Daily Evening Sentinel* in 1891: "We have two objects in view in starting the Carlisle School—one is to educate the Indians—the other is to educate the people of the country ... to understand that the Indians can be educated."[6]

Pratt circulated before-and-after images of Carlisle students as postcards, in letters, and in print media such as *Harper's Monthly* in order to garner public support, congressional appropriations, and private donations. Photographer J. N. Choate, who operated a shop in the town of Carlisle, photographed the students alone and in groups on their arrival at the school, and then again months or years later. Where the "before" photographs showed the students in their traditional clothes and long hair, in the "after" images they were carefully posed in uniforms, with hair cut short and skin tones often lightened (artificially, through front lighting, overexposure, filters, and powder makeup, or naturally as students lost their suntans).[7] Historian Brian Dippie concludes that "physical appearance was an obsession at Carlisle."[8]

These images do not represent their subjects as purely abstract bodies, nor are they anonymous. Because the Carlisle students were so well documented, we often know who the children were and even what happened to them during and after their school years, such as those pictured in figure 9.1: Lakota students Richard "Wounded" Yellow Robe, Henry Standing Bear, and Chauncey Yellow Robe (brother of Richard), whose photographs were taken in 1883 on arrival at Carlisle and again in 1886. The images impose both identification and anonymity, a contradiction that resembles what Allan Sekula calls the "biographical machine" of early police photography; although the captions identified specific individuals, the photographs were also intended to represent a generic type, and the two-image sequence was meant to demonstrate a replicable civilizing process.[9]

Carlisle's educational system originated in a military prison, which is important to its deployment of before-and-after pictures as well, for as Sekula argues, the "central issues of nineteenth-century penal discourse" were "the practical drawing of distinctions between incorrigible and pliant criminals, and the disciplined conversion of the reformable into 'useful' proletarians."[10] Sekula points out that early archives of police photographs returned obsessively to "that privileged figure of social reform discourse: the figure of the child rescued by a paternalistic medicosocial science."[11] The before-and-after sequential form was used by other reform organizations—including private charities, abolitionist organizations, and orphan centers—to raise funds (concurrent with a more specialized medical use of the form to illustrate surgical outcomes). As with the Carlisle Indian Industrial School, the visual rhetorics of these organizations turned on the image of the child. The Orphan's Shelter of Philadelphia produced before-and-after photographs of enslaved children "as we found them"—dressed in ragged, torn clothing on their removal from slave owners—and "as they are now," after education and care at the Orphan's Shelter, dressed in new clothes; these image sets were circulated in the 1860s by the abolitionist Society of Friends.[12] British reformer Thomas Barnardo ran a string of private charity homes for street children starting in 1866 and sold before-and-after images to help support the organization (court records

Figure 9.1a–b. Lakota students Richard "Wounded" Yellow Robe, Henry Standing Bear, and Chauncey Yellow Robe (brother of Richard), whose photographs were taken in 1883 upon arrival at the Carlisle Indian Industrial School and again after six months—or possibly longer—at the school. Courtesy of Archives and Special Collections, Dickinson College, Carlisle, PA; Carlisle Indian School Digital Resource Center (CC BY-NC-SA 4.0).

from a widely publicized 1877 lawsuit reveal that he sometimes used models and doctored the photographs to exaggerate differences in the children's appearance). Barnardo's images, a huge sensation at the time, may well have influenced Pratt's decision to deploy this visual discourse in the United States. While Indigenous images are not the only case of early comparative photography (the Barnardo images were certainly more widely seen in Europe), the Carlisle example shows us one way that visual sequence mattered for projects of persuasion and control.

The structure of before-and-after pictures is similar across these images of abolitionist rescue of enslaved children, charity homes for urban homeless English children, and the Carlisle images of Indigenous children, each documenting the result of custodial transfer. But the Carlisle images stand in a unique relationship to situated colonizing practices because the separation of Indigenous children from their communities was the official policy of the state, and Indigenous children were trafficked by the state itself. Their transformation was not from slavery or homelessness to better economic conditions or freedom from bondage; rather, the before-and-after images present the institution's justification of the breakup of intact tribal families and the recategorization of Indigenous children as wards of the state. Circulated as evidence of social progress, the image sequences foregrounded cosmetic changes intended to signal shifts in national allegiance, representing a settler colonial practice of expropriation. While the abolitionist images document the freeing of enslaved children, the Carlisle images document the subjugation of Indigenous children within a system of confinement at the same historical moment that tribes experienced a 90 percent loss of territory. Thus the Carlisle before-and-after images were articulated with broader forms of imposed individuation, particularly in connection with the expropriation and settlement of Indigenous land through contemporaneous policies of land allotment. This practice fragmented tribal territories into discrete parcels with allotted acres separable from reservations by sale or transfer of title.

Pratt's version of assimilation at Carlisle followed the model he developed for Apache prisoners of war, which retroactively incorporated Indigenous tribes into the military in the wake of violent conflict, occupation of Indigenous territories, and coercive treaty negotiations between the US government and tribal nations. Tuscarora scholar Jolene Rickard asserts that the Carlisle images "signified the end of the 'Indian' wars and evoked security. They are not overtly photographs of the 'land' but are documents of the systematic removal of Indians from their homelands."[13] The photographic isolation of the children from their environments and from Indigenous forms of social organization also "disguised the sense of community" and "implied erasure of 'Nation.'"[14] Curtis Marez argues more broadly that mass-produced photographic images of Indians facilitated "the photo-conversion of Indians into property," while early westerns catalyzed a form of "ritual imperial spectatorship" that encouraged viewers to take on a "proprietary relationship to images of Indians."[15] This transactional sense of ownership created by the commodity status of the photograph (what Vivian Sobchack, following Jean-Louis Comolli, calls the "money of the real") duplicates the discourse of possession underpinning the images of custodial transfer in the before-and-after pictures circulated by social advocacy organizations.[16]

Before-and-after images envision the state reorganization of Indigenous families and imply their political consent by excluding conflict and resistance in the space "in between" the two photographs. This ellipsis or interval naturalizes colonization as a function of the passage of time rather than the effects of active policies. Omitting images with parents and community, images of separation, and images of return, the photographic sequences visually eradicate tribal and parental rights along with processes of change. What such processes might look like—the removal of children from their homes, their journey away from family and into institutional space, their confrontation with or adjustment to institutional education—is nowhere in the carefully staged linear narrative of the image sequence.

Comparative Photography and Early Cinema

Before-and-after pictures stand in a unique relationship with Indigenous images because their signature formal element—the interval—has everything to do with colonial timelines: when the story begins, when it ends, and what it leaves out. The photographic interval matters because it elides crucial narrative action. Despite the extensive body of scholarship demonstrating how instantaneous photography formed a technostructural origin point of cinema, we have not accounted for the expansion of the interval in before-and-after pictures as a co-circulating public discourse. To understand how comparative photography works, we must pay attention to this interval and its articulation with other protocinematic image technologies, and with early cinema itself. Like other forms of sequential imagery, before-and-after pictures manipulate elements of time and space, and especially the compression of time. The spatial sequencing captures, orders, and displays its subjects, gridding the narrative of social rescue in cellular parts and structuring the inchoate space of developing social identity in visually physical terms. Before-and-after pictures also codified an artificial differentiation between tradition and modernity as discrete spheres. The imagined development (of traditional to modern) is presented by the before-and-after structure as a unified linear process that follows an expected trajectory over time. The Carlisle School images manifest "a visual form that rationalizes the fragmentation and sequencing of temporal frames into a legible organization suggestive of modern industrial production."[17] The photographs effect an intersection of fact (the removal of Indigenous children) with early cinema's melodramatic plots around "a central event of a lost, exchanged, recovered, re-identified child."[18]

This logic of sequence is also the logic of cinema, as scholarship on motion studies and sequential photography has shown for early film. Like Eadweard Muybridge's images, before-and-after pictures record bodily actions, and like Félix-Louis Régnault's images, they also try to record racial differences. Étienne-Jules Marey may have seen the interruption of movement—the too-great photographic interval—as a problem to solve, but in before-and-after pictures that interruption is the central engine of the form. Chronophotography demonstrated what Tom Gunning calls "the new mastery of the incremental instants of time" that characterized modernity, while also "creating new regimes of bodily discipline and regulation based upon a new observation of (and knowledge about) the body."[19] If motion studies capture and slow down rapid movement, before-and-after pictures speed up time to measure social engineering, the production and regulation of bodily identity, and colonial timelines. Yet, like chronophotography, before-and-after pictures stand in an uneasy relationship with narrative.

Before-and-after pictures underwrite cinema's colonial projects in a different way than Muybridge's, Regnault's, Marey's, and other motion studies do. Their qualities involve posed stillness rather than frozen movement, and the elision of action rather than deconstruction of action. Unlike motion studies, they necessarily embed a narrative, and that narrative is one of imagined progress—specifically, in these early instances, colonial rescue. They have more in common with time-lapse photography than the protocinematic motion studies of Muybridge, yet they also partake of less documentary, more fantastic forms of temporal progression. Like time-travel narratives, they pulse forward, flashing between moments of stasis with the gradual details of change suppressed. Because before-and-after pictures so selectively present moments of change, they convey a strongly moral order and distill structural dichotomies, such as civilization and savagery, that are critical to the development of film genres such as the western.

In this gridlike mapping of motion—the act of fracturing and regimenting action into discrete photographs that are incomplete on their own—there is the potential to resequence the story. Before-and-after pictures invite the temporal continuity of progression and, simultaneously, make available a structural space for alternative sequencing, disruptions of the progression that include a reversed time frame (reading right to left), and the imaginative "filling in" of not only the interval between the before-and-after but also around the boundaries of the sequence itself—before the "before" and after the "after." Jonathan Crary has remarked on the interdependence of images in chronophotography as well as the resulting "temporal mutability," noting that Muybridge's images "at least suggest the possibility of novel social/historical intuitions, 'flashing up' amid their disruptions of presumed continuities or their shattering of the self-sufficiency of an autonomous image."[20] In the case of the Carlisle images, the before-and-after pictures' artificially differentiated typology of primitive and civilized reinforced evolutionary, developmental models. Yet while the images narrate assimilation when read in sequence, the photographs could also be disarticulated, decontextualizing the images in order to renarrate them. The Carlisle "before" images, in particular, frequently circulated this way, sold separately as souvenirs to the crowds who gathered to watch the children disembark from the train on their arrival at Carlisle, or more widely as postcards feeding public interest in traditional regalia. Resequencing images might be done for a number of purposes, not all of which are necessarily politically radical or disruptive of dominant narratives, but the potential exists for new narration to emerge from disordered sequence. And beyond simple reordering, I argue, films that engage with comparative photography's visual discourses can flesh out the narrative space of the interval, completing the missing parts of the story in either expected or surprising ways. Thus comparative photography embeds in itself—in its formal qualities of sequence and interval—possibilities for expansion and opposition as well as control and containment, possibilities that are exposed and exploited by cinematic storytelling.

Early film, emergent from chronophotography, expands narratively into the space of comparative photography's interval. Cinema occupies the colonial timeline laid out in before-and-after pictures by filling in the missing action with various fantasies and even documentary scenarios of that suppressed action. The narrative vacuum of the interval becomes an invitation to the narrative excess of cinema. While comparative photography documents change over long periods of time, cinema reveals time in its fleeting, unfolding moments. Making slow, incremental change more rapid creates drama and affective connection—the logic of the time-lapse—while activating static images into the temporality and shape of narrative. Mutually constitutive of our larger social history and our developing range of visual narrativity, before-and-after images represent a significant (if underestimated) addition to the cluster of other experiments in precinematic and extracinematic photography and image sequencing.

And by imagining the stories of departure, transformation, and return that are suppressed in the Carlisle before-and-after images, early westerns inundate the ellipsis with the melodrama of colonial rescue, repurposing documentary, evidentiary photo-sequencing for the work of frontier fantasy. Cinema's frontier melodramas return obsessively to contact scenarios, but before-and-after photographs unfailingly avoid envisioning them, and where before-and-after images cloak the violence of contact, westerns are notorious for showing it. The structural space of the interval in before-and-after pictures opens up an arena of free play for settler colonial imaginaries—especially scenarios of contact—as well as for scenes and performances of Indigenous visual sovereignty.

Narrating the Interval in Frontier Melodramas

Keyed to before-and-after pictures as a prior and coexisting public discourse, early actualities and frontier melodramas build and reflect on—and frequently disrupt—the visual politics and linear temporality of before-and-after sequencing. Because this sequencing is so strongly tied to narratives of progress from savagery to civilization—and to racial staging through costume—the resequencing activated by early film scenarios can destabilize these very notions, as well as the idea of developmental progression itself. Across nonfiction, reformist, and melodramatic modes of address, spectacles of separation and return depict Indian characters leaving and returning to reservations and families. Frontier melodramas that depict Indian familial rupture and reunion take up theatrical contrasts in costume to make visible what is repressed in the interval of the photographic sequence—Indian parents and tribes, emotional and physical stresses, and actions of resistance and accommodation. Early nonfiction films such as *Club Swinging at Carlisle Indian School* (American Mutoscope and Biograph, 1902) and

Viewing Sherman Institute for Indians at Riverside, California (Keystone, 1915) as well as later films sponsored by the government or private organizations, such as the Harmon Foundation's 1933 film *The American Indian: Government Education*, frequently depict the assimilation process in scenes of institutional instruction, or even groups of students demonstrating traditional skills or dances.

Frontier melodramas activate and engage narratives of "progression" and "reversion," subjecting the stasis of before-and-after portraits to the fluidity and play of cinema. While before-and-after photographs employ staging that resembles melodramatic tableaux in their stillness, the postures of restraint in the portraits contrast with early cinema's histrionic performative styles conveying emotional excess through gesture and expression. Many early films extend the story of the before-and-after or reverse the before-and-after sequence in order to depict movement from the residential school back to a reservation community (what school officials derided as going "back to the blanket"). Scenarios of "reversion" gain traction from the before-and-after pictures' baseline arrangement of forward "progression." For example, in these stills from D. W. Griffith's *Call of the Wild* (American Mutoscope and Biograph, 1908) we see Charles Inslee as George Redfeather in his boarding-school dinner clothes courting an upper-class white woman, while a later scene reveals his "reversion" to traditional costume (a blanket and headdress) when rejected by his beloved (figure 9.2). (The presence of a Chinese servant in the earlier sequence invites viewers to assess Redfeather's assimilation in a calibrated racial and class comparison.) Scenes of Indian familial rupture represent the violence that goes unseen in the Carlisle before-and-after photographs—for example, when a settler father threatens to take his mixed-blood child away from his Indian wife in Cecil B. DeMille's *The Squaw Man* (Lasky, 1914) and the Young Deer film *For the Papoose* (Pathé, 1912).

Films like *Maya, Just an Indian* (Frontier, 1913), *Strongheart* (Biograph/Klaw and Erlanger, 1914), *The Last of the Line* (Mutual, 1914), and *The Lure of Woman* (World Film, 1915) translate the theatrical poses of before-and-after pictures into scenes of generational confrontation, with the reunion of a returned boarding-school student with a traditional tribal community represented in the manner of a contact narrative. These films imagine the personal and familial suffering from generational rupture that goes unseen in before-and-after pictures, while dramatizing tropes of frontier contact and imperial logics of tradition and modernity within Indian families divided by institutional education. The films bring the two-image sequence of before-and-after photographs together into one cinematic frame (and, thus, a unified temporal moment) through two-shots and other compositional elements, reiterating the characters' entrapment in trajectories of loss using the constrictions of the film frame and mise-en-scène, and through changes of costume.

Figure 9.2. Charles Inslee as George Redfeather in two stills from D. W. Griffith's *Call of the Wild* (American Mutoscope and Biograph, 1908). Image courtesy of the Library of Congress.

While the melodramatic schema of limited options and no-win situations very often foreclose the narrative potential for Indian characters to act out autonomous self-invention, imaginative agency, or adaptation, that same cinematic system can provide the means to "dismantle, reverse, confuse, ironize and otherwise unravel" the linear straitjacket of before-and-after pictures.[21] "In mobilizing and animating the static portraiture of the photographs, Indian dramas also open up the representational field to imagine moments of trauma, resistance, circulation, substitution, hybridity and exchange."[22] The photographic interval in before-and-after pictures represents a rupture, reiterating in a structurally formal way the colonial ruptures that media scholar Faye Ginsburg describes when she argues that contemporary Indigenous media attempts "to heal disruptions in cultural knowledge, historical memory, and identity between generations."[23] Early cinema creates further possibilities and spaces for what Seneca scholar Michelle Raheja calls "visual sovereignty," or Indigenous representational self-determination.[24] Just as before-and-after images of Indigenous children have been reclaimed and rerecognized as family photographs by descendants, the potential for visual sovereignty, or the "space between resistance and compliance" across systems of visual signification on-screen, creates opportunities for reimagining Indigenous agency in the work of performers such as Lillian St. Cyr (Winnebago) or Nipo Strongheart (Yakama).[25] Integrating the study of comparative photography in the history of North American early cinema offers an opportunity to better understand the visual politics of settler colonialism and its contestations, especially in relation to melodramatic modes (unleashing of the repressed, trafficking in excess) and cultural problem solving.

Studying the political work of the Carlisle before-and-after pictures shows how this more temporally stretched form of sequential photography undergirds the development of some of the most influential twentieth- and twenty-first-century representational forms, and reveals once again how the didactic strategies echoing from colonial practices remain with us in our visual rhetorics. Before-and-after photographs bring together fantasies of colonial rescue with evidentiary discourses of the actual in order to incite viewers to action and influence their beliefs, mapping visual schemas of temporal progress onto the bodies of Indigenous youth. Propagandistic and instructional, they model developmental logics that are both about education and also themselves educational. We should count before-and-after pictures among the proliferate origins of cinema narrative, and as a foundational image structure in the history of the genre film—the documentary, the frontier melodrama, and the western.

JOANNA HEARNE is Associate Professor of Film Studies in the English Department at the University of Missouri, where she also directs the Digital Storytelling Program. She is author of *Native Recognition: Indigenous Cinema and the Western* and *Smoke Signals: Native Cinema Rising*.

Notes

1. The quotation in my title is from Giorgio Agamben's essay on Guy Debord's films, "Difference and Repetition," in which he describes narrative techniques of repetition and stoppage (or interruption) as the "conditions of possibility" in cinema. Giorgio Agamben, "Difference and Repetition: On Guy Debord's Films," in *Guy Debord and the Situationist International*, ed. Tom McDonough (Cambridge, MA: MIT Press, 2002), 314, 315–16.

2. Joanna Hearne, *Native Recognition: Indigenous Cinema and the Western* (Albany: SUNY Press, 2012), 27.

3. Ibid.

4. David Wallace Adams, *Education for Extinction: American Indians and the Boarding School Experience, 1875–1928* (Lawrence: University Press of Kansas, 1995); Brenda Child, *Boarding School Seasons: American Indian Families, 1900–1940* (Lincoln: University of Nebraska Press, 1998); Jacqueline Fear-Segal, *White Man's Club: Schools, Race, and the Struggle of Indian Acculturation* (Lincoln: University of Nebraska Press, 2007); Amelia Katanski, *Learning to Write "Indian": The Boarding-School Experience and American Indian Literature* (Normal: University of Oklahoma Press, 2005); Tsianina Lomawaima, *They Called It Prairie Light: The Story of Chilocco Indian School* (Lincoln: University of Nebraska Press, 1994). On settler colonialism, see Patrick Wolfe, "Settler Colonialism and the Elimination of the Native," *Journal of Genocide Research* 8, no. 4 (2006): 387–409.

Several studies (e.g., by Lonna Malmsheimer, Hayes Peter Mauro, Jolene Rickard, and Joanna Cohan Scherer) have analyzed the Carlisle before-and-after pictures specifically, situating them within the long history of photography of American Indians. The photographs were concurrent with the aesthetic of primitivism in portraits by Edward Curtis, for example, who, far from documenting transformation, is known to have regularly removed or erased evidence of modernity, such as umbrellas, clocks, books, and wristwatches. Lonna M. Malmsheimer, "'Imitation White Man': Images of Transformation at the Carlisle Indian School," *Studies in Visual Communication* (September 1985): 54–75; Hayes Peter Mauro, *The Art of Americanization at the Carlisle Indian School* (Albuquerque: University of New Mexico Press, 2011); Jolene Rickard, "The Occupation of Indigenous Space as 'Photograph,'" in *Native Nations: Journeys in American Photography*, ed. Jane Alison (London: Barbican Art Gallery, 1998), 57–71; Joanna Cohan Scherer, "You Can't Believe Your Eyes: Inaccuracies in Photography of North American Indians," *Studies in the Anthropology of Visual Communication* 2, no. 2 (1975): 67–79.

5. Adams, *Education for Extinction*, 52.
6. Malmsheimer, "Imitation White Man," 63.
7. Fear-Segal, *White Man's Club*, 163–64.
8. Brian Dippie, *The Vanishing American: White Attitudes and U.S. Indian Policy* (Lawrence: University Press of Kansas, 1982), 116.
9. Allan Sekula, "The Body and the Archive," *October* 39 (Winter 1986): 3–64.
10. Ibid.
11. Ibid., 14.
12. The Getty collection image set includes a brief narrative that provides the backstory of the children's mother and their rescue from slavery, with the bottom of each card reading, "Profits from sale, for the benefit of the children."
13. Rickard, "The Occupation of Indigenous Space," 60.
14. Ibid., 63–64.
15. Curtis Marez, "Aliens and Indians: Science Fiction, Prophetic Photography and Near-Future Visions," *Journal of Visual Culture* 2 (2004): 340.
16. Vivian Sobchack, "The Scene of the Screen: Envisioning Photographic, Cinematic, and Electronic 'Presence,'" in *Materialities of Communication*, ed. Hans Ulrich Gumbrecht and K. Ludwig Pfeiffer (Stanford, CA: Stanford University Press, 1994): 92.
17. Hearne, *Native Recognition*, 25.
18. Tom Gunning, "Tracing the Individual Body: Photography, Detectives, and Early Cinema," in *Cinema and the Invention of Modern Life*, ed. Leo Charney and Vanessa R. Schwartz (Berkeley: University of California Press, 1995), 42.
19. Ibid., 16.
20. Jonathan Crary, *Suspensions of Perception: Attention, Spectacle, and Modern Culture* (Boston: MIT Press, 2000), 147.
21. Hearne, *Native Recognition*, 31.
22. Ibid., 31–32.
23. Faye Ginsburg, "Indigenous Media: Faustian Contract or Global Village?" *Cultural Anthropology* 6, no. 1 (1991): 104.
24. Michelle Raheja, *Reservation Reelism: Redfacing, Visual Sovereignty, and the Representation of Native Americans in Film* (Lincoln: University of Nebraska Press, 2010), 193–94.
25. Ibid., 193.

Part III
Performing Bodies

Introduction

As Jonathan Auerbach writes in his 2007 study *Body Shots: Early Cinema's Incarnations*, "Practices of cinema during its first decade came to rely most crucially on the dynamic language of body movement—gestures, comportments, and attitudes . . . lending a special kind of materiality to motion pictures." This remark aptly describes the core role of the performing body in early cinema. The two delineated notions of body language and physical materiality provide essential guidelines for this section, devoted to early cinema as a way of displaying the body. What Anthony Paraskeva calls the "symbolic properties of the gesturing body" has been recognized as the main expressive subject of cinema from the first film theories promoting film as a universal language. Moreover, the idea of a body language implies codifications, references, and intermediality, all at the heart of the texts in this section, which take a transdisciplinary and comparative approach.

The "materiality" of the human body that, according to Auerbach, "contaminated" early film, highlights the central question of indexicality and realism. The moving body on-screen seemed unusually present, close, and real, acquiring a new quality and a specific power of fascination. Its capture by the movie camera exposed it as a "living" object of voyeurism, eroticism, or identification. Issues of gender and class were thus fundamentally involved in early cinematic spectacle of bodies, either epitomizing the masculine, codifying the feminine, or making way for a modern, urban, and intense physicality that was emerging within the new body culture of the 1900s.

While early film has already been studied as the reign of the scopic drive, this section looks at the other end of the camera and examines how early cinema put the body on display—and threw it into question. In the first essay, Charlie Keil and Denise McKenna reveal how the appeal of early Hollywood's mixed-gendered performing bodies proved to be not only the basis of its success but also "one of the industry's most persistent problems." Focusing on the slapstick actresses' body, they demonstrate how their intrepid physicality challenged gendered norms and became "a site for the negotiation of profound social change," promoting the bravery, freedom, and ambition of comediennes.

Focusing on dancing and boxing attractions in Norwegian early fiction films, Gunnar Iversen argues that the modern, exotic, and liberated female dancing body delineated a new femininity for the newly independent Norway. The male boxing body, similarly "young and hyper-kinetic," is correspondingly presented by Iversen as the expression of the new international body culture, contributing to the Norwegian representations of masculinity and shaping its new cultural identity.

The display of fighting naked male bodies is further examined by Ivo Blom, whose contribution focuses on the *forzuti*, strongmen who emerge as key figures in Italian films in the 1910s. Through the case study of the *forzuto* Ausonia, Blom shows that this display of the muscular "sons of Sandow" drew on traditions outside the cinema. Centering on the reference to *poses plastiques*, the author progressively outlines the whole intermedial nexus (including scenic shows of strongmen, postcards of bodybuilders, living-statue performances, sculptures, and *tableaux vivants*), which determined this early-cinema iconography of the perfect male body.

The perfect female body has not been left behind. The following essay by Valentine Robert explores the first cinematic appearances of the naked body—which proved to be mainly feminine. Robert analyzes this early display of undressed bodies through a theoretical ambivalence between an illicit and obscene "nakedness" and an artistic and ideal "nudity"—on the one hand, cultivating the immediacy, rough mobility, and crudeness of the indexical naked body; on the other hand, idealizing the nudity with artistic references, academic poses, and elaborate *tableaux vivants* staging. At the crossroad between erotic voyeurism and (more or less fallacious) erudite contemplation, the naked body emerged as a subversive but not illegitimate early-cinema subject.

Sébastien Dupont-Bloch concludes the section with a notable "body performance affair." Aiming to carve the body of a man caught in quicksand, the sculptor Paul Capellani asked his brother, the famous filmmaker Albert Capellani, to record his own submersion with a movie camera. Paul then made his sculpture based on the film footage. Albert Capellani also built an entire film around this scene, which was even transposed into a painting for the film poster. This vanishing-body performance thus generated sculpted, painted, and filmed bodies, epitomizing the intermedial nexus shaping representations of the body in early cinema. But why did this artist want to model his motionless work on a cinematic performing body? Because the recorded experience was said to be "real," relying on a "material," indexical, and moving quality. The loop is completed; Auerbach's concepts are wholly actualized. Paul Capellani, indeed, proclaimed to have risked his life performing, caught in the quicksand as truly as by the camera.

10 Risky Business

The Early Film Actor and Discourses of Danger

Charlie Keil and Denise McKenna

WHAT DID IT mean to "work" in the motion-picture industry during its first decades? And what were the risks associated with film labor? From the outset, the laboring body proved central to the cinematic experience, both on-screen and off. One of the most visible workers was the actor, the performing body duly registered by a newly minted medium predicated on indexicality. Discussions of early screen acting often noted the arduous nature of film performance, especially in "body genres" such as slapstick comedy or the numerous variants of early action films.[1] The thrill of "body genres" that required scenes of physical mayhem to stage comedic threats or that showcased spectacular feats of physical daring was reinforced by "real" stories about film stars who leaped from trains, fell off bridges, and cozied up to wild animals in the name of screen acting. Aside from the pleasurable spectacle of danger, the visceral appeal of actors at risk was enhanced by their flagrant disregard for social conventions predicated on bodily propriety. Indeed, filmmaking's perilous physicality—its comic pratfalls and daring stunts—helped define early film's excitement and appeal even as it tied certain genres and performers to working-class identity and culture.

Strategies to manage and contain these different dangers helped define the parameters of the industry's uplift movement from 1907 to 1915, perhaps most clearly in the promotion of cinema's educational potential and in the gentrification of exhibition spaces and social practices.[2] The discourse of danger, then, broadly encompasses the film industry's development—from the moral dangers of screen content to the licentious temptations of darkened theaters, and from the financial risks of film producing to the very real dangers of flammable nitrate. Danger as a fantasy and as a material effect establishes a narrative logic for the film industry, placing risk management at the center of its industrial expansion in the form of problems to be resolved and surmounted by filmmakers, reformers, and bureaucrats alike. Danger also made good copy. A 1915 cartoon for *Motion Picture Magazine* depicts a hapless would-be hero whose misguided attempt to

BRUTAL PARTY (to Jones, who has just rescued a young woman against her will)—
You big chump! You've just spoiled forty feet of film.

Figure 10.1. "Brutal Party," *Motion Picture Magazine* (September 1915), 134.

rescue an actress merits only disdain from the sopping-wet performer and wrath from the director. This cartoon exploits the comedic disjunction between film-world priorities (in which 40 feet of film supersedes physical danger) and outdated modes of gendered chivalry.

Notions of bodily imperilment pervaded the discourse on early acting, while a suggestion of danger informed representations of the production process itself, yet these formulations of risk are multivalent, even contradictory. An apparent tension in such discourse arises from the competing aims of actors defending their trade and the film industry promoting a positive image of the emerging studio system, all with an eye to the negotiation of slapstick comedy's opprobrious appeal. Thus, rhetoric emphasizing an individual actor's exceptional dedication to his or her craft despite its dangers is undercut by descriptions of film production that portray studio labor in terms of hyperbolic physicality.

In the years immediately following the advent of screen stardom, women who achieved a degree of fame working in the early film industry found themselves uniquely positioned to account for their own labor to an expanding audience. As Jennifer Bean has demonstrated, female players helped fuel the inflated publicizing of the early star system and the celebratory excess that surrounded "thrilling modern film genres."[3] Such rhetoric singled out female stars for their spectacular physicality and emotional fortitude. And as Bean makes clear, "realist hype" that conflated screen stunts with offscreen risk supported these assertions, shifting attention away from cinema's institutional expansion and onto the extraordinary body of the female performer.[4] Yet in acknowledging screen acting's physical demands, female stars spoke to the difficulties of their work even as they sang its praises. Certainly, the focus on risk constructed knowledge of filmmaking as spectacle, but the discourse of danger also constituted a new understanding of what women's labor could look like. Whereas most of the crafts necessary for film production were rationalized by gendered divisions—meaning men worked as grips or constructed sets while women typically labored in costume departments and editing rooms—acting remained open to both sexes in roughly equal numbers. Accordingly, female performers engaged in physically demanding stunts or comic pratfalls that rivaled those of their male counterparts.

The cartoon "Brutal Party" is typical of images that humorously exploit the tensions between the viewer's misguided expectations of film work and the "reality" of film labor, but it also reiterates the visual evidence on the screen: if dangerous, film work was equally risky for both men and women—as was the choice they made to leave "happy homes" to work in photoplays. Undoubtedly, the kind of work that women performed on-screen often confounded societal expectations, especially when associated with the genre norms of slapstick comedy or action serials. Famous comedic actors such as Florence Turner and Mabel Normand wreaked havoc on themselves and their environment, challenging gendered mores with their antics as they traversed middle-class and working-class cultures and spaces—at once "dainty" and capable of appealing moments of reserve and at the same time disruptive, anarchic, and subversive in their physicality.[5] Similarly, serial queens expanded gendered norms as they defied both gravity and nefarious villains while racing through cities and across countries to solve a new crime each week. At the level of performance and genre, the disregard for decorum along with filmmaking's perilous physicality—whether it be frenetic knockabout comedy or the derring-do of action stunts—established parameters for cinema's success, but it also inextricably linked these genres (and their key performers) to a working-class culture associated with bodily excess, urban mobility, and violence.[6]

At the same time that genre conventions established expectations concerning the types of labor that female actors could perform on-screen, the emergent studio system was becoming a highly visible and distinctly modern heterosocial workspace, one that epitomized the possibilities—and problems—of male and female employees working together. The conjunction of the physicality of female on-screen performance and the mixed-gender working conditions at film studios required forms of discursive negotiation that become manifest in the trade press

Figure 10.2. "And Yet . . . Lots of Young Men and Women, Living in Happy Homes, Want to Be Photoplayers!" *Motion Picture Story Magazine* (March 1913), 128.

and fan magazines of the day. From interviews with actresses that focused on fashion or culinary accomplishments to cartoons lampooning workplace conditions, early Hollywood's nascent publicity machine devised strategies to defuse the potentially problematic implications of the laboring female body. Another *Motion Picture Magazine* cartoon from October 1914, "A Day with the Players," explicates common misunderstandings of film work in some detail, conveying sarcasm through wordy text as it mocks in equal measure the female star who leaps into water despite not knowing how to swim and the audience that mistakes screen labor for "play." The valorization and critical scrutiny of on-screen female labor ultimately throws into relief the material tensions and symbolic possibilities of Hollywood's emerging studio culture and the images it created.

The very basis of the industry's success—the appeal of its on-screen performers—also proved to be one of the industry's most persistent problems. Film acting posed certain challenges for those wishing to cast cinema as a respectable art form during this period. Articles about film actors that began circulating around 1907 often described performing for the screen as a particularly demanding form of labor; coverage of motion pictures evidenced a shift from a technical understanding of film to a more personality-driven account of the medium.[7] As Richard deCordova notes, many of these early articles grappled with the problem of reconciling screen acting's broad physicality—the prevalence of "lying down, rolling over and jumping"—with established theatrical traditions.[8] Attitudes toward motion-picture work as a valid artistic form with its own requirements and standards of practice gradually shifted during the following decade, especially as production companies and actors promoted cinema's artistic and uplifting possibilities. Slapstick, however, remained resistant to such revisionism since the "lying down, rolling over and jumping" never really went away; the expectation that performers accepted such risks, in turn, had physical consequences for the actors themselves. The "Answers to Inquiries" and "Greenroom Jottings" in *Motion Picture Magazine*, which tracked the minutiae of actors' lives for their readers, are also a compendium of injuries and illnesses incurred on sets. In interviews, actors would confirm the risks that screen acting entailed, and some of their mishaps became the stuff of legend: Mabel Normand suffered head trauma while working at Keystone in 1915; Wallace Reid was injured on location (or while in transit to location) in 1919, which likely contributed to his morphine addiction, and probably to his death;[9] also in 1919, Harold Lloyd mistook a live bomb for a prop and blew some fingers off his right hand. Not coincidentally, two of these decidedly unfunny incidents occurred in the service of producing comedy: clearly, the work of making people laugh entailed a high degree of bodily risk.

How, then, should we describe the relationship between labor, the gendered body, and slapstick comedy? The slapstick body is often the abused body and, as

Figure 10.3. "A Day with the Players," *Motion Picture Magazine* (October 1914), 88.

Scott Balcerzak suggests, this traumatized comic body promotes an understanding of "slapstick as [a] social mechanism . . . one that reflects . . . comedy's potential to deconstruct industrial society through its 'types.'"[10] Accordingly, we can see slapstick's bodily violence as emblematic of the technological machine age's dehumanizing effects. Studies of these abused comic bodies have often focused on Charlie Chaplin and Buster Keaton, particularly the relationship between man and modern mechanization, satirically literalized in *Modern Times* when the machine swallows Chaplin. However, the recent work of Maggie Hennefeld, among others, has shifted our attention to the multivalent significance of early *female* comic performers, identifying the slapstick comedienne's body as a site for the negotiation of profound social change.

With female performers as the focus, slapstick could explore domestic space's potential for carnivalesque confusion, often featuring housemaids as a fulcrum for comic misunderstandings based on ethnic, racial, and class stereotypes. Housemaids were, after all, a constitutive feature of working-class life; domestic service remained the single largest occupation for women between 1870 and 1940.[11] As a figure whose mobility was connected to the problems of immigrant labor and racial difference, and whose work life required that she traverse the public/private divide, the housemaid possessed a functional malleability that the industry exploited on- and offscreen.[12] In 1911, in an attempt to bolster cinema's progressive appeal, *The Moving Picture News* praised motion pictures as a psychological palliative for the working classes, as a space that could "let tired women forget the dishpan and scrub pail."[13]

This kind of imaginative appeal transforms later in the decade into stories about the "extra girl" who wanted to abandon domestic chores for greasepaint and the camera. The throngs of dislocated hopefuls arriving in Los Angeles partially justified the notion that women could escape working-class drudgery via the film studio.[14] And the discourse of danger that typified the early star system certainly suggested that a willingness to take physical risks was one road to success. Despite articles and cartoons that proclaimed film acting's labor-intensive legitimacy, celebrity interviews could also add the gloss of leisure to motion-picture work. As Winifred Kingston told *Photoplay* in 1915, filming in "fashionable homes" with "friendly" people was so "delightful" that she did not feel as if she were working.[15] Kingston's coy glamour on the magazine's cover further reinforces the seductive appeal of acting's extrafilmic rewards at the same time that it visually distances actors from a working-class typology. Kingston's pleasant characterization of her work life notwithstanding, actors often disputed accounts that effaced the true labor that film performing entailed. Accordingly, the desirable dimensions of screen acting that animate celebrity interviews overlap with cautionary tales directed at young women imagining an escape from menial work in the studio; these advisories insistently stress the dangers that

Figure 10.4. Winifred Kingston, *Photoplay* (January 1915).

await those who have failed to "break in." Such struggles to account for film work point to its novelty as an occupation, to its precarious class affiliations, and to its potent, fantastical appeal.

The 1913 comedy *Mabel's Dramatic Career*—with Mabel Normand as a kitchen maid who finds a happier life in the motion pictures—plays on many of these associations. *Mabel's Dramatic Career* brings together several strands of inquiry pursued here—the laboring body, the woman as comic performer, and the relationship between genre and audience—not surprisingly, all issues that the industry had to negotiate as it learned to promote stars and to build its system. The film quickly establishes Mabel as klutzy and hapless but deserving of the audience's sympathy when her buffoonish boyfriend (played by Mack Sennett) cruelly dumps her in favor of a more sophisticated city girl. In a scene where art may have imitated life, Mabel has a flamboyant fight with Mack. Then she is dismissed from her position and summarily thrown out of the house, essentially forced to leave home again to look for work. Mabel finds her way to the city, wanders past a film studio (labeled as Keystone), ends up on set, and becomes a film star. Later, Mack recognizes her face on a billboard and goes to see her film; once he sees her on the screen he remembers his first true love's worth, even though he cannot seem to distinguish between fiction and reality, as he viscerally reacts to the story with the directness of *Uncle Josh at the Moving Picture Show*. Normand's performance throughout the film is equally physical. She attacks and chases her worthless beau, his would-be girlfriend, and even the disapproving mother. And, as it is a Keystone film, she takes a fall in almost every scene. Mabel's penchant for disruption has its charms, but that talent is only recognized for its potential when she reaches the motion-picture studio.

Slapstick chaos laid siege to the home under various comedic guises, but housemaids like Mabel legitimated slapstick's invasion of domestic space by exploiting the situatedness of working-class life as a comic milieu, while the housemaid's proletarian roots aligned slapstick comedy with its supposed target audience. In the case of *Mabel's Dramatic Career*, comedic transformation comes in the form of studio success, as Mabel stumbles into a filmmaking context that solves all the problems posed by her failed romance—she finds a career, becomes successful in ways impossible for a maid, finds a husband (as revealed in the last scene), and, albeit unwittingly, makes her unfaithful fiancé realize his loss. The film is self-reflexive on a number of levels and plays with Mabel Normand's own star story and the indelible contribution of physically oriented slapstick to Normand's star persona. As Charlie Keil has argued, "To become useful to Keystone, Mabel the maid must abandon any pretence toward legitimate acting and release the physical energy within her that was already on abundant display in the film's first half. To put it another way, in the scene [where Mabel engages in a pratfall for the Keystone cameras] the actress Mabel Normand must convey the persona she has already established for herself in a series of Keystone comedies in order to allow the Mabel of the diegesis to become the Mabel of Keystone fame."[16] *Mabel's Dramatic Career* presents the Keystone Company as the ideal home for Mabel's actorly talents, precisely because the studio can accommodate the unrestrained physicality that Mabel has already demonstrated "in real life." The film imagines the studio as a place where new identities and careers are fashioned out of chance, need, and the idiosyncratic appeal and skills of the individual aspirant.

Hollywood studios have long been mythologized as the place where dreams of stardom are realized through filmmaking's magical process. But the early manifestation of the studio myth in *Mabel's Dramatic Career* adds an intriguing element of physicality to the equation, suggesting a comic inversion to the supposed transformational properties of the camera. *Mabel's Dramatic Career* evokes this early period in the developing star system because it presents the performer's laboring body as essential to success at Keystone and points to other dimensions of studio life often occluded in fictional representations of filmmaking. But if one examines a fuller range of representations of studio life and acting, one can see that this discourse encapsulated ideas about work and career that reveal the studio as a worksite embodying novel forms of labor. The studio could enact changing attitudes toward work, becoming, even for women like Mabel's beleaguered maid, a place to find a new kind of job and a satisfying life. Privileging the studio as a site of self-fulfillment through a career is a narrative that has many corollaries in star interviews of this period, in which actors acknowledge the challenges and toil of motion-picture acting. This rhetoric of hard work validated screen acting as a specialized and respectable profession, although comedy still presented certain problems for the industry's uplift movement. As Rob King succinctly describes it, slapstick was "resoundingly opposed to cultivated standards,"[17] and persistent critiques of the genre confirm its beleaguered status. Yet associations between slapstick and the industry extended beyond the screen into representations of the studio itself.

The pratfalls of comedy served as a mechanism for depicting the dangers of filmmaking. Those dangers quickly became a trope exploited in numerous cartoons that spoofed the disjunction between on-screen glamour and on-set reality. A cartoon entitled "A Quiet Day" exploits the humorous potential of various genres, depicting the comical extremes of life behind studio walls as physically demanding and perilous. But in its manic energy, this "quiet day" draws a clear parallel between slapstick comedy and studio production practices as a whole, setting up film production as the butt of a joke that depends on bodily threat. This cartoon also recalls Ben Singer's analysis of melodrama (a genre referenced in the cartoon) and the possible—and problematic—connections between violent film culture and the "vulnerable" proletarian body. As Singer argues, beyond its appeal to a working-class audience, the spectacular violence, excess, and "volatility" of urban existence that typified the sensational melodrama and action serials profoundly connected with the physicality and dangers of workers' lives.[18] The comic carnage of a "Quiet Day" suggests that the studio, like the screen, is another staging ground for the types of perils that define contemporary working-class life. An assortment of dangers confers a sense of excitement and vibrancy on the studio as a work environment, quite distinct from the allure that Hollywood would increasingly cultivate as the decade progressed, in its carefully controlled depictions of filmmaking as a specialized and hierarchical process.

Envisioned as the nexus of working-class physicality and occupational mobility, as well as a site of heterosocial fluidity, Keystone becomes a signal studio in this regard. Actors of both sexes, physically invested in body comedy, contribute to this optimistic outlook on novel workplace demands. The Keystone comic embodies the enthusiasm of the committed employee. Enthusiasm is manifest in the representation of the rigors of screen work, such as diving into

Figure 10.5. "A Quiet Day in a California Movie Camp," *Photoplay* (July 1915), 153.

rivers or jumping over walls or taking a pie in the face. The actor's intrepid physicality may connect film labor with its working-class roots, but it also expresses a commitment to the inherent and sometimes excessive requirements of film production. As one reporter said of Keystone's Louise Fazenda, she "is a Keystone comedienne, therefore it is needless to say that she is brave."[19] As Kristen Anderson Wagner has discussed, many comic performers were ambivalent about their own connection to slapstick, voiced in interviews or expressed in action as they exchanged one studio for another. Comediennes, in particular, negotiated a position that allowed them a subversive freedom, but they often tempered this modern mobility with an appeal to tradition by insisting on the conventionally feminine trappings of delicate domesticity, or at least in an aspirational desire for more emotively acceptable dramatic work.[20] However, enthusiasm for their work grounded the ambition to transcend the limitations and humiliation of working within slapstick—particularly for women—within an understandable and relatable context. In effect, the desire to escape slapstick created a forum in which women could speak about having ambition, an idea that confounded gender norms already troubled by the physical excesses of their screen labor. And as we can see in the "Quiet Day" cartoon, along with other representations of film production in print and on the screen, studio space finds itself conflated with slapstick's comedic spectacle to define film labor. And no studio proved more emblematic of shifting ideas about work, risk, and ambition than Keystone.

If we can understand slapstick as a form that offers a mordant morphology of contemporary life—a kind of gallows humor of modern mayhem and everyday risks—it also symbolizes the American film industry's most disreputable qualities. Slapstick was the inherent contradiction in uplift arguments about the film industry's social value and remained a problem demanding a solution as much as it was a genre ripe for exploitation. And as slapstick's greatest proponent, Keystone Studios can stand as a metonym for the most persistent critiques of the film industry as a whole. It churned out lowbrow entertainment, lacking in refinement or social worth, supposedly appealing to the most debased audience; yet it was also a studio whose employees committed their bodies to the company good despite slapstick's dangers.

Keystone also represents another aspect of the film industry's economic imperative: how to transform labor into entertainment. Rob King observes that the studio's founder, Mack Sennett, opposed the notion that filmmaking should emulate the rationalized practices of industrialized efficiency; instead, he crafted a mythology that positioned Keystone as a carnivalesque counterpoint to mechanized labor. As King argues, "Sennett's publicity department worked hard to depict the Keystone lot as a zany counterweight to the rationalization of American industry, a place where the lines separating work and play, productive labor and dynamic disorder, became hopelessly entangled."[21]

Figure 10.6. Detail from "West Coast News of National Significance," *Photoplay* (February 1917), 64.

Eliding evidence of production processes proved essential to the industry's institutional development, a tendency as apparent in the increased emphasis on diegetic integrity in storytelling techniques as in the building of walls around the studios. Keystone confirms how the industry's initial strategy for managing the star system during the transitional era—primarily collapsing on-screen and offscreen identities to project a coherent persona—could prove adaptable to managing a studio's image. Keystone's unique relationship to one genre facilitated an approach to representing the studio that conflated all aspects of its production into humorously appealing imagery. Defining studio culture emerged as a critical business strategy, a process that unfolded concurrently with both developments in the star system and the hierarchical structuring of studio labor and management. Complicating these institutional ambitions, however, were the gender and class anxieties that inform the reception of early film acting, the pleasure in problematic genres, and the challenges that the nascent star system posed to controlling and protecting the actor's image and the excitement of manufactured thrills. But in the years before glamorized Hollywood lifestyles thoroughly dominated the discourse of celebrity, actors' enthusiasm for their craft and their dedication to their home studio tied a nebulous new occupation to other forms of middle-class life—and helped to demonstrate how screen acting was a worthwhile pursuit, even as actors would seemingly risk life and limb just to get a laugh.

CHARLIE KEIL is the Principal of Innis College and a Professor in the History Department and the Cinema Studies Institute at the University of Toronto. He is editor of *A Companion to D. W. Griffith*, *Editing and*

Special/Visual Effects (with Kristen Whissel), and the forthcoming *Oxford Handbook of Silent Cinema* (with Rob King).

DENISE MCKENNA is part-time faculty in the Cinema Program at Palomar College. She has published on gender and studio culture in the early American film industry and is the editor of a special issue on labor for *Feminist Media Histories*.

Notes

1. Jennifer Bean, "Technologies of Early Stardom and the Extraordinary Body," *Camera Obscura* 16, no. 3 (2001): 9–57. Linda Williams expands on Carol Clover's concept of horror as a "body genre" to include melodrama and pornography. These body genres deploy tropes of gendered and "ecstatic excesses" to evoke visceral responses from their audience; see "Film Bodies: Gender, Genre, and Excess," *Film Quarterly* 44, no. 4 (Summer 1991): 2–13.

2. Anne Morey discusses educational reform and its approach to cinema as "both a danger to be mastered and a vehicle for improving society" in *Hollywood Outsiders: The Adaptation of the Film Industry, 1913–1934* (Minneapolis: University of Minnesota Press, 2003), 2.

3. Bean, "Technologies of Early Stardom," 12.

4. Ibid., 18.

5. For more on the disruptive potential of women in silent comedy, see Kristen Anderson Wagner, "Pie Queens and Virtuous Vamps: The Funny Women of the Silent Screen," in *A Companion to Film Comedy*, ed. Andrew Horton and Joanna E. Rapf (Malden, MA: Wiley-Blackwell, 2013), 39–60; see also Maggie Hennefeld, "Miniature Women, Acrobatic Maids, and Self-Amputating Domestics: Comediennes of the Trick Film," *Early Popular Visual Culture* 13, no. 2 (2015): 134–51.

6. Ben Singer, *Melodrama and Modernity: Early Sensational Cinema and Its Contexts* (New York: Columbia University Press, 2001). See also Kathy Peiss, *Working Women and Leisure in Turn-of-the-Century New York* (Philadelphia: Temple University Press, 1986).

7. Richard deCordova, *Picture Personalities: The Emergence of the Star System in America* (Urbana: University of Illinois Press, 2001), 30–45.

8. Ibid., 35. DeCordova is quoting from *Moving Picture World* in 1907. As he notes, we can interpret much of this discourse as asserting that performers on-screen were actually acting. By the end of the decade, such assertions that screen art was a particular kind of performance art became more explicit.

9. For more on this, see Mark Lynn Anderson, *Twilight of the Idols: Hollywood and the Human Sciences in 1920s America* (Berkeley: University of California Press, 2011).

10. Scott Balcerzak, *Buffoon Men: Classic Hollywood Comedians and Queered Masculinity* (Detroit, MI: Wayne State University Press, 2013), 12.

11. Janet M. Hooks, *Women's Occupations through Seven Decades*, Women's Bureau Bulletin No. 218 (Washington, DC: US Department of Labor, 1947), x. There are also statistics that put the number of women in domestic service at 3 out of 10; see "Working Women

in the 1930s," in *American Decades Vol. 4: 1930–1939, U.S. History in Context* ed. Judith S. Baughman et al., (Detroit: Gale, 2001), http://ic.galegroup.com.

12. For more on anxiety about women's leaving home for work, see Joanne J. Meyerowitz, *Women Adrift: Independent Wage Earners in Chicago, 1880–1930* (Chicago: University of Chicago Press, 1991).

13. Mary Lawton Metcalfe, "Psychological Power of Moving Pictures," *Moving Picture News*, November 11, 1911, 8.

14. In the 1910s, the migration of women to Los Angeles outpaced that of men. See Frank L. Beach, "The Effects of Westward Movement on California's Growth and Development, 1900–1920," *International Migration Review* 3, no. 3 (Summer 1969): 25–28.

15. Lucy Davis, "The Girl on the Cover," *Photoplay*, January 1915, 36.

16. Charlie Keil, "1913: Movies and the Beginning of a New Era," in *American Cinema of the 1910s*, ed. Charlie Keil and Ben Singer (New Brunswick, NJ: Rutgers University Press, 2009), 105.

17. Rob King, *The Fun Factory: The Keystone Film Company and the Emergence of Mass Culture* (Berkeley: University of California Press, 2009), 24.

18. Singer, *Melodrama and Modernity*, 53. For more on connections between slapstick and death, see Muriel Andrin, "Back to the 'Slap': Slapstick's Hyperbolic Gestures and the Rhetoric of Violence," in *Slapstick Comedy*, ed. Rob King and Tom Paulus (London: Routledge, 2010), 226–35.

19. "She Quit at the Altar," *Photoplay*, August 1917, 26. Even so, she did marry Noel Smith in 1917—and turned the wedding into a Keystone film.

20. Kristen Anderson Wagner, "'Have Women a Sense of Humor?': Comedy and Femininity in Early Twentieth Century Film," *Velvet Light Trap* 68 (Fall 2011): 35–46.

21. King, *The Fun Factory*, 34–35.

11 Bodies in Motion
Dancing and Boxing in Early Norwegian Cinema

Gunnar Iversen

THE CONNECTIONS BETWEEN dance and early cinema, and between boxing and early cinema, have received considerable attention, especially in American, French, and German contexts; however, less is known about these connections in other countries and other national cinemas. Numerous films included scenes of dancing or boxing, exploring movement and gesture, corporeal expression and physical display, either as an attraction itself or integrated into different narratives. These scenes not only foreground the medium specificity of film by representing movement and physical presence, but they also explore notions of bodily liberation, physical culture, rhythm, physical performance, morality, beauty, and eroticism. Different performers helped audiences to navigate social and cultural transitions and transformations through moving bodies.

In Norway, as in many other countries, the medium of film was introduced in the form of representations of bodies in motion. The very first films shown in Norway in April 1896 were the Bioskop films by Max and Emil Skladanowsky, which had premiered at Berlin's Wintergarten on November 1, 1895. Thus, the medium was introduced in Norway through films showing acrobatic and athletic performances, including dancing and boxing. When the first fiction films were made in Norway in the 1910s, scenes of dancing and boxing were incorporated into the narratives and played a central role in the stories that were told. These scenes represented a different and new body culture that made an impact in Norwegian society.

In this short essay, I will discuss the role of dancing and boxing in early Norwegian cinema. I will focus mostly on the role of dance performances in the earliest surviving Norwegian feature film, *Under the Law of Change* (*Under forvandlingens lov*, 1911), made by cinema owner, composer, and musician Halfdan Nobel Roede, as well as the role of boxing in *The Daughter of the Revolution* (*Revolutionens datter*, 1918) by cinema owner Ottar Gladtvet. I will also take a more cursory look at other Norwegian feature films of the 1910s in which dancing and fight scenes were important.

Dance as a Cultural Point of Encounter

Even though cinemagoing became a major popular form of entertainment in Norway during the first decade of the twentieth century, domestic film production remained small and resulted mainly in actualities. Fiction-film production started in Norway in 1911, but between 1911 and 1919, only sixteen fiction films were made. This occurred in two short, eruptive periods. Between 1911 and 1913, eight feature films were made. However, the municipalization of cinemas in Norway after 1913 caused insecurity and upheaval in the film business, which halted until 1917. At that point, another eight feature films were made between 1917 and 1919.[1] From 1920 onward, fiction films were produced regularly in Norway, although only a few features were made each year. Although there are many similarities between the films in these two short periods of fiction filmmaking in Norway in the 1910s, there are also important differences. The people and production companies who made the films were different in the two periods, as were the stories they told. However, in both periods, scenes of bodies in motion were an important attraction in the narratives of Norwegian films.

The fiction films made in the earliest period, between 1911 and 1913, took their inspiration from the Danish erotic, sensational, or "social" melodramas. *The Abyss* (*Afgrunden*, Urban Gad, 1910), in particular, was a huge success in Norway. The film not only made Asta Nielsen and Poul Reumert into stars, but the famous erotic "gaucho dance" led to discussions about cinema's supposedly harmful effects, especially on children. The Norwegian feature *The Demon* (*Demonen*, Jens Christian Gundersen, 1911) included an erotic "apache" dance that triggered local censorship there.[2] *The Demon* is a melodrama about love and gambling. The young daughter of a general is wooed by both a young count and an older baron. She chooses the young count and marries him. The older baron decides to take revenge by ruining the young count through gambling. The count not only loses most of his family's money at a casino but also becomes enamored with a young dancer, Cleo, and goes with her to a brothel. When his wife learns about this, she decides to commit suicide, but she is saved and then hides until her husband mends his ways. They reunite at the end.

In an important sequence in Gundersen's film, the count, Werner von Falkenstein, watches a couple dance in a brothel. This central dance scene in *The Demon* is obviously modeled on *The Abyss*; it shows a man and a woman dancing closely and rubbing their bodies against each other. It is obviously erotic. The man, played by the famous painter Per Krohg, the son of the even more famous painter Christian Krohg, is dressed as a Pierrot in white, and his knee is pressed between the legs of the all-black-clad female dancer as they slowly gyrate. It is obviously an *Abyss*-like erotic bodily display, and local police immediately cut the scene. Ironically, today the dance is one of only two surviving scenes from the film; the rest is lost.

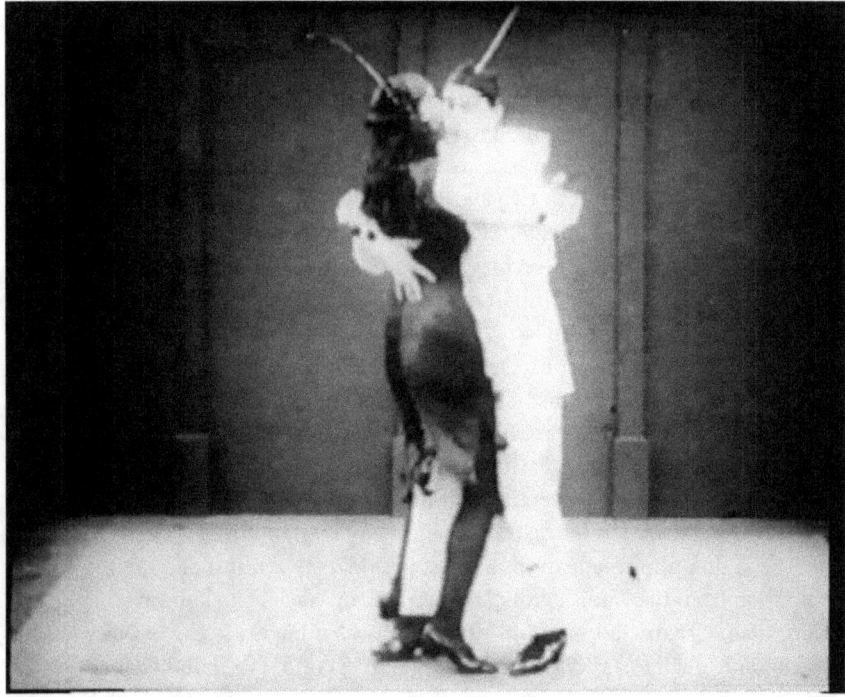

Figure 11.1. Dance inspired by *Afgrunden* from *The Demon*.

Even more interesting is *Under the Law of Change*, made in 1911, the same year as *The Demon*. The story is simple: Camillo sees his best friend, Arthur, give his wife, Julia, a letter. He looks through her purse, finds the letter, and discovers that his wife is having an affair with Arthur. He shows the letter to Arthur's wife, Franziska, and the two deceived spouses decide to punish Arthur and Julia. They put sleeping powder in their champagne at a party and then put them in two big iron cages while they are unconscious. Camillo and Franziska then travel abroad and visit an outdoor *varieté* show, during which three women perform three different solo dances. Camillo and Franziska return home to find that the passion between Julia and Arthur has cooled during their imprisonment, and they release them. The last intertitle is brief and ambiguous: "Homecoming and reconciliation. The triumph of marriage."

The three dances that Camillo and Franziska watch at the outdoor variety show on their trip abroad are part of the story; they are motivated by the story, inserted into the narrative to create a pause and to express different ideas about bodies and movement. However, this sequence, which takes up more than one fourth of the whole twenty-minute film, also halts or stops the narrative. The

Figure 11.2. Bertha Raestad's cakewalk in *Under the Law of Change*.

dances are only partly integrated into it. Even more central than in *The Demon*, the dances in *Under the Law of Change* are not erotic; instead, the sequence represents a variety of dance styles and movement vocabularies. The three dancers are photographed against a simple backdrop in three single, mostly unedited scenes. However, between the dances we cut to shots of Camillo and Franziska at the outdoor *varieté*, weaving the two spaces together into a unified performance. The dances become an attraction in and of themselves but not only for showing off the female body in motion. The dancers also represent different performances of femininity, and they have different corporeal and kinesthetic meanings that represent distinct individual and cultural identities.

The first is a cakewalk, performed by the actress Bertha Raestad. Her dance is expressive and kinetic; she moves rapidly around the stage, moving her arms and legs wildly. At the end of the dance, she lifts her skirt as she kicks her legs, in an exaggerated fashion typical of the cakewalk. Even though this part is an obvious erotic spectacle, the dance itself is hardly erotic. It is very different from the couple dancing in *The Demon*, and the female dancer does not come off as a dancing seductress. It is more of a silly and spirited dance than an erotic one. The cakewalk is usually danced by a couple and derives from African American slave

Figure 11.3. Botten Soot's Egyptian dance from *Under the Law of Change*.

caricatures of their masters' European-style dances on the plantations; later they became a popular part of minstrel shows and musical revues in the United States. By 1911, it was regarded by many as the American national dance.³ The white Norwegian dancer, Bertha Raestad, imitates a black dance that parodies older white dance styles, in a "curious mixture of caricature and authentic dance."⁴ Or as Megan Pugh writes about the cakewalk in Europe in the early years of the twentieth century: "Amateur white European cakewalkers were imitating white minstrel cakewalkers imitating black slaves imitating their masters, who were unable to recognize that they were being mocked."⁵ Exotic and new in a Norwegian context, the dance allows the performer to express herself in an unusually expressive way.

The second dance is an exotic "Egyptian dance," as defined by an intertitle, performed by the actress Botten Soot. This is also an exotic dance, slower than the cakewalk, and consisting of a combination of wild, rapid gyrations and poses that reference Egyptian hieroglyphics. The dance ends in the only medium shot in the film, and the only cut in the presentation of the three dances, showing the smiling actress after the dance is over. Probably inspired by the well-known Egyptian dances of Ruth St. Denis, Soot's performance added dance images from another ancient or exotic culture.⁶

Figure 11.4. Hedvig Dietrichson's Chopin dance in *Under the Law of Change*.

The third dance is different from the previous two. Solo dancer and dance teacher Hedvig Dietrichson performs a "Chopin dance." This is obviously inspired by Isadora Duncan, the legendary American pioneer of modern dance who often used works by Chopin as musical accompaniment to her dances.[7] Not only does Miss Dietrichson perform barefoot but her loose white Grecian tunic and uncorseted body clearly reference Duncan. She also performs in a Duncanesque style, with slower and more fluid movements that spread seamlessly throughout adjacent body parts as each action evolves seamlessly into the next.[8]

The female dancing body in *Under the Law of Change* delivers a set of performances and practices through which a variety of cultural issues such as race, ethnicity, gender, self, art, physical culture, and Norwegian national culture are negotiated. The dances are very different from the erotic display in *The Demon*, or the Norwegian folk dances so important at this point in Norwegian history and culture—as they would be in later Norwegian films during the so-called national breakthrough in the early 1920s.[9] The dances in *Under the Law of Change* represent either the latest dance types, as in the Duncanesque Chopin dance, or exotic and ancient dances, like the cakewalk and the Egyptian dance.

Dance historians Ann Daly and Mary Simonson see the dancing body as a "meeting ground" or "a point of encounter," where different discourses are played out.[10] According to Daly, dancing in this period is "a potent barometer of cultural transition."[11] The dances in *Under the Law of Change* represent different meeting points between tradition and modernity, and between Norway, the continent, and the United States. Being very different from Norwegian traditions, all the dances represent something new, foreign, modern, energetic, and exciting. The dancing body in this film is not only a female spectacle, put on display for the audience in the film's narrative and for the audience in the theater, but also a young and hyperkinetic body, expressing different examples of new and modern femininity.

An article about German dancer Rita Sacchetto in the Norwegian women's magazine *Hjemmet* (*The Home*) from January 1911 points out that Sacchetto's dance is a result of hard training, and that ballet would soon be replaced by a simpler and freer dance.[12] In Halfdan Nobel Roede's film, movement, physical culture, and femininity are reimagined through three dances that represent different modern free-dance styles and models of body movement. The dances explore aspects of the dancing body as well as femininity that are linked very loosely to the main narrative of the film, but to the display of the female body they add a discourse of becoming modern in the newly independent Norway.

Boxing, Masculinity, and Class

When Norwegian filmmakers resumed film production in 1917 after a three-year fiction-film hiatus, it seems that the male body was more important than the female body. In several films we see the male body in motion, but there are no female dance scenes. Although the chase and boxing scenes in the Norwegian films of the late 1910s are more integrated in the narrative than the dances in the films by Gundersen and Nobel Roede are, they are still special attractions that stop, freeze, or halt the narrative.

One example is Peter Lykke-Seest's *The Story of a Boy* (*Historien om en gut*, 1919). The main character is young Esben, who is falsely accused of stealing a wristwatch at school. When his parents do not believe he is innocent, Esben decides to run away from home. He takes on different jobs, but is threatened by a group of thieves who want him to join their gang. Instead of helping the band of criminals, Esben runs away once more, and the film ends in a long sequence in which he is chased by the thieves, who are chased by a policeman and some scouts. The chase scene is not only the high point of the action-filled story but also a way of displaying a number of male bodies in motion, overcoming different obstacles. The chase ends in a fight where the scouts help out, suggesting that their physical education in nature makes them better men than big-city thieves. This long sequence explores masculinity through the moving male body taking on different natural obstacles or fighting.

The exploration of masculinity through the male body in motion is even more central in Ottar Gladtvet's *The Daughter of the Revolution* (*Revolutionens*

Figure 11.5. The boxing match in *The Daughter of the Revolution*.

datter, 1918). In this film, Claire, the daughter of a rich factory owner, meets Albert, a metalworker. He saves her from a mob during a revolution, and, dressed as a boy, she crosses the border into a neighboring country with his help. Claire lives as a guest in the house of the upper-class Dalton, who is actually on the edge of bankruptcy. His son, Jack, woos Claire, though he does not love her. He is only interested in her money, which he needs in order to save both himself and his father from poverty. Jack wants Albert out of the picture, so he stages a boxing match against him at the Olympia Club. The winner will get Claire's hand in marriage. After four rounds of boxing, and considerable time, Albert knocks out his rival. In an epilogue, five years later, we see Albert teaching his and Claire's son how to box and become a real man.

Even though the boxing match in *The Daughter of the Revolution* is integrated in the narrative in a slightly different way than the dances in *The Demon* and *Under the Law of Change*, in that it actually has consequences for the ending of the story, this sequence is still like a film within the film. The match is eight minutes long, nearly a fifth of the forty-four-minute-long film. It shows off the male body, exposing the two fighters' bare chests and legs, and negotiates aspects of class and masculinity. The match is not only an attraction in itself, showing off the men's exposed bodies in motion. Although they are stripped of their outer class symbols of clothes and manners, their fight is clearly a metaphor for the class struggles that the film's narrative thematizes.

The working-class metalworker, Albert, has a rougher and less graceful boxing style, often crouching and evading the punches of the more elegant, upper-class pugilist, Jack. His body is also darker, having been exposed to sunlight and weather at work in a shipyard, than that of his paler, upper-class rival. The two men embody the two classes that fight for power in society at large, and even though the workers are negatively portrayed during the chaos of the revolution, in the end it is the working-class Albert who wins Claire. Albert is like a modern fairy-tale figure, an "Askeladd," a trickster from Norwegian folklore who wins the princess and the kingdom through hypermasculine bodily performance. The epilogue with his son underlines that the fight is all about manliness and defining it through bodily display.

Overall, the exploration of the male body in motion in the films by Peter Lykke-Seest and Ottar Gladtvet in the second half of the 1910s is more complex than the dance scenes in the Norwegian films from the first half. However, the chase, fistfight, and boxing scenes also represent different meeting points between tradition and modernity, expressing different examples of masculinity on display for the audience.

Performances of Self

Dance scholars have pointed out that modern dance in the early twentieth century presents not a performed character but rather performances of the self.[13] The dancing body participates in the production of cultural identity. The same is true in the case of boxing, as scholars Dan Streible and Lee Grieveson have shown.[14] The filmic representation of bodies in motion served as an imaginary or fantasy space onto which both female and male audience members could project their desires but also their own reimaginations of body and self.

Dancing and boxing in Norwegian cinema in the 1910s can be seen as two different ways of transmitting and discussing different ideas about bodies, movement, physical culture, masculinity, femininity, modernity, and class. The change from female dancing to male boxing probably has a number of causes: first, the shift from Danish erotic melodramas to American films as the model for domestic film production; second, the change of attitude toward narrativity and a tighter integration of attractions and spectacles. Both of these are important for understanding the refocusing from female dancing to male boxing, chases, or fistfights. The First World War and the Russian Revolution, the last echoed in the narrative in *The Daughter of the Revolution*, may also have been an additional cause of the change from focusing on the female to the male body.

In the Norwegian cinema of the 1910s, dancing and boxing can be seen as points of encounter where different discourses and performances of self and attitudes to the body are played out. The different dances in the films from the early

Figure 11.6. Dance scene from *The Demon*.

1910s, and especially the long boxing sequence in *The Daughter of the Revolution*, can be seen as a meeting ground where new international discourses of body culture meet older Norwegian body discourses in order to produce and negotiate cultural identity.

The dance styles of Isadora Duncan, Ruth St. Denis, and Rita Sacchetto were new to Norway in these years and were regarded as innovative, exciting, and liberating for women dancers. The same goes for boxing. The first boxing club in Norway started in Kristiania in 1909, but the activity was prohibited between 1910 and 1911, so even by the end of the 1910s it was new and contested. When the ban was lifted, however, national boxing championships were arranged with little opposition. The different dances in the films by Gundersen and Nobel Roede, as well as the boxing in Gladtvet's film, represent meeting points between Norway and the continent, tradition and modernity, where cultural identities were performed. Bodies in motion became an important way of discussing and performing modernity on- and offscreen during these years.

In the 1920s, there are no boxing scenes in Norwegian films, and the traditional folk dances that appear in some of the rural melodramas work in a very different way than the exotic, modern, and foreign dances of *The Demon* and *Under the Law of Change*. Bodies in motion are also no longer highlighted; instead, they are seamlessly integrated into well-tempered narratives. Dance and boxing in the Norwegian cinema of the 1910s highlighted bodily presence, but they also explored modernity and helped audiences navigate social and cultural transitions and transformations in a very different way than the later films of the 1920s did.

In early Norwegian cinema, bodies in motion were important, as attractions and as corporeal and kinesthetic models, in that they demonstrated how to move and behave in the modern world. Dancing and boxing became a window onto another, more modern realm of masculinity and femininity. The moving bodies became performances of the self, mapping out new possibilities and cultural identities in a newly independent country that was trying to navigate between tradition and modernity.

GUNNAR IVERSEN is Professor in Film Studies at Carleton University in Ottawa and former Professor of Film Studies at NTNU in Norway. He has published books and essays on Norwegian film history, documentary and factual television, and sound studies.

Notes

1. Gunnar Iversen, "The Norwegian Municipal Cinema System and the Development of a National Cinema," in *Early Cinema and the "National,"* ed. Richard Abel, Giorgio Bertellini, and Rob King (London: John Libbey, 2009), 195–98.
2. Gunnar Iversen, "Cutting Bordello Scenes and Dances: Local Regulation and Film Censorship in Norway before 1913," *Film History* 17, no. 1 (2005): 106–12.
3. Brooke Baldwin, "The Cakewalk: A Study in Stereotype and Reality," *Journal of Social History* 15, no. 2 (1981): 208–14; Mary Simonson, *Body Knowledge: Performance, Intermediality, and American Entertainment at the Turn of the Twentieth Century* (Oxford, UK: Oxford University Press, 2013), 39; Megan Pugh, *America Dancing: From the Cake Walk to the Moon Walk* (New Haven, CT: Yale University Press, 2015), 10–28.
4. Baldwin, *The Cakewalk*, 212.
5. Pugh, *America Dancing*, 23.
6. Karl Toepfer, *Empire of Ecstasy: Nudity and Movement in German Body Culture, 1910–1935* (Berkeley: University of California Press, 1997), 175; Ann Daly, *Done into Dance: Isadora Duncan in America* (Middletown, CT: Wesleyan University Press, 1995), 103, 105.
7. Daly, *Done into Dance*, 66–67, 150.
8. Ibid., 35.
9. Gunnar Iversen, *Norsk filmhistorie: Spillefilmen 1911–2011* (Oslo: Universitetsforlaget, 2011), 35–69.
10. Daly, *Done into Dance*, 4; Simonson, *Body Knowledge*, 4.
11. Daly, *Done into Dance*, 5.

12. "Rita Sacchetto," *Hjemmet*, January 29, 1911, 66.

13. Emma Doran, "Figuring Modern Dance within Fin-de-Siècle Visual Culture and Print: The Case of Loïe Fuller," *Early Popular Visual Culture* 13, no. 1 (2015): 31; Daly, *Done into Dance*, 68.

14. Dan Streible, *Fight Pictures: A History of Boxing and Early Cinema* (Berkeley: University of California Press, 2008); Lee Grieveson, "Fighting Films: Race, Morality, and the Governing of Cinema, 1912–1915," *Cinema Journal* 38, no. 1 (1998): 40–72; Lee Grieveson, *Policing Cinema: Movies and Censorship in Early Twentieth-Century America* (Berkeley: University of California Press, 2004).

12 The Beauty of the *Forzuti*
Irresistible Male Bodies On- and Offscreen

Ivo Blom

In the 1910s the international film audience was set alight by a new phenomenon: the *forzuto* or cinematic Italian strongman. At the end of the Victorian age, men started stripping off their three-piece suits and tails to reveal perfect bodies. Cinema audiences loved it. Where did this male exposure come from and how was it displayed? The Italian film journal *La Vita Cinematografica* praised actor Mario Guaita, aka Ausonia, for "the plastic beauty of his appearance, the attraction and at the same time the power and swiftness of his perfect body, his penetrating glance, and his perfect acting,"[1] in his role as a Roman gladiator in the epic film *Spartaco* (Enrico Maria Vidali, Pasquali 1913). Shot in late 1913, *Spartaco* was first released in Rome in February 1914, along with intense publicity. Ausonia accompanied the film's first nights abroad in places like Vienna and Budapest, where he would flex his muscles in public, "causing a new, strange sensation among the spectators," as one Hungarian daily stated.[2]

When researching Italian and foreign films starring Italian strongmen, I was struck by how innovative they were in *displaying male flesh* in an era when the male nude was hardly seen in fiction films. Released a year before *Spartaco*, Bruto Castellani's Ursus, in the epic blockbuster *Quo vadis?* (Enrico Guazzoni, Cines 1913), was still prudently dressed in a tunic. Yet in *Spartaco* the camera often focuses on Ausonia's naked torso, muscular arms, and stern look. His body is that of an athlete and bodybuilder, quite unlike another *forzuto*, Bartolomeo Pagano (Maciste), whose massive body and bull's neck were both products of hard labor on the docks of Genoa.[3] *Spartaco* was arguably the first Italian feature to display Ausonia's type of male physique, and cinema proved to be an excellent medium for sculpting it with light. The new medium also called on a rich tradition of displaying the male physique on stage, particularly in *poses plastiques*, which Ausonia himself had performed. He would go on to refer to the male display in both his theatrical career and his subsequent epic and adventure films. Ausonia's film career illustrates well the embodiment of the male in silent cinema, its *transmedial* pedigrees, and how it served as a basis for future *intramedial* references.[4] Finally, in this context of cinema and popular culture, antiquity served as an important pretext for displaying the male body.

In art and popular culture, male nudity or seminudity had become quite common around the turn of the century. It was visible in the bare chests and legs of the gladiators in Jean-Léon Gérôme's epic painting *Pollice verso* (1872, Phoenix Art Museum), or the full nudes in the allegoric paintings made for unions and cooperatives, such as Alfonso Quarantelli's fresco *La marcia dei lavoratori*, part of the triptych *Il lavoro redento* (1898), at the Sala della Mutua Ferrovieri in Milan. Male nudity was also represented in Belle Époque poster design, such as Marcello Dudovich's famous poster, *Fisso l'idea. Inchiostro per scrivere. Federazione italiano chimico-industriale* (1899), and Leopoldo Metlicovitz's poster for the *Mostra del Ciclo e del Automobile* (1905). The clothed Ursus in the film *Quo vadis?* contrasts with the character's *pictorial* imagining from Henryk Sienkiewicz's classic epic novel, for example, and on postcards from around 1900 that depict Ursus in the arena in *Quo vadis?* as painted by Jan Styka and Piotr Stachiewicz. While Stachiewicz's Ursus still wears a loincloth that accentuates his buttocks, Styka's Ursus is shown stark naked. Both are seen from the back, denying the spectator their faces but accentuating their physique.

Postcards of male nude sculptures were also common, as were photographs and postcards of professional wrestlers such as Giovanni Raicevich (1881–1957) and George Hackenschmidt (1877–1968), and early bodybuilders such as Eugen Sandow (1867–1925). The latter were amply displayed in the new physical-culture magazines such as *La Culture Physique*, founded in 1904 by the then-famous physical-culture teacher Edmond Desbonnet (1867–1953).[5] As Tamar Garb indicated in *Bodies of Modernity*, "It was the newest of pictorial media, photography, which became an important vehicle through which modern endeavours could establish their links with an ancient and noble past. The modern body-building or 'physical culture' movement as it was then called, depended on photography for its publicity and for propagating an image of ideal masculinity based on ancient prototypes."[6] Thus, people were regularly confronted with the male nude or seminude, though rarely in fictional cinema—that is, until Ausonia and Maciste came along around 1913–1914.[7]

To date, the literature has focused on Maciste's innovative type and the attention to his body.[8] Bartolomeo Pagano's character, Maciste, originated as the *black* (African) helper of the Roman hero in Giovanni Pastrone's antiquity film, *Cabiria* (1914). After the film's enormous success, Maciste was launched as a modern *white* hero in various Italian and a few German action and adventure films of the 1910s and 1920s. The first of these films, *Maciste* (Vincenzo Denizot, 1915), begins in a cinema auditorium where *Cabiria* is being screened. After the film title, the name "Maciste" appears, foregrounding his character. Then we see, first on the auditorium screen and then as two separate shots without the auditorium framing, Maciste bending the iron bars to free his Roman buddy and himself from prison. The female lead in *Maciste*, helpless and harassed by evil

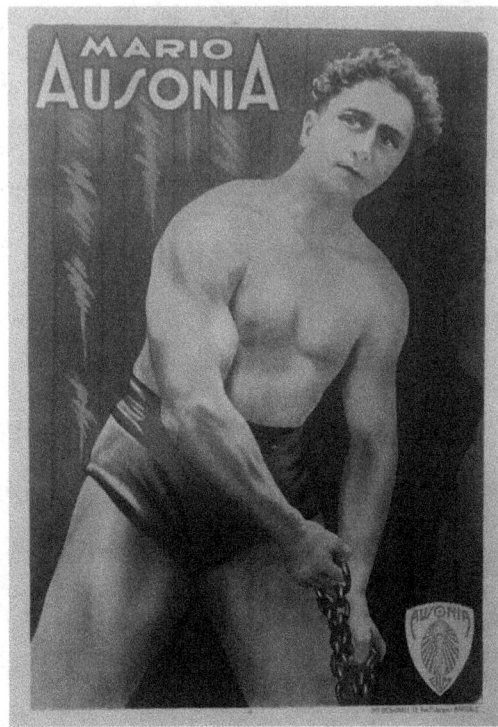

Figure 12.1. Mario Ausonia, Ausonia Film. Undated poster. Courtesy of David Chapman.

men, watches the film, and Maciste's escape convinces her that he is the guy to help her out. The spectators in front of her, clearly stand-ins for us viewers, nod to convey their enjoyment of Maciste's act. Afterward, we see Maciste training at the Itala film studio, doing his daily exercise of lifting weights and flexing his muscles between shootings.

Months before *Cabiria*'s release, a similar bar-bending moment had already appeared in a key scene in *Spartaco*. When Spartacus is unjustly imprisoned, falsely accused of murdering Crassus, he hears a voice nearby that turns out to belong to his sister (Cristina Ruspoli). She is also imprisoned, but for overhearing the real culprits discussing the conspiracy. Desperate to free her, Spartaco rips off his tunic, showing his massive arms and bare back. Like a strongman from the circus, he bends the iron bars one by one with all his might. While most of the film is framed in a long shot, *this* scene is a medium shot, allowing us to get a closer look at him flexing his muscles. This bar-bending feat, which allowed him to strip and show muscle, was so successful that Ausonia repeated it in his subsequent epic, *Salambò* (Domenico Gaido, 1914), released in 1915 and based on Flaubert's novel. Antiquity gave the camera an opportunity for showing beefcake.

Playing the gladiator in *Spartaco* was a natural follow-up to Ausonia's previous career striking artistic poses on stage, the so-called *poses plastiques*, with the Trio Ausonia, the "Gladiators of the Twentieth Century." In Ausonia's diaspora film *Dans les mansardes de Paris* (Mario Guaita/Ausonia, 1924),[9] he plays a young Parisian who drops out of medical school to seek fame and fortune, first in the circus and then through *poses plastiques*, clearly mimicking Myron's *discobolos* and Leone Leoni's statue of *Emperor Charles V as Virtus Subduing Fury*. This trajectory parallels Ausonia's real-life story.[10] Mario Guaita (1881–1956) was a member of a well-to-do Milanese family. His father, Raimondo Guaita, was a respected surgeon and podiatrist who specialized in treating children. Guaita refused to follow in his father's footsteps, so he left his medical studies and dedicated himself to athletics and vaudeville. He began his stage career as a solo performer and then later formed the Trio Ausonia, which mimicked Roman gladiators by showing off their physique. While Garb writes, "Reproductions of ancient sculptures and modern men could be happily juxtaposed in the two-dimensional world of the photographic print, thereby setting up analogies and invoking comparisons between ancient and modern that were perfectly sustainable in the photographic medium,"[11] on stage they chose a synthetic alternative to this juxtaposition, showing modern and ancient in one single image. From the start of the nineteenth century, *poses plastiques* were staged in theaters where men and women imitated classical statues, either Greek and Roman originals or famous neoclassicist ones, or at least created visions of classic mythology with well-formed bodies, poses, draperies, and settings. These images echoed bourgeois taste and its craving for a tasteful naturalism.

Poses plastiques were different from *tableaux vivants* in that they did not need to explicitly refer to any pictorial or sculptural model; they merely suggested artistic or classical connotations and focused more on the mobility/immobility effect. Contrary to popular belief, it is less about a difference between sculpture versus painting than it is between nonreferential and referential to an artwork.[12] Moreover, it is not a simple question of either/or; there are examples in which both terms are applicable.[13] Indeed, the references to Myron and Leoni in *Dans les mansardes de Paris* could be called both *poses plastiques* and *tableaux vivants*. The sources are not mentioned in the intertitles, but the audience in the film clearly recognizes and appreciates the citations, suggesting that the spectators watching this film share a frame of reference.[14] A remarkable detail is that the references to Myron and Leoni in *Dans les mansardes de Paris* were reproduced exactly on stage by 3 Olympier, competitors of Trio Ausonia, as we can see from postcards.[15] *Poses plastiques* had been popular throughout the nineteenth century and continued to be in the early twentieth century.[16]

Tableaux vivants and *poses plastiques* were much appreciated around 1900 and well into the 1910s as an antidote to hectic life in the modern city and to the grotesque acts on display in vaudeville houses.[17] This was due to their setting; an almost complete absence of motion, the dark auditorium, and spectacular lighting effects were important for making the *tableaux vivants* into a stunning attraction while at the same time creating a mood of contemplation, similar to looking at a painting or sculpture in a museum. For the *poses plastiques*, white powder would sometimes be used as a kind of body paint to make the human bodies look as marble-like and statuesque as possible.[18] Curtains were usually lifted for every tableau, and programs were often very explicit about which artworks and which artists had been used. The *tableaux vivants* and *poses plastiques* were crowd pullers because they showed seminude figures on stage (bare-chested men and bare-legged women in tight-fitting tricots that suggested nudity, and from around 1903 even completely in the nude). Surely eroticism was involved, though movement was prohibited during the show, thus presenting the nude on par with nineteenth-century academic painting: situating the nude in antiquity or mythology and frozen in motion. While some called it art reduced to pornography, others cherished it as art for the middle classes, as Nicole Anae has written. Furthermore, she notes, "As a stage tableau with its own 'exclusive, imagistic language of performance,' the *poses plastiques* style offers itself as a predecessor of the so-called 'physical' theatre of today, which embraces mime, acrobatics and other circus skills, mask, commedia and visual theatre."[19] We could surely add silent film as well.

As mentioned before, with Trio Ausonia, Mario Guaita was successful not only in Italy but all over Europe as well.[20] The oldest sources on Trio Ausonia date from December 1907, when the trio performed at the Casino de Paris,[21] and they went on to perform frequently in France, with shows in May 1908 in Paris and in both 1908 and 1909 in Lyon. A critic in Lyon wrote, "The Trio Ausonia deserves special mention for their superb poses plastiques, which complement their strength exercises and draw the attention of all."[22] The trio mixed poses with physical exercise on the stage. They toured Europe between 1907 and 1914, and the United States in 1913–1914 as well, based on ads from the time.[23] In 1908 the French magazine *La Culture Physique*, one of the oldest physique magazines, published a short text on the Trio along with a photo.[24] While the text mentions athletes and exercises but not explicitly *poses plastiques*, the photo does show them in furs and Roman sandals, with gladiator helmets visible behind them.[25] After a break during the First World War, which may have had to do with Guaita's sparse film acting in 1917–1918 or military service, Trio Ausonia began performing again in 1919. Ausonia's action and crime films for the new company De Giglio Film, such as *Atlas* (Mario Guaita-Ausonia, 1920), were shown simultaneously in the cinemas from 1919 to 1920, while the gladiator trio performed five

Figure 12.2. Trio Ausonia. Undated French postcard. Collection Ivo Blom.

times for one to two weeks at the Turin variety theater, Maffei, and returned there occasionally until 1924.[26] In the years 1922–1924, the Trio Ausonia performed again in Paris and also in Algiers,[27] as Guaita had also become a film star in the meantime. By then, Guaita started passing his prime and moved from Italy to Marseille, where he made a few modest but still interesting films with Gina Relly and Léon Mathot for Lauréa Films.[28] In this context it is also challenging to connect Ausonia's French film *Mes p'tits* (Paul Barlatier, Charles Keppens, 1923), set in the world of the wandering circus and fairground, with the gradual downfall in his professional career. In 1927, Guaita still performed solo as a strongman at the Apollo theater in Paris. Even in 1930, Ausonia returned on his own to Algeria to perform as a music-hall strongman in the anteprogram of film projections in Oran and Algiers.[29]

Two important and partly converging elements shaped the framework of the *forzuto*: fairgrounds and sports. The strong men, called *les Hercules* in France, were a regular feature at the fairgrounds. *Mes p'tits* explicitly works this into its plot.

Ausonia plays a widowed circus athlete who loses his job after the circus director dies and his wife sells off the circus. He starts performing as a strongman at the fairgrounds but is falsely accused of murder and loses his children. Surviving as a wandering strongman and working odd jobs, one as a stevedore (reminiscent of Pagano's original job), for example, he keeps searching for his children. While both on- and offscreen, fairground strongmen were often depicted as bad guys and antagonists who mistreated women, in films like *Mes p'tits* strongmen are the heroes.[30]

After *Salambò*, Guaita made a variety of rather undistinguished films. He relaunched himself as an action hero with the film *L'atleta fantasma* (Raimondo Scotti, 1919), about a masked hero who, just like Don Diego or Bruce Wayne, leads a double life as a milquetoast to avoid attracting attention. At the beginning of *L'atleta*, Guaita makes a visible connection with his epic films but also with his earlier career in Trio Ausonia, as if they were his artistic pedigree. We first see Ausonia pose in antique attire, leaning on a column, reminding us of his previous feats on and off the screen. The image transforms into Ausonia dressed as gentleman in tails. Finally, we see him wearing the knitted hood over his "frac," changing him into the "phantom athlete" from the film's title. The *pose plastique* motif returns when a reproduction of the statue of the famous Dying Gaul or Dying Gladiator is at risk of being stolen. The statue is clearly a *pose plastique*, pretending to be marble, and woven into the plot as a real statue. Ausonia prevents the theft by imitating the statue, covered in white powder and a white wig, and coming to life Pygmalion-like when the thieves try to steal it.[31] He imitates the extra who poses as a real statue, which is itself a reproduction of a classical original, highlighting the layers of intermediality.

We can conclude that the antiquity films such as *Spartaco* and Ausonia's later action and adventure films consciously play with displaying the male body, building on traditions outside the cinema, either more generally in art and popular culture, or in Ausonia's case, his own *poses plastiques*. In this he rivaled Maciste, despite their different backgrounds and different typologies. In the 1920s the *forzuti* Carlo Aldini and Luciano Albertini would go even further by posing almost fully nude for photographs, which were reproduced on postcards. Full frontal nudity was not permitted, so they were shot from the side, with the occasional fig leaf. Like Ausonia's, Aldini and Albertini's films would often start with reminders of their perfect bodies, after which they would be seen well dressed. But audiences would still remember what was under those fashionable outfits. Again, antiquity enabled the showing of beefcake.[32]

IVO BLOM is Assistant Professor of Comparative Arts and Media Studies at Vrije Universiteit, Amsterdam. He is author of *Jean Desmet and the Early Dutch Film Trade*, and in 2015 he organized the retrospective "Italian Muscle in Germany" at the Giornate del Cinema Muto, Pordenone.

Notes

1. Eliseo Demitry, *La Vita Cinematografica*, Turin, February 14, 1914, cited in Aldo Bernardini and Vittorio Martinelli, *Il cinema muto italiano. I film degli anni d'oro: 1913*, vol. 2 (Roma: Centro Sperimentale della Cinematografia/Nuova ERI, 1994), 262.
2. Ibid., 264.
3. Ivo Blom, "Spartaco ovvero Il gladiatore della Tracia," *Il Cinema Ritrovato XXVII edizione*, Bologna 26 giugno–6 luglio 2013 (Bologna: Cineteca di Bologna, 2013), 39.
4. Jens Schröter, "Discourses and Models of Intermediality," *CLCWeb: Comparative Literature and Culture* 13, no. 3 (2011).
5. On Raicevich, see Arnaldo Ferraguti, "Il più forte," *Il Secolo XX* 7, no. 4 (April 1908): 282–92. See also George Hackenschmidt, *The Way to Live in Health and Physical Fitness* (1908; repr. O'Faolain Patriot LCC, 2011), and David L. Chapman, *Sandow the Magnificent: Eugen Sandow and the Beginnings of Bodybuilding* (Champaign: University of Illinois Press, 2006). Chapman also writes about Desbonnet and *La Culture Physique*.
6. Tamar Garb, *Bodies of Modernity: Figure and Flesh in Fin-de-Siëcle France* (London: Thames and Hudson, 1998), 55.
7. Occasionally, the male (semi-)nude was visible in early nonfiction. For the Sandow kinetoscope and mutoscope films, see Elaine Mancini, "Ricerche americane: Maciste manca ma pornografia c'è," in *Gli uomini forti*, ed. Alberto Farassino and Tatti Sanguineti (Milano: Mazzotta, 1983), 75. Other nonfiction displays can be found in early filmed boxing matches, such as Messter's "living sculpture" films of 1903 and Pathé's films of athletes exercising at the military school at Joinville (ca. 1911).
8. Jacqueline Reich, *The Maciste Films of Italian Silent Cinema* (Bloomington: Indiana University Press, 2015); Monica Dall'Asta, *Un cinema musclé* (Crisnée, Belgium: Editions Yellow Now, 1992). See also Monica Dall'Asta, "Les extraordinaires aventures de Maciste autour du monde," in *Les racines populaires de la culture européenne*, ed. Stéphanie Delneste et al. (Brussels: Peter Lang, 2014), 139–58.
9. Vittorio Martinelli and Mario Quargnolo, *Maciste & Co. I giganti buoni del muto italiano* (Gemona, Italy: Cinepopolare, 1981), 38; Micaela Veronesi, "Molta fantasia per un unico uomo. Le sceneggiature avventurose di Renée Deliot," *Bianco e nero* 2 (May–August 2011): 83–91.
10. Martinelli and Quargnolo, *Maciste & Co.*, 37. See also Martinelli's biography of Ausonia in Farassino and Sanguineti, *Gli uomini forti*, 15.
11. Garb, *Bodies of Modernity*, 55.
12. Valentine Robert, *L'origine picturale du cinéma. Le tableau vivant, une esthétique du film des premiers temps* (Lausanne: University of Lausanne, 2016), 49–55.
13. Ibid., 49–55, 74–75. *Tableau vivant* was not limited to the stage, as it continued in the new medium of cinema, too easily forgotten in contemporary research (ibid., 74–75).
14. Schröter, "Discourses and Models of Intermediality," stresses how important this recognition is for transmedial intermediality.
15. Around 1906–1913 they were popular, though the *Echo d'Alger* still mentions them performing in the Casino Music-Hall as late as 1931. A picture of the *pose plastique* drawn from Leone as published in *Das Programm* in 1905 was republished in Daniel Wiegand, "Früher Film, Tableaux Vivants, und die 'Attraktion des Schönen,'" in *Film Bild Kunst: Visuelle Ästhetik des vorklassischen Stummfilms*, ed. Jörg Schweinitz and Daniel Wiegand (Marburg, Germany: Schüren, 2016), 95.

16. Nicole Anae, "Poses Plastiques: The Art and Style of 'Statuary' in Victorian Visual Theatre," *Australasian Drama Studies* 52 (April 2008): 112–30, particularly 122–23 for the terminology. Anae focuses on performances by women instead of by men.

17. Wiegand, "Früher Film, Tableaux Vivants," 93–102.

18. Exceptionally, the 3 Olimpier used green to imitate bronze.

19. Anae, "Poses Plastiques," 126.

20. Martinelli and Quargnolo, *Maciste & Co.*, 37; Michele Giordano, *Giganti buoni. Da Ercole a Piedone (e oltre) il mito dell'uomo forte nel cinema italiano* (Roma: Gremese, 1998), 17–18.

21. Earlier Italian examples may exist, but the online version of the Turin daily *La Stampa* does not mention the Trio Ausonia before 1915.

22. For the December 1907 show at the Casino de Paris, see *Gil Blas*, December 18, 1907; *Le Figaro*, December 18, 22, and 27, 1907; *Le Journal*, December 18, 1907; *L'Humanité*, December 18, 1907; *L'Orchestre*, January 2, 3, 5, 6, 7, 8, and 9, 1908. For the May 1908 show at the Théâtre des Ambassadeurs in Paris, see *Comoedia*, May 24, 26, 27, 28, and 29, 1908. For the July 1909 show in Lyon, see Alègre, "Lettres de province: Lyon," *L'art dramatique et musical*, July 1, 1909, 18.

23. For the Fövarosi Orpheum show in Budapest, see *Das Programm. Artistisches Fachblatt*, March 6, 1910. In *Das Programm. Artistisches Fachblatt*, 1913, page 581, an ad for Trio Ausonia states that the trio was doing a successful tour in North America and was fully engaged until April 1914.

24. "Notre Galerie Athlétique. Trio Ausonia," *La Culture Physique*, October 1, 1908, 1386.

25. For the connotation of *poses plastiques* with Roman gladiators, see also a picture of Luciano Albertini's early vaudeville group, Les Albertini, showing the men as gladiators. Mario Quargnolo, *Luciano Albertini, un divo degli anni 'venti* (Udine, Italy: CSU, 1977), 20. The theme of the gladiator fight between *mirmillo* and *retiarius*, popularized by Gérôme's painting *Pollice Verso* and its manifold reproductions, was published by *La Culture Physique*. Georges Dubois, "L'escrime dans l'Antiquité," *La Culture Physique*, January 15, 1908, 826–28.

26. This was in January, April, and August 1919 and May and September 1920. See the online version of *La Stampa*. Sometimes these performances coincided with projections of Ausonia's films, which in the early 1920s in Turin were always at the Cinema Teatro Vittoria.

27. For the show at the Casino Music-Hall in Algiers of November 1922, see *L'Echo d'Alger*, November 26, 1922, and *Annales africaines*, November 23, 1922. For the one at Olympia in Paris in July 1923, see *Comoedia*, July 24, 26, and 28, 1923 and *Le Journal*, July 20, 1923. For the show at Olympia in May-June 1924, see *Comoedia*, May 24 and 29, and June 11, 1924, and *Le Journal*, May 24, 1924.

28. These were distributed by Méric, a French distribution company specializing in strongmen films. In 1926 Guaita made his last film: *La donna carnefice nel paese dell'oro*.

29. *Le Petit Parisien*, December 16, 1927; *Le Journal*, December 14, 1927. *Les Spectacles d'Alger*, November 3, 1930; *Oran Spectacles*, February 15, 1930; *L'Echo sportif de l'Oranie*, February 14, 1930. In Oran, he preceded the film *Minuit ... Place Pigalle*. After his last film production, Guaita settled for good in Marseille. He opened up a small cinema at the Pointe Rouge, which he ran until 1947.

30. Another version of physical exercise that became popular in the nineteenth century was gymnastics. See Simon Martin, *Sport Italia: The Italian Love Affair with Sport* (London: Tauris, 2011), 11–52. The army, schools, and the state all believed gymnastics had value,

leading to the founding of gymnastic schools and societies, military athletic schools, and physical-culture clubs. Several of the Italian *forzuti* had roots here. Luciano Albertini's claims to have trained at gymnastic associations in Forlí and Bologna and at the Lyon-based physical-culture club École de Pechin are unconfirmed, but proof exists that Carlo Aldini was at one time a member of the still-existing Bologna sports club Virtus.

31. For the Pygmalion motif in early cinema, see Ivo Blom, "Of Artists and Models: Italian Silent Cinema between Narrative Convention and Artistic Practice," in *The Cinema of Sensations*, ed. Ágnes Pethő (Cambridge, UK: Cambridge Scholars, 2015), 121-36.

32. This shows in particular in Aldini's Achilles in *Helena* (Manfred Noa, 1924). See my general text and entries in the catalog of the Giornate del Cinema Muto 2015 (Pordenone 2015), 79–90.

13 Nudity in Early Cinema; or, the Pictorial Transgression

Valentine Robert

LET ME BEGIN with a song, written by Joseph Flynn in 1894 and titled "*McGinty at the Living Pictures*":[1]

> Dan McGinty went to the opera show with his old wife Mary Ann,
> And took a front seat in the middle aisle amongst the bald-headed clan;
> But he wasn't prepared for the sights he saw and he laughed with might and main
> When the living pictures came to view, why he nearly went insane.
>
> When he saw the Sleeping Beauty, why he got such a shock
> You could hear his heart ticking like an eight-day clock.
> Then he danced and he pranced,
> and said he, "I've been to France,
> But that's the finest sight I ever saw;"
>
> Then his eyes bulged out, he began to shout;
> The gallery boys hollered, "Put that Zulu out."
> Then his wife grabbed his feet,
> pulled him under the seat.
> So he couldn't gaze upon the living pictures.
>
> When the girl who posed as Venus, with her form so grand,
> You could hear McGinty holler a way above the band.
> Then said he, "Mary Ann,
> you will lose your old man
> If you don't be quick and take me out entirely."[2]

Luke McKernan, on his remarkable blog thebioscope.net, first thought that this song was about McGinty's discovery of early cinema, telling us "how excited some

---

My warmest thanks go to Louis Pelletier, whose linguistic corrections and scientific discussions invaluably contributed to this article.

could be at what they saw on the screen."³ But McKernan later corrected in brackets: "This song refers to tableaux vivants, not motion pictures."⁴ Indeed, instead of *moving pictures*, this song is about proper *living pictures, tableaux vivants*—that is, theatrical imitations of works of art that very often involved nude figures, as shown in our illustrations of Venus living pictures (figure 13.2 below), surely similar to the one that made McGinty holler! But as I will argue here, and as these photographs, which in reality are *cinematic frames*, reveal, Luke McKernan was not really mistaken in connecting these lyrics with early cinema. This chapter aims to show why.

Nude or Naked on Stage

Basically, this song is about discovering nakedness. McGinty, who had only seen his wife's undressed body, can suddenly ogle other women's forms. This music-hall song exaggerates this erotic shock, which drives McGinty to a grotesque form of madness. But this caricature is not groundless. One of the main reasons for the worldwide success of living pictures at the end of the nineteenth century was, indeed, the erotic power of these exhibitions of real nude bodies, mostly women, standing undressed before the viewers and the *male gaze*, the "bald-headed clan" described in the song. We can easily recognize them in illustrations of *tableaux vivants*, such as the 1848 engraving of "*The Three Graces*, as exhibited by the Model Artists of New York,"⁵ where this male gaze was even helped by binoculars and opera glasses, rather reminiscent of McGinty's eyes "bulging out." But what made these shows appropriate for the opera house (not just the bawdy house) was the "fig leaf" of respectability: their *artistic quality*, or the accuracy and perfection of these "living" copies. In the *New Yorker* illustration, the three naked girls posing on stage are imitating Antonio Canova's *Three Graces* in absolutely every detail, from hairstyle to toe position, leading us to reconsider the front-row bald-headed spectators using binoculars. Are these gazing men really *voyeurs*, eagerly ogling the naked models and their most intimate anatomy? Or are they, on the contrary, art history *connoisseurs*, testing the details of the artistic copy, in line with the nineteenth-century trend of inspecting works of art with magnifying glasses, which became as compulsive for experts such as Bernard Berenson as for the general museum visitor.⁶

One may think that this question is in bad faith. But, whether an alibi or not, the argument did exist,⁷ and the quality of the imitation of the work of art was a key issue in these performances, which were discussed in the newspapers, impacting on the longevity and the reputation of the shows. This ambivalence between lustful voyeurism and artistic contemplation was later theorized as an opposition between the words *naked* and *nude*. While other languages, like French, make no distinction (using the same word "*le nu*" for both translations), English does. Kenneth Clark has theorized this dissimilarity in the following polarization: On the one hand he links "nakedness" with "artless," obscene exhibition and illicit voyeurism. On the other, he identifies "nudity" as an artistic category that deals with ideal beauty and deserves legitimate contemplation.[8] The attraction of living pictures precisely rested on this oscillation between nakedness and nudity, on the one hand de-idealizing the painting that takes shape in the flesh, on the other hand transfiguring the actors' bodies into works of art. The fact is too often overlooked, but thanks to this nude alibi, *tableaux vivants* were *the* means by which, historically, the naked body got on stage.[9] And the same story occurred on screen: the *naked* came into view under the guise of the *nude*, shaped by pictorial codes. Motion pictures became the direct heir of living pictures.

Pathé's Saucy but Pictorial Scenes

Let us return to our illustrated living Venus, taken from an 1899 Pathé production titled *Birth of Venus* (*La naissance de Venus*) (see figure 13.2a). In the Pathé Catalogue, the film appears in a series called *scènes grivoises d'un caractère piquant*, literally meaning "saucy scenes with a hot quality." In addition to this title, a warning advises exhibitors to "exclude children from the exhibition of these pictures."[10] The tone is set. The detailed descriptions of these films then systematically refer to undressed bodies: "barely dressed"; "half dressed"; "dressed with a negligee"; "undressed"; "unclothed"; or "entirely naked."[11] The exhibition of flesh is the main selling point. Furthermore, almost all these quotations refer to *female* undressed bodies. We can then surmise that when Pathé asked exhibitors to exclude children, the implication was that mothers and maids were also to stay outside with their flock.

It is somewhat different in English. The series title is simply translated as "Scenes for Smoking Concerts" in the London catalog.[12] It could seem chaster than the "hot" and "saucy" original title, but "Smoking Concert" implies explicit conditions of reception: for men only. Then, not only children but women are also excluded, raising fascinating issues about the varying status of the female spectator of these first erotic films and shows (recall the role of McGinty's wife, for example). This terminology also reveals the filiation between these early legal and official productions and the illegal pornographic films that would soon be called "stag movies"—"stag" being a synonym of "smoking concert." Unfortunately, the summaries describing the undressed quality of these scenes are not translated in the extant English catalogs (at least the ones I had access to), preventing us from knowing if the chosen word would have been "naked" or "nude." The hesitation is justified, because these film descriptions not only praise their transgressive undressed bodies, they also advertise their artistic and cultural references.

The catalog summaries make constant reference to art, literature, mythology, and famous iconic nude figures in a lyrical literary style, with sophisticated adjectives, elaborated grammar, and a touch of poetry quelling any suspicion of vulgarity.¹³ And several surviving films of this not-for-children-list prove that the reference was visually significant. *La Naissance de Vénus* (Pathé, ca. 1899) is inspired by William Bouguereau's painted Venus; *Le Jugement de Phryné* (Pathé, ca. 1899) is arranged after the famous painting of the same title by Jean-Léon Gérôme; and *Le Réveil de Chrysis* (Pathé, ca. 1899) has much in common with Ferdinand Roybet's *Odalisque*.¹⁴ One of these 1899 nude films (a second one appeared a few years later¹⁵) is even openly described in the catalog as a "reproduction of Garnier's famous painting."¹⁶ In my research, I found many *tableaux vivants* in early cinema (particularly in historical or biblical early films).¹⁷ But my findings also suggest that catalogs seldom cited the pictorial sources of the pictures they described—*except* for films displaying naked figures. In this risqué realm, reference goes hand in hand with prudence. Framing the film as a copy of a work of art shifts the responsibility for its undressed staging to the artist, and at the same time it justifies nudity as part of an artistic tradition, far from gratuitous and reprehensible exhibitionism. Similarly, on stage, quoting the artistic sources played a significant role in the legitimizing strategy of the living pictures, which had always struggled with censorship.¹⁸

Gaumont's Secret but Perfect Engravings

It is no surprise, then, to discover that an entire series of early naked films secretly produced by Gaumont in 1907 was composed only of meticulously referenced living pictures. This series was demonstratively called "Vieilles Estampes," meaning "Old Engravings." The clandestine catalog in which they were sold reprised the titles of the "original" painting and made sure to brandish the names of their reputable creators.¹⁹ Moreover, the reference was explicit even in the screenplays of these early nude films, deposited with the Bibliothèque Nationale de France. The action of these contemplative pictures is so limited that their two-line descriptions could well hold the record for shortest screenplay ever. But this nonexistent narrative is offset by the attributions added to the titles ("after Fragonard," "after Baudoin," "after Dennel"). The entire plots of these "old engravings" are there, in the actualization of the image.

The real action is in the eye of the beholder, who recognizes these "engravings" and relishes the sight of these *half-nude, half-naked* bodies put on cinematic display. The real narrative is in the imitative staging, as shown by the exactitude of the Gaumont living picture after Dennel, which manages to keep each element and detail of the composition while adapting the image to the enlarged format of the screen. The same degree of accuracy can be seen in the embodiment of a Baudoin painting considered in all its baroque details, from furniture—even including wall molding and the drape of the curtain—to the smallest accessories such as an upside-down high-heeled shoe left in a corner. This example is all the more mesmerizing in its content. Titled *Le modèle honnête*, Baudoin's painting—reproduced down to the smallest detail and even in its title by *Le modèle honnête* (Gaumont, 1907)—depicts an artist's model crying of modesty as she poses undressed in front of a painter, hiding her face while also exhibiting her breast (in a paradoxical gesture typical of Gérôme's *Phryne*).[20] This cinematic *tableau vivant* then creates a perfect mise en abyme of the blurring of the boundary between the naked and the nude.

Biograph's Naked but Covered Pictures

This intermedial process becomes still more visually striking in the Biograph series of nude films explicitly called *living pictures*. The production catalog also precisely cites the original and "faithfully represent[ed] well-known art master-pieces [by Sarony, Landell, Delaplanche, etc.]."[21] But these films are not simply framed as paintings, as they are listed in the "vaudeville" section of the catalog and even explicitly stated to be "shown exactly as in first-class vaudeville theatres."[22] This entrenchment of references is made concrete visually (see figure 13.1).

The living pictures are not only incredibly accurate and motionless,[23] but in the illustrated example the black background even highlights the precision of the body stances and the foreground details. A giant frame is set around the scene, sealing the pictorial origin of the image. Still, a second level of intermedial interplay appears: around the frame's golden border, we can see the edge of a theatrical scene, with stagehands opening and closing the curtains. The same double device appears in most of these Biograph living pictures, "covering" the naked body with the double "protection" of the theatrical *and* pictorial reference, twice legitimizing the nude tradition, twice exonerating the film production of the undressing gesture.

These nude bodies have yet another proper cover: the Biograph models are not really naked but wearing a flesh-colored leotard. This semitransparent bodysuit, which became widespread in early American and English films to represent naked women, comes directly from theatrical living pictures. Nineteenth-century audiences discovered these props in the *tableaux vivants*. Victor Hugo described this novelty at a living-pictures show he attended for the first time in Paris in 1846. "The pink silk tights that covered [the models] from the feet to the neck were so thin and transparent that you could see not only the toes, the navel, the nipples, but also the veins and the colour of every mark on the skin in every part of the body. Toward the pelvis, however, the tights were thicker and you could make out only the shape."[24] While Hugo obviously scrutinized this leotard very closely(!), the Biograph camera remains more distant. They are, nevertheless, the same kind of tights that dressed (or should we say *undressed*) the Biograph's living-pictures models.

Figure 13.1a–b. Comparison between the original nude painting by Louis-Maurice Boutet de Monvel, *La leçon avant le sabbat*, 1880 (h/t, 165 × 132 cm, Nemours, Château-Musée, d.r.), photo © RMN-Grand Palais/Philippe Fuzeau, and its cinematic tableau vivant in *Living Pictures: "Departure for Sabaoth"* (Arthur Marvin, Biograph, 1900).

Venus in the Washroom

The comparison between Pathé's *Birth of Venus* and the Biograph version of the same subject emblematically shows the two main ways of staging the naked body in early cinema.

Most of the time, the explicitly "saucy" French productions revealed the breasts and buttocks entirely. In the 1899 film (figure 13.2a), the Pathé Venus does an ostentatious, slow spin to exhibit her naked bottom in addition to her breasts. But like most of these early French nude films, underwear conceals the model's pubis.

The traditional Anglo-Saxon way of half-veiling the body with the living-pictures leotard may appear more modest (see figure 13.2b). It may seem to echo the way in which academic painters (such as Bouguereau or Cabanel, who also bequeath *Births of Venus* to posterity) depicted a pearly, slick flesh to idealize their nude figures. Émile Zola hilariously satirized this code of "goddesses drowned in milk" and bodies made of "almond paste."[25] But it was the sculptural quality of cold, classical marble that this pictorial convention mainly sought.[26] The leotard had a similar effect, even more so on the screen, where the black-and-white image "sculpts" shadows and gives the flesh-colored tights a marblelike whiteness.[27]

However, the Pathé Venus is cast in such a powerful contrast between light and shade that (on purpose or not, we will never know)[28] the overexposed naked body is also covered with a smoothing brightness, a "veil of light" concealing and shrouding the body. The modesty of the Biograph Venus is not so obvious. First of all, the flesh-colored leotard was sometimes considered, at the time, "worse" than proper nakedness.[29] And Victor Hugo's description shows how much the

162 | *Corporeality in Early Cinema*

Figure 13.2a-b. Comparison between an almost naked Venus by the French Pathé Company in *La naissance de Vénus* (Pathé, ca. 1899, frame grab) and an almost (but differently) naked Venus by the American Biograph Company in *"Birth of the Pearl": Living Pictures* (Frederick S. Armitage, Biograph, 1901).

spectators were irresistibly led to test the actual presence of this second skin in the most intimate parts of a body far more *revealed* than *concealed*. This phenomenon is emphasized in these early films with zenith lighting, high contrast, and unsteady images, notably creating with this Biograph Venus an extremely ambiguous shadow in the pelvic area.

Moreover, the very way in which viewers encountered these Biograph living pictures must be considered, because they were primarily made for the mutoscope—that is, for private peep-show devices made for solitary viewing, with a handle and a loop structure (the come-and-go of the curtain) allowing for feverish repetition. This suggestive connection with "solitary vices," which immediately tarnished the reputation of the mutoscope,[30] reached its high point when the puritan city of Rhyl decided, in 1899, to place the mutoscopes in . . . the men's room![31] One may easily assume that in the washroom (which quickly became overcrowded and forced the mutoscope business to stop) the whole "bald-headed clan" was probably as unrestrained as McGinty.[32]

The Voyeur behind the Connoisseur

The audience is precisely the point with which I will end this chapter. For the difference between the naked and the nude is, ultimately, a pure matter of looking. And here lies the scandal, or legitimacy, of early nude films. How else could the first known example of censorship have concerned *Studio Troubles* (British Biograph, 1899)?[33] First, the woman's body is covered with a leotard. Second, the scene takes place in a painter's studio, following an early cinema tradition that provided narrative *and* aesthetic justification for the model's exhibition.[34] Last of all, the scene *is* a living picture, modeled on an academic English painting by Frank Hyde titled *The Artist's Studio*.[35] But all these legitimizing arguments collapse when confronted with the description of the McGinty-esque behavior of the viewers, especially the "youths and men who, with leering eyes and base language, supplement[ed] any vicious suggestions these pictures had already made."[36] Here, the mutoscope viewing hood seems to have been used much more like a voyeuristic device than a tool for art experts.[37]

On the contrary—and lastly—how could such a film as the 1903 Oskar Messter production *AktSkulpturen* (*Live Sculptures*) *not* have been banned? It uses iconic references with no accuracy, no leotard, and no set, and it distinctly exhibits nakedness. The totally naked and well-lit models stand on a turntable and each pose lasts for a full rotation, allowing an unrestricted, voyeuristic view of the breasts, buttocks, and pubis. The answer to this *nakedness* is *nudity*, or, in other words the artistic argument, this time directly applied to the audience. Indeed, this film was not so much a film *after* than *for* painters. The subtitle identified the production as a *Studienfilm für bildende Künstler* ("Film study for pictorial artists").[38] These early nude films' best alibi was, therefore, in the viewer's eye, and in his ability (which McGinty lacked) to hide the voyeur behind the art connoisseur.

VALENTINE ROBERT is Lecturer in Film Studies at the University of Lausanne. She is editor with Laurent Le Forestier and François Albera of *Le Film sur l'art. Entre histoire de l'art et documentaire de creation*.

Notes

1. While an original score can be found at the New York Public Library, there is an audio recording sung by Edward M. Favor (ca. 1902) at the Library of Congress on an Edison Gold Moulded Record (#1066).
2. Joseph Flynn, *McGinty at the Living Pictures* (sheet music) (New York: Spaulding and Gray, 1894).
3. Luke McKernan, "Since Mother Goes to the Movie Shows," Bioscope, May 18, 2011, https://thebioscope.net/2011/05/18/since-mother-goes-to-the-movie-shows.
4. Ibid. This correction was added after a comment by Rich Markow, bottom of the page.
5. Quotation of the title of this engraving published by James Baillie (New York City, 1848). I reproduced and commented on this illustration in Valentine Robert, "Le tableau vivant ou l'origine de l'"art' cinématographique," in *Le tableau vivant ou l'image performée*, ed. Julie Ramos (Paris: Mare and Martin/Inha, 2014), 262–82.
6. See Ernest Samuels, *Bernard Berenson: The Making of a Connoisseur* (Cambridge, MA: Harvard University Press, 1979), 95, 103, 149. This common practice was most notably commented on and satirized by Emile Zola, *Ecrits sur l'art* (Paris: Gallimard, 1991), 177–87, 363–94.
7. One of the best examples I found was a review of a *tableaux vivants* performance in Paris in 1849, where the art critic swears to have looked at "each of these pictures," with "pleasure," "regarding art only." According to him, he needed to be disturbed by the colorful reactions of his neighbors to realize that this pleasure could be erotic: "Judging by the vivid impressions they seem to be feeling, [they] were likely looking at the same pictures in a fully other perspective" (*Journal des Beaux-Arts*, April 22, 1849, 63).
8. Kenneth Clark, *The Nude, A Study in Ideal Form* (New York: Doubleday Anchor, 1954), 23ff.
9. See G[ustave]-J[oseph] Witkowsky & L[ucien] Nass, *Le Nu au Théâtre, depuis l'Antiquité jusqu'à nos jours* (Paris: Daragon, 1909), 222–23.
10. "Exclure les enfants pour l'exhibition de ces tableaux," *Pathé Catalogue* (Paris, 1900), 50.
11. "à peine vêtu, à demi vêtue, habillée d'un saut de lit, déshabillé, dévêtue, entièrement nue," *Pathé Catalogue* (Paris, 1900), 50–51.
12. *Pathé Catalogue* (London, 1903), 69.
13. *Pathé Catalogue* (Paris, 1900), 50–51.
14. For a visual confrontation of *Le Réveil de Chrysis* and Roybet's painting, see Maria Magdalena Brotons Capó, *El cine en Francia, 1895–1914: Reflejo de la cultura visual de una época* (Santander, Spain: Genueve Ediciones, 2014), 190–91.
15. See *Pathé Catalogue* (London, 1903), 70, or *Pathé Catalogue* (Paris, 1904), 97.

16. "Reproduction du célèbre tableau de Garnier, " *Pathé Catalogue* (Paris, 1900), 51.

17. See Valentine Robert, "L'origine picturale du cinéma. Le tableau vivant, une esthétique du film des premiers temps," PhD diss., University of Lausanne, 2016.

18. Among the remarkable collection of living-pictures programs that Jack W. McCullough sets up in his book *Living Pictures on the New York Stage* (Ann Arbor, MI: UMI Research Press, 1981), most quote their sources, such as the program for "Madame Warton's tableaux vivans" [sic] (pompously claimed to be "under the patronage of the Royal Academy"), which lists every original title of the works and every artist's name (43). Concerning the struggle living pictures had always waged with censorship, the best example is the Victorian one, well described by Joseph Donohue, *Fantasies of Empire: The Empire Theatre of Varieties and the Licensing Controversy of 1894* (Iowa City: University of Iowa Press, 2005).

19. This precious document was discovered by Maurice Gianati, commented on in his chapter "Alice Guy a-t-elle existé?" in *Alice Guy, Léon Gaumont et les débuts du film sonore*, ed. Maurice Gianati and Laurent Mannoni (New Barnet, UK: John Libbey, 2012), 14–15.

20. See Bernard Vouilloux, *Le tableau vivant. Phryné, l'orateur et le peintre* (Paris: Flammarion, 2002), 245–56.

21. The Biograph series of living pictures is heterogeneous (composed of various subseries made several years apart with different directors, models, sets, and modalities), and the explicit listing of the original artists occurs only for one section of the series, filmed by Arthur Marvin in August 1900. *Biograph Catalogue* (New York, 1902), 61.

22. These living-pictures films are even said, in the catalog introduction, to be the most representative of this "vaudeville" section, staged "with as great care as . . . any of the largest productions of this order"—reflecting the success and reputation of the music hall contemporary productions of *tableaux vivants*, such as Kylanyi's. *Biograph Catalogue* (New York, 1902), 54.

23. The question of the movement or stillness of these cinematic living pictures is fundamental but highly complex and cannot be treated in the limited scope of this paper. See Robert, "L'origine picturale du cinéma," 304–60; and Valentine Robert, "Filming Stillness: The Movement of Living Pictures," in *Archaeology of Movement*, ed. Benoît Turquety and Maria Tortajada (Amsterdam: Amsterdam University Press, forthcoming).

24. Victor Hugo, translated by E. H. Baltimore and A. M. Baltimore, in *The Essential Victor Hugo* (Oxford, UK: Oxford University Press, 2004), 176.

25. Zola, *Ecrits sur l'art*, 182.

26. See Alison Smith, *Exposed: The Victorian Nude* (London: Tate, 2001), 90.

27. The appearance of the flesh in early films was an immediate issue for actors and cameramen, related to film-stock sensitivity (the blue-sensitive film that dominated the production until the 1920s rendered flesh tones darker and suspiciously dirty). Makeup strategies were developed to whiten the filmed skin, and stage conventions were redesigned. See James Bennett, "Early Movie Make-up," Cosmetics and Skin, May 15, 2016, http://www.cosmeticsandskin.com/cdc/early-movie.php.

28. We can, however, be almost certain that the original copies had that much contrast. The illustration is indeed an official still photograph, and the contrast of the copies and duplicates I have seen in archives was even stronger, to the point of being almost indecipherable.

29. Dominique Bonnaud, "Enquête sur le Renouveau du Café-Concert," *La Renaissance: politique, littéraire et artistique*, February 7, 1914, 16–17.

30. Richard Brown and Barry Anthony, *A Victorian Film Enterprise: The History of the British Mutoscope and Biograph Company, 1897–1915* (Wiltshire, UK: Flicks, 1999), 223.

31. Ibid., 99–100.

32. This men's lavatory story raises again the issue of the female viewers' status. Brown and Anthony, as well as Dan Streible, showed that the exhibition of mutoscope pictures to women was condemned as of 1899 as pure indecency, and the Rhyl "male" measure was precisely meant to avoid offending any women or girls. See Dan Streible in "Children at the Mutoscope," *CINéMAS* 14, no. 1 (2003), 91–116. But, except in Rhyl (where, sarcastically, the most feverish toilet visitors seem to have been youths from twelve to fifteen years old), girls had access to these licentious attractions. Neither must one forget that the first ad for the mutoscope presented a feminine spectator. Certainly, this starlet, Anna Held, known to strip on stage and to initiate Ziegfeld Follies, held out the promise of a foxy undressed show, but she also associated the mutoscope with the woman's gaze, outside of the smoking concert.

33. Brown and Anthony, *A Victorian Film Enterprise*, 102–7.

34. See Kaveh Askari, *Making Movies into Art: Picture Craft from the Magic Lantern to Early Hollywood* (London: British Film Institute, 2014), 44–70.

35. I was put on the track of a *tableau vivant* and discovered the link with Hyde's *The Artist's Model* thanks to Tim Batchelor, who suspected that the film was "probably inspired" by another Frank Hyde painting called *The Eton Boy*. Tim Batchelor, "The Nude in Early Film," in Smith, *Exposed*, 179.

36. "The Lantern Record," *British Journal of Photography* 46, no. 2057 (October 6, 1899): 73.

37. The opposite assumption could have been made. For example, Kaveh Askari assumed that "the exhibition format [and] sustained viewing [of these looped *tableaux vivants* films] might have encouraged the same kind of gaze that art-appreciation groups sought to cultivate at the turn of the century." Askari, *Making Movies into Art*, 50. But as soon as nudity is concerned, voyeurism comes into play.

38. This excuse was also used in photography (at least on the French legal market, where nude photographs were only authorized to be published and sold for so-called artistic use, in particular in reviews such as *Le nu esthétique* [Paris, 1903–1905] pretending to be read by artists and connoisseurs only). And this alibi will last for decades in the film industry. Some nude films of the 1940s produced by Criterion Films or Candid Cinema [*sic!*] still carry the warning "This picture has been produced exclusively for the use of classes in graphic arts, art students and others who are using motion pictures instead of living models for study. It is not intended for public exhibition." (Quotation of the title appearing as a "Foreword" of *The Fabulous Figure, The Body Beautiful, Doctor's Office, Bed Time*, and other short films of a series produced by Criterion Film, 1940s, private collection.).

14   Paul Capellani

The Body Put to the Test by Cinema

Sébastien Dupont-Bloch
Translated by Timothy Barnard

"How an actor uses the kinematograph to make sculpture." This was the title of an article appearing on July 3, 1909, in the weekly magazine *L'Ilustration* devoted to *L'Enlisé*.[1] Not the Pathé film *L'Enlisé du Mont Saint-Michel* (*Caught in Quicksand on Mont Saint-Michel*), released in early 1908—the article does not even mention its title—but rather *L'Enlisé* (*Caught in Quicksand*), a sculpture by Paul Capellani (brother of film director Albert Capellani) on exhibit at the 1909 Salon des Artistes Français. And yet the article claims that this sculpture was, indeed, *based on* the film, or more precisely what we might call a *study of the filmed body*.

According to the article, reprinted by the daily newspaper *L'Ouest-Eclair* on July 12 of that year, Paul Capellani wanted to experiment and film himself sinking into the ground. He wanted to "synthesize the movement of the projected figure" so as to understand and better transcribe the expression of these near-death moments in order to create a sculpture.[2]

Photographs taken by Charles Gerschel illustrate the article, showing the actor actually sinking into the ground on the film shoot, and the sculpture being completed. These mirroring pictures demonstrate how *Enlizé*[3] embodies an astonishing act of intermediality. Capellani had, in fact, transformed a cinematic shot, a dynamic object without depth, into a sculpture, a static object without time. He had transformed flat yet animated images into a three-dimensional static object. In this way, a body was projected from one expressive space to another by substituting quantifiable parameters that could not be confused with artistic interpretation. The sculpture was presented as the sought-after product of a drama that the artist experienced himself, as Paul Capellani did not want to simulate the action by using a model, or by acting, as he himself was an actor. According to the article, the film shoot almost cost the artist and his crew their lives. When the actor and then the equipment began sinking into the ground, the crew had to call for emergency assistance, which arrived "just in time."

Figure 14.1. Paul Capellani performing in the film of his brother Albert Capellani, *L'Enlisé du Mont Saint-Michel* (1908)—photograph by Gerschel published in *L'Illustration* 3462 (July 3, 1908): 12.

The Film

Today the film is believed to be lost, but traces of it can be found in print sources. On January 26, 1908, for example, the editor of the newspaper *Le Sémaphore algérien* made reference to "*L'Enlize du Mont Saint-Michel*, a great drama with a highly poignant effect, among the films that had won 'great favor' at the Kursaal Omnia in Alger."[4] It had been released a few days earlier at the Pathé-Grolée cinema in Lyon, and circulated for at least a year, as it was still being shown at the Omnia in Rouen in October 1908. This 150-meter film was produced and published by Pathé Frères.[5] Although it was not credited to him, it may have been directed by Albert Capellani, who began his career as a director at Pathé in 1906 with a fiction film, *Le Chemineau*, featuring Paul Capellani and inspired by *Fantine*, the first part of *Les Misérables*.[6] Only one thing is certain, because he is physically recognizable: the role of the sinking man was, indeed, played by Paul Capellani (1877–1960), Albert's younger brother. The catalog description situates the scene of Capellani sinking into the ground in a broader series of dramatic events, but it constitutes the climax of the film, as this description suggests by depicting it as the final scene, and as it is confirmed by the film's poster showing Paul Capellani sinking in quicksand.[7]

Figure 14.2. E. Marche, poster of *L'Enlisé du Mont Saint-Michel*, 1908—lithography edited by Pathé, 160 × 120 cm. Courtesy Bibliothèque Nationale de France.

The poster is signed "E. Marche," who was not among the professionals working for Pathé at the time, such as Cândido de Faria and Adrien Barrère. The choice and use of colors and the skillful composition of the drawing show the hand of an accomplished artist and illustrator who was able to synthesize spectacular attraction, dramaturgy, and narrative.[8] The depiction of fright in Paul Capellani's posture and features has lived on through the ages. After the newspaper *Le Rire* put it on its July 31, 1909, cover,[9] the poster was plagiarized in 1994 for the cover of a novel by Lucien Vibert, titled *Le fleuve de soie* (Editions Le Grand Livre du Mois), that has nothing to do with the story or film of 1908.

Figure 14.3. Paul Capellani, *L'Enlisé*, 1909—plaster preserved at the Musée Historique du Mont Saint Michel, photographed by the Neurdein Brothers (private collection, reproduced with permission of the Roger-Viollet Agency).

The Sculpture

Enlisé has been exhibited since 1909 in a corner of the Mont Saint-Michel museum with the sole description, "Sinking in quicksand." This sculpture, made in 1909 by Paul Capellani, recalls the dangers of the Mont Saint-Michel bay, which for a long time was known as "Mont Saint-Michel, peril of the sea." The sculpture, in an academic style, is made of plaster. The face and eyes clearly express terror, and the parts of the body that stick out of the quicksand evoke both muscular strength and helplessness.

Nevertheless, a comparison of the sculpture and the film images makes the artistic endeavor announced in the article somewhat suspicious. Unlike the photographs, the sculpted model has neither a mustache nor a beard. He resembles neither the photographed actor nor the character on the poster. Did the actor wear a fake beard? Did the sculptor shave it off, change it, get rid of it?

As the possible externalization of a traumatic event, the sculpture represents an act of intermediality. It is a special form of *sculpturation*, as defined by Michel Delage, "a clinical psychological tool used to express emotions through the body alone."[10] In this case, the projection of a modal space to another is not merely dimensional; it gives form to a mental representation by way of the body. The figure is shown alone, and we cannot know either to whom he is crying out or whether anyone can even hear him. The essential information is expressed through the face, the part of the body closest to the senses and to consciousness. Looking at this face, we are as close as possible to the perception of imminent death. Here the only clothing we see is the shirt, glued to the body; we cannot truly distinguish the skin except through the folds representing veins bulging from effort. A hand thrusts powerfully against the murderous substance, which we sense to be as resistant as stone; the other hand slides uselessly along this same substance, which slips away when one seeks, on the contrary, to make use of its resistance. Here the body is useless, an actor in its own imminent death, a machine powerless to save itself.

Embodiment

L'Enlisé du Mont Saint-Michel, whether in the form of a picture, a film, or a sculpture, can also be seen as the fatal impotence of the wretched in the face of blindly unrelenting social and natural injustice—something that André Antoine, founding father of naturalist theater and modern stagecraft, would not have disavowed. Paul Capellani acted for him at the Odéon throughout the year *L'Enlisé* was shot in 1907.[11] According to Jacques Richard, Paul Capellani was more than Antoine's actor: he was Antoine's disciple, retaining "the stamp of his master" in the films he acted in, directed by Albert Capellani.[12]

By immersing his body in quicksand in front of a movie camera in the search of a true and natural depiction, Paul Capellani went beyond Antoine's precepts,[13] for whom "the surroundings determine the characters' movements, rather than the characters' movements determining the surroundings."[14] And if naturalism may be defined, as Aurélie Gendrat does, as "an authentic and expressive depiction of nature and bodies,"[15] it is precisely this that shaped the actor/sculptor Paul Capellani's performance.

It is possible that the sculpture was only a secondary product of the film— that the film shoot was autonomous, and the sculpture was not premeditated but an improvised and therapeutic result that gave material form to a traumatic event. The film was released in January 1908 and the sculpture was shown at the Salon des Artistes Français in May 1909. More than a year passed, then, between the film's release and the sculpture's exhibition. During this interval, Capellani was able to find cathartic release from an event that truly did almost cost him his life.

Whether intentionally or not, therapeutic or not, this sculpture—like the film—depicts the recorded agony of a body. The change in the body's coordinates in its migration from cinema to sculpture is a temporal crystallization but also an amplification of anatomical details. If we accept, moreover, that Paul Capellani actually did risk his life during the film shoot and that his later sculpture is a firsthand, unambiguous document, we can see it as an illustration of the gravest test to which a body can be put in the name of film art.

SÉBASTIEN DUPONT-BLOCH is a doctoral student at Paris 1 Panthéon-Sorbonne University and a lecturer at the Université Normandie-Caen.

TIMOTHY BARNARD is a translator, author, and book publisher. He has translated and published volumes by André Bazin and Jean-Luc Godard and is author of the short volume *Découpage*.

Notes

1. *L'Illustration*, July 3, 1908, 12.
2. "A conscientious sculptor entered quicksand to give his work greater realism and life," *L'Ouest-Eclair*, July 12, 1908, 1.
3. Spelling of the work's title varies from author to author in the different newspapers that announced the film screening. In 1908 the spelling changed, with *"enlisé"* seeming more modern and gradually replacing *"enlizé,"* which was used for a time, specifically with reference to quicksand (thanks, undoubtedly, to Victor Hugo in *Les Misérables*). I will retain the spelling each author used.
4. *Le Sémaphore Algérien, organe de la marine, du commerce, de l'industrie, de l'agriculture et des travaux publics*, January 26, 1908, 3. The film was screened between *His First Cigar* (*Le premier cigare d'un collégien*, Pathé, 1908) and *Gendarme Has a Keen Eye* (*Le gendarme a bon oeil*, Pathé, 1908).
5. Henri Bousquet, *Catalogue Pathé des années 1896 à 1914* (Bures-sur-Yvette, France: Editions Henri Bousquet, 1994), 68.
6. Lucien Logette, "De l'écrit à l'écran: Les Misérables," *1895* 68 (December 2013): 57.
7. "A wretchedly-dressed man asks for charity in the streets of Mont Saint-Michel. He receives nothing. A family takes him into their poor home, however, and gives him something to eat. The oldest child welcomes him but unfortunately falls and suffers a serious head injury. The father writes a note for the doctor. The tramp decides to take it to him. He must cross the channel separating the Mont from the mainland. But he takes the wrong path, is caught in quicksand, and dies. (Script based on viewing.)" *Catalogue Pathé des années 1896 à 1914*, 68.
8. This may be the painter Ernest Gaston Marché (1864–1932), who studied in Paris at the École Nationale Supérieure des Arts Décoratifs. Like Paul Capellani, Ernest Marché frequented and exhibited his work at the Salon des Artistes Français during this same period.
9. My thanks to Jérémy Houillère for this reference.
10. Michel Delage, *La résilience familiale* (Paris: Odile Jacob, 2008), 203.
11. Édouard Noël and Edmond Stoullig, *Les Annales du théâtre et de la musique* (Paris: Librairie P. Ollendorff, 1907), 179, 194, 198.
12. Jacques Richard, "Des acteurs qui échappent au théâtre," *1895* 68 (December 2013): 121.
13. From the first shot of his first film, *Le Chemineau* in 1905, Paul Capellani threw himself into cinema as he had done with the theater. Not hesitating to transgress cinematic codes in order to extend the work of Antoine's Théâtre Libre to cinema, as a tramp Paul Capellani appears fragile and, without ceasing to look at the camera, moves closer to it to literally provoke a close-up of his face, immersed in the role.
14. André Antoine, "Causerie sur la mise en scène," *La Revue de Paris* 10, no. 2 (March–April 1903): 603.
15. Aurélie Gendrat, *Zola, l'Œuvre* (Paris: Bréal, 1999), 16.

Part IV
Bodily Features

Introduction

The essays included in this section focus on a series of particular fragments of the body. They offer interpretations of how the on-screen depictions of bodily features came to carry specific meanings depending on cultural and historical contexts. In turn, the essays demonstrate how such notions about filmic depictions of the body came to define the very possibilities of how cinema's representation and aesthetic were conceived in its early years.

The section opens with two texts that concern the first years following the introduction of the cinematograph and the kinetoscope. Jean-Claude Seguin takes on the themes of hair and hairiness in a survey of early films on beards, barbers, and shaving. In correspondence to how hair has been considered a signifier of gender and social codes, early films—starting with some of the earliest productions of the Edison company—took particular interest in depicting themes such as the homosocial space of the barbershop and the delicate art of handling a straight razor. As Seguin demonstrates, the cinematic concern with hair provided proper context for commentary on the always-threatened bourgeois social order as well as on socially acceptable appearances and grotesque transformations.

John Fullerton's essay examines two early films that were shot by Lumière cinematographers in Mexico. The films, which depicted scenes of an execution and a deadly duel, as well as photographic records of the aftermath of Emperor Maximilian I in 1867, highlight early cinema's status as a modern memento mori that could represent instances of death and dying like no other medium. In Fullerton's account, the eye of the dying man is charged with an uncanny, self-reflexive meaning, as the duel film makes visible to the spectators how a match held near the dying person's eye is used to confirm whether it is dilating—that is, whether it is a living eye or one immortalized by film.

The two essays that follow share a concern with the reproduction of the human face on the screen. Oksana Chefranova, in her essay "Breathing Faces, Twinkling Eyes," explores critical and theoretical commentary on the face in close-up in the context of Russian cinema of the 1910s, particularly focusing on the films of celebrated director Evgenii Bauer. Concerning the discourses on the face from before the canonical writings of Béla Balázs and Jean Epstein, Chefranova shows how the face in close-up appeared as a medium-specific trait of cinematic expression that continuously balanced the oppositions of form and formlessness, narrative and abstraction, stillness and motion, exterior surface and spiritual interiority, and expressivity and restraint. In the early Russian writings on the face in close-up, the face is regarded as what Chefranova calls an elemental medium, with emotions acting on its features like natural elements on a landscape.

The face is also revisited in Alice Maurice's contribution, here in connection to the application of makeup on the stage and film set during transitional-era Hollywood. As Maurice notes, as a key element in early writings on acting, stardom, and film style, "makeup becomes an important tool for translating and re-coding persistent attitudes about realism, transformation, and mutability," as it codifies facial features and skin color, and corresponds to changes in cinematographic and acting styles. In this discussion, once again, the face appears not merely as an objective entity to be reproduced but as a medium for expression itself, a surface to be written on.

15   Hair and Hairiness in Early Cinema

Jean-Claude Seguin

Translated by Timothy Barnard

HAIR AND HAIRINESS hold a special place in cultural history as gender markers, social indicators, and civilizational codes.[1] Thus, to examine the presence and role of hair in early cinema is both to consider how it was incorporated into brief film narratives between 1896 and 1906 and to study its social meaning and functions—particularly how it delineates (and can then threaten or deconstruct) a character's gender, identity, and even humanity. Exploring the place of hair in popular early films makes it possible to compose a reasonably accurate portrait of what defined a fin-de-siècle "man" and to highlight an important feature of the body as depicted by early cinema.

The Barber

Let's begin our journey through the realm of hair with the person who has long had the duty of taking care of it, both on our faces and our heads: the barber. In late 1893, William Heise produced *The Barber Shop* in the Black Maria for W.K.L. Dickson. According to the Edison filmography established by Charles Musser,[2] this was the eighteenth motion picture Edison made, which is far from irrelevant. That the barber was one of the first tradesmen depicted (along with the blacksmith and the cobbler) shows the social importance of this profession at the time. Despite its brief length, the film depicts a genre scene similar to one we would find in an eighteenth-century engraving or painting.

The limited space of the Black Maria was a constraint, overcome in this case by overlap perspective: the set in the background, the barber and his client in the middle, and the two customers closest to us. The camera operator thus plays exclusively on depth of field. But what does this short sketch show us? If its purpose had been simply to show a customer coming to get a shave, it would have been less interesting. One of the main attractions of *The Barber Shop* lies in the two customers in the foreground. They tell us much more about the social space the barbershop represents. First of all, we are in a male space, where a woman's figure would cause disturbance and disorder. The barbershop is a place of sociability, where the wait and its fulfillment are essential. It molded not only the body but also the behavior. In this space, male identity is defined both physically and socially. The success of the original film led Edison to produce a remake in January 1895; slightly more elaborate and complex, it had three overlapping actions: a barber and his customer, a shoe shiner and his customer, and two other people.[3] The catalog claims that "this is one of the most popular film ever produced."[4]

The popularity of these films, which materialize the "established social order" spatially and physically, speaks volumes about their conventionality. And this established order is jeopardized by the appearance of female legs in another Edison production, from 1898 (and remade in 1901), *What Demoralized the Barber Shop*.[5] Here the comedy is based on the sudden appearance of the "feminine" in the "masculine" world, a disorder that is clearly eroticized—there is no doubt that the legs belong to women of easy virtue who walk the streets—and that gives rise to extreme agitation in not only the customers but also the barber, who appears to be on the verge of slitting the throat of one poor and particularly manhandled customer. It is noteworthy that in this "disordered" barber space, the women occupy a dominant position in the frame.

While the barbershop could be depicted as a highly structured social space where the intrusion of women sowed trouble, other pictures focused on the barber-customer relationship for purely comic ends, with or without the use of trick effects. Another reason early cinema paid special attention to the figure of the barber is the unequal relationship between the barber as the dominant figure and the customer as the dominated and submissive one. The gag was born out of this unequal situation. This was the case in the famous film *Le Barbier fin de siècle* (*The Up-to-Date Barber*, Pathé, 1896), a picture that combines two early genres: the trick scene and the comic scene.

The trick effect used here—a man literally losing his head—is a classic in the world of prestidigitation and, of course, in the films of Georges Méliès. What may be of greater interest is the choice of the barbershop as background. Between the lines, it played on the fears that the barber's instruments may instill: the straight razor, scissors, and so on. Any of these objects could become a weapon and threaten the bodies that are subjected to them—not only their masculine attributes, but their very life. The trick thus gives the film both a comic and a more troubling effect.

This is just one example among many that work with multiple variations of related themes but that are all based on the principle of "disrupting" an established social and spatial order. This, as Petr Král has shown, would become the form of "disorder" found in the slapstick comedy.[6] The customer in *Le Barbier facétieux* (*The Barber's Revenge*, Pathé, 1903), half shaved because he arrived late, or the injured customer in *El Barbero* (1898), a splendid Spanish flip-book by Pablo Audouard, are variants that could almost take an infinite number of forms and could sketch the outlines of an early film "genre."

Hair, however, is not at the center of film depictions of the barbershop, an enclosed space whose décor never changes. Control over hairiness becomes a symbol of social power over masculinity, legitimating the dominant/dominated relationship between the barber and his client. But the beard, along with the mustache, has been featured as the essential element of some early moving pictures.

The Beard

The beard is a marker of virility that early cinema would put to use in many films. I will of course make no attempt here to inventory the films in which a male character is adorned with a significant beard but rather will limit myself to a few examples where beards have an iconic role.

By focusing the viewer's attention on a hairy feature that defines "maleness," the films play to varying degrees on a man's relationship with his virility, or at least with his masculinity. Thus, every attack—cutting, shaving, and so on—can be read symbolically as playing on castration, reactivating the symbolic dimension that empowered the figure of the barber. The fact that today beards have become chic and that the barbershop—and no longer the hair salon—is in vogue are signs of a return of the physical assertion of masculinity. At the turn of the twentieth century, beards were considered more "natural," and every attack on their integrity took on meaning. Take the case of the film *Ah! La barbe* (*Funny Shave*, Pathé, 1905), attributed to the Spanish filmmaker Segundo de Chomón. This curious film puts shaving, or rather self-shaving, at the heart of the story, something given even greater effect by placing the character in front of a large mirror.

As it was practiced at the time, shaving was a complex operation that required dexterity, know-how, and patience. Entire treatises were devoted to the "art of shaving," which was related to a sense of pleasure.[7] Our character, looking into the mirror, evidently takes great pleasure in spreading the soap on his face, to the point that he even greedily tastes the lather, as if it were ice cream or candy. A few seconds later, he sharpens his razor with delight on the leather strop. This delight and eroticization tend to liken the art of shaving to onanism, or something close to it. Everything is ready for the gallant man to give himself up to this solitary pleasure. And the way the film is set up, the mirror plays a central role: it is the witness to the shaving. Of course, its main role is functional—it is preferable to shave oneself in front of a mirror to avoid accidents—but we cannot overlook the fact that the character is, in a sense, creating a self-portrait, a kind of selfie. As soon as the man, entirely devoted to his own image, begins to use his cutthroat razor, figures appear in the mirror, like "alternative" faces.

These three heads are all monstrous, in the Latin sense of the term *monstrum*: "a divine omen"; "a supernatural appearance." The first head looks like that of a clown, the second that of an elderly professor, and the third that of a stupid child sticking out its tongue. If we leave aside the trick effect, of which Segundo de Chomón had become a master, these three portraits appear to loom into view as alternatives that the mirror is proposing to the character, creating a before-and-after shaving effect. The question of identity is thus at the very heart of the act of shaving, which the young man will bring to an end by smashing the mirror. The goal of this brief sketch (barely 40 meters long) was to make the audience laugh at the trick effects, but it also drew on the art and vanity of shaving, the fantasy of sculpting one's own face and identity, defying the order of nature.

Hair and Hair Pieces

The head of hair or its substitute is the primary subject of many films, a few exemplary cases of which I will discuss here. In most of these films centered on the head of hair, the basis of the story is the question of growing hair or replacing it. Unlike the beard, whose "virile" or "masculine" nature I pointed out earlier, here the head of hair is a *human* attribute with a primarily aesthetic function.

In the early-cinema era, baldness was seen as a handicap, even a tragedy, whetting the appetites of merchants of miracle products, such as the one used by the character in *Lotion miraculeuse* (*Miraculous Shampooing*, Pathé, 1903), a remake of *L'Eau merveilleuse* (*A Wonderful Hair Restorer*, Pathé, 1901). The gag is based on out-of-control and anarchic hair growth, but the cure is worse than the disease. Whereas films about beards were concerned with questions of male/female identity, in the present case the human/animal relation is at the center of the film. The dual disorder—the absence or abuse of the hair on one's head—calls the person's integrity into question.

The body can also be threatened by hirsutism, or more specifically hypertrichosis, an archaic fear found in naturalist treatises, such as the seventeenth-century *Monstrorum Historia* by Ulisse Aldrovandi, the most famous of its kind. Individuals suffering from hypertrichosis—the genetic peculiarity of the famous Gonzalez family, who circulated in the royal courts of sixteenth-century Europe—were likened to half-human, half-animal monsters. In the nineteenth century, most of these people were sent to the circus, where they performed alongside hybrid creatures (such as Julia Pastrana, the Mexican monkey-woman; Fedor Jeftichew, the boy with a dog's head; and Stephan Bibrowski, the man with a lion's head) and bearded women—these emblematic characters whose hairiness precisely located them in a no-man's- (and no-woman's-) land, between genders and on the borderline of animality. In early cinema, the sudden and tricky growth of hair on the head, and in some cases on the rest of the body, was like a cinematic variant of the werewolf legend.

Behind the comic effect one cannot help but see a kind of "moral." Even bald human beings should be content with their lot and beware of charlatans and mad scientists who take advantage of their weaknesses to subject them to diabolical experiments. This was an undoubtedly conservative moral, if it were not for the "cinematic experiment" prevailing.

Early films also enjoyed "scalping" their characters by targeting and removing their hairpieces. *La Perruque* (*The Wig*, Pathé, 1905) is a classic that, in a humorous mode, exposes false pretense and fakery of every sort. A fop tries to battle the ravages of time in order to seduce his lady friend. The old rake, a classic figure from Molière to Max Ophüls, tries to find subterfuges to conceal his decrepitude. The most interesting figure is that of the little imp who, in jest, slips among grown-ups to expose, through the fakeness of their hair, their vanity. *La Course à la perruque* (*The Wig Chase*, Georges Hatot, Pathé, 1906) returns to the figure of the mischievous child who, for fun, upsets the normal order. Taking advantage of the drowsiness of an elderly lady and a balloon seller, two scamps attach his balloons to the lady's wig. Redeployed in a manner for which they were not intended, they rise up in the air, taking the wig with them. Following this opening scene, we are treated to a classic film chase that constitutes most of the film. But female baldness does not appear in early cinema, as far as I have been able to determine, or if it is present, it is purely marginal. Unlike male baldness, it is less conducive to humor and pranks. Hatôt thus resolved the matter by using a man to play the role of the old woman, which is also a classic technique in comedy, from Shakespeare to Buñuel. The comic effect of cross-dressing is operative as long as it is a man dressed as a woman and not a woman dressed as a man.[8] In this way, the "old lady" can leap, jump, and turn somersaults as much as "she" likes, a sure-fire way of making the audience laugh, at least back then. *La Course à la perruque* thus speaks to the question of gender in contemporary society, the respective territories of masculinity and femininity, and the ways in which they are "breached."

Conclusion

The films we examined, mostly of a comedy type that would be reactivated in the following decade in the form of slapstick, implicitly carry out a reflection on the gender codes that shaped the contemporary society. Hair is one of the main "secondary sexual characteristics," to borrow terminology from anthropological studies, where the topic of hair has grown in importance over recent years.[9] Today we see an increase in theoretical literature focusing on the hair and its absence.[10] But there is no book exploring this issue in film, and even less so concerning early cinema.[11] However, the head of hair and beard are central in many comic early film narratives, just a sample of which was highlighted in this study.[12] This body of works calls into question or parodies gender norms and some divides between male and female. With the tacit complicity of the spectator that is involved in the comedy film genre (and with the normative strength of collective laughing), the gendered stereotypes and masculinity attributes of the time turn out to be, at times, reaffirmed and at others, as we hope to have demonstrated, shaken.

JEAN-CLAUDE SEGUIN is Professor Emeritus at the University Lumière Lyon 2. He is author of *Histoire du cinéma espagnol, Pedro Almodóvar o la deriva de los cuerpos*, and *Alexandre Promio*. He is editor with Michelle Aubert of *La Production cinématographique des Frères Lumière*.

TIMOTHY BARNARD is a translator, author, and book publisher. He has translated and published volumes by André Bazin and Jean-Luc Godard and is author of the short volume *Découpage*.

Notes

1. See Marie-France Auzépy and Joël Cornette, eds., *Histoire du poil* (Paris: Belin, 2011); Yve Le Fur, ed., *Cheveux chéris, frivolités et trophées* (Paris: Actes Sud/Musée du Quai Branly, 2012); and Christian Bromberger, *Trichologiques* (Paris: Bayard, 2010).
2. Charles Musser, *Edison Motion Pictures 1890–1900: An Annotated Filmography* (Washington, DC: Smithsonian Institution Press, 1997), 18.
3. According to Charles Musser, this description may correspond to a third version, because here the shoe shiner is white. Musser, *Edison Motion Pictures*, 168.
4. Ohio Phonograph Co., *The Edison Kinetoscope*, price list, August 1895, 9 (*Barber Shop*).
5. The American Mutoscope and Biograph Company would again plagiarize this film four years later under the title *The Barber's Dee-light* (1905).
6. Petr Král, *Le Burlesque ou Morale de la tarte à la crème* (Paris: Stock, 1984) and *Les Burlesques ou Parade des somnambules* (Paris: Stock, 1986).
7. Georges Malet, *Théorie de la barbe ou comment il faut se raser* (Paris: Les Éditions Orah, 1928).
8. On women dressed up as men, see Laura Horak, *Girls Will Be Boys: Cross-Dressed Women, Lesbians, and American Cinema, 1908–1934* (New Brunswick, NJ: Rutgers University Press, 2016).
9. See Bromberger, *Trichologiques*; Le Fur, *Cheveux chéris*, and Lucinda Hawksley, *Moustaches, Whiskers & Beards* (London: National Portrait Gallery, 2014).
10. About the "slick tyranny," see Jean Da Silva, *Du velu au lisse, histoire et esthétique de l'épilation intime* (Paris: Complexe, 2009), and Stéphane Rose, *Défense du poil, contre la dictature de l'épilation intime* (Paris: La Musardine, 2010).
11. Though Antoine de Baecque pioneered the field with his chapter "Projections; la virilité à l'écran," in Alain Corbin, Jean-Jacques Courtine, and Georges Vigarello (dir.), *Histoire de la virilité*, vol. 3 (Paris: Seuil, 2011), 431–60.
12. Ongoing release of early film catalogs (see "Los orígenes del Cine," https://www.grimh.org) will lead to a more complete corpus. The question of intimate hairiness lies beyond this chapter's focus on slapstick.

16 Lumière Agents in Mexico
The "Body" of Film as a Late-Nineteenth-Century Discourse

John Fullerton

For Aurelio de los Reyes

As is well known, the day after the *Cinématographe* was first exhibited to a paying audience at the Salon Indien, a review in *La Poste* observed, "Death will have ceased to be absolute."[1] In a similar vein, Tom Gunning has argued that the motion picture, along with the photograph and phonograph, were technologies that variously "claimed to preserve human traits . . . after the subject had died."[2] These technologies not only represented media forms that were thought to overcome death through movement, expression, and voice; they also marked, in the case of the *Cinématographe*, an uncanny aspect that identified a deeper ambivalence, one that delivered "an uncanny foretaste of death," a modern memento mori.[3] These observations form the theme of this essay, which compares two films and a photograph. The films were made by the Lumière agents Gabriel Veyre and Fernand Bon Bernard, who worked in Mexico between August and December 1896, while the photograph was taken by François Aubert of Emperor Maximilian (Maximiliano) shortly after his embalmment following his execution in Mexico on June 19, 1867. As we will see, the concern with death, embalmment, and the uncanny were common elements in the two Lumière films and the photograph by Aubert.

In the early morning of Monday, October 12, 1896, two Lumière agents filmed the execution of Antonio Navarro, a fusilier, in the *plazuela* de Santiago in Mexico City. The event was covered in the Mexican press and in French- and English-language newspapers published in the capital. *The Two Republics* reported, "There was one American woman in the crowd of spectators, who were there to witness the execution, and when the first volley was fired she fainted away. An itinerant photographer was also there with a newly invented camera that takes every motion, and as soon as the condemned man was in position the mechanical action of the camera was set in motion and continued until the execution was over."[4] News of Navarro's execution was also carried in *L'Echo du Méxique*. Over the next two days, *L'Echo du Mexique*, *El Universal*, and *El Globo* announced that Lumière agents would show the film in a forthcoming presentation, and that proceeds would be donated to the family of the fusilier.[5] The film, however, does not appear to have been shown in public, as there are no notices of its exhibition in the daily press. Given that a film with this subject was not included in the Lumière catalog, it seems likely that the Lumière company in France and its agents in Mexico withdrew or, indeed, suppressed it, despite the frisson such events customarily offered spectators in the late nineteenth century.

The last film that Veyre and Bernard shot in Mexico, unlike the footage of Navarro's execution, has survived. Although *Duel au pistolet*, shot in December 1896, staged a "simulated duel" (*simulacro de duelo*), as the title of an article in *El Nacional* clarified,[6] the film almost certainly left spectators uncertain of its resolution. In the closing moments of the film, a lighted match is held in front of the eyes of one of the duelists who, apparently "shot" by his opponent, has fallen to the ground. Staged parallel and close to the lower frame line, the action renders the outcome of the examination of the duelist's eyes unclear. The inspection (to see if the eyes dilate) demonstrates that they were understood to be central to the process of determining whether the duelist was alive (figure 16.1). The outcome of this process, however, was uncertain since it took place in the last frames of the film, offering the spectator little opportunity to verify if the duelist was alive at the end of the film.

Although *Duel au pistolet* was exhibited in France and Venezuela the following year, it was not shown in Mexico.[7] To understand this decision, we may turn to what was still a significant moment in the collective memory of the nation: the execution of Emperor Maximilian with two of his generals on the Cerro de las Companas (Hill of the Bells) to the west of the city of Querétaro.[8] What the execution of Maximilian and the Lumière film have in common is a concern with ascertaining death by means of inspecting the protagonist's eyes, a process recorded in a photograph by François Aubert after Maximilian's eyes were replaced with glass ones during embalmment (figure 16.2). In contrast to the animation that would have accompanied the dilation of the duelist's pupils in the Lumière film, Maximilian's glass eyes present an uncanny, fixed, and awkwardly embodied "gaze," one that draws attention to the fact that the passing of time was variously articulated in photographs and film. In this respect, the photograph was analogous to the making of a mummy, a process that aspired to preserve the body from decay.

André Bazin famously addressed this issue in his essay "The Ontology of the Photographic Image." Opening with an analogy that compared the plastic arts with psychoanalysis, Bazin argued, "At the origin of painting and sculpture there lies a mummy complex."[9] For Bazin, photography arrested the moment in which

Figure 16.1. Frame grab, Gabriel Veyre and Fernand Bon Bernard, *Duel au pistolet (longueur: 12 mètres)*, 1896. Reproduced with thanks to Angel Martínez Juárez, Head, Departamento de Catalogación, Filmoteca de la UNAM.

the photograph was taken. Cinema, however, added the trace of duration to the photographic image, a process that Bazin compared with the mummy, where change was "mummified as it were" (*"comme la momie du changement"*).[10] The photograph by Aubert and the Lumière film thus represented different temporal regimes. In the case of the photograph of Maximilian, the image presents an effect secured *outside* the medium (i.e., at some later moment) since interpretation by the viewer relied on reports printed in the daily press to clarify action. *Duel au pistolet*, on the other hand, secured effect *within* the film, since action, even when the film lacked a clear narrative outcome, was the only means available to spectators to determine the closing moments of the film. Whereas the photograph of Maximilian arrested the moment in which the image was made, the film embodied mutability given that the outcome of the narrative is unclear. Anticipation of the outcome of the film on the part of the spectator was thus integral to the process of viewing the film. Shortly, of course, intertitles in concert with filmic devices would advance narration in a process increasingly embodied in the medium, but at this point in development, filmic discourse did not have recourse to such strategies.

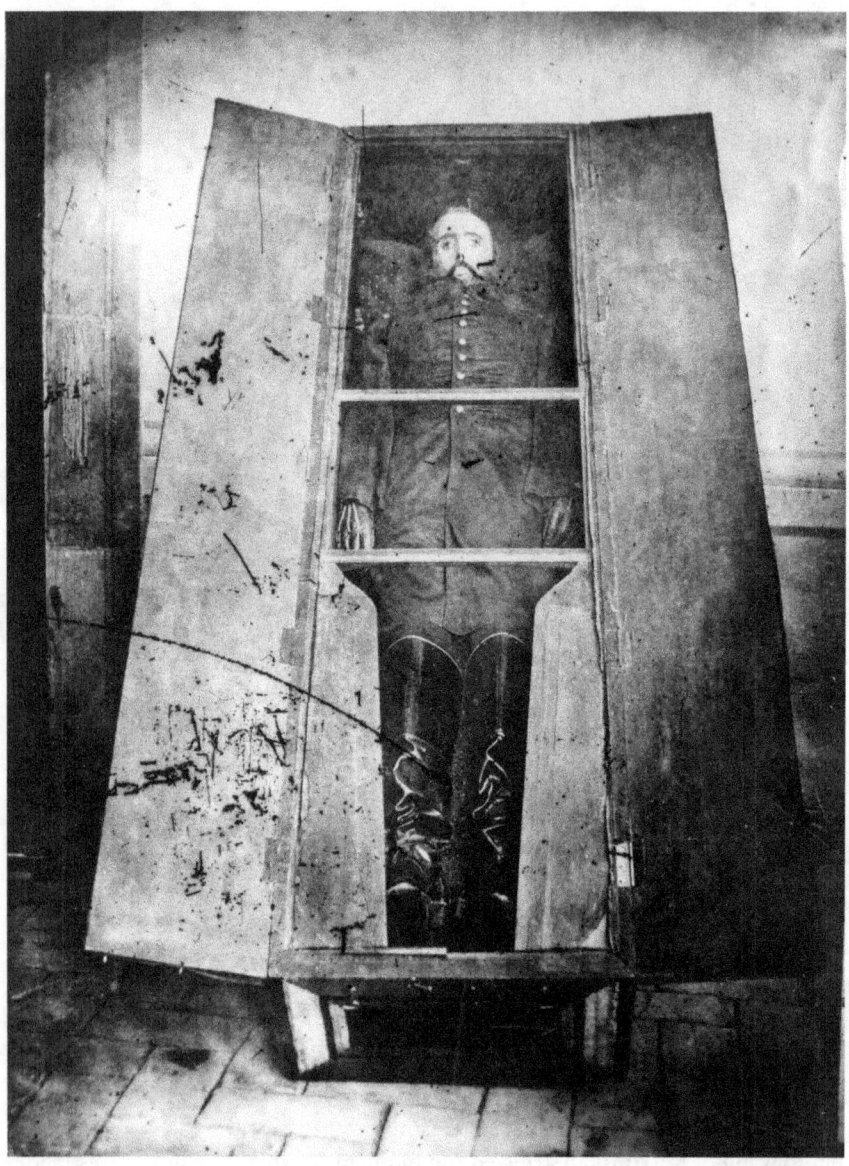

Figure 16.2. François Aubert, print from original glass plate [The body of Maximilian in his coffin after the first embalmment], 1867, 24 × 17.8 cm. Reproduced by permission of the War Heritage Institute, Brussels, Nr inv WHI: DB-a14.049.

Consider further the comparison of the Lumière film with the photograph by Aubert. The earliest account of the process in which Maximilian was embalmed was published on August 11, 1867, in the French newspaper *Le Figaro*, almost two months after the execution: "I'm sending you photographs taken at Querétaro after the execution. That is, pictures of Maximilian's servant's waistcoat and frock coat, which the emperor, whose clothing was stolen, wore at the execution, as well as portraits of the firing squad that shot Maximilian. I acquired these photographs from the army's chief doctor who embalmed Maximilian or rather who stuffed him, for he gave him two large, black glass eyes, since he had no blue ones. These photographs were taken in secret."[11] A letter from the same source, translated into Spanish, was published in Mexico six weeks later.[12] Could the process of replacing Maximilian's eyes with glass have resonated as late as 1896, when the eyes of the duelist were examined at the end of the Lumière film? Since the film was not shown in Mexico, it is impossible to pronounce whether this was the case. The illustrated press, however, returned to the execution of Maximilian on a number of occasions in the early twentieth century. We may propose, therefore, that memories of Maximilian's execution were fostered in the public mind by articles published in the illustrated press.[13]

As the report in *The Two Republics* indicates, executions constituted a public spectacle in Mexico City at the end of the nineteenth century. Although the account of what occurred during Maximilian's execution is not clear, there is general agreement that the firing squad botched the execution and the coup de grâce required to dispatch Maximilian.[14] After the execution, Maximilian's body was embalmed in Querétaro, a process that took almost eight days to complete, according to the account published in the memoirs of Maximilian's private secretary, José Luis Blasio.[15] Since the physicians responsible for the process had no naphtha, Maximilian's veins and arteries were injected with zinc chloride after his intestines, heart, liver, and lungs had been removed. The body was then dressed in black trousers; military boots; the blue campaign coat that Maximilian had worn, with gilt buttons secured up to the neck; a black necktie; and black kid gloves. Black glass eyes were placed over his natural eyes since glass eyes of the color of Maximilian's could not be obtained. The removal of a portion of beard from his face and some hair also disfigured the remains, in which state Aubert photographed Maximilian's embalmed body.

The body was placed in a cedar coffin lined with zinc, with Maximilian's head supported on a black velvet pillow trimmed with gold thread. The coffin also contained two small compartments at its foot. In one of these, the heart, liver, and lungs were placed; the other compartment held the remainder of the substances that had been taken from Maximilian's body, all materials being mixed with charcoal and chloride of lime. After a month, it was evident that the body had been badly preserved. It was transported to the hospital of San Andrés in Mexico City, from where, after further intervention, his body was transported to Veracruz and taken by ship to Trieste in January 1868.

Il Tiempo Semanario reported a news story relating to Maximilian on June 17, 1901, thirty-four years to the day after the execution. The magazine reproduced photographs of monuments on the Cerro de las Companas alongside the chapel, consecrated in 1901, that was built to commemorate Maximilian in response to a request from the Austrian government.[16] Since the technical conditions of photography made it impossible to record the moment of the execution (because shutter speeds were too slow), Aubert could only record events after the execution had been completed.[17] Notwithstanding the difficulty of recording the execution, the subject continued to interest the illustrated press. In June 1905, *El Tiempo Ilustrado* published an article that printed photographs of the convents where Maximilian was held before his court martial, with photographs of memorials on the hill outside Querétaro and a composite photographic print by Adrián Cordiglia.[18]

Cordiglia's photo montage, prepared in 1867 and evidencing disparities in scale between location, protagonists, and participants, combined heterogeneous sources (Aubert's photograph of an adobe wall on the Cerro de las Companas and a print of the execution squad) with images of Maximilian and the two generals executed alongside him. The composite print, showing men grouped in a photo montage, marks a radical departure from the morally exemplary *tableaux* typical of history painting in late-eighteenth-century France.[19] Perhaps in recognition of this transformation, a handwritten text, barely visible in the print that *El Tiempo Ilustrado* reproduced, provides narrative and dramatic intelligibility: "The last words of Maximilian: Mexicans! May my blood be the last which shall be spilt, and that it regenerates this unhappy country."[20]

Given that the technical conditions available for making photographic images could not record events instantaneously until the latter part of the nineteenth century, we may propose that action at the close of the Lumière film casts into strong relief the immediacy that film and photography introduced in visual culture in the closing years of the century. Thus, the concluding moment of *Duel au pistolet*, unlike the photographic medium at the time of Maximilian's execution, displays a capacity to record images almost as fast as visual perception itself. We can observe, therefore, that for a short period, before other devices were innovated in filmic discourse, cinematographic images conferred affect with an immediacy that was represented in the "body" of film itself. This process, as we have observed in *Duel au pistolet*, stimulated a response in the spectator, one that anticipated narrative resolution irrespective of the film's indeterminate ending. As Bazin argued, film added the trace of duration to the photographic image, yet in the case of *Duel au pistolet*, that process was shown to be mutable, inaugurating a desire for narrative resolution that exceeded what was represented in the closing moments of the film.

JOHN FULLERTON is Emeritus Professor of Cinema Studies at Stockholm University. He is author of *Picturing Mexico: From the Camera Lucida to Film*, editor of *Screen Culture: History and Textuality*, and editor with Jan Olsson of *Allegories of Communication: Intermedial Concerns from Cinema to the Digital.*

Notes

1. *La Poste*, December 29, 1895, cited in Noël Burch, "Charles Baudelaire versus Doctor Frankenstein," in *Life to Those Shadows*, trans. and ed., Ben Brewster (London: British Film Institute, 1990), 21, and in Maurice Bessey and G. M. Lo Duca, *Lumière l'inventeur* (Paris: Editions Prisma, 1948), 48.

2. Tom Gunning, "Re-Newing Old Technologies: Astonishment, Second Nature, and the Uncanny in Technology from the Previous Turn-of-the-Century," in *Rethinking Media Change: The Aesthetics of Transition*, ed. David Thorburn and Henry Jenkins (Cambridge, MA: MIT Press, 2003), 48.

3. Ibid.

4. "The Execution of Antonio Navarro. A Soldier Was Shot in the Square at Santiago," *Two Republics*, October 13, 1896, 5.

5. "Exécution du soldat Navarro," *L'Echo du Mexique*, October 13, 1896, 3; "Le Cinématographe 'Lumière,'" *L'Echo du Mexique*, October 14, 1896, 3; "Donativo a la familia del fusilado Navarro," *El Universal*, October 15, 1896, 7; "El Cinematógrafo Lumiere [sic]," *El Globo*, October 16, 1896, 3.

6. "Simulacro de duelo," *El Nacional*, December 14, 1896; Felipe Garrido, ed., with the collaboration of Jorge Gallardo and María Sánchez de Tagle, *Luz y sombra. Los inicios del cine en la prensa de la ciudad de México* (Mexico City: Consejo Nacional para la Cultura y las Artes, 1997), 71. The film was reported in one other newspaper on December 14, 1896: "Don Francisco Romero hiere en duelo á Don Fernando Veraza [sic]. Intervención de la Policía" in *El Imparcial*. Fought with pistols and with the permission of the police, the duel was played by two professional actors who took the roles of Mexican politicians, Francisco Romero and Fernando Verástegui, "with the object of taking a view for the cinématographe Lumière" (*"con el objeto de sacar una vista para el cinematógrafo Lumière"*). *El Nacional* observed that the police "took part in the simulation to add life and movement to the view" (*"que tomaron parte en el simulacro para dar más vida y movimiento a la vista"*). Translation from Spanish by the author unless otherwise indicated.

7. *Duel au pistolet (longueur: 12 mètres)*, Lumière catalog no. 35, was exhibited in Lyon, France, on February 21, 1897, and in Caracas, Venezuela, on July 29, 1897. *Lyon républicain*, February 21, 1897, cited in Michelle Aubert and Jean-Claude Seguin, eds., *La Production cinématographique des Frères Lumière* (Paris: Bibliothèque du Film (BiFi)/Editions Mémoires de cinéma, in collaboration with Centre national de la Cinématographie and Librairie du Premier Siècle, 1996), 362; *El República* (Caracas), July 28, 1897, cited in Philippe Jacquier and Marion Pranal, eds., *Gabriel Veyre, opérateur Lumière. Autour du monde avec le Cinématographe. Correspondance (1896–1900)* (Lyon: Institut Lumière, 1996), 92. The French title of the film (*Mexique: un Duel au pistolet*) specifically identifies Mexico as the location

of the film. Had the film been shown in Mexico, a different interpretation of the concluding action would have been available to viewers in Mexico since the duel between Francisco Romero and Fernando Verástegui (duels were banned under Mexican law in 1895) echoed the closing scene of a novel that Heriberto Frías published in 1896 before the Lumière agents shot the film in Mexico. With knowledge of the outcome of Frías's novel, viewers would have known that Verástegui died at the conclusion of the duel. For further consideration, see Aurelio de los Reyes, *Los orígenes del cine en México 1896–1900*, 2nd ed. (Mexico City: Fondo de Cultura Económica, 1983 [1972]), 13–14, 77.

8. In 1864, Ferdinand Maximilian Joseph, Archduke of Austria and member of the House of Hapsburg, was persuaded by Napoleon III of France to be proclaimed emperor of Mexico in order to support French military intervention in Mexico. When this ambition was not secured, French forces were pulled out of Mexico in 1867, and Benito Juárez, whom the French had deposed as president, regained control of the country. Maximilian was taken prisoner in Querétaro, where, charged with treason for helping a foreign army invade Mexico, he was executed by Republican forces.

9. "*A l'origine de la peinture et de la sculpture, elle trouverait le 'complexe' de la momie.*" André Bazin, "Ontologie de l'image photographique," in *Qu'est-ce que le cinéma?*, Vol. 1 (Paris: Editions du Cerf, 1958), 11. The metaphorical analogy of the psychoanalytic complex with the remains of the mummy is marked in the French by the use of quotation marks, an analogy not signaled in the English translation. André Bazin, "The Ontology of the Photographic Image," in *What Is Cinema?*, Vol. 1, trans. Hugh Gray (Berkeley: University of California Press, 1967), 9. Bazin's essay was first published in *Problèmes de la peinture*, ed. Gaston Diehl, in 1945.

10. Bazin, "The Ontology of the Photographic Image," 15; "Ontologie de l'image photographique," 16. For further discussion of this distinction, see Philip Rosen, "Belief in Bazin," in *Opening Bazin: Postwar Film Theory and Its Afterlife*, ed. Dudley Andrew with Hervé Joubert-Laurencin (Oxford, UK: Oxford University Press, 2011), 107–18, 110 in particular. The photograph of Maximilian's glass eyes with their uncanny gaze brings to mind late-eighteenth-century waxwork studies of human anatomy by Clemente Susini, studies that draw corporeality forcefully to attention. See, in particular, Susini's waxwork anatomical study of the human eye and visual cortex in Museo Zoologico La Spècola, Florence, Italy.

11. Albert Wolff, trans. Jeanine Herman, "Gazette du Mexique" with extracts from a letter signed by "X ...," *Le Figaro*, August 11, 1867, in "Newspaper Excerpts" selected by Anna Swinburne in John Elderfield, *Manet and the Execution of Maximilian* (New York: Museum of Modern Art, 2006), 189.

12. In English translation, the passage reads, "He sent the photographs taken in Querétaro following the execution, the one of the vest of Maximilian's servant—worn by the emperor, whose clothing had been stolen—as well as group portraits of the squad of soldiers who shot him. These photographs were given to me by the doctor in charge who embalmed Maximilian or, better said, packed him—since he put big black eyes [into the sockets] for lack of blue ones. These photographs were made in secret." Olivier Debroise, trans. and rev. in collaboration with the author by Stella de Sá Rego, *Mexican Suite: A History of Photography in Mexico* (Austin: University of Texas Press, 2001 [1994]), 169. The Spanish text reads: "*Envío las fotografías que se tomaron en Querétaro después de la ejecución, es decir, la del chaleco del criado de Maximiliano, que portaba el emperador, a quien se había robado su ropa, así como los retratos del grupo de soldados que le fusilaron. Me ha proporcionado estas fotografías*

el médico en jefe que embalsamó a Maximiliano o, por mejor decir, quien le embaló, pues le puso grandes ojos negros a falta de ojos azules. Estas fotografías han sido hechas en secreto." "Captura y ejecución del emperador Maximiliano," La Revista Universal, September 23, 1867, 2; Claudia Canales, "A propósito de una investigación sobre la historia de la fotografía en México," *Antropología e Historia. Boletín del Instituto de Antropología e Historia* 3, no. 23 (July–September 1978): 67, cited in Olivier Debroise, *Fuga Mexicana. Un recorrido por la fotografía en México* (Barcelona: Editorial Gustavo Gili, 2005), 249, note 9, 289.

13. In addition to articles in the illustrated press, accounts of the execution of Maximilian were published throughout the latter part of the century. One of the earliest accounts of the embalming of Maximilian was written by Prinz Felix zu Salm-Salm, General, First Aide-de-Camp and Chief of the Household of the Emperor. Salm-Salm's diary, *Querétaro. Blätter aus meinem Tagebuch in Mexiko. Nebst einem Auszuge aus dem Tagebuch der Prinzessin Agnes zu Salm-Salm*, was published in Stuttgart in 1868, the same year in which an English translation appeared.

14. Newspaper reports that circulated in Parisian newspapers between July 1, 1867, and October 10, 1867, are included in "Newspaper Excerpts," selected by Anna Swinburne in Elderfield, *Manet and the Execution of Maximilian*, 182–91. The reports provide conflicting accounts of events on the Cerro de las Campanas.

15. The account, in José Luis Blasio's memoirs, was published in Mexico in 1905 and in English translation in 1934. See Appendix III, "Disposition of Maximilian's Body," in José Luis Blasio, *Maximilian Emperor of Mexico Memoirs of his Private Secretary José Luis Blasio. Translated from the original Spanish by Robert Hammond Murray. Foreword by Carelton Beals* (New Haven, CT: Yale University Press, 1934), 204–9.

16. "Aniversario 19 de Junio de 1867," *Il Tiempo Semanario*, June 17, 1901, 287–89. The anonymous article recalled moments that led to the execution of Maximilian before going on to describe the consecration of the chapel. One short paragraph comments on the photographs that accompanied the article: "An old picture, of which we publish a copy today, reproduces the sad scene on the Cerro de las Campanas" ("*Una pintura antigua, de la que publicamos una copia hoy, reproduce la triste escena del Cerro de las Campanas*") (288).

17. Photographs taken by Aubert include images of Maximilian's bloodstained shirt and clothing, a studio portrait of the execution squad standing at ease, an adobe wall on the Cerro de las Campanas, and three makeshift memorials where Maximilian, General Miguel Miramón, and General Tomás Mejía were executed. Aubert's photographs circulated widely in Europe and Mexico as albumen prints and *cartes de visite*. See photographs reproduced in Elderfield, *Manet and the Execution of Maximilian*, 10, 14, 34, 90, 98, 190. Aaron Scharf dates the introduction of "instantaneous photographs" to 1858 when exposures of 1/50 of a second were innovated. Faster exposures "beyond the capabilities of the unaided eye" became available to photographers in the 1860s and 1870s. Aaron Scharf, *Art and Photography* (Harmondsworth, UK: Penguin, 1974 [1968]), 181.

18. The composite photographic print was published in *El Tiempo Ilustrado* 5, no. 234 (June 18, 1905), 386.

19. Examples of this tradition known in Mexico include Jacques-Louis David, *The Oath of the Horatii* (*Le Serment des Horaces*, 1784, oil on canvas, Louvre, Paris) and Jacques-Louis David, *Lictors Returning to Brutus the Bodies of His Sons* (*Les licteurs rapportent à Brutus les corps de ses fils*, 1789, oil on canvas, Louvre, Paris). See Rafael de Rafael's discussion of David in articles published in *El Espectador de México* in 1851 on the third exposition of

the Academia de San Carlos, reprinted in Ida Rodríguez Prampolini, ed., *La crítica de arte en México en el siglo XIX*, Vol. 1, 2nd ed. (Mexico City: Universidad Nacional Autónoma de México, Instituto de Investigaciones Estéticas, 1997 [1964]), 239–40.

20. "*Últimas palabras de Maximiliano: Mexicanos, que mi sangre sea la última que se derrame y que ella regenere este desgraciado pays* [sic]." The text, lower right, is readable in the print reproduced in Arturo Aguila Ochoa, *La fotografía durante el Imperio de Maximiliano* (Mexico City: Universidad Nacional Autónoma de México, Instituto de Investigaciones Estéticas, 2001), 55, also reproduced in Elderfield, *Manet and the Execution of Maximilian*, 90. Variant versions of Maximilian's final speech exist. Salm-Salm records that the speech, part of a longer address, concluded: "Mexicans! May my blood be the last which shall be spilt for the welfare of the country; and if it should be necessary that its sons would still shed theirs, may it flow for good, but never by treason. Viva independence! Viva Mexico!" Prince Felix zu Salm-Salm, *My Diary in Mexico in 1867, including the Last Days of the Emperor Maximilian . . .*, 2 vols. (London: Richard Bentley, 1868), I, 308.

17 Breathing Faces, Twinkling Eyes

On the Cinematic Visage in Russian Films of the 1910s

Oksana Chefranova

THE FACE CONSTITUTES a privileged object of cinematic representation and is itself a moving image before it becomes an image on the screen.[1] This article explores the "aesthetic significance of the face"[2] in Russian cinema of the 1910s, in the transitional period between earlier films' curiosity about the face and its transformation into a theoretical figure during the 1920s. In the cinema, the face emerges as a locus of paradoxes through persistent evocations of sculpture on one hand and metaphor of elemental media such as water and air on the other. What does the face's suspension between form and formlessness, ideality and individuality, suggest about its expressive ability? How does the face's duality of stillness and motion, visible and invisible, and internal and external help to elucidate the reciprocity between the face and the film image? This chapter focuses on three major faces of early Russian cinema—Vera Karalli, Ivan Mosjoukine, and Vera Kholodnaya—with examples from the films of one of the most prominent and influential Russian filmmakers of the silent era, Evgenii Bauer, whose distinct ability to work with the actor's presence on screen was acknowledged by his contemporaries.[3]

The Ballerina's Smile: Water and Deformation

In one of Bauer's morbid melodramas, *The Dying Swan* (Khanzhonkov & Co., 1916), the heroine's father consoles his daughter, the mute ballerina Gizella (Vera Karalli): "Surely, you are not crying because you cannot speak? You have your face, which speaks more than words. You have a soul which is more beautiful than words." The next intertitle explains: "Gizella loves to dance. Dancing is her whole life, her soul." While this familiar interconnection between the soul and expression designates the face as a nonverbal, expressive medium of the human

---

I am grateful to Tom Gunning for offering invaluable comments on my talk during the Domitor conference in Stockholm, 2016.

personality, it seems also crucial to look at interactions between the face and dance, brought together here by a ballerina from the Imperial Bolshoi Theater, Vera Karalli, a dark-haired beauty who lent her gray eyes and classic profile to the screen in 1914.[4] In the course of the 1900s, choreography, especially ballet, grew into a metamodel for cinematic performance, for the body moving on screen, and, as I suggest, for the cinematic face.[5] The cardinal point of intersection between the two media of ballet and cinema lies in the mutual muteness and the art of rhythmic movement, as a writer for the Alexander Khanzhonkov studio's trade magazine *Pegas* observes: "Ballet, with the silence of its personages, is destined for direct service to the kinematograph by fate itself. These two 'mute' breeds of art perfectly amplify each other."[6]

In the essay "The Ballerina's Smile," Alexander Cherepnin, one of the first Russian theoreticians of dance from the beginning of the twentieth century, admires classical ballet choreography as "the highest stage of dance culture . . . free from the soul's excesses, and governed by that which is common to all arts—the law of emotional economy—whose ideal is the calm and smooth sea surface of the soul, a reticent sense of being withdrawn. Remember the passionless, empty, expressive-of-nothing faces of antique sculptures of the classical period. Mimics are out of place here."[7] Praising the empty, motionless visages of antiquity, the sameness of its sculptural faces,[8] Cherepnin considers "the ballerina's smile"—a stereotypical frozen smile held across different dances, a grimace in between the face and the mask—the wrong face for ballet, while the ideal would be fulfilled by "the ballerina without the face, or with the face covered by a mask or tulle veil. . . . An easy compromise may be achieved: to create a single expression which would correspond to the nature of each individual dance or style of a ballet. Thus, Karsavina in Shopeniana dances with half-closed eyes and lashes looking down, with the face enveloped by a diaphanous veil of melancholy. The sorrow imprinted on the face of Karalli-Odetta is convincing as well."[9]

This facial architectonic of sorrow becomes Karalli's signature appearance, a perfect ballerina's face that found its way into Russian cinema's paradigm of the restrained visage that seems to downplay expressive variety.[10] External immobility, calm, and slowness became the equivalents of truthfulness, sincerity, and naturalness in cinematic performance, reflected as well in the notion of the model (*naturshchik*), a term borrowed from the plastic arts of painting and sculpture and epitomized in the method of choosing actors for their peerless look, the sculptural neutrality of the face, or the ability to control all movements, rather than for acting talent. Bauer was among the first to recognize the film actor as the "model of the screen."[11]

The proclivity to reduce and subdue such a complicated text as the human face in ballet and cinema transpires in different media as well. In modern theater, as Gordon Craig, moving toward his theory of the Über-Marionette as the perfect actor, stated around 1908, "In most cases, the human facial expression does not have any value, and the theater art urges me to acknowledge that it would be better if a performer instead of six hundred expressions holds just six."[12] The Symbolist "total theater," creating unity out of figures, light, and forms, subordinated natural human expression to the faces of sleepwalkers, while the idea of the face as mask became one of the theatrical techniques Vsevolod Meyerhold used throughout his creative career, finding its way to the director's cinematic experiment, *The Picture of Dorian Grey* (Timan & Reinhardt Studio, 1915).[13] Russian Symbolist poet Maximilian Voloshin, fascinated by the pervasive sameness of faces spawned by modernity, particularly by theater and the department store, developed a theory of the mask as a translucent layer-veil that, reducing the face, allows it to gleam through, both covering and revealing the face at the same time. For the poet, paradoxically, it is only with this mask, performing the face's "spiritual cloth" and "an artificially created mechanism that, representing a living human, possesses its own gestures, intonations, words, tastes," that the face comes into being.[14]

With this reduction, the face as a signifying system based on the classification of expressions or types gives way to a face as a surface of perpetual transformations. The double analogies for the ballerina's face that Cherepnin poses—the immobile visage of a statue and the calm and smooth water of the sea—both embody this reduction and, at the same time, foreground the surface as one of the face's main expressive constituents. The metaphor of water, conveying the ephemerality of the ballet, renders the face as a dynamic façade of forces, streams, and tensions, a subject of deformation—that is, a dynamic process or a trace of motion inscribed on the surface from inside or outside. In *Cœur fidèle* (Pathé, 1923), Jean Epstein creates "the fluid world of the screen"[15] by superimposing two surfaces—the woman's pale visage and the sea—enabling different water movements, from light ripples to streams and crashing waves, to supplement the immobile mask with the perpetual motion and unrest of the living human face. The cinematic layering of the images of water and the expressionless, "photogenic" mask together produce the face. Elsewhere, Epstein, for whom cinema is composed of small movements, describes a face in close-up as revealing breezes and waves of feeling: "Muscular preambles ripple beneath the skin. Shadows shift, tremble, hesitate.... A breeze of emotion underlines the mouth with clouds.... Capillary wrinkles try to split the fault. A wave carries them away."[16] Emotions act on facial features as natural events act on a landscape; the face transforms into a surface at the power of these elemental forces.

In Bauer's melodrama *After Death* (Khanzhonkov & Co., 1915), the close-up of the heroine Zoia (Vera Karalli) reveals the "ballerina's face"—the white surface, vacant of significant deformations from emoting or acting, with the wide-opened unblinking eyes. With the progression of the close-up, the face stays

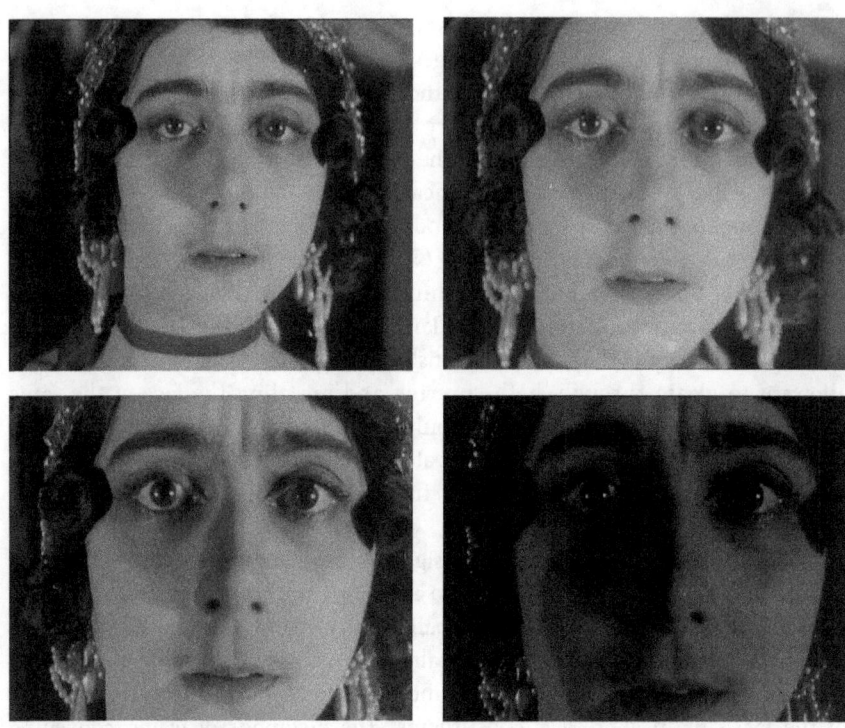

Figure 17.1a–d. The Close-Up of Vera Karalli. *After Death*, dir. Evgenii Bauer (Khanzhonkov & Co., 1915).

immobile; Karalli just slightly lowers her eyelids and raises her chin. When the camera tracks in, the face enlarges until it fills the entire screen, strangely reciting another moving close-up from Bauer's *Happiness of the Eternal Night* (Khanzhonkov & Co., 1915): Medusa's stone face with grotesquely frozen eyes, a mask of shock that visualizes the face that has already reached the limit of its expressive power. The face advancing toward the spectator reiterates the Phantasmagoria ghosts or unusual creatures and monsters forcefully approaching the screen's surface from the "inside" of the image in the magic lantern shows, repeated in tracking to the face of the moon in Georges Méliès's *A Trip to the Moon* (1902). Karalli's explicitly frontal close-up belongs to the set of stylistic conventions that approximate early cinema and sacral imagery, as in the Byzantine icon or acheiropoetic image of the Veil of Veronica.[17] The viewer is not drawn into the space of the image by the frontality of the icon, as Noa Steimatsky notes, but the space "is directed forward: depth is conceived not as behind but in front of the icon."[18] The frontally positioned face no longer offers a depth to reveal, but rather everything happens on its surface or is being pushed forward into the zone between the face and its interlocutor. With its frontal assault on the camera, Karalli's face attains a nearly ceremonial significance, magnifying almost to the level of monstrosity and conveying the face's power to enthrall and transfix.

When Karalli presses forward, her face is rendered as progressively distorted by being layered with shadows, the fleeting traces of surface deformation not unlike ripples of water.[19] The more the face is eclipsed and "deformed," the more the facial relief is graphically pronounced, the more the visage beckons expressively: shadows around the eyes and folds between the brows disturb the initial stasis and supplement the face with the imprint of emotion, transfixing it onto a surface for pictorial reading. Within the film, Karalli's white, luminous face reverberates with the glowing and empty screen, whose vacuity exists as a surface of pure potentiality, waiting for shadows to be projected through it: the film's protagonist, Andrei (Vitold Polonsky), an amateur photographer, tries to uncover the mystery of already dead Zoia by examining a glass daguerreotype of her portrait, letting the light from the projector pass through its translucent surface to cast an elusive shadow on a white screen. With Zoia's "absent" interiority, whose enigma remains hidden and unattainable, her face emerges as the vacuous center of the film, as a neutral surface. In its frontality, the face speaks directly, yet still fails to become an entry to the soul that resides behind the facial features; rather, with Bauer's pictorializing strategies, the face promises an elusive interiority through a contingent articulation of shadows and reflections. The ballerina's face, in reciprocity between sculpture, water, and the screen, becomes the reflective surface of deformation, on which external reads as internal. The ballerina's empty face echoes Stéphane Mallarmé's ideas on ballet dance as completely dissolving the personality of a performer. Mallarmé's ballerina translates meaning outside herself, and the ballerina's emptiness secures her fleeting existence solely as a passive carrier of another's script, a surface for the projection of any kind of meaning.[20] Perhaps it is this metaphoric transparency that grants dancers, Vera Karalli and Vera Kholodnaya, the power to become Bauer's exceptional screen performers.

Mosjoukine's Eyes: The Face as Sky-Gazing

"His Gaze," an essay written by Ksenia Mar about Ivan Mosjoukine in 1918, contains a number of assumptions on the nature of the face:

> This superhuman steely gaze instantaneously pierces me. . . . After a tormented scene, the screen grew dim. And from this darkness, his face has been emerging. . . . Framed by grey hair, with pursed lips, barely noticeable lightning of wrinkles crossing his beautiful forehead, this motionless face belongs to a marble statue. . . . And only his eyes are animated by incomprehensibly monstrous life. They stare straight at me, penetrating my soul, speaking of some depthless sorrow, of unearthly tension of emotions. . . . These

several moments during which this gaze has been burning my soul, seem like an eternity. . . . His gaze, consumed by shadows, was fading, and finally dissolved, completely swallowed by this darkness. . . . On the street, trying to avoid petty artificial electrical lights, I gaze at the sky, looking for faraway stars. I saw their pale twinkling and it reminded me of his gaze—his eternal gaze looking from afar. . . . A city tram passing, and for a brief moment strange unfamiliar faces flashed by behind its glass window—such bizarre faces, completely lifeless, dead.[21]

The sky's human incarnation in this essay reveals contemplation of the face in kinship with sky-gazing, folding the Romantic paradigm of a sublime, solitary encounter with nature into the modern experience of the face through the cinematic apparatus. Iconographically and pictorially, the sky invokes a similar awe of immensity as the face in close-up does, while metaphorically embodying a host of ideas such as flux, absence, distance, metamorphosing of reality, and transcendence to an imaginary sphere. Mar's vision of Mosjoukine's gaze, seducing from the sky, accentuates the role of distance in the cinematic experience, while the text's folding of intimacy and remoteness, the detail and the gigantic, highlights an essential quality of the close-up. The face, sky, and screen images live in sympathetic resonance; the face becomes the filmic close-up and then the eternal celestial realm, whose heavenly fogginess suspends the face between appearance and disappearance. Modernity is abundant with representations of the atmospheric, formless faces in a state of flickering instability, on the verge of dissolution, the face as a milky nebula in which two eyes can be distinguished by their twinkling. Voloshin finds this face in the paintings of Eugène Carrière, whose black-and-white portraitures show the face made of bundles of matter not yet figured: "For Carrière, the human face is the twinkling of a celestial planet, mysterious, unknowable. The face is the celestial dust of the Milky Way; it is whirlwinds of unformed celestial nebula. The celestial landscape of the face. Every face of Çarrière is infinitely close, desirable, yet unattainable, like the native face of the Earth seen from the freezing depth of a Moon crater."[22]

Despite Mosjoukine's versatility as an actor (his repertoire includes diverse roles from comical incarnations of women to romantic heroes to neurasthenics), the plastic nature of his facial features, covered with white makeup, acquires the qualities of sculpture. Instead of a living face, Mosjoukine initially emerges out of Mar's description as the ideal image, fixed in the immobility of statue, the ultra-face (his sculptural blankness is later used by Lev Kuleshov in his experiment) whose hair, lips, and forehead form the frame for this face's essential feature—the actor's famous eyes. The more Mar immerses herself in the kinetic energy of the actor's ecstatic gaze, the more the face disappears from her ekphrasis, until his eyes become his face, living on after the crystalline sculptural visage dissolves.

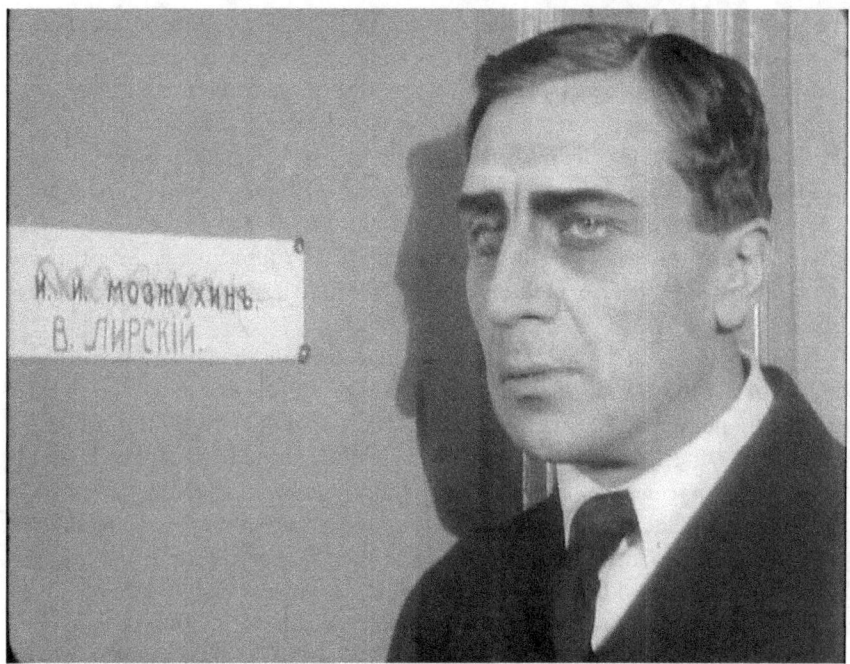

Figure 17.2. Ivan Mosjoukine. *Behind the Screen*, dir. G. Azagarov (?) & A. Volkoff (?) (Co. "I. Ermoliev," 1917).

Mar's description comes closer to the Romantic tradition that sees the eyes as "the mirror of the soul," a point where one's soul is able to speak most directly to another.

But to what degree does Mosjoukine's expression owe to his inner emotions and acting skills, and to what degree does he take his expression from the effective lighting? While Mar recites here the disorienting experience of the cinematic close-up, by which proximity and enlargement entails the loss of unity of the face, the text exposes one of the basic dualities of the face that rests on the ambiguous relations of the skin's surface and the eyes: in their mobility, contrasted with the immobility of the rest of the face, and light shining on the eyeball, the eyes are singled out from the facial totality, creating a plastic conundrum for the medium of sculpture. Being the most difficult facial part for sculptural rendering, the eyes also cannot be copied or imprinted on the death mask. The metaphoric potential of the eyes, lost in the discourse of sculpture, finds its likeness in atmospheric and celestial events with the pale twinkle of stars standing for light twinkling in the eyes. Gaston Bachelard notes how this twinkling quality suggests the gaze; for him, the starry night sky is a realm of absolute slowness, of imperceptible movements of celestial bodies, in which everything that shines and twinkles acquires the gaze.²³ The expressive potentiality of the tiny dot of trembling light reflected in the iris to animate the eyes and create the gaze, long-recognized in painting and photography, reappears in cinematic acting: Evgenii Petrov, directly linking the expression of the eyes to the power of reflecting light, states in his book on the film actor that "the most crucial quality for the screen performer's eyes is not their color but their capability to gleam, which constitutes expression."²⁴ The particular quality of Mosjoukine's light-blue eyes to gleam, their "pale twinkling," and their ability to easily overflow with tears, supplemented by virtuosity in manipulating the gaze and amplified by effective lighting, all constitute this "magnetic gaze."

Mixing inside and outside, the eye's convex mirror emerges as an interface, on the surface of which a reflection appears as a promise of the soul. The eye's virtual depth, not unlike the depth of the cinematic screen, paired with the illusory power of moving light, figures the apparatus of film as a medium of light. From his experiments in scenography in the technological theater of operetta-*féerie* during the late 1890s, Bauer was quite familiar with the ability of the twinkling light to create a moving image. One of the pieces in Bauer's repertoire was the mysterious spectacle of twinkling and moving lights, so-called wandering lights, often linked to the motif of resurrection of the dead and the animation of inanimate bodies, such as statues coming to life.²⁵ The theatrical light becomes dispersed throughout the multitude of different sources of illumination that, twinkling and shining everywhere, animated the space in one kinetic kaleidoscope, so the entire stage environment appeared vitalized with the vibration, scintillation, and flickering of numerous lights. In its pure electrical brilliance in the operetta-*féerie*, light as such received a visibility of its own, as its power exceeded the function of illumination and became an apparatus for animation and stage illusion.²⁶ Tom Gunning, describing the meaning of "flickering" as a rapid movement of light, originally referring to flames or the reflection of light, points to "light's ability not only to reveal, illuminate, and enlighten, but also to conceal, cast shadows, and create illusions."²⁷ In the same vein, twinkling refers to the power of light to animate and create an illusion of the gaze. It is the twinkle—a trembling, unsteady, spasmodic light switching repeatedly between bright and pale—that obliterates the stasis of Mosjoukine's and Karalli's stare. Transforming the Chronos of the motionless sculpture to the Kairos of the passing moment, the twinkle introduces time and creates expression, while the ideality of the sculptural visage in its aesthetic sublimation gives way to a contingency of individuality narrated through the volatility of nature. Mar's aligning of Mosjoukine's face with the spectacle of nature also contains an assumption about cinema: unlike the artificiality of the tram window transforming faces into a vision of the dead, cinema appears capable of rendering the transience of life—the darkness of the screen, which is the darkness of the night sky, is transfigured into a living environment.

Ephemeral/Ethereal/Elemental: Air and Breathing

The major face of the cinema belongs to the first Russian film star, and a discovery of Bauer, Vera Kholodnaya, whose rare photogenic qualities, her *kinogenie*, made this "supreme model of the screen" into a sensation. She lacked dramatic acting experience but was trained as a ballet dancer who occasionally performed in *tableau vivant*; thus, Kholodnaya's screen appearance communicates a captivating presence rather than any psychological fulfillment of a character. In *The Song of Love Triumphant* (Khanzhonkov & Co., 1915), Kholodnaya's first film, Bauer broke the scene of her close-up into separate disconnected fragments, "nuances of emotions as laughter, a calm mask, grief, tears, sobbing," alternating them with images of objects and natural elements—"landscapes, vases, clouds."[28] What is particularly intriguing in the reflective face, born through montage in anticipation of the famous experiment of Bauer's pupil Kuleshov, is this juxtaposition between the face on-screen and the elusive phenomenon of a cloud, sharing with the face perpetual subtle transitions from invisibility to visibility and so on. Metaphorizing ideas of flux and revelation, the cloud translates the experience of the aesthetic instability of the face that, in its nebulous image, morphs and mutates, slowly undulating and continuously changing.

Kholodnaya figures a paradox: while compared to the "marble Madonna" (the screen name "Kholodnaya," meaning "cold," implies the coldness of marble and a restricted register of emotions—in the cinematic mise-en-scène she is often juxtaposed with statues and sculptural figurines), her statuary perfection and pale visage become animated by a life force—her intense, ecstatic breathing. Impalpable, yet existing, breath is corporeal excess, an elusive presence that stands for the inside-out dynamic, for the soul, a kind of Platonic essence. Communicating between inside and outside, breath blurs the opposition of visible and invisible, and through breath this relation between seen and unseen comes to be visceral.[29] "A breeze of emotion underlines the mouth with clouds";[30] breath manifests itself via its surface deformation as Kholodnaya's facial gesticulation seems to be generated by an internal force finding its way out of her body, haunted by involuntary spasms. But what becomes more apparent is how through its production and kinship with air, breath exposes the face's relationship with the body, objects, and the environment surrounding the face. Throughout her films and photographs, Kholodnaya's face often appears enveloped in layers of translucent, airy materials, ephemeral fabrics of white tulle, gauzy veils, and fuzzy feathers undulating in the filmic wind, a seeming continuation of her breathing, as in the lengthy, tumultuous scene of the heroine's suffering during the wedding ball in Bauer's *Life for a Life* (Khanzhonkov & Co., 1916).

The natural rhythm of breathing merges with the artificial wind—generated by Bauer's beloved wind machines—and both translate into the affective shaping of cinematic rhythm; the face, the environment, and the image itself are suffused

Figure 17.3. Vera Kholodnaya. *Life for a Life*, dir. Evgenii Bauer (Khanzhonkov & Co., 1916).

with the moving air.[31] The exaggerated breathing moves air that, together with the wind, exposes Kholodnaya's centrifugal face (contrasting with Mosjoukine's centripetal face) and environment as being in reflexive correspondence. When Roland Barthes in *Camera Lucida* describes something reverberating from a photographic portrait as "a sudden awakening, completely, outside of likeness, . . . a kind of intractable supplement of identity . . . stripped of any importance,"[32] he refers to it as the "air" of a photographic image. While Barthes's air is undoubtedly different from Bauer's, they both point beyond resemblance and iconicity and are part of the aerial imagination ruled by equivocation between the visible and the invisible.

The Face between the Death Mask and Elemental Media

Through the three faces that repeat a certain pattern—immobile sculptural blankness animated by the flux of deformation, twinkling, or breathing—cinema does not merely fashion the face as a text for affective reading but reveals the face as continuously mediated. In 1913, a Russian illustrated magazine published a collage of nine photographic images of tango performers in which the plastic qualities of the dancers, the power of light of the photographic medium, and the skills of the photographer transform and stylize the moving figures into antique

Figure 17.4. Vera Kholodnaya. *Life for a Life*, dir. Evgenii Bauer (Khanzhonkov & Co., 1916).

sculptural reliefs. Throughout the images, the dancers hold the same expression and have their eyes closed, wearing what would be Cherepnin's ideal "ballerina's face"—the face as the death mask. These photographic sculptural ghosts certainly call to mind André Bazin's insight into the very origin of the photographic image that lies in the desire to preserve the body and face, shared by cinema as a medium for recording physical reality.[33] The face fleetingly appears in a review on *The Song of Love Triumphant*:

> The screen images that photograph reality are as less real as a book illustration or as a dream weaved from snatches of what one has experienced while awake. This sense of unreality is amplified by the fast alternation of cinematic pictures and their uniform grey tone, similar to a uniform tone of images created by a poet's inspiration. In most cases, these poetic images have only a face, a form, and being born in imagination, the images no longer stay still, but become blurred, indistinct, flickering: a perfect semblance of the movie screen.[34]

In the reciprocity here between the images of imagination and the images on the movie screen, the latter, for a moment, receives form—the elusive façade of the close-up—only to dissolve back into gray and formless flickering. The face seems like the only form possible for the scintillating flow of imagination, while the film image mirrors the face's suspension between figure and formlessness, the sculptural logic and the atmospheric logic, pictorial closeness and elemental openness. In the face's suspension between the artifice of sculpture and the volatility of nature, sculpture figures the face as an aesthetic totality, form, copy, and imprint of the death mask, while the contingency of the elemental media invokes the face's shifting immediacy, which escapes copying and may even lie beyond representation. The ephemerality of the face points beyond resemblance and iconicity and invites a conceptualization through water, air, and cloud that are among the natural sources of figuration, in which appearance is reduced to imagination without images. Their elemental formlessness, and then polysemy as signs, exposes the face as a self-manifesting and malleable text. In the cinema, the face's expressive power transcends psychological motivations; rather, these transient supplements to the sculptural visage, evoked through the metaphorics of elemental media, suggest the passage from fleeting appearance to essence and render the face's ability to be expressive. The elemental media help to explain not merely the fragile stability of the face, but how the face operates, to uncover its technologies—the surface deformations and creation of the gaze via twinkling and reflection. This work of the face supports itself by the process of breaking form, which belongs, according to Georg Simmel, to the fundamental logic of the face. It is this breaking of form, narrated through elemental media, that implies the medium specificity, as it stands for the flickering instability of the face that only cinema can promise to show.

OKSANA CHEFRANOVA is Lecturer in Film and Media Studies at Yale University, where she is also the Director of Film Programming. She is currently working on a book manuscript, *From Garden to Kino. Evgenii Bauer, Cinema, and Russian Visual Culture Circa 1900*.

Notes

1. The face has a long history and art history, being linked to nonmimetic expressivity, universal language, visual knowledge, scientific exploration, and discipline. Some significant contributions on the face include Noa Steimatsky, *The Face on Film* (Oxford, UK: Oxford University Press, 2017); Noa Steimatsky, "What the Clerk Saw: Face to Face with the Wrong Man," *Framework: The Journal of Cinema and Media* 48, no. 2 (2007): 111–36; Jacques Aumont, "The Face in Close-Up," *The Visual Turn: Classical Film Theory and Art History*, edited and with an introduction by Angela Dalle Vacche (New Brunswick, NJ: Rutgers University Press, 2003): 127–48; Mary Ann Doane,

"The Close-Up: Scale and Detail in the Cinema," *Differences: A Journal of Feminist Cultural Studies* 14, no. 3 (2003): 89–111; Tom Gunning, "In Your Face: Physiognomy, Photography, and the Gnostic Mission of Early Film," *Modernism/modernity* 4, no. 1 (1997): 1–29; Mikhail Yampolsky and Larry Joseph, "Mask Face and Machine Face," *TDR: The Drama Review* 38, no. 3 (Autumn 1994): 60–74.

2. Georg Simmel, "The Aesthetic Significance of the Face," in *Georg Simmel, 1858–1918: A Collection of Essays, with Translations and a Bibliography* (Columbus: Ohio University Press, 1959): 276–81.

3. Valentin Turkin, "Evgenii Bauer," *Pegas: Zhurnal Iskusstv/Pegasus: A Journal of Arts* 5 (1916): 49–51.

4. Praising Karalli's rhythmic subtlety and gestural expressiveness, as well as her luminous face, Aleksandr Khanzhonkov notes, "With her beautiful gray eyes and classic profile she made such a sensation that she became at once a 'kino-star,' rising on the Russian film horizon." A. A. Khanzhonkov, *Pervye gody russkoi kinematografii: vospominaniia* (Moskva: Iskusstvo, 1937), 86 [my translation].

5. On connections between ballet and cinema, see Lynn Garafola, "Dance, Film, and the Ballets Russes," *Dance Research: The Journal of the Society for Dance Research* 16, no. 1 (Summer 1998): 3–25.

6. Vedi Slovo, "Ballet and Kinematograph," *Pegas: Zhurnal Iskusstv/Pegasus: A Journal of Arts* 2 (1915): 94 [my translation].

7. Alexander Cherepnin, "The Ballerina's Smile," *Teatral'naya gazeta* (Moscow, 1913–1917), from a clipping file held by the Museum of Maly Theater, Moscow [my translation]. During the 1910s, when Cherepnin (pen name Li) was publishing in the art periodical *Theater Newspaper*, he was influenced by the ideas of Benedetto Croce's look at choreography through the prism of cultural theory.

8. The Silver Age's revival of interest in classical antiquity was pervasive, affecting literature, visual arts, dance, and popular media. Samuel N. Dorf, "Dancing Greek Antiquity in Private and Public: Isadora Duncan's Early Patronage in Paris," *Dance Research Journal* 44, no. 1 (2012): 5–27; Anna Frajlich, *The Legacy of Ancient Rome in the Russian Silver Age*, Vol. 48 (Amsterdam: Rodopi, 2007).

9. Alexander Cherepnin, "The Ballerina's Smile" [my translation].

10. On psychology conveyed in early Russian cinema through the static frozen face and immobile eyes, see Yuri Tsivian, "New Notes on Russian Film Culture," in *The Silent Cinema Reader*, ed. Lee Grieveson and Peter Krämer (London: Routledge, 2004).

11. The term "*naturshchik*/model" fully emerged in the 1920s, and Lev Kuleshov claimed to have coined it. Yet Bauer and Valentin Turkin began using the term during the early 1910s. See Nea Zorkaia, "Svetopis' Evgeniia Bauera," *Iskusstvo Kino* no. 10 (1997): 77–93. It is tempting to see Bauer's *naturshchik* as an anticipation of Robert Bresson's concept of the model and the French director's method. See Doug Tomlinson, "Performance in the Films of Robert Bresson: The Aesthetics of Denial," in *More Than a Method: Trends and Traditions in Contemporary Film Performance*, ed. Cynthia Baron, Diane Carson, and Frank P. Tomasul (Detroit, MI: Wayne State University Press, 2004), 71–93.

12. My translation from a Russian edition of Gordon Craig, *Vospominaniya, stat'i, pis'ma* (Moskva: Iskusstvo, 1988), 237.

13. On mask acting as a component of Meyerhold's aesthetics, see Robert Gordon, *The Purpose of Playing: Modern Acting Theories in Perspective* (Ann Arbor: University of Michigan Press, 2006).

14. Maximilian Voloshin, "The Face, Mask, and Nudity," in Maximilian Voloshin, *Liki tvorchestva* (Leningrad: Nauka, 1988), 399–404.

15. Jean Epstein, "The Fluid World of the Screen," in *Jean Epstein: Critical Essays and New Translations*, ed. Sarah Keller and Jason N. Paul (Amsterdam: Amsterdam University Press, 2012).

16. Jean Epstein, "Magnification," in *French Film Theory and Criticism*, Vol. 1., ed. Richard Abel (Princeton, NJ: Princeton University Press, 1993), 235. On Epstein's ideas of fluidity, see Jean Epstein, "Logic of Fluidity," in *Jean Epstein: Critical Essays and New Translations*, ed. Sarah Keller and Jason N. Paul (Amsterdam: Amsterdam University Press, 2012).

17. Within the Byzantine theology, the acheiropoetic image meant an image miraculously created by divine agency and "without the hand" and by direct imprint. On frontality in early cinema, see François de la Bretèque, "Les films hagiographiques dans le cinéma des premiers temps," in *Une invention du diable? Cinéma des premiers temps et religion*, ed. Roland Cosandey, André Gaudreault, and Tom Gunning (Sainte-Foy, Québec: Presses de l'Université Laval/Domitor, 1992): 121–30.

18. Noa Steimatsky, "Pasolini on Terra Sancta: Towards a Theology of Film," *Yale Journal of Criticism* 11, no. 1 (1998): 247.

19. Writing on Rodin, Rainer Maria Rilke compares the face of a living person posing for the sculptor, full of motion and unrest, to ripples and the crashing of waves that become shadows on the sculptural face. Rainer Maria Rilke, *Auguste Rodin* (New York: Sunwise Turn, 1919), 32.

20. Stéphane Mallarmé expressed his fascination with how the dancer's subjectivity can disappear in dance and the female body transfigured into the pure idea of movement and transformation, almost into "nothingness." Stéphane Mallarmé, "Ballets," in *Selected Prose Poems, Essays, and Letters*, trans. Branford Cook (Baltimore: Johns Hopkins University Press, 1956), 62. The ballet performer, unlike dramatic actors, does not need to project the presence of a character's personality but should remain empty, to be a passive carrier of another's script. Bauer's *The Dying Swan* fashions Karalli's mute ballerina Gizella as such a type of empty canvas for a decadent painter, who, possessed by panic over the unrepresentable, embodies the idea of death using Gizella's dead body. See also Tom Gunning on Mallarmé's ideas in Tom Gunning, "Loïe Fuller and the Art of Motion: Body, Light, Electricity, and the Origins of Cinema," in *Camera Obscura, Camera Lucida: Essays in Honor of Annette Michelson*, ed. Richard Allen and Malcolm Turvey (Amsterdam: Amsterdam University Press, 2003), 75–89.

21. *Kinogazeta*, no. 10 (1918): 6 [my translation]. Mar writes about the lost film *Sin* (1918), which belongs to the later phase of Mosjoukine's career in Russia, when he shifted to playing neurotic figures. For a comprehensive outline of the actor's career in Russian cinema, see Richard Abel, "The 'Magnetic Eyes' of Ivan Mozzhukhin," *Cinefocus* 2 (Fall 1991): 27–34.

22. Maximilian Voloshin, "Carrière," in Voloshin, *Liki tvorchestva*, 238. Marcel Proust's *In the Shadow of Young Girls in Flower* describes Albertina's face as a shapeless environment, atmospheric substance, comparing it to the white constellation of twinkling stars.

23. Gaston Bachelard, *Air and Dreams: An Essay on the Imagination of Movement* (Dallas, TX: Dallas Institute Publications, 1988), 161–74.

24. Evgenii Petrov, *Cho dolzhen znat' kinoakter* (Moskva: Kinopechat', 1926). Cited in Mikhail Iampolski, *Demon i labirint: diagrammy, deformatsii, mimesis* (Moskva: NLO, 1996), 262.

25. For Robert Planquette's operetta, *Rip Van Winkle*, Bauer designed the setting for the second act: "The tableau 'Wandering Lights' is magnificent, fantastic and beautiful—the abyss, deteriorated and ruined, enlivened by twinkling lights." *Novosti dnia*, August 18, 1895, 3 [my translation].

26. As Hans Blumenberg points out, the German word *Scheine* reflects the equivocal nature of the double meaning of light: "brilliance" and "irradiation," as well as "appearance," "illusion," or "semblance." Light is simultaneously a precondition of vision that makes everything visible and an object of visibility, an appearance itself. Hans Blumenberg, "Light as a Metaphor for Truth," in *Modernity and the Hegemony of Vision*, ed. David Michael Levin (Berkeley: University of California Press, 1993), 30–62.

27. Tom Gunning, "Flickers: On Cinema's Power for Evil," in *Bad: Infamy, Darkness, Evil and Slime on the Screen*, ed. Murray Pomerance (Albany: SUNY Press, 2004), 32.

28. Cheslaw Sabinski's memoir, translated by Yuri Tsivian, in Yuri Tsivian and Richard Taylor, *Early Cinema in Russia and Its Cultural Reception* (New York: Routledge, 2013), 192.

29. See Davina Quinlivan, *The Place of Breath in Cinema* (Edinburgh: Edinburgh University Press, 2012).

30. Epstein, "Magnification," 235.

31. The intensity of the wind machines grows in the scenes in which Kholodnaya breathes ecstatically. Kholodnaya's face offers a contradiction to Greta Garbo's visage, also interacting with the wind in the final close-up in *The Queen Christina* (dir. Rouben Mamoulian, 1933) as the gusts of wind cannot disturb Garbo's primordial face, which completely erases expression and is unsusceptible to deformation.

32. Roland Barthes, *Camera Lucida: Reflections on Photography* (New York: Hill and Wang, 1981), 109.

33. André Bazin, "The Ontology of the Photographic Image," in *What Is Cinema? Vol. 1*, trans. Hugh Gray (Berkeley: University of California Press, 2004), 9–16.

34. Incognito, "The Song of Love Triumphant," *Vestnik Kinematografii* 115, no. 17–18 (1915): 45–48 [my translation].

18 Making Faces

Character and Makeup in Early Cinema

Alice Maurice

For actors in the transitional era, a "character" was synonymous with "a makeup," and since actors typically did their own makeup, acting and "making up" were understood as complementary skills. Discussions of screen makeup practices in the trade and popular press become more prominent after 1910, which is perhaps not surprising given the changing conditions of the cinema in the transitional era—especially the increasing use of the close-up, the industry's push toward artistic status and respectability, and the rise of stardom. While discussions of makeup practices register these industrial and aesthetic shifts, they also reveal continuity with discussions of makeup and acting on the turn-of-the-century stage. In what follows, I focus on three common if somewhat contradictory threads: the disavowal or downplaying of the role of makeup in screen acting; the close association of disguise and authenticity in makeup, including the impact of gender norms and ethnic categories on how makeup was used and judged; and the relation between makeup and facial expression as often opposed tools for controlling and shaping the face. In these debates and discussions, we see how makeup becomes an important tool for translating and recoding persistent attitudes about realism, transformation, and mutability.

Transforming Human Features

James Young, a stage actor who would become a screen actor and director in the transitional era, was known as a master of makeup. In 1905, he published *Making Up: A Practical and Exhaustive Treatise on This Art for Professional and Amateur*. In addition to being a textbook and manual, the book also offered opinions about makeup from a number of the leading stage actors of the day. One of them, Sager Midgley Jr., offers up the following definition: "The art of making up is the art of being able to transform any given set of human features into an apparently different set, and is accomplished with the aid of cosmetics, powder, rouge, grease-paint, crepe hair, and sometimes wigs and beards."[1] This still seems like a useful definition, though tilted toward what was known as "character makeup" (as opposed to "straight makeup"). Straight makeup refers to makeup that is not meant to hide or significantly change the face of the actor; it is essentially beauty makeup, meant to make one look better, to show up well in the footlights or, in the case of cinema, for the camera. Character makeup focuses on creating characters and usually depends on transformation and disguise—on trading one set of features for another, as Midgley put it. But the line between straight makeup and character makeup is not always so clear, and certainly reshaping the features is part of both practices.

Young's book focuses on both, but there is a special emphasis on character makeup. The book contains detailed instructions on how to apply makeup, accompanied not only by step-by-step diagrams, but also—and this is what made it unique at the time—by photographs of well-known actors applying makeup, as well as photos of them with and without it. During this period on stage and screen, actors would often repeat a "makeup" for different characters that fit the same general type. Character types in Young's book include age makeup as well as ethnic and racial disguises, and the book is, of course, replete with stereotypes and stock characters. But it also includes instructions for specific characters—that is, classic figures (from Shakespeare, for example) that were repeatedly called for on the early twentieth-century stage (figure 18.1). You can see this variety of characters (and what is meant by "character") in the list of manufacturer's wigs (complete with order numbers) included in the volume. You could buy a wig for "Irish servant" or "Old woman, eccentric," but also for Marie Antoinette, Pygmalion, or Othello, along with all manner of racial and ethnic stereotypes. And the thing is, if you look at, say, a movie makeup textbook from 1927 (such as MGM makeup artist Cecil Holland's *The Art of Make-up for Stage and Screen*), the categories really do not change much at all.[2]

The list of greasepaint shades—ranging from "very pale flesh color" to "Negro"—shows how skin tones were codified to reflect the standard types and stereotypes circulated on the American stage. While the makeup toolkit of the screen performer remained much the same as that of the stage actor in many ways, there were differences as well, due to the various technological and stylistic elements of early film. Two of the most commonly cited differences for film actors were the proximity of the camera (such that makeup had to look natural "up close") and the color adjustments required for black-and-white orthochromatic film stock. The latter required experimentation with greasepaint shades, since skin tone (understood in terms of white actors) tended to register darker on ortho, and because reds registered as black, the use of rouge and lipstick had to be curtailed or adjusted for film.[3] As actress Edna Mayo put it in a 1915 article for *Picture-Play Weekly*, while rouge was a "beautifier" on stage, it was mainly used as an "alterer" for film, and "the altering is generally for the worse"; she emphasizes the use of rouge "in the make-up of the woman of the streets, the dissipated

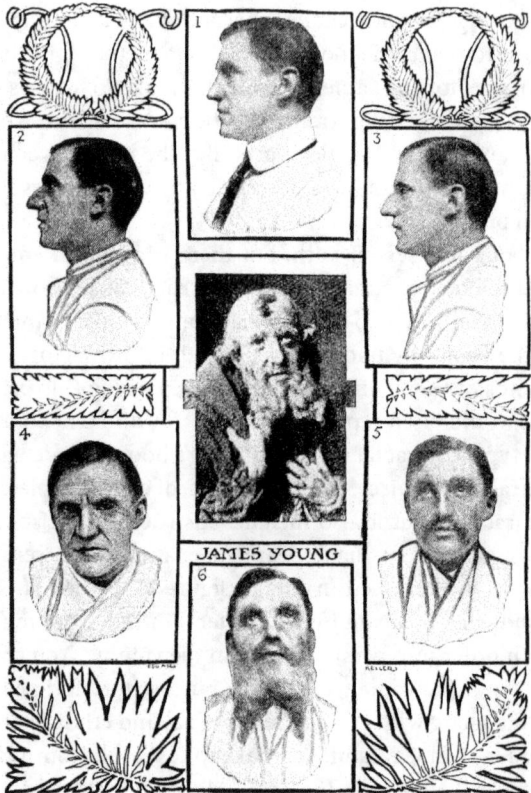

Figure 18.1. James Young showing the process of becoming Shylock.

man, the starving girl mother, the drug fiend, everyone who must show the ravages of dissipation or hardship."[4]

One might expect that Young's book, written in 1905 and geared for the theater, would emphasize more extensive and elaborate makeup. However, the first section of Young's first chapter is dedicated to realism and the exigencies of modern theater: "As the knowledge of the stage manager has advanced in supplying realistic effects, so the actor in his 'make-ups' has kept pace with modern realism."[5] He goes on to demonstrate the fine line between disguise and authentic impersonation, also a common theme in transitional-era discussions of screen acting: "Almost anyone can completely conceal his identity," he notes, but for "successful character impersonation," real skill is required.[6] Even in a text primarily meant for stage actors, some actors advise against too much makeup—notably prominent actor David Warfield, who suggests that acting and "making up" are, in fact, two different and even opposed skills. He gives actors the following simple advice: "Don't make up at all, except under conditions that render it an absolute necessity."[7] In part, he is reacting to the qualities of the makeup itself. While greasepaints were improved, they were still thick and heavy at this time, which is likely why he declares his faith in the actor "depending on the facial expression to convey the meaning of the part to the audience rather than the use of immobile paint."[8] This notion of makeup as a mask that hinders the mobility of the face comes up repeatedly in discussions of screen acting, especially later in the transitional period, when discussions of facial expression become popular—in large part because of the increased use of the close-up and the rise of verisimilar acting codes.[9] Warfield also does his part to deny or disavow his own use of makeup—insisting, for example, that he did not use "a particle of paint on [his] face"[10] for his most famous role, Simon Levy in "The Auctioneer." He then describes the makeup he did, in fact, use but which, he assures us, he could have "done without."[11]

"Making Themselves Up Ugly"

The denial or rejection of makeup continues in discussions of screen makeup, with commentators in trade magazines occasionally scolding actors for makeup mistakes or proclaiming the camera's preference for realism (i.e., less makeup). The disavowal of makeup takes a different form, however, when it comes to female actors. While instruction manuals specific to the screen do not appear until later in the teens, makeup advice in fan magazines is often either aimed at the aspiring (female) actors among the readership or presented in the revelatory tone of nascent celebrity culture.[12] Actresses themselves, when writing about their own makeup practices, often downplay them; in the period before 1915, screen actresses who discuss makeup typically reserve their comments for straight makeup rather than character makeup. When they downplay makeup, it is because they want to tout not their acting prowess as Warfield does (that is, the idea that they do not need makeup to create a character) but rather the photogenic properties of their faces—or what one commentator calls that "exceptional gift for 'registering.'"[13] As Edna Mayo put it, after giving a rather exhaustive treatise on how to apply makeup for *Picture-Play Weekly*, "I myself use very little makeup . . . my face, I am told, is the type that 'takes well.'"[14] After saying this, she details her "simple" makeup routine, which includes cold cream, greasepaint, powder, lip color, eyebrow liner, and the beading of the eyelashes (achieved with a "cosmetic pencil heated in a candle flame"). Here, beauty makeup counts as little or no makeup. She notes that having a face that takes well is not the same as being beautiful, since the camera "performs some weird stunts," such as making beautiful people ugly and vice versa. Of course when she says her face takes well, she refers to the way shadows and light, and black-and-white film stock, will render the features and the shape of the face, while also revealing the way certain offscreen beauty norms determine on-screen preferences and norms. For example, an actor with deep-set eyes will appear "blind or eyeless" to the camera, Mayo notes, while freckles or too "round" a face are generally lamented. On the other hand, the camera's demands can turn an "ugly duckling into a swan," as one fan magazine summed up the story of Mae Marsh. Thought by some too ugly for the camera, they report, she was discovered by D. W. Griffith, who, applying his own physiognomic principles, immediately recognized the screen potential of her "finely shaped head and intellectual forehead."[15]

When trade and fan magazines turn their attention to actresses who play character roles, interviewers typically go out of their way to inform the reader that the actress is, in fact, pretty. This approach seems, in part, to coincide with efforts (beginning around 1909) to position newly rising stars, and with the increasing demand from fans to "know" their favorite actors—by name but also as "personalities." In his study of early cinema stardom, Richard deCordova identified the "dual movement of concealment and revelation [through which] the player's name was constituted and valorized as a site of knowledge," arguing that withholding actors' names was part of the industry's larger strategy of "explicitly posing or revealing a secret" in the promotion of "picture personalities."[16] Indeed, we can see this tension between concealment and revelation play out in two articles about Florence Turner—one in *Moving Picture World* from 1910 (in which we are reminded that she is the "Vitagraph Girl") and one from the same journal in 1912, when she had already achieved fame. In the earlier feature, her "histrionic ability" is tied equally to her "curious blend of nationalities . . . Spanish, Italian, Scotch, and American" (a made-up lineage, which Sumiko Higashi has discussed in terms of Vitagraph's project of rebranding for middle-class taste)[17] and to her "powers of makeup," which allow her to "absolutely disguise her face or obliterate her own charming personality."[18] The 1912 interview, in contrast, emphasizes her willingness to play "homely" characters (while reminding us she is pretty), and credits her success to her "thousand fleeting expressions."[19] Here, her "personality" must shine through, over and against her stated appreciation for the "distortion of the human face." This assurance that actresses who play ugly are actually pretty becomes standard fare. In an interview with Mae Hotely (figure 18.2) from 1912, for example, we are told that she "bears no resemblance to the typical old woman, aggressive mother-in-law, or rampant suffraget [sic]; on the contrary, she quite won the admiration of us all."[20] Here, the larger promotional strategy of concealment and revelation is reiterated by the actor's talent for literal concealment—for disguises that contradict the requisite charm of the female picture personality.

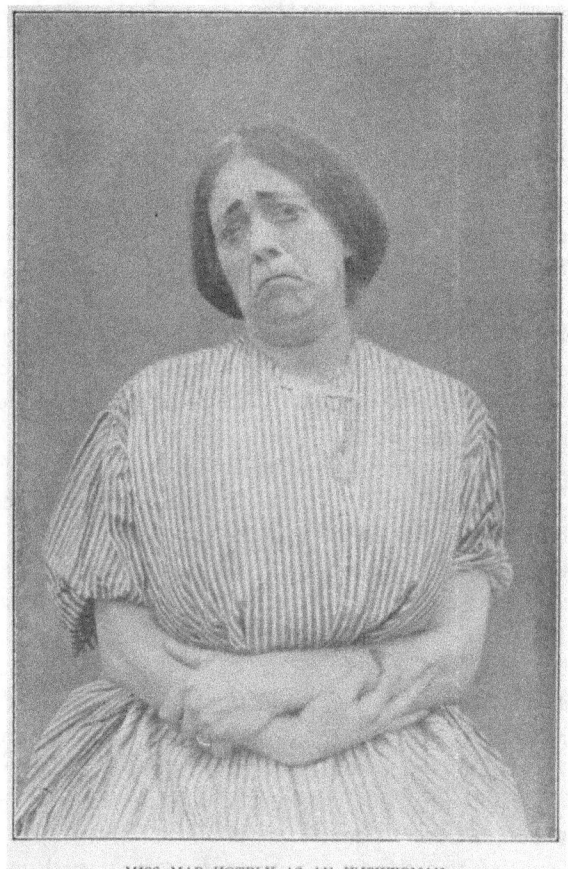

MISS MAE HOTELY AS AN IRISHWOMAN
(SHOWS WHAT CLEVER MAKE-UP CAN ACCOMPLISH)

Figure 18.2. From Francis Agnew's *Motion Picture Acting: How to Prepare for Photoplaying* (1913).

In general, there seems to be a distaste for or a tendency to disbelieve actresses who "make themselves up ugly"—especially young actresses. For his part, James Young, back in 1905, suggested that typage is *always* preferred when it comes to female actors, "owing to the fact that it is apparently impossible for a young woman to make-up effectively to appear matronly or middle-aged."[21] Theater managers must cast women who "looked the part."[22] This attitude lingers on in the effusive praise for nineteen-year-old Blanche Sweet in 1913: "A remarkable case is recorded on the film in which she played the part of a woman of thirty-four years of age and successfully changed to a woman of forty without the aid of makeup. She accomplished the difficult feat of showing the difference in years merely by her finished knowledge of the art of facial expression."[23] We see here not only the astonishing "effect" of a young woman playing "old," but also, again, the opposition between makeup and facial expression.

Disguise and Authenticity

While now and then commentators will praise an actress's makeup skills, it is typically men who are lauded as "masters" of makeup. And, despite multiple commentators calling for realism and typecasting, makeups and types remained common in the years between 1905 and 1915. Special praise was still reserved for the most radical transformations. Prior to Lon Chaney, who came to fame in the teens, numerous actors became famous for their astonishing transformations and complete disguises. Ralph Ince became famous for his Abe Lincoln makeup, featured in multiple Vitagraph films, including *The Battle Hymn of the Republic* (1911).[24] William West was praised as an "undisputed master" of makeup and singled out for his "remarkable make-up" in the 1913 film *To Abbeville Courthouse*, in which the white actor plays an elderly black man. The reviewer for *Motography* noted, "It is a fact that the southern darkies gathered around to watch the taking of the picture were dumbfounded by the realistic make-up which Mr. West so cleverly contrived."[25] Race, of course, was just one of the most obvious and egregious elements in that period that prevented using actors who "looked the part" rather than actors in makeup.

Indeed, in discussions of these makeup transformations, the "fooled-the-natives" test is often applied. Two examples of this suggest the way race, class, and gender expectations shape how makeup is judged and perceived, and also offer up different examples of how makeup for the screen looked on camera and off. One story from *Picture Stories Magazine* praises actor Robert Vignola for his work as Judas in Kalem's *From Manger to Cross* (1914), with the proof of his mastery of makeup found in the fact that he could "walk about the streets of Jerusalem" without attracting any attention.[26] The writer follows this up by telling us that Vignola also recently "crossed from one side of New York to the other when made up as a Jew, and no one saw through the disguise."[27] A 1913 feature on actress Gwendolyn Pates tells a similar story, but differently. Pates recounts shooting a picture in what she calls "the slummiest of slums," in which she plays an "Irish washerwoman's daughter." She tells the interviewer, "I had my makeup on, eyelids darkened and all that," and an "old Irishwoman comes out of one of the tenements." On seeing Pates, the woman concludes she has black eyes, and that she has been beaten "cruel hard" by her husband.[28] Pates gives the woman's reaction in Irish dialect. So the color adjustments that needed to be made for the black-and-white ortho film stock (compensating for eye shadow colors that would look white on film), and which would normally look unusual in real life, are here understood as making her "Irish" disguise all the more realistic off camera, one ethnic stereotype helping out another.

Makeup and Facial Expression

As facial expression became a favored topic during the early teens, many commentators identified a facility with facial expression as the primary skill for actors; they also warned, as *Motion Picture Magazine* did, that "greasepaint is objectionable, because it stiffens the muscles of expression,"[29] though this commentator also went on to detail the use of greasepaint. And although it is tempting to attribute the interest in facial expression solely to changing performance styles and the demands of realism in film, we must remember that this opposition was central to the theories of stage acting and realism that inspired James Young's commentary in 1905. But sometimes descriptions of, advice for, and reactions to acting reveal a more subtle and intricate relation between the expressive powers of makeup and the expressive powers of the face itself.

Beginning in July 1914, *Motion Picture Magazine* ran a series of articles (by the magazine's editor and co-founder, Eugene Brewster), called "Expression and the Emotions." The series draws largely on Darwin's *The Expression of the Emotions in Man and Animals* from 1872, with quasi-scientific explanations of facial muscles alongside philosophical musings about the human emotions. The author's stated purpose is to teach readers how to read facial expressions so that they might better enjoy the movies. Although partly advice for actors on how to best control their facial muscles, it is largely aimed at showing readers what certain emotions look like so that they can recognize them correctly. Brewster makes a passing reference to makeup when he notes, "Formerly, the faces on the screen were all chalky white and the art of make-up was not understood by the players. The best camera in the world cannot give perfect modeling to faces that are plastered with grease paint and white powder."[30] The technological conditions were now right, he says, for an actor to "make his or her face tell the story."[31] The articles feature photos of actors—sent in by the actors themselves—representing particular emotions. His focus is primarily on the mobility of the face, on the "capacity for expression."[32] And yet for all this emphasis on mobility, Brewster is fairly rigid in terms of which actors are capable of embodying which emotions; he calls them out by name, declaring which sorts of emotions they can express and which they cannot, and whether they have expressive faces at all: "The face of Cissy Fitzgerald is remarkably mobile. . . . Alice Joyce's face is not."[33] But he ends up relying on the more immobile qualities of the face—calling on physiognomy and even phrenology. He notes that certain kinds of faces (and heads) are limited to certain types and certain social meanings, saying that while "photoplay directors show cleverness in assigning parts in which racial peculiarities should dominate, they often err with regard to physiognomic and phrenological points."[34] He goes on to explain the (physiognomic) difference between a character who "accomplishes his designs by force of will" and one who does so "by brute strength." He notes that these characters' chins and foreheads will

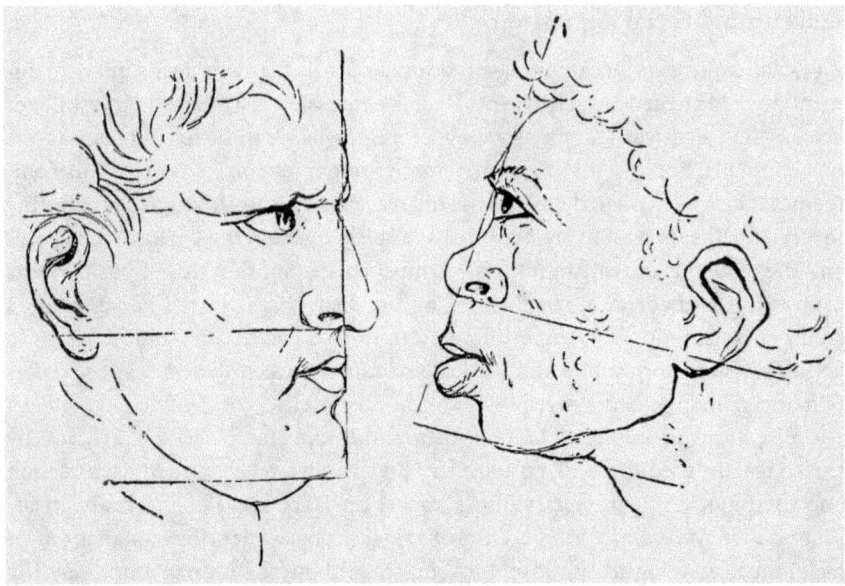

Figure 18.3. Physiognomic illustration from *Motion Picture Magazine*'s 1914 series on "Expression and the Emotions."

be set differently, and uses images to illustrate his point (figure 18.3), saying that they serve his purpose, *even though*, he notes, they were "originally designed to show racial differences."[35] Obviously the coincidence of the types he describes and racial taxonomies is no coincidence.

But this tension between the mobility or mutability of the face, on the one hand, and the notion of the features being set in stone, on the other, suggests the perceived limits of (and maybe even resistance to) the ability to remake the face and its meaning—a resistance, perhaps, to an endlessly fluid identity, a potentially monstrous shape-shifting. As a way of thinking about the combination of makeup and expressiveness, or the possible links between emotional expression and astonishing disguise (both seemingly different benchmarks for acting), I will conclude with a movie called *Miss Jekyll and Madam Hyde*, released by Vitagraph in 1915. The film's title promises a female version of Robert Louis Stevenson's famous story of transformation, but, based on descriptions, that does not quite seem to be what the film delivered. It tells the story of Miss Jekyll (played by Helen Gardner), a young woman whose father has been blackmailed into promising her hand in marriage to an unsavory character. Thinking that this man wants her for her purity, she dreams of becoming "hard, sophisticated, and reckless" in order to turn him off but gives up when she envisions herself as old and "dissipated."[36] So the film did apparently feature her in a "changed" appearance, envisioning a "loose" woman as the analogue to Mr. Hyde, except her transformation is not real, nor is it positioned as the most remarkable one in the film. That is reserved for Baron Stana, a satanic character (his name is an anagram of Satan) played by Paul Scardon, another actor acclaimed as a "master of makeup." An interview with Scardon identifies him as an actor who has "made a success of this art, not by the use of disguises, but by wonderful control over the features."[37] Only a few lines later, however, the writer notes that Scardon "has presented his characterizations in make-up so effective and completely disguising that it is almost impossible to recognize him."[38] Scardon is in makeup on the set of *Miss Jekyll and Madam Hyde* during the interview, and he describes the makeup he devised as one that "appears to change like the fleeting hues in a glass prism. This is accomplished by the use of proper colors and a trick of expression. One moment we have the benevolent old gentleman, and the next the sinister prince of evil."[39] He illustrates this "change of expression" for the interviewer, and "the effect was startling. Almost without any perceptible effort, the kindly old gentleman disappeared, and the speaker appeared to be the leering, evil representative of the infernal regions."[40]

What interests me here is the emphasis on movement, trickery, appearance, and disappearance—how the two characters, good and evil, coexist on his face, which shifts through a "trick of expression" that is also a "trick of makeup." Also, it is interesting that in a movie called *Miss Jekyll and Madam Hyde*, the supporting character is the one who achieves the astonishing transformation. Essentially, the definitive metamorphosis of the story (from good to evil) is safely displaced back onto the male character—while the woman's transformation is imaginary and shifted onto purely sexual "ruined woman" territory. The reviews barely mention the change in her or what it looked like, but Scardon's makeup work is central, the main attraction.

When makeup is visible—when it is actually seen—it is typically seen as additive, transforming, or disguising. But it is also an extension of the face—continuous and contiguous with facial features and facial expressions; as such, it foregrounds the face as a body part, and, like the magical satanic makeup described earlier, offers us flashes of the fluidity of identity and the mutability of flesh and bone. A critical history of makeup practices might reconnect the seemingly opposed histories of the face and the body in cinema, giving us a better sense of how fantasies of authenticity and transformation shape the screen face in ways both material and lasting. We might think about the screen face, then, not merely as a medium for expression, but as a sculpted object and a surface written—and rewritten—upon with makeup.

ALICE MAURICE is Associate Professor of English and Cinema Studies at the University of Toronto. She is author of *The Cinema and Its Shadow: Race and Technology in Early Cinema*.

Notes

1. James Young, *Making Up: A Practical and Exhaustive Treatise on This Art for Professional and Amateur* (New York: Witmark, 1905), 156.
2. Cecil Holland, *The Art of Make-up for Stage and Screen* (Los Angeles: Cinematex, 1927).
3. David Bordwell, Janet Staiger, and Kristin Thompson, *The Classical Hollywood Cinema: Film Style and Mode of Production to 1960* (London: Routledge, 1985), 518–22.
4. Edna Mayo, "Making Up for the Movies," *Picture-Play Weekly*, June 5, 1915, 2.
5. Young, *Making Up*, 6.
6. Ibid., 4.
7. Ibid., 148.
8. Ibid.
9. Roberta Pearson, *Eloquent Gestures: The Transformation of Performance Styles in the Griffith Biograph Films* (Berkeley: University of California Press, 1992).
10. Young, *Making Up*, 148
11. Ibid.
12. Francis Agnew's *Motion Picture Acting: How to Prepare for Photoplaying* (New York: Reliance Newspaper Syndicate, 1913) is an early example of a practical cinema-specific guide for aspirants. It includes makeup as a necessary skill but does not offer specific instructions on the topic.
13. "Velma Lefler," *Picture-Play Magazine*, January 1917, 15.
14. Mayo, "Making Up for the Movies," 1.
15. "Mae Marsh, of the Majestic Company," *Motion Picture Magazine*, August 1915, 118.
16. Richard deCordova, *Picture Personalities: The Emergence of the Star System in America* (Urbana: University of Illinois Press, 1990), 73, 82.
17. Sumiko Higashi, "Vitagraph Stardom: Constructing Personalities for 'New' Middle Class Consumption," in *Reclaiming the Archive*, ed. Vicki Callahan (Detroit, MI: Wayne State University Press, 2010).
18. "Picture Personalities," *Moving Picture World*, July 23, 1910, 187.
19. "Florence Turner Comes Back," *Moving Picture World*, May 18, 1912, 622.
20. "Mae Hotely," *Motion Picture Story Magazine*, October 1912, 150.
21. Young, *Making Up*, 37.
22. Ibid.
23. "Blanche Sweet with Mutual," *Motography*, December 25, 1913, 468.
24. "Ralph Ince, of the Vitagraph Company," *Motion Picture Story Magazine*, March 1913, 114.
25. "A Remarkable Makeup," *Motography*, July 12, 1913, 20.
26. *Picture Stories Magazine*, December 1914, 245.
27. Ibid.
28. "Gwendolyn Pates, of Pathé-Frères," *Motion Picture Story Magazine*, March 1913, 117.
29. "Answer Department," *Motion Picture Magazine*, August 1915, 133.
30. Eugene Brewster, "Expression and the Emotions," *Motion Picture Magazine*, August 1914, 107.
31. Ibid.
32. Eugene Brewster, "Expression and the Emotions," *Motion Picture Magazine*, July 1914, 113.

33. Eugene Brewster, "Expression and the Emotions," *Motion Picture Magazine*, October 1914, 119.
34. Eugene Brewster, "Expression and the Emotions," *Motion Picture Magazine*, September 1914, 102.
35. Ibid.
36. "Miss Jekyll and Madame Hyde," *Motography*, June 19, 1915, 1030.
37. Carl Rich, "Paul Scardon, Master Make-up Artist," *Picture-Play Weekly*, April 24, 1915, 8.
38. Ibid.
39. Ibid., 8–9.
40. Ibid., 9.

Part V
Embodied Audiences

Introduction

Modern conceptualizations of the human body not only found expression on screen in early films but also provided the key terms for debates about film spectatorship from the first days of cinema. The historical accounts in this section describe how the early film spectator was seen as a particularly modern subject and—in keeping with contemporary discourses about gender, adolescence, and physiology—as a crucially corporealized one. This spectator appeared to be uniquely susceptible to the effects of the moving images, already charged as he or she was with modern nervous energies; as such, movies became a source of social anxiety from the new phenomenon of cinema but also one of the attractions that cinema offered.

In the essay that opens this section, Mireille Berton traces popular discourses on the visibility and audibility of early female moviegoers. As Berton shows, the manner in which female audience members inhabited the darkness of the nickelodeons and other early film exhibition spaces became a source of moral concern in the early twentieth century. Commentators of the time described female spectators, time and again, not only as physically and mentally susceptible to the impressions of the motion pictures, but also as a seductive distraction to the male spectators. Thus, while the coming of cinema opened new possibilities for women with respect to visibility in the public sphere, it also quickly necessitated patriarchal society to articulate new oppressive expectations of women's public conduct as spectators. However, as Berton argues, the cultural anxiety that the alleged demeanor of female filmgoers caused points precisely to the emancipatory potential of female spectatorship.

The essays by Christina Petersen and Stephanie Werder demonstrate how such notions regarding the physical impressionability of the film spectator were also central in psychological and physiological research during the early-cinema era. Petersen's essay focuses on the work of noted American psychologist G. Stanley Hall, whose writing on the experience of film viewing during the first decades of the twentieth century anticipates several important conceptions of spectatorship in later works of film theory. Hall engaged with the topic of film spectatorship in his writings on adolescence, which he had described as "the most embodied period of life"; in his view, adolescence entails a form of mimetic relationship with one's environment. As Petersen shows, Hall found mimetic relationships to be an essential aspect of film viewing. For Hall, the cinema could offer everyone—not just young people—the experience of youth spectatorship, which enabled a renewed, embodied relationship to one's self through a playful exploration of actions and attitudes. In this sense, he put a positive twist on the conception of a susceptible or impressionable spectator, as the mimetic encounter with the cinema could, in Hall's view, allow for a reversal of the alienating experience of industrial modernity.

Exploring similar themes in the context of 1910s Germany, Werder's essay considers how the modern recurring topos of the "nervous modern age," which associated modernity with nervousness and sensory overload, found expressions in debates about the cinema. In these early discussions, the cinema—with its bright, flickering, and rapidly shifting pictures—was said to have shocking effects on its viewers' nerves, thus exposing them to mental and physical danger. This discourse may be understood as a variant of former cultural concerns about the effects of modern media, but as Werder argues, it could also attribute positive traits to the cinema: if the film spectator is understood to have a weak, impressionable body, the intense effect of motion pictures could also be seen as a shock therapy of sorts that may heal damaged or dull nerves.

Closing this section, Denis Condon's essay draws on another type of rare and infinitely rich historical resource that may help us come to terms with embodied experiences of film spectatorship—a detailed diary kept by Dublin architect and avid film fan Joseph Holloway, in which he kept records of moviegoing, complete with insights about the films as well as the exhibition spaces, starting as early as 1894. Condon's essay takes us on a journey around Dublin's theaters and movie houses, following the flaneur-diarist whose account offers a unique opportunity to read a firsthand meta-spectatorial commentary that proves to be particularly attuned to the working-class audiences' excitement and behavior during film screenings. With few such accounts still existing today, Condon's reading of the diary entries brings to life another impression of real bodies' encounters with projected images—as well as with one another—in early-cinema exhibitions.

19 "Keep It Dark"

The Fatale Attraction of the Female Viewer's Body

Mireille Berton

THIS ARTICLE AIMS at discussing the erotic appeal of the female spectator and the contrasting discourses generated by her nervous body, perceived as being at once excited and exciting. Blamed for disturbing the early screenings with their exuberant hats, loud laughter, interminable chatter, and breast-feeding when they came with their babies,[1] female viewers were also criticized for provoking disorder by offering an exciting distraction to male spectators. Chief among the concerns about female erotic power was the fact that the presence of women threatened to disturb other viewers, particularly men. Many scholars have examined the erotic function of dark viewing spaces that afforded privacy beneficial to romantic or sexual encounters. Competing discourses about the consequences of female (over)presence in projection sites such as nickelodeons reveal a set of fears related to the new visibility of women's bodies in the public sphere—bodies, as I would like to suggest, that were mainly conceived of as nervous organisms overloaded with contagious stimuli.

The semiobscurity of movie theaters, as well as the romantic atmosphere of some movies, led many commentators to condemn the amoral behavior not only of depraved men but also of women whose erotic appeal both distracted the audience and competed with the spicy scenes on the screen. A closer look at primary sources (articles, press illustrations, postcards, and movie pictures) from different countries (the United States, France, and Italy) reveals the anxiety related to the possibility of mimicry: that of female bodies instinctively imitating the moving images and thereby contaminating the audience. The discourse on women whose excessive visibility upset the smooth running of screenings should thus be situated within the larger context of a culture of the nervous body that feared not only the contagious effects of movies but also those male and female viewers who set a bad example for the others.

Indeed, the fear of female sexuality erupting at film screenings derived from the threat of women's mental and physical impressionability—as well as from the risk of this impressionability becoming widely contagious. In each of her distracting actions during the screening, the female viewer was implicitly described as a nervous body in a context where mass culture was read exclusively through its appeal to excitability, sentimentality, and social mimicry. Therefore, in what follows I will offer some considerations about the gendered and social issues raised by the relationship between the sexualized female viewer and the cultural imaginary of the nervous body as it circulated around 1900.

Cinema as Female Space

From its earliest days, the movie theater revealed itself as a site where people belonging to groups excluded from the dominant discourse and from positions of power could have access to a new kind of collective experience.[2] Whether in Italy, Germany, France, or the United States, the movie theater enabled women in particular to enter public spaces where people who differed in terms of their origins, age, gender, socioeconomic status, and so on mingled together. As the study conducted by the German sociologist Emilie Altenloh shows, in a context where the status of women was being redefined, cinematography offered them the opportunity of having an independent activity, which they greatly appreciated.[3] Interviews conducted with female moviegoers show that they felt perfectly safe and secure in movie theaters, in spite of arguments advanced by moralizers about the so-called dangerousness of movie screenings for "weak" subjects. This was the case of an article published in 1910 that reported the enthusiasm of a "nickelodeon fiend" who liked going alone to the cinema.[4] Therefore, one must distinguish between the social reality within which women, who consumed a great number of moving pictures, were happy to be able to enjoy a relatively unprecedented freedom, and discourses that brandished the specter of sexual, moral, and physical depravity through the symbolic figures of female spectators who were either neurotics, adulteresses, or rape victims.[5]

The fact of the matter is that underlying the moralizing discourse of those who were alarmed by the loosening of morals, cinema was supposed to have encouraged a certain unnamed fear that modern leisure activities might be a means to emancipation for women. For this reason, discourses about female moviegoers must, above all, be considered as discourses about the newfound visibility of women in public spaces that had been dominated by men up until then. What is at stake is not only the visibility of women in movie theaters but also their visibility on the silver screen, with actresses embodying models of femininity that had no precedent and that resisted traditional norms of respectability and morality—examples that were likely to inspire the female moviegoers themselves.

The unease caused by the significant number of women going to the movies finds its source in the excessive behavior of some female spectators who, according to documents, externalized their feelings in noisy fashion and commented constantly at full voice on the images being screened.[6] Thus, mentioning the expressivity and emotivity of women became commonplace in statements by men fantasizing about an ideal female moviegoer who would be as silent as she was invisible,[7] namely a mother with irreproachable moral standards or, better still, a woman escorted by a man (her brother, her husband, or her boss).[8]

One of the goals of the movements aimed at reforming cinema was precisely to create a disciplined viewer whose cognitive activity went unhindered and who respected the ritual of film screening. If during the first phase of film history, screenings were subjected to a process of hystericization in cinephobic and moralistic discourses that relegated them to the feminine sphere of mass culture, the institutionalization phase was associated with a masculinization of the model viewer (as well as exhibition venues, production modes, representation modes, etc.). The will to educate some members of the audience considered to be recalcitrant betrayed the underlying notion that before being a gaze, the female viewer was a body, desirable as well as desiring.

The Female Body and Sexual Desires

As a site fostering social interaction, the movie theater provided people of both genders with opportunities for romantic and sexual encounters.[9] As Richard Maltby points out, "Movies, amusements parks and dance halls created a heterosocial environment that provided young women with access to a wider range of evening pleasures, and produced a commercial relationship between sexes that rendered more ambiguous the connection between the exchange of money and the granting of sexual favors than the processes of direct purchase assumed in the red-light districts."[10]

As illustrated by a substantial iconography, darkness and promiscuity provided ideal conditions for more or less extensive flirtations.[11] Postcards of the 1910s commonly depicted the movie theater as a place of sexual license, where romantic scenes playing on the screen were reflected in the thoughts of audience members. Many of these play on the idea of the movie theater as a place for sexual license because it allowed people to gather in the dark. The thoughts of the audience are then complemented by the image on the screen.[12] Romantic confusion or subterfuge among audience members was a common subject in comic postcards of the early period of cinema, as was the correlation between romantic behavior on the screen and among those watching the film—or not, because they were busy kissing each other.[13] A man embracing his male neighbor rather than a female partner is meant to have occurred because of the darkness; it also shows the variety of sexual behavior depicted in filmic and parafilmic sources.

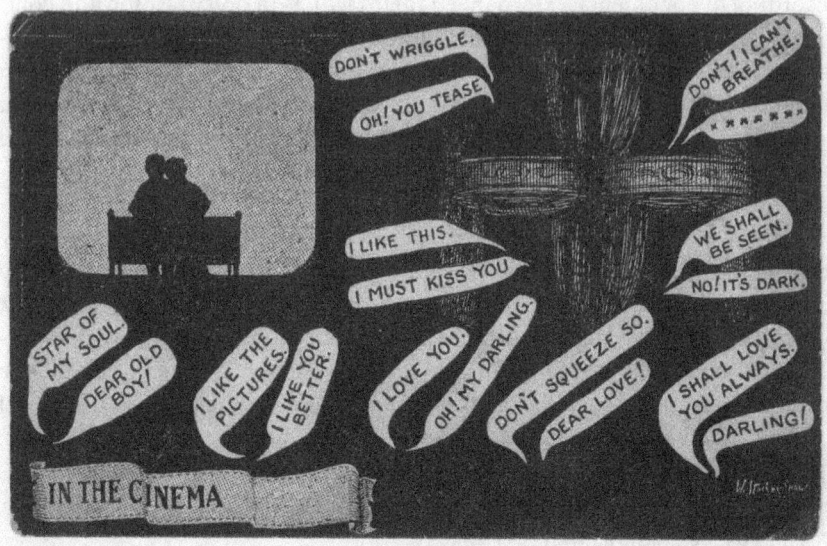

Figure 19.1. "In the Cinema," W. Stocker Shaw, postcard, ca. 1910. Nicholas Hiley Collection.

The sexual dangers of such new social alliances were readily apparent, and middle-class progressive reform activities from different countries targeting vice can be seen in this context.[14] Movie theaters appeared to be heterosocial and heterosexual places that were often described as "stations of vice,"[15] encouraging depraved behavior and white slave traffic.[16] The Chicago Vice Commission declared in 1911 that "vicious men and boys mix with the crowd in front of the theaters and take liberties with very young girls.... Many liberties are taken with young girls during the performance when the place is in total or semi-darkness. Boys and men slyly embrace the girls near them and offer certain indignities."[17]

In press articles about the moving picture shows, we can read that "darkness is a dangerous adjunct of propinquity."[18] Among the problems the reformers condemned were those occasioned by spectators who talked during the show, whistled or clapped at the kissing scenes on the screen, or even sexually harassed women in many ways. The physical presence of women in public screening sites was disturbing not only because they wore big hats, laughed, spoke loudly, or breast-fed their babies but also because their bodies acted as magnets that aroused desire and competed with the stars on the screen.

An article with a satirical tone reveals, "Of course it is not necessary to look at the picture,"[19] as there is another show going on in the movie theater itself, with women offering a display of charms and glamour. For instance, W. A. Scranton advises women to "always take your time and walk leisurely" in order to

Figure 19.2. "You May Make Mistakes Even at the Picture Palace," postcard, ca. 1910. Nicholas Hiley Collection.

mesmerize male viewers. Indeed, the German sociologist Emilie Altenloh points out in her investigation that whereas women went happily to the movies for the sake of the film itself, men's focus was more on their female companions: they watched them watching the movie.[20] Thus, not only were women supposed to be interfering with the proper screening of the film, they were also deemed to encourage, in a relatively active and willing way, licentious behavior. The female moviegoer appears thus as an object for the male gaze as well as an object of desire, on equal footing with the film that fascinates viewers; this competition highlights the implicit analogy between woman and the mesmeric power of the filmic image. As Richard Maltby reminds us, "The culture of consumption required extensive renegotiations of the ways in which women occupied public spaces, but for cinema the anxieties provoked by these renegotiations concentrated around 'realism' and 'imitation.' Films were censorially criticized for the excessive adequacy of their representations of the real, while it was their 'mesmeric' powers of influence that provoked concern over imitative behavior."[21]

The Nervous Body of Spectators

The turmoil caused by female viewers' sex appeal is but one of a set of discourses that depict cinema as an experience with the potential to feminize the viewer,

Figure 19.3. "Come and See the Pictures. Everybody's Doing It!" Donald McGill postcard, ca. 1910. Nicholas Hiley Collection.

which makes it conducive to daydreaming, being vulnerable to suggestion, and even neurosis (exposing one to the danger of a loss of contact with reality). Encouraging all manner of physical and psychological excesses, filmic projections shaped a viewer with a particular sensitivity to an environment fraught with excitement. And indeed, many primary sources describe the act of viewing films with words that connote femininity: emotivity, suggestibility, fickleness, sentimentality, and so on.[22] The insistence on the excesses of moviegoing as practiced by women is in fact a transposition, enabled by the use of different words, of one of the key stereotypes of positivist culture: the hysterical woman who overreacts to external stimuli. For instance, many medical and paramedical texts of the time condemn the contagious effects of moving images, thought to exert a strong suggestive power on so-called weak subjects, such as women, children, and neurotics.[23]

Rae Beth Gordon's work has shown the considerable influence that psychological theories of the imitation instinct and the cerebral unconscious had on early cinema, which integrated them through comedy, as exemplified by the Bous-Bous Mie, a dance with contagious effects on viewers.[24] The fear of female sexuality erupting at film screenings derived from the threat of women's mental and physical impressionability—as well as from the risk of this impressionability becoming widely contagious. Although women were far from being the only category of viewers concerned, commentators frequently singled them out by talking disapprovingly about their psychological and physical excesses and their propensity to interact with their surrounding environment.

Visited by a huge number of people considered to be vulnerable to the physical and psychic effects of moving images, movie shows became sites that were seen as being at once female and feminizing; in other words, they fostered hysteria and regression. The presence in the audience of large numbers of women and children, the very subjects deemed to be the most penetrable to the influence of the filmic image, is not unrelated to this process of feminization of the cinematic apparatus. The latter can even be said to be the subtext of the moralizing discourses that urged the development of regulatory strategies in the effort to transform cinema into a morally respectable art and the viewer into a disciplined subject. In order to regain control over filmic projections, the reform movements would impose rules of conduct more in keeping with the ideals of masculine subjectivity: temperance, moderation, and rationality. Thus, one of the goals of the movements aimed at reforming cinema was to absorb, as much as possible, the nervous body of the viewers—a sensory, mimetic, and desirable body that hindered the consumption of film.

Conclusion

However, female sexuality as it revealed itself at early film screenings was not simply feared as an obstacle to the progressive constitution of a disciplined show; rather, it also functioned as a modality for accessing new kinds of social and aesthetic experiences. Many discursive and iconographic sources depict the figure of the seductress who seeks to take advantage of the particular context of film screenings to entice men. As Shelley Stamp Lindsey points out, all female viewers were considered at once to be soliciting and solicited: "Cinemas were described by many observers as arenas of particular carnal license, where women were alternately preyed upon by salacious men who gathered around entrance ways, and themselves tempted to engage in untoward conduct."[25] According to Sharon R. Ullman, "In the world as on the screen, women came to be incorporated into a vision of desire and lust, both as object and participants."[26]

Many films showed women available to male desire, such as *Love in a Hammock* (Edison, 1901), *The Adjustable Bed* (American Mutoscope and Biograph, 1905), or *Always Room for One More* (American Mutoscope and Biograph, 1905), comedies where men and women try to occupy a physical space that is too small or too fragile at the same time. Inevitably collapsing on top of each other, the characters always end up laughing and then embracing and kissing each other. As Ullman notes, "many of the movies are remarkable in showing not only the sexual possibilities available to women but also the responsibility of initiation placed upon them.... [Thus,] the women and men viewing these short comedies could happily share responsibility for sexual encounters and enjoy the effects together."[27] We can see that "from the inception of film until the rise of serious censorship, a period encompassing the years 1896 to 1910, motion pictures demonstrated a surprising recognition of female desire and sexual availability."[28] These images created the impression of an active female sexuality and helped establish women as agents of desire; moreover, these movies "presented images of woman that rang true with many in the audience."[29] Therefore, moviegoing offered women the possibility of becoming eager participants in sexual desire, as this short text from 1910 illustrates: "How did it happen that these five men who were so angry with the woman in the nickelodeon for not taking off her hat became so friendly with her afterward? It was raining like fury when the show was over and she invited them to take shelter with her under her hat."[30]

This anecdote implicitly acknowledges the emancipatory power of female scopophilia, since the female viewer in question is not merely the object of the gaze but also its subject, a subject who moves autonomously in a public space and is sexually proactive. Finally, the "hysterical" sexual appeal of female spectatorship was seen not only as an obstacle to the progressive constitution of a disciplined show based on the masculine values of individualism, control, and temperance but also as an opportunity for living a new kind of social and aesthetic experience determined by the highly sensorial environment of modernity.

MIREILLE BERTON is Senior Lecturer in the Department of Film History and Aesthetics at the University of Lausanne. She is author of *Le Corps nerveux des spectateurs. Cinéma et sciences du psychisme autour de 1900* and editor with Anne-Katrin Weber of *La Télévision du Téléphonoscope à YouTube. Pour une archéologie de l'audiovision*.

Notes

1. Women disturbed the screening in various ways, such as keeping their hats on or standing up to look for friends. We can read in articles written in an ironic tone, "When you reach your seats, do not sit down immediately. Stand up and look around for your friends. It is dark, I know, but if you wait long enough your eyes become accustomed to the darkness, and you may then recognize the backs of some acquaintances. The people in back of you have X-ray eyes and can move to some other seat if they don't like it. When you sit down, be sure and do not remove your hat. That is only necessary in legitimate theaters and is not expected

here." W. A. Scranton, "Etiquette. On the Proper Way for Two Women to Spend an Evening in a Movie Picture Theater," *Motion Picture Magazine* 4 (May 1916), 67.

2. Silvio Alovisio, "La Spettatrice muta. Il pubblico cinematografico femminile nell'Italia del primo Novecento," in *Non solo dive, Pioniere del cinema italiano*, ed. Monica Dall'Asta et al. (Bologna: Cineteca di Bologna, 2008), 269–88; Anne Friedberg, *Window Shopping: Cinema and the Postmodern* (Berkeley: University of California Press, 1993); Sabine Hake, *The Cinema's Third Machine: Writing on Film in Germany, 1907–1933* (Lincoln: University of Nebraska Press, 1993); Andrea Haller, "Diagnosis: 'Flimmeritis': Female Cinema-going in Imperial Germany, 1911-1918," in *Cinema, Audiences and Modernity: New Perspectives on European Cinema History*, ed. Daniel Biltreyest, Richard Maltby, and Philippe Meers (London: Routledge, 2011), 130–41; Miriam Hansen, *Babel & Babylon: Spectatorship in America Silent Film* (Cambridge, MA: Harvard University Press, 1991); Frank Kessler and Eva Warth, "Early Cinema and Its Audiences," in *The German Cinema Book*, ed. Tim Bergfelder, Erica Carter, and Deniz Görktürck (London: British Film Institute, 2002), 121–28; Luca Mazzei, "Il cinematografo da sole. Il cinema descritto dalle donne fra 1898 e 1916," in Dall'Asta et al., *Non solo dive*, 257–68; Kathy Peiss, *Cheap Amusements: Working Women and Leisure in Turn-of-the-Century New York* (Philadelphia, PA: Temple University Press, 1986); Veronica Pravadelli, *Le Donne del cinema. Dive, registe, spettatrici* (Lecce, Italy: Editori Laterza, 2014); Lauren Rabinovitz, *For the Love of Pleasure: Women, Movies and Culture of in Turn-of-the-Century Chicago* (New Brunswick, NJ: Rutgers University Press, 1998); Heide Schlüpmann, *The Uncanny Gaze: The Drama of Early German Cinema* (Champaign: University of Illinois Press, 2009 [1990]); Heide Schlüpmann, "Cinema as Anti-Theater: Actresses and Female Audiences in Wilhelminian Germany," in *Silent Film*, ed. Richard Abel (New Brunswick, NJ: Rutgers University Press, 1996), 125–41; Janet Staiger, *Bad Women: Regulating Sexuality in Early American Cinema* (Minneapolis: University of Minnesota Press, 1996 [1995]).

3. Emilie Altenloh, *Zur Soziologie des Kinos. Die Kino-Unternehmung und die Sozialen Schichten ihrer Besucher* (Jena, Germany: Eugen Diederichs, 1914).

4. Adriana Spadoni, "An Interview with a Nickelodeon Fiend. What the Pictures Mean to a Lonely Woman," *San Francisco Call*, August 21, 1910, 12.

5. Pravadelli, *Le Donne del cinema*, 12–14.

6. Haller, "Diagnosis," 134; Pravadelli, *Le Donne del cinema*, 15.

7. Haller, "Diagnosis," 135. See also A. Walter, "Erzieht die Kinobesucher," *Lichtbild-Bühne* 8, no. 45 (November 6, 1915): 46–48.

8. Alovisio, "La Spettatrice muta," 283–84.

9. Mary Heaton Vorse, "Some Picture Show Audiences," *Outlook*, June 24, 1911, 441–47.

10. Richard Maltby, "The Social Evil, the Moral Order, and the Melodramatic Imagination, 1890–1915," in *Melodrama: Stage, Picture, Screen*, ed. Jacky Bratton, Jim Cook, and Christine Gledhill (London: British Film Institute, 1994), 218.

11. "Moving Picture Shows," *Los Angeles Herald Sunday Magazine*, August 7, 1910, 16.

12. "In the Cinema," W. Stocker Shaw, ca. 1910, from the Nicholas Hiley collection; "What Could Be Nicer?" Fred Spurgin, ca. 1917, from the Nicholas Hiley collection; "They That Go in Darkness," Fred Spurgin, "Cinema" series no. 250, November 1915, from the Nicholas Hiley collection. Dr. Nicholas Hiley is head of the British Cartoon Archive at the Templeman Library, University of Kent, Canterbury.

13. "You May Make Mistakes Even at The Picture Palace," postcard, ca. 1910, Nicholas Hiley collection.

14. Lee Grieveson, *Policing Cinema: Movies and Censorship in Early-Twentieth-Century America* (Berkeley: University of California Press, 2004).

15. "Recruiting Stations of Vice. A Libel on Moving Picture Theaters," *Moving Picture World*, March 12, 1910, 370–71.

16. "Mothers' Responsibility," *St. John Review*, February 2, 1913, 1: "The moving picture show is another source of downfall, not that the show of itself is bad but that the influence at work there. The white slavers gather here and watch her, and little by little lead her on until ruin is accomplished. Then, rather than face her parents and friends, she enters this den of vice and becomes dead to the world"; "Des femmes enlevées grâce à des injections de somnifères," *L'Impartial*, January 8, 1914, 1; "Stockades Where Girls Are Sold into White Slavery," *The Press* (Spokane, WA), May 5, 1910, 1.

17. Chicago Vice Commission, *Social Evil in Chicago* (Chicago: Gunthorp-Warren, 1911), 247.

18. "Moving Picture Shows," *Los Angeles Herald*, August 7, 1910, 16.

19. Scranton, "Etiquette," 67.

20. Altenloh, *Zur Soziologie des Kinos*, 95.

21. Maltby, "The Social Evil," 220.

22. Silvio Alovisio, *L'occhio sensibile. Cinema e scienze della mente nell'Italia del primo Novecento* (Torino: Kaplan, 2013); Mireille Berton, *Le corps nerveux des spectateurs. Cinéma et sciences du psychisme autour de 1900* (Lausanne: L'Âge d'Homme, 2015).

23. Amalia Campetti, "Il Cinematografo nell'educazione," *Rivista di Pedagogia* 5, no. 3 (1910): 73–79.

24. Rae Beth Gordon, "Les galipettes de l'Autre burlesque ou la mécanique corporelle du Double," *1895* 61 (September 2010): 129–48; *Why the French Love Jerry Lewis: From Cabaret to Early Cinema* (Stanford, CA: Stanford University Press, 2001).

25. Shelley Stamp Lindsey, "Is Any Girl Safe? Female Spectators at the White Slave Films," *Screen* 37, no. 1 (Spring 1996): 4.

26. Sharon R. Ullman, *Sex Seen: The Emergence of Modern Sexuality in America* (Berkeley: University of California Press, 1997), 28.

27. Ibid., 23, 27.

28. Ibid., 19.

29. Ibid., 42.

30. "How She Conciliated Them," *Carrizozo News*, August 26, 1910, 26.

20 "The Best Synonym of Youth"
G. Stanley Hall, Mimetic Play, and Early Cinema's Embodied Youth Spectator

Christina Petersen

While studies of early cinema's relationship to the spectator's body have long engaged with issues of gender, race, class, and sexuality, early cinema spectatorship and embodiment in relation to age, particularly adolescence and youth, continues to be a developing area of study.[1] As this essay will discuss, the concept of adolescence as a distinct life stage between childhood and adulthood came of age with the emergence of cinema. First defined in detail by child psychologist G. Stanley Hall, modern adolescence came to represent the most embodied period of life, marked by a mimetic relationship to one's environment. In this era, Progressive reformers and legal officials' attempts to reshape transitional-era American cinema popularized Hall's conception that America's young were susceptible to mindlessly imitating what they saw at the cinema. It is less well known that Hall also explicitly linked film to the distinction between adolescence as a delineated life stage and youth as a modern structure of looking and feeling.[2]

In 1904, Hall asserted that youth comprised a feeling of play, and in 1915 he explicitly connected this idea to the somatic experience of film spectatorship. This was one year before fellow psychologist Hugo Münsterberg published *The Photoplay: A Psychological Study* and twenty years before critical theorist Walter Benjamin explored the concept of playful mimetic innervation through cinema.[3] For Hall, with the rise of film as a mass medium and the advent of World War I, the cinema offered a cure for the sedentary lifestyle not only for the modern adolescent but for the spectator of any age who could return to a more primitive and embodied relationship to one's body. In this sense, moviegoing was considered akin to sports spectatorship. At first it represented the recreational equivalent of Taylorist modes of physical labor, namely an enervating and alienating experience that enforced a strict divide between spectator and participant. However, Hall's views eventually shifted toward an expanded notion of recreation in which a spectator could also be revitalized by watching other bodies at play. Hall's ideas thus formed the basis for the concept of what I term the "youth spectator," an embodied, susceptible, yet playful subject position accessible to the film spectator no matter their chronological age.

Born in 1844 in Ashfield, Massachusetts, Granville Stanley Hall graduated from Williams College and studied at Union Theological Seminary, where he was inspired by Wilhelm Wundt's *Principles of Physiological Psychology* to undertake doctoral work at Harvard with William James. In 1878 he earned the first American doctorate in psychology from Harvard, continuing his studies with Wundt before teaching at Antioch College and Johns Hopkins University. He became the first president of Clark University in 1889 as well as the first president of the American Psychological Association. Through his involvement with both organizations, Hall brought Sigmund Freud and Carl Jung to Clark for a series of lectures in 1909, an event that marked Freud's only visit to America.[4]

In addition to this distinguished biography, Hall is best known today for his unlikely two-volume bestseller, *Adolescence: Its Psychology and Its Relations to Physiology, Anthropology, Sociology, Sex, Crime, Religion and Education*, published in 1904, which redefined adolescence and youth for the twentieth century. In *Adolescence*, Hall described the stage between childhood and adulthood as a "marvelous new birth" in which the adolescent, like an infant, "awakes to a new world and understands neither it nor himself. . . . Character and personality are taking form, but everything is plastic."[5] For Hall, adolescence marked the most embodied period of life, an "age of sense" in which the adolescent explored "every possibility of action and innervation," as their senses were the most open to their environment.[6] Following Freud, Hall noted that because of adolescents' susceptibility to their environment, the "temptations, prematurities, sedentary occupations, and passive stimuli" of modern urban life sapped the life force of the young, causing anxiety and neurasthenia.[7] While Hall did not single out the cinema as one of these "passive stimuli," Progressive reformers such as Jane Addams and Louise de Koven Bowen took up his ideas in their agitations for more attention to the influence of the burgeoning mass medium of motion pictures on America's youth. Lee Grieveson has termed this strain of discourse, although he dates it to Münsterberg's *The Photoplay: A Psychological Study*, the "mimetic paradigm," as it linked discussions of hypnosis, suggestion, and subjectivity to the fledgling medium of the cinema.[8] According to this model, of which we can see strains in Hall's work, adolescents' mimetic engagement with the cinema was marked by a loss of individuality through an unconscious susceptibility to the film image.

For Hall, one of the hallmarks of this heightened mental and physical plasticity was the adolescent's propensity toward emulative social behavior as he or she groped toward a new sense of self. Hall considered adolescence the period of life when "imitation reaches its acme," especially "if we include its psychic as well as its merely attitudinal and motor forms."[9] Hall noted that adolescents constantly and consciously aped "positions, expressions, gait, and mien in order to understand" their new world and their place in it.¹⁰ While such imitation was necessary to natural human development, Hall found the malleability of the young most disturbing in contemporary America. Most often Hall wrote about this acceleration in terms of precocity, in which "to assume the responsibilities, ideas, amusements, and passions of adults, when character is plastic and unformed, gives an unconscious sense of having been robbed of the just rights and immunities due to childhood."¹¹ Precocity in *Adolescence* represented less a mark of intelligence or sophistication than a pathological condition in which fears about premature development went hand-in-hand with those of arrest and reversion.

However, precocity was not solely a disease of the young. With the advent of Fordism and Taylorist scientific management techniques, Hall diagnosed premature aging in adults, who now suffered from an unprecedented alienation from their bodies and a resulting depletion of energy, an ailment that he termed "Americanitis."¹² Although a chronic condition of modern life, Americanitis could potentially be cured by a return to the ancient roots of the human race. In this, like his contemporaries, Hall was a strong adherent of the nineteenth-century theory of recapitulation, namely the idea that an individual, over the course of his or her individual psychic and physical development, could be said to reiterate the path of human evolution.¹³ In this formulation, adolescence constituted a new birth not only because of the individual's tremendous pubertal growth but also because it represented a step up on the ladder of human evolution. If, as recapitulation theory held, children could be considered modern savages, adolescents had more in common with contemporary "primitives" (as well as women and the lower classes) than white Euro-American adults. Yet although adolescence could be likened to an earlier stage of human evolution, Hall did not view it in a negative light, since adolescence also represented what he termed "the apical stage of individual human development."¹⁴ Adolescence may have signified modern atavism, but it also held the promise of genius and the "superanthropoid that man is to become."¹⁵

How, then, could one counter the premature aging due to the alienating and divisive nature of modern life and work? For Hall, the means lay in play. Following Friedrich Schiller, Hall argued that "'man is whole only when he plays,'" and he understood the term according to the prevailing theory of recreation in the early twentieth century: as a means for "creating anew, restoring lost powers, both physical and mental."¹⁶ This rejuvenating aspect of play most interested Hall in the wake of modern, industrial labor practices and the debilitation of modern adolescents. In *Adolescence* he claimed that "play is always and everywhere the best synonym of youth" and that "all are young at play and only in play, and the best possible characterization of old age is the absence of the soul and body of play."¹⁷ In Hall's theory, while adolescence now represented a distinct period of life between ages fourteen and twenty-four, the concept of "youth" no longer simply indicated physiological age; it became a quality of experience achieved through play.[18]

For Hall, play was a rejuvenating experience because it allowed a means to commune with the ancients. Rejecting Karl Groos's theory of play as preparation for later life, Hall argued that play reinvigorated the player by returning him or her to a prior stage of human evolution and development—much like adolescence.[19] In 1901, Hall wrote that play offered a "reversion to outgrown states and in the repetition, with variations, of acts and the expression of instincts that growth has left behind."[20] And the activities he defined as play were similarly reversionary. In *Adolescence*, he discerned ancient and rejuvenating roots in activities such as hunting, fishing, and boxing, but originally and importantly *not* in watching such pastimes. However, in the wake of World War I and the rise of film as a mass medium, Hall's writings on sports and the cinema reflected a substantial shift in his theory of recreation. Play was now transformed from a solely participatory activity into one that also included the act of spectating; or rather, spectatorship now became a form of participatory recreation.

Prior to World War I and the advent of film as a mass medium, Hall diagnosed both participation and spectatorship of professional and collegiate sports as another symptom of Americanitis, as "the propensity to codify sports, to standardize the weight and size of their implements, and to reduce them to . . . regimentation, is an outcrop of uniformitarianism that works against that individuation which is one of the chief advantages of free play."[21] Serious athletics did not constitute play in Hall's eyes, since they forced players to become merely segments of a larger entity and transformed spectators into an undifferentiated mass. For Hall, players and fans were "too often animated by the same zest that has sustained ancient gladiatorial contests in modern bull-fights and pugilism."[22] With Hall's discovery of the cinema, though, he reversed his position on sports spectatorship. In "Recreation and Reversion" (1915), Hall considered football the most atavistic of all modern recreation, not only as "a prize fight multiplied by eleven" for the players, but "the spectators, too, relapse and perhaps yell and dance like aborigines. The issue of the game is of little import and has no relation to the life of the spectators, but the emotion is intense and suggests gladiatorial combats in the arena."[23] While ten years earlier Hall had disliked such regression to Roman times, now athletics' ability to return spectators to a previous stage of human history became "re-creative and re-generative."[24]

The shift seems to stem from the transformation of the participant experience in the wake of the application of Fordism to the new machines of war. After this sea change, Hall now found spectatorship of human conflict somatically restorative, since actual participation now offered bodily perils as never before. Athletics as "mimic struggle" made apparent the nature of life-and-death struggle obscured in civilized life yet did not share the same stakes. Football, baseball, horse and boat racing, and "indeed every drama and romance pivots on a conflict ending in the triumph of one and the defeat of the other force or person, and the zest of it all is that the conflict is more intense and the issues are more clearly drawn and palpable than in real life about us. Here all ends well, and we are refreshed because the primal emotions of our forebears in us have been relieved for a time."[25] It is in this refreshing aspect of witnessing clear-cut drama and conflict with no import in real life that Hall first located the re-creative and re-generative aspects of the cinema. Like footraces, children's theater, gambling, and "the passion of impersonating other people and animals," "the moving picture seen by millions daily" was a popular form of recreation because it offered elements that harked back to "primitive or pre-historic life" by positioning the spectator as an embodied participant.[26]

After this first consideration of the rejuvenating potential of cinema, Hall, who would become a dedicated filmgoer in his later years, further explored the nature of modern recreation through film, in particular the holistic imbrication of mind and body in slapstick comedy.[27] In a 1922 essay, "Notes on the Psychology of Recreation," Hall wrote, "Amusement is often more than rest; it is *rejuvenation*."[28] In response to the on-screen antics of Charlie Chaplin, Mack Sennett, and Roscoe "Fatty" Arbuckle, he argued that these new clowns served up "a new concoction of childish naiveté, downright imbecility and odd drollery utterly impossible in real life, and the laugh is at the original creation of a depth of preposterousness *beneath the level* of the lowest intelligence."[29] For Hall, seeing the childish slapstick comedian performing sight gags produced an involuntary somatic response—laughter—in the spectator that triggered a reversion to a preintellectual state. Much like Walter Benjamin's discussion of the innervating experience of watching slapstick comedies in an early version of his essay, "The Work of Art in the Age of Its Technological Reproducibility," Hall argued that Chaplin and his colleagues' ability to incorporate the jerky rhythms of the assembly line offered a means of reviving the "aloof, apart and desiccated" modern human subject.[30] The slapstick comedian represented an image in which the moviegoing public could recognize itself as ruled by the same cadences and witness a way to combat their deadening effects. Watching these modern clowns could innervate spectators by inciting a physical response such as laughter merely by watching other bodies on the screen.

Hall made his most explicit link between his theory of play and the spectator's mimetic engagement with the cinema in his only essay dedicated to film, which extended the regenerative potential of the slapstick comedian to the screened body in general. In "Gesture, Mimesis, Types of Temperament, and Movie Pedagogy" (1921), Hall employed Freudian terms to describe the cinema's ancient origins in the art of gesture. In the modern era, the primacy of speech had suppressed the previously central role of gesture as the medium of the unconscious in human communication. With the decline of gesture, communication had become increasingly less directly expressive of internal emotional states. For this reason, Hall heartily approved of gesture's recent resurgence in silent cinema, since, as "a form of expression more primitive and fundamental than language," the return of gesture could make life "not only more expressive but more sincere and interesting."[31] Film, therefore, offered not only a means to record gesture for study but also the pedagogical potential to return to a more forthright and embodied form of communication. In gestures, defined by Hall as "movements addressed to the eye," we both reveal our inner selves through our outer bodies and sense the internal states of others based on their external demeanor.[32] Gestures represented, then, not only a more truthful form of human contact but also the aspect of cinema that made it the most like play.

Like play, gestures restored wholeness to the human subject who used them to communicate, but with the added dimension that correctly *reading* a gesture could also revitalize a person, since through this process one reconnected to a more ancient form of interaction. In this aspect Hall accounted for the draw of the cinema—in the rush of excitement the spectator felt when confronted with genuine individuality or emotion expressed through the body. In Hall's words, "How the discriminating spectator is thrilled by a really new dance with original features, which does not depend on or lapse to mere athleticism or acrobatics but shows a true artistic spirit and flash of originality! Still more is he stirred by expressions of grief which do not depend on sprayed-on tears and a face turned away or hidden because the actor is inadequate to do justice to the emotion, or to portray real psychic anguish."[33] Here Hall linked the reaction of the spectator to authentic, individual sentiment and his concept of unconscious, automatic mimetic reaction, divided into what he termed "reflex" and "associative" mimetic movement. In Hall's formulation, physical manifestations like laughter or trembling could occur because of external reflex factors, such as tickling or cold, but also because of internal, associative stimuli, such as witnessing something comic or feeling afraid.[34] In both, the physical response was the same, and the act of watching such emotions could have the same effect on the body as originally feeling them. In this sense, as Hillel Schwartz has discussed, gesture became more than an expressive form of communication, it also became operative, working on the spectator as much as conveying emotion.[35] The viewer's bodily response to images rendered them less passive observers than active participants. In this aspect of the cinema, Hall located a restorative and rejuvenating potential for the film spectator, returning him or her to a previous state of development and a more primitive relationship to the body through susceptibility and play. Similar to his pre–World War I theories on adolescence, Hall's postwar writings on film emphasized the reversionary, embodied aspects of this new medium that could reconnect spectators to their alienated bodies and make them feel young again.

In this way, while Hall's discussion of the rejuvenating aspects of early cinema remains an unexplored historical and theoretical byway, we can see aspects of his ideas in more recent scholarship on embodied spectatorship. Among others, Laura Marks has argued for film spectatorship as a form of "tactile visuality" that "draws upon the mimetic knowledge that does not posit a gulf between subject and object, or the spectator and the world of film."[36] In this she builds on Vivian Sobchack's assertion that film viewing is at once a carnal and conscious experience that relies on cinematic technology to create a reversible model of vision.[37] And Sobchack's work further draws on Walter Benjamin's writings on the cinema, particularly his notions of aura, innervation, and the "mimetic faculty," namely the ancient capacity for seeing and producing "similarities" that connect the perceptual world of the human subject with nature.[38] For Benjamin, the mimetic faculty had diminished in modernity but could still be discerned in children's play, dance, and language, all modern forms of play with ancient roots.[39] In Benjamin's view, film served as a new source of innervation, which possessed, as Miriam Hansen has discussed, "the potential to reverse, in the form of play, the catastrophic consequences of an already failed reception of technology" through its ability to copy reality and captivate its viewer at a somatic level.[40]

What is striking is that all of these aspects of embodied spectatorship are present in Hall's scattered discussions of adolescence, youth, play, mimesis, and the cinema in the early twentieth century. After the advent of World War I and film as a mass medium, Hall considered film spectatorship a palliative for the ills of modern life, as it allowed for a more holistic relationship to one's own body, collapsing the distinction between body and mind reinforced by Fordism and Taylorism. For Hall, in the wake of modernity, "the best synonym for youth" was not only play but also the cinema.

CHRISTINA G. PETERSEN is Christian Nielsen Chair and Associate Professor of Film Studies at Eckerd College.

Notes

1. See, for example, Miriam Hansen, *Babel and Babylon: Spectatorship in American Silent Film* (Cambridge, MA: Harvard University Press, 1991); Jacqueline Stewart, *Migrating to the Movies: Cinema and Black Urban Modernity* (Berkeley: University of California Press, 2005); Jennifer Bean, "Technologies of Early Stardom and the Extraordinary Body," in *A Feminist Reader in Early Cinema*, ed. Jennifer Bean and Diane Negra (Durham, NC: Duke University Press, 2002), 404–43; and Lauren Rabinovitz, "The Coney Island Comedies: Bodies and Slapstick at the Amusement Park and the Movies," in *American Cinema's Transitional Era:*

Audiences, Institutions, Practices, ed. Charlie Keil and Shelley Stamp (Berkeley: University of California Press, 2004), 171–90. For a discussion of the importance of the suggestible child and youth audience to early and classical cinema, see Lee Grieveson, *Policing Cinema: Movies and Censorship in Early-Twentieth-Century America* (Berkeley: University of California Press, 2004).

2. For more on the concept of a "structure of feeling," see Raymond Williams, *Marxism and Literature* (Oxford, UK: Oxford University Press, 1977), 132. For Williams, "The term is difficult, but 'feeling' is chosen to emphasize a distinction from more formal concepts of 'world view' or 'ideology.' It is not only that we must go beyond formally held and systematic beliefs, though of course we have always to include them. It is that we are concerned with meanings and values as they are actively lived and felt, and the relations between these and formal or systematic beliefs are in practice variable.... An alternative definition would be structures of experience."

3. See Hugo Münsterberg and Allan Langdale, *Hugo Münsterberg on Film: The Photoplay—A Psychological Study, and Other Writings* (New York: Routledge, 2002); Walter Benjamin, "Doctrine of the Similar," in *Selected Writings: Volume 2, 1927–1934*, ed. Michael Jennings (Cambridge, MA: Belknap Press, 1999), 694–98; and Benjamin, "On the Mimetic Faculty," in *Selected Writings: Vol. 2*, 720–22.

4. For more on Hall's biography, see Dorothy Ross, *G. Stanley Hall: The Psychologist as Prophet* (Chicago: University of Chicago Press, 1972).

5. G. Stanley Hall, *Adolescence: Its Psychology and Its Relations to Physiology, Anthropology, Sociology, Sex, Crime, Religion and Education*, Vol. 1 (New York: Appleton, 1904), xv.

6. Ibid., 310, 316.

7. Ibid., xv, 278, 290.

8. Lee Grieveson, "Cinema Studies and the Conduct of Conduct," in *Inventing Film Studies*, ed. Lee Grieveson and Haidee Wasson (Durham, NC: Duke University Press, 2008), 3–37.

9. Hall, *Adolescence*, Vol. 1, 316.

10. Ibid.

11. Hall, *Adolescence*, Vol. 1, 384. According to youth historian Joseph Kett, at the turn of the century adolescence had become "not merely a dangerous time of life that needed careful watching, but a stage marked too often by overpressure and an acceleration of experiences." Joseph F. Kett, *Rites of Passage: Adolescence in America, 1790 to the Present* (New York: Basic Books, 1977), 135.

12. G. Stanley Hall, "Student Customs," *American Antiquarian Society Proceedings* 14 (1900–1901): 116–18; G. Stanley Hall, "Recreation and Reversion," *Pedagogical Seminary* 22 (1915): 510. For more on the effects of Fordism and Taylorism on the filiarchal system, see Gilman M. Ostrander, *American Civilization in the First Machine Age: 1890–1940* (New York: Harper and Row, 1970).

13. Ross, *G. Stanley Hall*, 89–93. In addition to Charles Darwin, Ross notes that Hall was particularly influenced by Ernst Haeckel's *The Evolution of Man* (1883) and Henry Drummond's *The Ascent of Man* (1894) (92, 261).

14. Hall, *Adolescence: Its Psychology and Its Relations to Physiology, Anthropology, Sociology, Sex, Crime, Religion and Education*, Vol. 2 (New York: Appleton, 1904), 361.

15. Ibid., 90–94.

16. Friedrich Schiller, *On the Aesthetic Education of Man*, quoted in Hall, *Adolescence*, Vol. 1, 203; Hall, "Student Customs," 96. See also Karl Groos, *The Play of Animals* (New York: Appleton, 1898), 15–16.

17. Hall, *Adolescence*, Vol. 1, 206.

18. Ibid., xx.

19. Groos, *The Play of Animals*, 7–8. See also Bill Brown, *The Material Unconscious: American Amusement, Stephen Crane, and the Economies of Play* (Cambridge, MA: Harvard University Press, 1996), 185.

20. Hall, "Student Customs," 96.

21. Hall, *Adolescence*, Vol. 1, 230.

22. Hall, *Adolescence*, Vol. 2, 411.

23. Hall, "Recreation and Reversion," 513. Hall took his ideas on football from G.T.W. Patrick's claim that sports spectatorship satisfied a present need to be savage for a limited period of time. G.T.W. Patrick, "The Psychology of Football," *American Journal of Psychology* 14, no. 3/4 (July–October 1903): 117.

24. Hall, "Recreation and Reversion," 512.

25. Ibid., 515.

26. Ibid., 516–17.

27. Lorine Fryer Pruette, *G. Stanley Hall: A Biography of a Mind* (New York: Appleton, 1926), 50, 72.

28. Hall, "Notes on the Psychology of Recreation," *Pedagogical Seminary* 29 (1922): 73 [emphasis added].

29. Ibid., 97 [emphasis added].

30. G. Stanley Hall, "The Muscular Perception of Space," *Mind* 3, no. 12 (October 1878): 435; Ross, *G. Stanley Hall*, 70; Miriam Hansen, "Benjamin and Cinema: Not a One-Way Street," *Critical Inquiry* 25, no. 2 (Winter 1999): 332; Walter Benjamin, "The Work of Art in the Age of Its Technological Reproducibility: Second Version," in *Selected Writings: Volume 3, 1935–1938*, ed. Howard Eiland and Michael Jennings, trans. Rodney Livingstone et al. (Cambridge, MA: Harvard University Press, 2002), 31, 38; and Hall, "Notes on the Psychology of Recreation," 97.

31. G. Stanley Hall, "Gesture, Mimesis, Types of Temperament and Movie Pedagogy," *Pedagogical Seminary* 28 (1921): 171.

32. Ibid., 172.

33. Ibid.

34. Ibid., 193–94.

35. Hillel Schwartz, "Torque: The New Kinaesthetic of the Twentieth Century," in *Incorporations*, ed. Jonathan Crary and Sanford Kwinter (New York: Zone, 1992), 77.

36. Laura Marks, *The Skin of the Film: Intercultural Cinema, Embodiment, and the Senses* (Durham, NC: Duke University Press, 2000), 140–51.

37. Vivian Sobchack, *Carnal Thoughts: Embodiment and Moving Image Culture* (Berkeley: University of California Press, 2004), 76–83.

38. Ibid., 288–89.

39. Benjamin, "Doctrine of the Similar," in *Selected Writings: Vol. 2*, 694–98; and "On the Mimetic Faculty," in *Selected Writings: Vol. 2*, 720–22.

40. Miriam Hansen, *Cinema and Experience: Siegfried Kracauer, Walter Benjamin, and Theodor W. Adorno* (Berkeley: University of California Press, 2011), 139; Michael Taussig, *The Nervous System* (New York: Routledge, 1992), 146–48.

21 Perils of Cinema?
The German Cinema Debate and the "Nerve-Racking" Medium

Stephanie Werder

IN 1912, THE German psychologist Robert Gaupp explained that films have a different psychological effect than books. Because of the temporal concentration, spectators do not have time to process the moving images. Gaupp links not only certain filmic content but also the medium's specific features to nerve damage: "The horrifying and grotesque 'dramas' torturously shock the nervous system, especially with adolescents and sensitive viewers, but they don't grant the viewer the means with which he would otherwise be able to resist the attacks on his nervous system: he has no opportunity for calm reflection and mental processing, for sober criticism."[1]

In German-speaking countries, the idea that cinema could somehow inflict damage on spectators was widespread during the 1910s. Many believed that going to the cinema, far from having a relaxing effect, instead caused tension. Especially among the medium's adversaries and members of the Cinema Reform Movement (*Kinoreformbewegung*), cinemagoing was often described as a severe risk to physical and mental health. One common topos was the notion that cinema could cause nervousness, reverberating contemporaneous medical concepts surrounding "neurasthenia"—an illness that was, at the time, conceived as a weakness of the nerves.[2]

It is remarkable that such claims reached well beyond the field of psychiatry. For example in 1912, Klara Müller, who is in the source identified as a secretary, responds to a survey on the general public's opinion on cinema published in the reformist journal *Bild und Film*. Her answer suggests that the notion of cinema being able to influence nervous health was common knowledge. Müller stated the following: "In my opinion, more serious films shouldn't be too long, because they tire the nerves, which are already dull when you return, worn out, from work in the evening."[3] In the "German Cinema Debate," the notion of the "nerve-racking"—or just nerve-affecting—medium crops up very frequently. This debate had its peak in the early 1910s and was mostly carried out among members of the German-speaking educated bourgeoisie (*die Gebildeten*, as they referred to themselves), such as teachers, lawyers, or journalists, as well as by literary writers. In all manner of published forums and texts ranging from trade journals and newspapers to dedicated pamphlets or books, they discussed the nature of the new medium and its social and aesthetic implications.[4]

By analyzing the larger discursive network surrounding such positions, this chapter sets out to explore how the conception of cinema as a medium that affects the nerves proved to be so popular among the writers of the German Cinema Debate in the 1910s. First, I will consider the larger discursive historical context, namely the general concept of modern nervousness around the turn of the century. I will then turn to texts within the Cinema Debate as well as advertisements and film reviews in trade journals that claim cinema is "nerve-affecting," which show that for proponents of cinema, the medium's unique potential lay in its ostensibly intense effect on the nerves. Lastly, by comparing statements on cinema to descriptions of overstimulation in the "nervous modern age," I will attempt to reconstruct "nervous perceptual qualities," arguing that for historical viewers, cinema was likely to be seen as incorporating these qualities.

Discourse on Modern Nervousness

By the end of the nineteenth century, neurasthenia—or nervous exhaustion—had become something of a fashionable affliction. Throughout America and Europe, numerous psychiatrists and physicians were interested in and concerned about nervous afflictions and sent their patients for cures in sanatoriums. Neurasthenia was seen as resulting from the conditions of modern life (the fast pace and excitement of daily life and nightlife in the modern metropolis, increasingly burdensome working conditions, modern technology, etc.). Subjects were thought to have functional nerve damage, which made them highly irritable and caused them to experience many disparate symptoms such as headaches, stomachaches, heart trouble, or dizziness.[5]

As Mireille Berton has shown, within the psychiatric field there was a broad interest in cinema.[6] This scientific knowledge also informed public, less specialized discourses (like the German Cinema Debate). The psychologist Naldo Felke, for example, carried out experiments that attempted to determine cinema's effect on neurasthenic subjects, the results of which were then published in the popular scientific journal *Die Umschau*.[7] Felke concludes that the moving pictures' intensity of stimuli harms the eyes and nerves of the spectators, and that cinema is especially dangerous for people who already suffer from nervous weakness.

Since nervous exhaustion was seen as being caused by the modern way of life and as a disease of civilization, the subject of modern nervousness, unsurprisingly, was present throughout a broad range of discourses. In Germany, the affliction was often linked to the fear of degeneration in the modern age and was referred to in many political and public cultural debates outside the medical field.[8] The concept of modern nervousness was often employed to criticize certain factors of the modern environment—for example, in the debate on the noisiness of cities or in connection with school reforms.[9] Indeed, cultural critics regularly referred to the present as the "nervous age."[10] Today, the evocation of neurasthenia and modern nervousness is usually seen as an expression of cultural anxiety among the German educated bourgeoisie, in particular, which at the time was facing social and cultural changes as an effect of modernization.[11]

Thus, cinema was by far not the only phenomenon that was conceived of or described as nerve damaging around the turn of the century. Rather, the authors of the German Cinema Debate joined a certain tradition (in popular and medical discourses) of ascribing nerve-damaging effects to modern and urban forms of entertainment and nightlife such as gambling and going to concerts or vaudeville shows, going so far as to claim that certain styles of modern visual art or literature were a sign of the modern nervous age.[12] According to one common topos, modern humanity's nervous constitution influenced their cultural tastes: they both needed and enjoyed hyperstimulating experiences.

This rich discursive network might explain, at least to a certain degree, why the notion of the nerve-racking cinema proved to be so popular among adversaries of the medium and cinema reformers. I would argue that the discourse on nervousness was naturally suited to debates on cinema—a medium that was seen as emblematic of modernity. The attribute of "nervousness" was already being used as a discursive weapon to criticize a number of phenomena and betrayed a certain cultural bias against the modern age and contemporary culture. Arguably, however, this did not prevent cinema enthusiasts from interpreting the medium's effect on the nerves in positive terms.

A Medium That Affects the Nerves

As described previously, the notion of the cinema as nerve-racking was not limited to psychiatrists studying film, such as Robert Gaupp or Naldo Felke, but was taken up by many adversaries of the medium and members of the Cinema Reform Movement. For example, as Scott Curtis has shown,[13] the idea of potential damage to the nerves of the spectators was central to the theoretical writings of the prolific cinema reformer Hermann Häfker and informed his normative views on the formal construction and the proper—and artful—exhibition of films. In order to avoid excessive strain on the viewers' nerves and to ease their perceptual process, Häfker called for breaks between films as well as projections of stills for the viewers to rest their eyes on, to name just two suggestions.[14]

Aside from such elaborated concepts that indicate some basis in contemporary physiological and psychiatric knowledge, numerous texts contain much

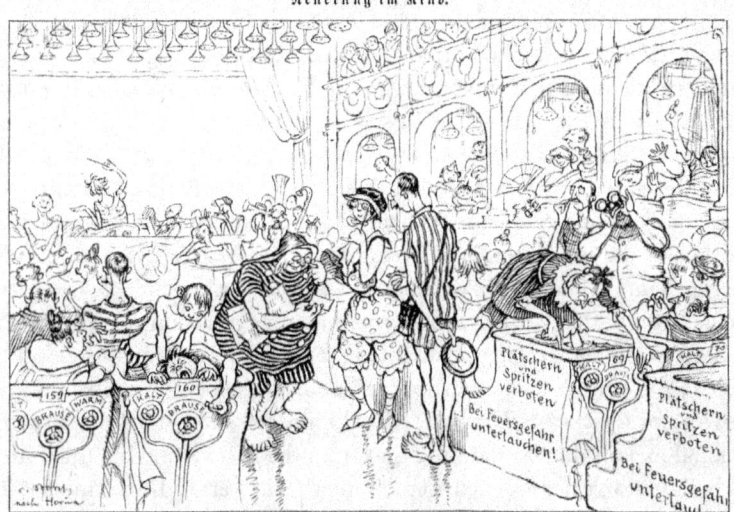

Figure 21.1. Carl Storch, "Neuerung im Kino," *Fliegende Blätter* no. 155, 1921. The caption reads: "Innovation in the Cinema. The rapid decline in attendance during the hot summer months in the cities has helped realize a long-held plan: the combination of cinema and bathhouse. The concept pursues a number of great goals. The attendee saves not only money but time; furthermore, the risk of fire is minimized; lastly, however, the attendee is able to cool his nerves from the agitation caused by the cinema drama, or heat himself with one turn of the faucet, should the program be too cool for his tastes." Universitätsbibliothek Heidelberg.

more cursory statements about cinema's nerve-racking effect, suggesting that this notion was widespread enough that it could be employed by a number of different people or parties. For instance, the Prussian minister of education, in a decree quoted in the trade journal *Lichtbild-Bühne* in 1912, uses it to medically justify moral objections to films by citing their supposedly corrupting effect. After raising general hygienic concerns for the bodies and minds of children who visit cinemas, the minister states that inappropriate and brutal scenes "spoil the youths' aesthetic sensibility, the senses get accustomed to strong and nerve-exciting impressions, and joy in calm contemplation of artworks is lost."[15]

However, notions of cinema's effect on the nerves were by no means limited to claims that the medium posed a danger to nervous health. Examining the context of the German Cinema Debate as well as advertisements and film reviews, for example in the trade journal *Lichtbild-Bühne*, it becomes clear that the spectrum of ideas on cinema and nervousness is extremely broad.[16] For example, many sources present the metaphorical and sometimes rather vague idea of cinema as a modern medium that in some way expresses or accompanies the nervous modern age. In articles, as well as in sensationalistic ads and reviews, one also encounters the notion that cinema's special potential lies precisely in its intense effect on the nerves: by being able to excite and entertain the dulled nerves of the blasé modern audience, it is well suited for the nervous modern spectator.[17] The author of the 1910 *Lichtbild-Bühne* article "Die Karriere des Kinematographen," for example, characterizes cinema by its "feverish aesthetics" (*Ästhetik des Fiebers*), claiming that with its rapidity and its concentrations of events, cinema (as well as *varieté* theater) is well adapted for the "nervous impatience" of modern people.[18] A similar idea often appears in advertisements. For instance, a 1915 film review for *Il jockey della morte* (Alfred Lind, 1915) advertises the suspenseful sensational melodrama by claiming that from the first second on, this film provoked breathtaking nervous tension among the viewers.[19] Thus, cinema's effect on the body is conceptualized as unreservedly positive, lending the medium its ability to sustain an audience's attention. In other articles and film reviews, we encounter the idea that cinema can counteract nervousness (much like the hydratherapeutic or electrotherapeutic cures[20] that were offered in sanatoriums at the time): that it can either heal the nervous spectators through stimulation or calm irritated nerves.[21]

This by no means exhaustive overview shows that the rather pessimistic statements about cinema's nerve-damaging effect represent only one variation in a much broader discourse. What all these differing ideas share is the notion that cinema is a medium that affects the spectators' nerves. It seems that cinema's adversaries, cinema reformers, proponents of the medium, and advertisers each had their own interest in reasserting this claim.

"Nerve-Affecting" Features—Nervous Perceptual Qualities

Aside from the context of broader discursive traditions and the convenient flexibility or adaptability of the concept of cinema having an intense effect on the nerves, its prevalence can be explained even further. As we can see by examining which cinematic or filmic features were associated with an effect on the nerves, the authors of these texts share common ground. A close reading of the texts demonstrates that such characteristics appear on different levels. First, there are general pictorial qualities of the filmic image that were thought to affect or damage the nerves, such as the constant movement of the image, the brightness of the screen, or certain technical deficiencies like flickering. Second, writers frequently mention certain "creative means" such as editing or the fast-paced narration of short films. Third, many texts critical of the medium typically associate nervousness with certain filmic content—such as brutal and bloody scenes or highly suspenseful narrative structures—or with genres such as the sensational melodrama (*Sensationsfilm* or *Sensationsdrama*), the crime film, or the "gothic" film (*Schauerdrama*). Interestingly, nerve-exciting effects are often emphasized in a positive way for the same genres in advertisements and reviews (as we saw in the example of *Il jockey della morte*). Finally, the sources mention certain characteristics of the theater experience and practices of exhibition: the abrupt changes the spectator experiences when watching a short-film program, the lack of breaks between the films, the sounds of the projection machine or "inappropriate" musical accompaniment, and even the profusion of olfactory stimuli in the cinema theater.[22]

In spite of the variety of features that were said to affect the nerves across different textual sources, their selection hardly seems arbitrary, especially when one considers the ways in which perceptual phenomena as well as contemporary artistic styles (such as impressionism[23]) were associated with the "nervous modern age." The nervousness of the modern metropolis is probably the most common topos in this realm, often surfacing in hygienic texts such as Willy Hellpach's 1902 "Nervosität und Kultur"[24] and Ludwig Wilhelm Weber's 1918 article "Grossstädte und Nerven,"[25] or Georg Simmel's 1903 sociological study, "Die Grossstädte und das Geistesleben."[26] At the turn of the century, the modern city—with its traffic, its noise, and its crowds, or all the unexpected events that could happen when crossing a street—is typically described as an environment of sensory overstimulation,[27] which is seen both as a result of and a catalyst for modern nervousness.

When one compares, on a more abstract level, such descriptions of perceptual phenomena described as nerve-affecting with the accounts from the German Cinema Debate, we can try to reconstruct *nervous perceptual qualities*, as I will call them—that is, perceptual qualities that were at the time associated with nervousness or conceived of as nerve-stimulating. These include such properties as an abundance of stimuli, constant motion, unexpected change, a somehow fluid or ephemeral quality, a lack of structure, or a fragmentary nature. It can be argued that for contemporary spectators, the perceptual experience of cinema incorporated most, if not all, of these qualities. While today's viewers might not be able to relate to such a perception (films from the 1910s do not seem particularly "nervous" today), for the original audience, cinema's "nervous qualities" must have been readily apparent considering the omnipresent discourse on the nervous modern age.

Moreover, this attempt at a reconstructive summary suggests that such nervous perceptual qualities preclude contemplation—the German, educated bourgeoisie's traditional ideal mode of the reception of art, one that demands a recipient to be concentrated and intellectually immersed and disembodied.[28] The notion of cinema affecting the nerves could be seen as a resistance to attempts under way at the time that sought to align cinema with traditional art discourses and educational concepts that called for a calm and contemplative audience.[29] Resistance to these efforts constitutes another reason for the great number of texts discussing the issue. More progressive voices, on the other hand, seemed to discern the potential for a modern, new kind of attention in cinema's intense effect on the nerves.

Conclusion

The notion of cinema as a nerve-racking medium is scarcely representative of the way German audiences of early cinema reacted to the new medium. In other words, taking these statements too literally would be a mistake, as they do not provide proof of an actual bodily effect on historical audiences.[30] Instead, it is first and foremost a biased attribution. It belongs to a larger discursive tradition that was prevalent especially among the German-educated bourgeoisie and symptomatic of their confrontation with modernity. As the warnings of the danger to nervous health were exploited in a number of different contexts, the references to cinema's nerve-damaging effect must be seen primarily as a convenient tool with which adversaries of the medium could stoke fears, or for cinema reformers to support their claims with reference to popular medical knowledge. As has been shown, these statements represent just one side of a larger discursive network within both the German Cinema Debate and advertisement, which also included a variety of positive ideas about cinema's intense effect on the nerves. Lastly, the popularity and prevalence of such ideas cannot be explained without considering the historical perception of the medium's specific features and specific tendencies that were associated with other presumably nerve-affecting phenomena of the time. The discourse on nervousness shaped the perception of cinema as an incarnation of such "nervous perceptual qualities"—and thus as an epitome of the modern nervous age.

STEPHANIE WERDER is a doctoral student at the University of Zurich's Department of Film Studies.

Notes

1. Robert Gaupp, "Der Kinematograph vom medizinischen und psychologischen Standpunkt," in *Der Kinematograph als Volksunterhaltungsmittel*, ed. Robert Gaupp and Konrad Lange (München: Callwey, 1912), 9.

2. See Joachim Radkau, *Das Zeitalter der Nervosität. Deutschland zwischen Bismarck und Hitler*, (München: Econ Ullstein List, 2000 [1998]), 52–66. The disease pattern "neurasthenia"

became a popular diagnosis and was picked up quickly by German-speaking physicians after George Miller Beard's studies: *A Practical Treatise on Nervous Exhaustion (Neurasthenia): Its Symptoms, Nature, Sequences, Treatment* (New York: Wood, 1880) and *American Nervousness: Its Causes and Consequences* (New York: Putnam, 1881).

3. "Wie das Publikum über kinematographische Vorstellungen urteilt. Das Ergebnis einer Umfrage," *Bild und Film* 2, no. 2 (November 1912): 37–41.

4. Texts from the German Cinema Debate are compiled in the following anthologies: Anton Kaes, Nicholas Baer, and Michael Cowan, eds., *The Promise of Cinema: German Film Theory, 1907–1933* (Oakland: University of California Press, 2016); Anton Kaes, ed., *Kino-Debatte. Texte zum Verhältnis von Literatur und Film, 1909–1929* (München: DTV, 1978); Jörg Schweinitz, ed., *Prolog vor dem Film: Nachdenken über ein neues Medium, 1909–1914* (Leipzig: Reclam, 1992); Fritz Güttinger, ed., *Kein Tag ohne Kino. Schriftsteller über den Stummfilm* (Frankfurt am Main: Deutsches Filmmuseum, 1984).

5. See Joachim Radkau's foundational study on the German discourse on nervousness: *Das Zeitalter der Nervosität*. See also Michael Cowan, *Cult of the Will: Nervousness and German Modernity* (University Park: Pennsylvania State University Press, 2008); and Andreas Killen, *Berlin Electropolis: Shock, Nerves, and German Modernity* (Berkeley: University of California Press, 2006). A transnational perspective is offered in Marijke Gijswijt-Hofstra and Roy Porter, eds., *Cultures of Neurasthenia: From Beard to the First World War* (Amsterdam: Rodopi, 2001).

6. See Mireille Berton, *Le corps nerveux des spectateurs. Cinéma et sciences du psychisme de 1900* (Lausanne: L'Age d'Homme, 2015).

7. Naldo Felke, "Die Gesundheitsschädlichkeit des Kinos," *Die Umschau* 17, no. 13 (1913): 254–55. On Felke, see also Michael Cowan, "Theater and Cinema in the Age of Nervousness," in *CINEMA & Cie* 5 (Fall 2004): 73–75.

8. See Volker Roelcke, "Electrified Nerves, Degenerated Bodies: Medical Discourses on Neurasthenia in Germany, circa 1880–1914," in Gijswijt-Hofstra and Porter, *Cultures of Neurasthenia*, 177–97.

9. See Radkau, *Das Zeitalter der Nervosität*, 334–49.

10. See Gilbert Merlio, "Kulturkritik um 1900," in *Krisenwahrnehmungen in Deutschland um 1900: Zeitschriften als Foren der Umbruchszeit im wilhelminischen Reich*, ed. Michel Grunewald (Bern: Peter Lang, 2010), 122–37; and Volker Roelcke, *Krankheit und Kulturkritik: psychiatrische Gesellschaftsdeutungen im bürgerlichen Zeitalter (1790–1914)* (Frankfurt am Main: Campus, 1999), 122–37.

11. See Roelcke, *Krankheit und Kulturkritik*, 122–37; and Radkau, *Das Zeitalter der Nervosität*, 60–66.

12. See, for example, Willy Hellpach, *Nervosität und Kultur* (Berlin: Räde, 1902), 127–58.

13. Scott Curtis, "The Taste of a Nation: Training the Senses and Sensibility of Cinema Audiences in Imperial Germany," in *Film History* 6, no. 4 (Winter 1994): 461–63. See also Scott Curtis, *The Shape of Spectatorship: Art, Science, and Early Cinema in Germany* (New York: Columbia University Press, 2015), 184–89.

14. Hermann Häfker, *Kino und Kunst* (München-Gladbach: Volksvereins-Verlag, 1913), 53.

15. "Die Stimme von zwei Ministern," *Lichtbild-Bühne* 18, May 4, 1912.

16. The analysis is part of my doctoral thesis in progress and is based on sources from the trade journals *Lichtbild-Bühne* (1909–1918) and *Kinema* (1911–1919); the Cinema Reform

magazine *Bild und Film* (1912–1915); texts collected in anthologies by Kaes, Schweinitz, and Güttinger; and several other relevant sources such as Hermann Häfker's writings on cinema.

17. For instance, Ferdinand Hardekopf refers to the cinema audience as a nervous "visorium" (which for him is the visual counterpart of an "auditorium"). He characterizes this audience as one that wants to see as many different things as possible in a short time. This text was published under the pseudonym Stefan Wronski, "Der Kinematograph," *Nord und Süd. Deutsche Halbmonatsschrift* vol. 34, no. 412 (1910): 326–28 (cited after Schweinitz, *Prolog vor dem Film*, 157).

18. "Die Karriere des Kinematographen," *Lichtbild-Bühne* 124, December 10, 1910.

19. "Der Todesjockey," *Lichtbild-Bühne* 34, August 21, 1915.

20. See Radkau, *Das Zeitalter der Nervosität*, 114–29; and Killen, *Berlin Electropolis*, 127–61.

21. See, for example, "Die Kinokur," *Lichtbild-Bühne* 7, February 14, 1914. This short article claims that a very nervous man was healed from his illness by the distractions he received during his daily visits to a cinema theater.

22. See, for example, the humoristic article "Die Nase im Kino," *Lichtbild-Bühne* 28, July 13, 1912.

23. See, for example, Hellpach, *Nervosität und Kultur*, 127–58. On the concept of impressionism as an aesthetics of will impairment, see Cowan, *Cult of the Will*, 31–39.

24. Hellpach, *Nervosität und Kultur*, 24–38.

25. Ludwig Wilhelm Weber, "Großstadt und Nerven," *Deutsche Rundschau* 177 (October, November, December 1918): 391–407.

26. Georg Simmel, "Die Großstädte und das Geistesleben," in *Die Großstadt. Vorträge und Aufsätze zur Städteausstellung* (Jahrbuch der Gehe-Stiftung zu Dresden, vol. 9), ed. Karl Bücher et al., (Dresden: v. Zahn und Jaensch, 1903), 185–206.

27. On the relation of hyperstimulus, the metropolis, and cinema, see Ben Singer, "Modernity, Hyperstimulus, and the Rise of Popular Sensationalism," in *Cinema and the Invention of Modern Life*, ed. Leo Charney and Vanessa Schwartz (Berkeley: University of California Press, 1995), 72–99.

28. On the concept of contemplation, see Curtis, *The Shape of Spectatorship*, 193–241.

29. On the relation between the preclassical filmic images and the arts, see Jörg Schweinitz and Daniel Wiegand, eds., *Film Bild Kunst. Visuelle Ästhetik des vorklassischen Stummfilms* (Marburg, Germany: Schüren, 2016).

30. On this subject, see Ben Singer, "The Ambimodernity of Early Cinema: Problems and Paradoxes in the Film-and-Modernity Discourse," in *Film 1900: Technology, Perception, Culture*, ed. Annemone Ligensa and Klaus Kreimeier (New Barnet, UK: John Libbey, 2009), 37–51.

22 "The Taste of the Moment Seems All for 'Pictures'"

Irish Historical Bodies before the Early Cinema Screen

Denis Condon

"I WAS SURPRISED TO come across James Joyce with a lady and gentleman in Fleet street this afternoon," Irish architect Joseph Holloway wrote in his diary entry for December 24, 1909. "I thought him away in Trieste on the borders of Italy. I think he had forgotten me—he looked so dazed & 'blank' when I took off my hat as I passed."[1] Joyce had left Ireland for Trieste in 1904, in part to relieve his perennial money problems. He had returned in 1909 with funds from Triestine businessmen to set up the Cinematograph Volta, one of Dublin's first picture houses.

Much has been written about Joyce's brief foray into cinema management,[2] but unique insights into what it was actually like to sit before the screens of Dublin's first picture houses are contained in the diary of the relatively obscure figure whom Joyce blanked as he passed with raised hat—a black bowler to match his dark suit and neatly trimmed mustache. Joseph Holloway is best remembered as the architect who, in 1904, had designed the first incarnation of Dublin's Abbey Theatre, Ireland's self-declared national theater. With that building long demolished and replaced, Holloway's more lasting legacy is his largely unpublished diary in which he recorded in detail his opinions not only on every Abbey opening night but also on the very many theatrical shows he saw in Dublin during a theatergoing career that stretched from the 1880s to the 1940s. The diary was, in a sense, Holloway's life's work, and it has been estimated as running between 15 and 25 million words, the disparity indicating that nobody has counted it accurately in any way. A searchable digital transcription would be a boon not only for theater scholars but also for film researchers, as Holloway also recorded his attendance at film shows beginning in 1896 and was a deputy Irish film censor in the 1920s and 1930s.

Not all commentators have been enthusiastic about Holloway's diary. Although Joyce's opinion of him is not recorded, other literary figures were far

Figure 22.1. "While waiting in the 'trying on room' at the West End Clothiers Co's shop in Dame Street, I caught my profile in one of the numerous mirrors that lined the little room & jotted it down on the back of '*The Leader*' which I happened to have in my hand at the time (Oct 6th—Thur)." NLI MS 1810, Joseph Holloway Diaries, October 6, 1910, n. p. Courtesy of the National Library of Ireland.

from complimentary. The playwright Sean O'Casey thought that Holloway's diary was "an impossible pile of rubbish," while the short-story writer Frank O'Connor referred to it as "that donkey's detritus."³ Others have been less disparaging. "In every way but one, Joseph Holloway of Dublin was a thoroughly unremarkable man," begins the introduction to a selection of his diary focused on the Abbey Theatre, "but in that one way he was, without exaggeration, astounding. For most of his almost eighty-four years, he was a man as completely dedicated to art as his country has ever seen."⁴

One of the diary's treasures is the fact that it is the only source offering sustained insights into the embodied experience of Dublin's first picture houses, written by a man who was himself becoming—somewhat despite himself—a regular cinemagoer. Holloway was interested in visual art, music, and literature, but his first love was theater of all kinds, from the Abbey's theater of the Irish literary revival to the offerings of commercial theaters ranging from legitimate playhouses to variety theaters. He titled his diary "Impressions of a Dublin Playgoer," and it frequently offers his appraisal of theatrical productions. However, these are embedded in his discussions of many other topics, not only issues relevant to the arts but also his own daily doings and the political occurrences of the day. His curiosity extended to the emerging cinema, and although briefer than his "playhouse impressions," these "picture-house impressions" frequently focus less on the films shown than on the audience's embodied experience.

Thus Holloway's observations constitute a form of "metaspectatorship," which in Jan Olsson's formulation concentrates "both on screen representations and audience members' bodily and physiognomic engagement with screen matters."[5] Olsson posits five phases for journalistic engagements with cinema that are distinguished less by a strict chronology than by the dominance of a certain mode of reporting on film spectatorship in the United States. Following an initial period of encounter in the mid-1890s, columnists rediscovered the first dedicated film shows in the early to mid-1900s as part of a wider flaneurial exploration of the city. In the later 1900s, the journalistic flaneur's glance at early cinema audiences was replaced by the more searching gaze of the campaigning reporter allied with movements intent on reforming the nickelodeons; these reform-minded discourses were, in turn, replaced by a more mixed mode. Finally, around 1914, columns were fully invested in cinema culture.[6] Olsson notes different timelines for the shifts between modes in countries other than the United States; this was the case in Ireland, where newspapers paid little attention to cinema before 1914.

Holloway's diary does display some of the patterns Olsson describes, but as the diary of an individual—albeit one used to seeing his opinions in print—it cannot reflect wider shifts in the relationship between established and emerging media. Nevertheless, flanerie and the moralistic middle-class gaze that gave rise to reform discourses do frame Holloway's metaspectatorial commentary on the bodily, active, social event that was cinemagoing in the period between 1908 and 1910, when Dublin's first full-time film venues were opening.

The diary's insights are certainly limited by their author's perspective. In this period, Holloway was in his late forties and living in the wealthy suburb of Pembroke, close to the city, in a large house with his eighty-year-old mother, Anne; his twenty-year-old niece, Eileen O'Malley; and a servant.[7] Although an architect by profession and president of the Architectural Association of Ireland in 1906–1907, he practiced little, relieved of the necessity of working by a small, private income. Unmarried, he was an Irish, middle-class, Catholic nationalist privileged enough to have been able to indulge his passion for theater almost limitlessly. Leisured, middle-class, and male, he was, in many ways, the very archetype of the flaneur, strolling the city, chatting with strangers and his many acquaintances, and inhabiting by turns the seemingly incongruent sites of Dublin's high and low culture.

A short journey brought him from his house to the city center, where the theaters that he spent much of his life attending and writing about were found. Specializing in new Irish plays that consciously contributed to the formation of a distinctly Irish culture, the Abbey largely defined itself against the city's commercial theaters: the Theatre Royal and Gaiety, which hosted internationally touring legitimate drama and musical theater; the Queen's, which was a melodrama house that periodically staged popular Irish plays; and the Tivoli and Empire variety theaters. The Rotunda was the exhibition and concert hall built as a source of funding for the city's oldest maternity hospital. Apart from the Abbey, all of these venues showed films at least occasionally. At the Rotunda, the Irish Animated Picture Company (IAPC) had, since 1900, mounted film and variety shows that often ran for several months before touring the country. Film shows were an established part of the programs at the variety theaters, and when the Royal and Gaiety introduced seasons of supposedly high-class variety they called "hippodrome," films appeared in these theaters with increasing regularity.

The nearest thing Dublin had to a dedicated film venue by the start of 1908 was the IAPC's seasons at the Rotunda. These shows benefited from the prestige of the venue itself as a site of elite and middle-class concerts and charity events, and the IAPC's advertising emphasized education as well as entertainment, thereby prominently associating filmgoing with edification and respectability.

The emergence of dedicated picture houses in Dublin can be quickly outlined. In March 1908, the Colonial Picture Combine leased the Queen's and turned it into the People's Popular Picture Palace (PPPP), which ran until January 1909. After this, the city again had no dedicated film venue until Joyce opened the Volta in December 1909. By April 1910, this had become unviable, and in June, Joyce's backers sold out to Provincial Cinematograph Theatres, a British company that on April 8, 1910, had also opened the Sackville Picture House on O'Connell Street.

Holloway's metaspectatorial observations of the first of these dedicated picture houses—the PPPP at the Queen's—depict a primarily working-class entertainment with a bodily active spectatorship. He could not have been very surprised by this, given that the Queen's had long been where mainly working-class Dubliners went to experience together the excessive stimulation of sensational stage melodrama.[8] These performances featured bodily imperilment and hairsbreadth escapes designed to draw gasps, villainous behavior that invited hissing, and comic turns that encouraged a tension-expelling laughter. Audience interaction with stage performers in these and other less structured ways was crucial to the nature of melodramatic entertainment; members of the audience were not expected to sit quietly in their seats.[9] Although many of the sensational melodramas staged at the Queen's were international touring productions, the theater had also been—and would be again after its year as a picture house—the home of Irish political melodrama, a popular nationalist theater.[10] Often drawn to the Queen's by these Irish plays, Holloway was familiar with and appreciative of the liveliness of its audiences, and it was this kind of audience he found at the PPPP.

Holloway's account of his attendance at its opening evening of March 2, 1908, is worth quoting at length to convey both the embodied experience of this key early show and the access the diary provides to early Irish film spectatorship. "As I am always interested in all matters appertaining to the stage in Dublin," he begins,

> I went down to sample the first evening shows, & found the entrances to the cheaper parts of the house thronged with small boys eager to gain admittance—*The Story of the Kelly Gang* evidently was the attraction to these youthful minds who seem full of the horrors of the "penny dreadful," & who longed to see some of them realised before their eyes in "living pictures." The excitement in the street outside was fully maintained inside (I got standing room on the upper circle for 6d). The house was thronged in every part, & a series of pictures depicting the humours and excitement of a man's first row on the river. This was followed by "the sorrows of a clown" & "Her rival's necklace"—two dramatic shows. Mr. Alan Wright sang "The Boy on the Raft," to a series of pictures & then a three minute interval occurred, & the lights put up. Smoking was freely indulged in & the whole house was agog with excitement. The event of the programme—"*The Story of the Kelly Gang*" was then announced amid "sensation," as they say in a murder trial, & the story was dramatically and excitingly unfolding itself amid noisy approval as I left a little after eight o'clock. The street outside was a hive of childhood & from every quarter crowds swarmed to swell the number, long queues were already formed awaiting entrance for the 9 o'clock show. All this goes to prove that crude melodrama even in "living pictures" is what appeals to the youthful mind ever eager for thrilling events. Leaving the excitement of Brunswick St. I hastened to the calm of Mr. John J. Marshall's lecture on "*Old Belfast—Its Origin & History*" at National Literary Society. It proved most interesting and instructive & the series of lantern illustrations added greatly to its interest.[11]

The vividness of Holloway's description brings to life an auditorium where the bodily excess on the screen was mirrored by agitated bodies in the social space of the auditorium. Attracted to the Queen's by a desire to observe this new form of amusement and assess its contribution to Dublin's entertainment world, he presents himself as a detached observer who ends his evening in the calmness of an "interesting and instructive" historical lantern lecture. Nevertheless, what he observes at the Queen's places him in a maelstrom of bodily excess, crammed in among the packed audience on the upper circle. He finds the members of the audience for this new form of entertainment to be in a state of "excitement"—a word he uses continually in the course of this passage—before they have even entered the theater. He emphasizes his own detachment from the thrills of the show by stressing his difference in age, class, and taste from the "small boys" and "hive of childhood" who thronged and swarmed the cheaper entrances, and whose excitement was intensified by the three-minute smoking interval. Holloway arrived with no apparent knowledge of what he would see, but that was not the case for the young audience whose anticipation of the early Australian feature film, *The Story of the Kelly Gang* (Tait, 1906), was part of the thrill of the evening—undoubtedly enhanced by the fact that Ned Kelly was of Irish extraction. His departure before the film finished demonstrated his disdain for this "crude melodrama ... in 'living pictures,'" and the associated penny dreadfuls, sensational trials reported in newspapers, and sensational stage melodramas recently performed at the Queen's.

The opening night's experience did not deter him from returning to the PPPP. Confronted with other working-class body genres on screen and heightened animation among the audience, Holloway maintained a sense of alterity on subsequent visits to the Queen's during the year that it operated as a picture house. Although "faked comic incidents formed the bulk of the pictures shown," during his second visit on April 6, 1908, the feature was the *Burns-Moir Fight* (Urban, 1907), and the "audience became quite excited over it."[12] Holloway did not: "The contrast of a lot of men in boiled shirt fronts seated around the ring as two brutes violently pummelled one another was not a pleasing sight to behold. As a living picture even, the sight was far from nice." He presents it as catering to another type of audience: "The 'small boy' of Dublin finds it exactly to his taste!"

His comments on June 3, 1908, suggest that it was also not suitable for respectable young women. On that evening, his niece Eileen unexpectedly accompanied him when he decided to attend the Queen's because the program included R. G. Walshe's half-hour Irish play *Before Clonmel*. In her company, he found that although "a few of the pictures were most interesting, ... some two or three, I am sorry to say, were excessively vulgar, & ought not to have been shown!"[13] He does not describe whether the rest of the audience recognized and responded to these films as vulgar—presumably with some kind of mild sexual content. Nevertheless, he does suggest that the Queen's specialized in genres that presented scenes of bodily excess in the form of sensational melodrama, boxing, and vulgarity.

After a final visit on July 18, Holloway appears to have tired of its offerings and did not visit the Queen's during the last six months of its picture-house career. Between July 1908 and June 1910, he reverted to more accidental filmgoing. He continued to attend the music halls and other theaters where films were included as part of the program, and he went to the IAPC's show at the Rotunda twice, in January and September 1909. The most significant development in Dublin cinema in this period, however, was Joyce's opening of the Volta in December 1909. Holloway and Joyce knew each other; they moved in similar intellectual circles in Dublin, and Holloway kept one eye on Joyce's career after he moved to Trieste in 1904. Despite this, Holloway did not attend any shows at the Volta during Joyce's two-week tenure as manager, from its opening on December 20, 1909, to his departure for Trieste on January 2, 1910, or during the following four months up to April 1910, when Joyce's partners decided to sell it.[14] In June 1910, it was sold to Provincial Cinematograph Theatres, the company that had opened the Sackville in April.

It was the Sackville rather than the Volta that Holloway patronized first, and he was apparently reassured enough that it would be respectable to do so with his niece. On June 18, 1910, he went to the Sackville "with Eileen for the first time in the evening." Duly recorded by Holloway, the visit seems barely notable otherwise and really only is for the lack of features so apparent in visits to the Queen's and Volta: metaspectatorial commentary on audience excitement. Instead, he reveals that at the Sackville, "the show of pictures were good on the whole but the screen on which they were displayed was on the small side. There was a good audience—there seems to be money in cinematograph shows just now. I like the scenes from passing events best—the made up 'story' pictures bore me as a rule! The little hall is nicely gotten up, & comfortable. Mr Huish, the manager was acting as money taker when we were going in."[15] Although the show at the Sackville was not wholly satisfactory—with the size of the screen and the uninteresting fiction films drawing criticism—there appears to have been nothing that put it beyond consideration for a future night's family entertainment.

This was not the case when a month later, on July 16, 1910, he paid his first visit to the Volta. Managed by the Sackville's Walter Huish, the Volta was having difficulties that including attracting higher-paying, middle-class patrons. "The 3d seats were well filled," he finds, "but the sixpenny ones were mostly unoccupied."[16] Although the size of the screen affected his experience at the Sackville, the technical problems at the Volta more seriously compromised his engagement with the films shown. "The operators had not quite got the hang of the place," he observes, "& some of the pictures were very blurred or frequently vanished momentarily from the screen often as if something was going wrong with the rollers & when a gramophone 'picture' was placed on the screen—they did not quite work together."

Despite the attractively decorated premises, the technical and audience-related problems were compounded by location and middle-class feelings of bodily danger from the kind of people who may have been in this part of the city at night. Although Mary Street was a shopping area with a major department store just a few doors from the Volta, it was also adjacent to some of the city's worst slums. So, in what might be called a moment of meta-metaspectatorship, Holloway commented not so much on the Volta's audience but on the people a patron might encounter on leaving the Volta at night. "A great crowd of Saturday night gazers were stand[ing] outside as I left the hall," he notes, "& a big crowd of youngsters mostly followed an 'outside' [carriage] bearing an accident case to Jervis St Hospital round the corner. Mary & Henry Street are busy & crowded thoroughfares on a Saturday night!" He was clearly not used to being in this part of the city at night, and presumably less adventurous members of his class would have been more disinclined to be there at all.

This altogether unsatisfactory entertainment experience made him reflect on the decline in Dublin's theater world. "Fancy I been driven to seek amusement at the 'Volta,'" he marvels, "& then you may know to what a state Dublin has fallen as an artistic centre. The Queens is the only house carrying on theatrical entertainments, the Gaiety & Abbey are closed, & the Royal given over to music hall work. . . . [T]he taste of the moment seems all for 'pictures' or vulgar turns—the vulgarer the better!" Therefore, he presents his cinemagoing at this point as a consequence of the fact that several theaters were closed for summer and others had replaced dramatic entertainment with variety acts, however vulgar. Nevertheless, the opening of the Sackville was a turning point for him. He went to it twelve times between July and December 1910. Unlike the Volta, it was in a part of the city that was thoroughly respectable. And it specifically courted a largely female matinee and early-evening audience by offering free tea. In the same period, he visited the Volta just twice, going back in November despite his reaction in July.

The second Volta visit is worth contrasting with the Sackville visits, which are notable precisely because he often went with his mother, Anne, and/or his niece, Eileen. On July 21, less than a week after his first unhappy experience at the Volta, the three generations of Holloways visited the Sackville: "Mother, Eileen & I went down to the *Picture Theatre* after tea & thought the programme good—a few American dramatic pictures were very effective. The place was crowded as usual. Pictures are rapidly taking the place of the plays with the ordinary amusement seeker."[17] For a self-described playgoer, that last statement was not to be taken lightly, and his own patronage of pictures rather than plays formed part of this general trend.

The most remarkable incident at the Sackville occurred on a visit in September 1910, as the result of sensory disorientation caused not by the behavior of the audience—which appears to have been as unremarkable as usual—but by the film. "One of the pictures—'*A Story of the Wireless*,'" he reveals, "almost made mother seasick by the realism of its sea-scenes."[18] His mother was by no means put off by such experiences of bodily discomfort, and he sometimes specifically went to the Sackville on her request. On October 17, for example, when Eileen and two female companions went to the Theatre Royal to see stage star H. B. Irving in the play *Dr Jekyll & Mr Hyde*, he writes, "I intended going also later on but Mother expressing a wish to see the pictures in O'Connell Street I went there with her instead."[19] While there, he saw Edwin S. Porter's *The Attack on the Mill* (Edison, 1910), which he praised as "exceedingly well enacted & beautifully 'set.'" Beyond his recognition of the work of a canonical early filmmaker—albeit without naming him—such instances show that cinemagoing had become habitual for the Holloways, forming part of the regular entertainment choices of this middle-class family.

His experiences at the Volta contrasted markedly with those at the Sackville. Like the Queen's before it, the Volta became one of the early picture houses that working-class patrons frequented. For this reason, Holloway did not attend it often, and on the few occasions he did, he went without his female companions and without really intending to be there. This is true of his Volta visit of November 5, 1910, when he began the evening with the intention of attending a variety show. "After tea I went down to the Tivoli only to find the 'Full' boards outside each entrance door & many turning away disappointed," he records. "There was a sharp wind blowing, & as it was then only a few minutes past seven, I sought the 'Volta' picture show in Mary Street to put in the time until 8.30."[20] Beyond a need for shelter until the Tivoli's second show, it is not clear what attracted him back to the Volta, given his experience in July, but the programming showed little difference from the Sackville: "A series of pictures representing an unsuccessful love affair of Messalina, ending in the Emperor's destruction was on as I entered. The place was full & I had to be content with a seat near the canvass. A tragic 'drama' *The Stepdaughter*, & a comic 'love story' occupied the canvass before I left & also an interest picture of Japanese life."

Holloway himself was paying more attention to screen matters than previously, but he was not alone. If the program of classical drama, tragedy, and travelogue may have seemed too edifying, too distant from the body genres previously offered to working-class audiences at the Queen's, this did not appear to bother the Volta's large crowd, which "was quite pleased with the 'story pictures' & followed them with ejaculations just like at the Queens." It seems that a negotiation was taking place between audience and exhibitor in which the proletarian audience would accept this kind of programming so long as an active spectatorship was accommodated.

As part of that active spectatorship, Holloway describes an unfolding entr'acte live drama of romance and conflict. During reel changes, an altercation occurred between the young female accompanist and two laborers. "When the lights were up between the pictures," he reveals, "the little girl presiding at the piano was addicted to looking up smilingly at the cinematograph operator, to the annoyance of two working men behind me who kept saying 'she was badly brought up' & at last one of them said quite loudly—'If you want the young fellow so badly you better go up to him decently." Although the Volta's predominantly working-class audience resembled the one at the Queen's in its voluble engagement with screen matters, it not only viewed a different kind of programming but also was more generationally and gender diverse. In this context, the pianist's attraction to the projectionist, her public display of desire, was unwelcome. Early cinemagoing at Dublin's working-class venues may have had fewer strictures on aspects of audience behavior, but it placed limits on women's comportment that closely resembled middle-class rules of respectability.

Holloway's diary uniquely records bodily active, working-class cinemagoing at Dublin's first picture houses. Written by a man who was himself—however reluctantly—becoming a regular picture-house patron, its metaspectatorship provides a rich context for framing the experiences of Irish bodies in front of the early cinema screen.

DENIS CONDON is Lecturer in Irish Film at the Departments of English and Media Studies, Maynooth University, Ireland. He is author of *Early Irish Cinema, 1895–1921*.

Notes

1. Joseph Holloway Diaries, December 24, 1909, National Library of Ireland (NLI) MS 1808: 687.

2. Richard Ellmann, *James Joyce*, new and rev. ed. (Oxford, UK: Oxford University Press, 1982), 300–311; Luke McKernan, "James Joyce's Cinema," *Film and Film Culture* 3 (2004): 7–20; Kevin Rockett, "Something Rich and Strange: James Joyce, Beatrice Cenci and the Volta," *Film and Film Culture* 3 (2004): 21–34.

3. Diarmaid Ferriter, "Holloway, Joseph," *Dictionary of Irish Biography Online* (Cambridge, UK: Cambridge University Press, 2009), http://dib.cambridge.org/.

4. Robert Hogan and Michael J. O'Neill, eds., *Joseph Holloway's Abbey Theatre: A Selection of His Unpublished Journal "Impressions of a Dublin Playgoer"* (Carbondale: Southern Illinois University Press, 1967), xi.

5. Jan Olsson, *Los Angeles before Hollywood: Journalism and American Film Culture, 1905 to 1915* (Stockholm: National Library of Sweden, 2009), 38.

6. Ibid., 69–93.

7. Census of Ireland, 1911, http://www.census.nationalarchives.ie/reels/nai000127292/.

8. Chris Morash, *A History of Irish Theatre* (Oxford, UK: Oxford University Press, 2009).

9. Ben Singer, *Melodrama and Modernity: Early Sensational Cinema and Its Contexts* (New York: Columbia University Press, 2001).

10. Deirdre McFeely, *Dion Boucicault: Irish Identity on Stage* (Oxford, UK: Oxford University Press, 2012); Cheryl Herr, *For the Land They Loved: Irish Political Melodramas, 1890–1925* (Syracuse, NY: Syracuse University Press, 1991); Stephen Watt, *Joyce, O'Casey, and the Irish Popular Theater* (Syracuse, NY: Syracuse University Press, 1991); and Richard Pine, ed., *Dion Boucicault and the Irish Melodrama Tradition* (Dublin: Irish Theatre Archive, 1985).

11. Joseph Holloway Diaries, March 2, 1908, NLI MS 1806: 220.
12. Joseph Holloway Diaries, April 6, 1908, NLI MS 1806: 377–78.
13. Joseph Holloway Diaries, June 3, 1908, NLI MS 1806: 574.
14. Kevin and Emer Rockett, *Film Exhibition and Distribution in Ireland, 1909–2010* (Dublin: Four Courts, 2011), 17.
15. Joseph Holloway Diaries, June 18, 1910, NLI MS 1809: 795.
16. Joseph Holloway Diaries, July 16, 1910, NLI MS 1810: 50.
17. Joseph Holloway Diaries, July 21, 1910, NLI MS 1810: 76.
18. Joseph Holloway Diaries, September 12, 1910, NLI MS 1810: 272.
19. Joseph Holloway Diaries, October 17, 1910, NLI MS 1810: 475.
20. Joseph Holloway Diaries, November 5, 1910, NLI MS 1810: 583.

Part VI
Bodies in Exhibition Spaces

Introduction

As the previous section demonstrated, interrogating the body in relation to early cinema implies going beyond the screen and considering the corporealized viewer. Yet at these times, before the institutionalization of cinema and when film exhibition was considered as a performance (as explored in the Domitor volume *Performing New Media, 1890–1915*), screen environments could take many different forms. This section concentrates on specific viewing patterns and exhibition spaces developed to enrich the spectator's physical involvement with early cinema. Considering, following Donald Crafton, "the end-use as part of the 'cinema system,'" and the audience as "less unitary and passive" and tainted with "discretionary behavior," the contributions in this section partake in the most recent historiographical renewals of the apparatus theories. They shine a three-way refracted light on the underestimated, multisensorial experiences of the early audience.

Martin Barnier studies early spectators' immersive experience in the exhibition space. Setting a wide historico-technical framework, he recalls how much the three-dimensional illusion was part of the attraction of early-cinema images, exalted by such apparatuses as phantom rides and Hale's Tours. He also turns to proper 3-D devices, including the 1915 stereoscopic film series by Edwin S. Porter, which required cardboard eyeglasses—in other words, a tool that directly touched and altered the viewer's senses. Barnier finally leads us far beyond the screen, to its disappearance, by way of the animated 3-D bodies of the Kinoplastikon. Tricked in his or her haptic experience, the viewer experienced these bodies, made only of light, as tangible.

Kristina Köhler concentrates on a specific and exemplary genre in terms of problematizing the spectator's physicality: early dance-instruction films. Proclaiming to teach the audience to dance, these films were structured as if the spectators were synchronically mimicking the performers, following the screened body gestures. However, as Köhler finds out, most of these films were screened in regular movie theaters with an audience, either spatially confined and having to postpone their practice or to only move their feet; the films sometimes acknowledged these exhibition constraints. But some of these films were screened at home and even led to the creation of new exhibition spaces, such as the Tanz-Kinema. Köhler's case study of this cinematic ballroom culminates in the identification of the production of a film not only made for, but also by and with, the audience. The spectator's body, encouraged to "dance with the screen," thus finished by penetrating it.

As a conclusion to this final section, Alison Reiko Loader definitively overturns our conception of the place of the spectator, disclosing overlooked dimensions of the camera obscura. Though Jonathan Crary established the camera obscura as an icon for the decorporealized vision predating the nineteenth-century advent of a bodily conception of the viewer, Loader shows that the device lived on in a "splendid, tangible, and re-created format," exploring what she calls the "tactile and sensual qualities of an apparatus long associated with disembodiment." This final essay thus casts the newly corporealized camera obscura as an emblem of the paradigm shift and new concern about the spectator's body—from which early cinema was to emerge.

23 The Viewer's Body in Motion

Physical and Virtual Effects of Three-Dimensional Spectacles

Martin Barnier

Translated by Timothy Barnard

THE BODY IN the space of the cinema venue is not only that of the person looking at a flat screen. We know that many early cinema events in which fixed or moving images were projected were accompanied by voices, sounds, and music,[1] which set the spectator's body and senses in motion. Even in silence, each person could detect the bodily presence of those around them, if only by their breathing. In addition, in the midnineteenth century, various devices showing three-dimensional images brought the viewer's body into the space of the representation. This immersion could be magnified through technical devices that moved the spectator's body in such a way that provoked a heightened sense of reality. In light of the importance and variety of these "presences," we must ask ourselves how the senses were used to involve the viewer, and how early cinema "incorporated" the spectator.

In this chapter, I will situate the body with respect to screenings and images in Western countries before 1914. What was the role of the viewer's body in the space of the venue? Michel de Certeau, in an interview with Georges Vigarello in *Esprit* in 1982, defined the body as a system of gestures and perceptions. For de Certeau, "each 'body' is the combination of determinations" that essentially affect its "limits" (where this body stops) and the development of its "senses (hearing, smell, sight)."[2] In France, the study of the social history of the spectatorial body began to develop a decade or so ago in the wake of work on the history of the body.[3]

The viewer's body sits in the venue—but the way the spectator perceives the three-dimensional image can shift that body into a virtual space. Numerous devices emerged in the nineteenth century to make it possible to immerse the viewer in a fictive three-dimensional environment. Here I will trace a chronological thread showing how these various stereoscopy techniques attempt to position the body of the spectator in concrete and virtual space.

The Immersed Spectator

Looking at images with an accentuated depth gives the viewer the sense that he or she is "entering" the depicted space. The brain projects one's body into the picture. This process is enhanced with viewing glasses or cabinets, which separate the spectator from the "real world" around him. The simplest and most rapidly expanding device for creating 3-D images was stereoscopic photography. Its great popularity began in the midnineteenth century. In 1851, David Brewster gave a stereoscope to Queen Victoria, and by the First World War, millions of stereoscopic images had been sold. The London Stereoscopic Company sold one million three-dimensional pictures in the year 1862 alone.[4] The public was fascinated with the feeling that one's entire body seemed to be drawn into the depth of the space when each eye was shown a slightly different image.

In the second half of the nineteenth century, while many other devices were developed to enable the audience to see pictures in 3-D and to imagine themselves in a three-dimensional space,[5] even pictorial conventions attempted to invoke that sensation. Academic paintings, called *pompier* in France, depict almost life-sized scenes with extreme realism. In museums and galleries, viewers of immense painted canvases could project themselves into historical locations,[6] imagining their bodies confronted with the gladiators in Jean-Léon Gérôme's *Pollice Verso* of 1872. The physical sensation of proximity to the depicted space enabled the artist's contemporaries to understand the artistic feat. The body of the observer of an ultra-realist, giant painting seems able to cast itself into an immense landscape. Academic painting had an influence on cinematic iconography.[7] We should relate this painting tradition to the image technology that seeks to immerse its viewer's body—of which the panorama is among the most spectacular example.

The growth of panoramas in the same period enabled the spectatorial body to enter a virtual world, providing the sensation of being on the rooftops of a large city or on a battlefield. The construction of virtual depth made the body feel like it could move through a landscape. In film projection, the creation of the stereo window was a continuation of this principle.

The Overwhelmed Spectator

Sitting in a dark room in front of huge, changing, and moving pictures, the spectator experienced another kind of immersion. Magic lanterns improved over the course of the nineteenth century, and some shows were especially illusionistic, such as Robertson's fantascope. Robertson notably projected images of phantoms onto smoke, creating a striking impression. The audience could see a three-dimensional spectral shape floating in the room, moving forward in the dark. Spectators felt not only fear but also the impulse to lean back, becoming aware of their bodies. The fantascope could indeed provoke concrete muscular movement—compelling the spectator to stand up, crouch down, or flee to avoid the illuminated smoke. In addition, the viewer of Robertson's shows was subjected to kinesthetic and multisensory effects: a glass organ accompanied the projection of phantoms and, in addition to the music, the fragrance of burning herbs created a peculiar atmosphere. At some shows his assistants, dressed in black, glided among the viewers holding a mask lit from the inside to appear like an approaching ghost.[8] All the senses were brought into play to make the public react physically.

A specific consideration of the observer's body and senses was implied in these shows. Charles D'Almeida, another lantern showman who offered anaglyphic stereoscopic projections in 1858, wrote that his "images in three dimensions can be seen from different places in the room."[9] He thus considered the audience's bodies in their plurality and even in their movement. The spectators could move about as they looked at the three-dimensional image. About three decades later, as scientific articles and patents around projection in relief proliferated, Alfred Molteni took up D'Almeida's anaglyphic principle. Using a single magic lantern equipped with two lenses on which green and red filters were placed, he made an anaglyphic stereoscopic projection that became a landmark because of the reliability of its material.[10] The viewers were given glasses with red and green lenses to see each image in relief. In other words, and in the same way as D'Almeida's, Molteni's device changed their sight, controlled their senses. A letter from Molteni to Étienne-Jules Marey gave a few more details about the feeling this provoked: "The three-dimensional sensation is created immediately and in the case of some images is quite pronounced."[11] The spectators in the room are thus able to "cast" themselves into the "reachable" scenes. They can imagine an interaction between the 3-D space unfolding on the big screen and their own bodies. The full-size landscape made one want to move into this "virtual" world.

The body of an individual viewer could also be moved by stereoscopic animated views. A great many devices displayed images in 3-D and in movement (using a series of still images) for a single observer. These included Jules Duboscq's Stereo-fantascope of 1852, Coleman Sellers's Kinematoscope in 1861, and Charles-Émile Reynaud's Stereo-Cinema in 1907.[12] In each case, the viewer had to lean over a device, not look at a projection on a screen. The body was involved as the spectator put his or her eyes in the visor and, most often, turned a crank. Some stereoscopic views were particularly stimulating to the senses. We know that many images seen through these stereoscopic viewers were "risqué." The body of a male viewer—or at least a part of it—could be set into motion by the erotic appeal of the pictures.

Screening moving images, which increased without stereoscopy after 1896, provoked a strong reaction in the audience's bodies. In the long line of "realism

Figure 23.1. *La Nature*, December 27, 1890.

through perspective," the sensation of a spectatorial body drowning in and moving through a very large space—a landscape with vanishing lines—was heightened in travelogues and so-called phantom rides. As a corollary, Louis Lumière's *L'arrivée du train en gare* (*Train Entering a Station*, 1897) and the many other train-arrival films were often described as having a realistic or three-dimensional effect. It is significant that, forty years later, in 1935, Louis Lumière placed his camera in the same spot, in the La Ciotat train station, for a remake of his film *in anaglyphic relief*.[13] Nevertheless, the early and nonstereoscopic films had an essential impact on bodies. Jean-Pierre Sirois-Trahan has identified how some spectators moved in reaction to the locomotive and other spectacular vehicles or cavalry as they sped toward the camera.[14] In the depiction of his first screening, Maxim Gorki very precisely explained how it felt to be "touched" by the picture: "Suddenly something clicks, everything vanishes and a train appears on the screen. It speeds straight at you—watch out! It seems as though it will plunge into the darkness in which you sit, turning you into a ripped sack full of lacerated flesh and splintered bones."[15]

Sirois-Trahan found many other examples of articles that testified to the movement of the viewers' bodies in reaction to the moving pictures, such as the arrival of the cavalry in Lumière film nr. 883, which made the audience comment: "we're almost afraid. We want to make room for them. . . . [Y]ou're going to be run over."[16] Sirois-Trahan highlights that "haptic reactions (leaning back, flinching, jumping, shouting) were frequent at the time."[17] Examples of movement in the room proliferate: "A horse-drawn cart comes straight into the spectators. My neighbor is so spellbound that she leaps up . . . and sits down again only after the cart turned and disappeared";[18] "I squirm in my seat"; "ladies . . . move back with horror," etc.[19] While debate continues over whether the viewers of the first Lumière train films cried out or not, it is clear that "life-sized" screenings of a machine moving through a space with depth of field caused the viewer's body to react, at least with a slight movement to offset the explosive perspective effect.[20]

Following the "sensational" success (referring to a strong bodily sensation) of the train and other vehicles arriving, the "phantom rides," referring to footage shot from the front of a train or subway, multiplied. "One holds his breath," an article in the *New York Mail and Express* of September 25, 1897, said of the Billy Bitzer film *Haverstraw Tunnel*.[21] Viewers thus become aware of their bodies and have the impression of being swallowed up by a tunnel. This is one of the highly sought-after effects of stereoscopic films, which I have described elsewhere as the "tunnel effect" and the "vortex effect."[22] In travelogues shot from the train's cowcatcher, the kinesthetic effect of reality gives the viewer the sensation of speed. These films were both a description of a landscape unfamiliar to the viewer and an immersion in reality. Their perceptual attraction was greatly increased in Hale's Tours programs (1905–ca. 1915), a fairground attraction in which the viewers sat in a real wagon that moved, as air was blown onto the audience.[23]

The body of the viewer could be moved even more effectively by combining techniques inherited from an entire tradition of immersive contemplation.[24] One specific case, the Maréorama, fused many elements: using hydraulic cylinders so that the public could feel the movement of waves on a fake boat, music, sound effects with whistles, wind and fog effects, and variations in light.[25] The virtual recreation of a journey undoubtedly reached its high point with the Maréorama. Painter Hugo d'Alesi designed this immense apparatus for the World's Fair in Paris in 1900. With its spooled canvases, the Maréorama recreated travel by ship but without the use of film.[26] We could say that the designers of this attraction went further than the usual panoramas in seeking out realism. Although for some viewers the effect was not pronounced enough, the passenger's body was incorporated fairly strongly through the pitching and rolling, among other effects. The latest technologies of immersion were constantly being updated, and the Maréorama is emblematic of the research being put into "moving" the body to please the senses.[27]

The Unsettled Spectator

While the Maréorama could potentially cause seasickness, three-dimensional and moving images could also cause discomfort; such was the case with Pepper's Ghost. The technique, which had existed since 1862, mainly consisted of embodying phantoms on stage during a play. Pepper's Ghost was combined with films in the 1910s. Under the title of Kinoplastikon, it met some success in London in 1913, mingling real bodies on stage with animated 3-D bodies screened on a glass. A journalist described it in the following manner: "Never before had I witnessed such a moving picture show. It was practically the illusion of life, remarkable and astonishing, almost *uncanny* in its realness."[28] This malaise caused by an excessive realism would return with projections "in relief." A very recent example can be found in a 2012 article on an identical technique, based on Pepper's Ghost (the so-called hologram). Commenting on Tupac Shakur, the murdered rapper, who "came back" through this device to perform "on stage" six years after his death, the journalist reused the term "uncanny."[29] The three-dimensional and animated body was thus explored in all its disturbing qualities, defying reality, physicality, and life.

What is most interesting about the Kinoplastikon is the lack of any visible screen. Figures seem to float like ghosts directly on the stage. The *Times* of London explained in 1913: "Visitors of the Scala Theater last week were able to see the latest development of the cinematographic art—living stereoscopic pictures shown without a screen."[30] The absence of a screen transforms the usual cinematic perception, enhancing the haptic quality of the images. These were, in addition, accompanied synchronously by the Vivaphone (a sound-reproduction device used before the 1920s). The advertising outside the theater proclaimed: "Singing, Talking, Moving Picture Figures in Solid Stereoscopic Relief, Without a Screen."[31] Sounds and images thus contributed to the "uncanny" impression of reality in this space, mixing performed and recorded voices, real and immaterial bodies. The eyes and ears of the viewers were as much stimulated as misled.[32]

Fooling the spectator's senses was a playful issue. Seeing a three-dimensional film might lead to the desire to "touch" what "protruded." Children were not the only ones who wanted to catch the Haribo candies that "sprang" out of the 2010 stereoscopic advertisement. Already one century earlier, journalists described being tempted to grip the foliage that seemed to sprout from the screen during the exhibition of stereoscopic films by Edwin S. Porter, which some called "forerunners of a new era in motion picture realism"[33] (once again, the excessive "reality effect" took center stage).

Known for his moving pictures of trains and gangsters (didn't the spectators duck to avoid the gun pointing at the camera in *The Great Train Robbery* [Edwin S. Porter, 1903]?), Porter was also one of the first to perfect anaglyphic stereoscopy using a standard projector, which he presented at the Astor Theater in New York on June 10, 1915. He said that it took him ten years of research, but he gave only a general explanation of his method, no precise technical details.[34] We know that there were cardboard eyeglasses, something that annoyed the *Moving Picture World* correspondent and made him hope that a future stage projection, in relief, could be viewed with the naked eye. While the glasses bothered his face, his body did participate in the experience: "Holding these glasses before the eyes, one gains a truly stereoscopic effect that is nothing short of startling in lifelikeness. The screen seems to be brought to within a few feet of the onlooker and the objects animate and inanimate stand out in correct perspective, quite as though the vision were centered on an actual room, a landscape or whatever the subject may be."[35]

By re-creating perspective, inventors made it possible to feel as though one were in an "actual room" or a true natural landscape. This gives the impression that the body is in a virtual space. While the image, when seen without glasses, is described as distorted because of the superimposition of the red and green images, with glasses "the reds and greens are neutralized into an even tone and out of the chaos, a duplicate life emerges."[36] As the *Moving Picture World* journalist explains, this "duplicate life" is essentially made up of landscapes. The three-reel series, small films in relief produced by Adolph Zukor and edited together, was composed of travelogues and excerpts of action films. Viewers were thus able to feel as if their bodies were in contact with vast three-dimensional spaces, or in the presence of spectacular natural phenomena such as Niagara Falls.

Whereas the *Motion Picture News* correspondent was too annoyed by the eyeglasses to be won over,[37] the *Motography* correspondent admired the new technique, especially when he saw trees in the foreground whose branches "appeared to extend right out over the stage." This gave the impression that a viewer in the first row could reach out and "[grab] one of the branches."[38] Objects thus leaped out of the screen with an almost haptic effect, creating an impression of nearness between the filmed objects and the viewer's body.

Each spectator's subjectivity should be considered here. The three records of the screening show different bodily reactions. Both the *New York Dramatic Mirror* and *Moving Picture World* reported that rapid action looked blurry.[39] Lynde Denig, for *Moving Picture World*, reported that the worst section (and thus the one that made him leave the film) was an Oriental dance "in which the performers were blurred and the film in its entirety shimmered, something like a reflection on a lake. Then there were other instances in which quick moments failed to register."[40] The anonymous *Mirror* author, however, had the impression of seeing

MOTION PICTURE NEWS   Vol. 11. No. 26.

Stereoscopic Pictures Give Sense of Depth to Images

Invention of Porter, of Famous Players, and Waddell, Late of Edison, Recently Shown at Private Exhibition in New York, Promises Revolutionary Improvement in Screen Vision

STEREOSCOPIC motion pictures, an invention on which Edwin S. Porter, of the Famous Players Film Company, has been working for about eight years, the last two of which have been in collaboration with William E. Waddell, formerly of the Edison company, have advanced so far that they were shown recently at a private exhibition.

The pictures really achieve the third dimension on the screen. That is to say, the figures have the apppearance of depth, or perspective, as well as breadth and height. They were viewed through colored lenses, green for the right eye and red for the left. The lenses may be made from glass celluloid or any transparent matter. Thus viewed the pictures have color value, but not full tones. Also, due to the eyes superimposing two images, as they do constantly in every day life, it is hard to portray action quickly crossing the lens by this stereoscopic photography. For instance, a horseman could ride at full speed straight toward the camera and be distinct, but he could not ride across the field of vision and be distinct.

From this it follows that many times, when the stereoscopic pictures portray action, the registration is indistinct. The figures seem to have three dimensions, but, through some illusion, they seem very close to the eye but small. Also the eyes feel the strain of viewing the pictures through differently colored lenses.

The stereoscopic process, according to Mr. Porter, is entirely in the film by the time it reaches the exhibitor, and may be projected on any projection machine or on any size screen.

But, because of the need for colored lenses and the sometimes imperfect registration, it is fair to say that stereoscopic pictures are not yet ready to be a commercial success. But those shown by Messrs. Porter and Waddell are far ahead of any others yet seen; so far ahead that it seems likely that the hardest obstacles have been overcome, and that perfecting the process for commercial use may be only a matter of a few months.

A stereoscopic effect can only be seen with two eyes. The reason for this lies in the fact that the distance between the eyes causes the two optics to see any article, a chair leg for instance, at slightly differing angles. The right eye sees the chair leg, and the left eye sees it. But the brain only gets one impression. So, to some extent, two eyes see around behind the chair leg, and so demonstrate, ocularly, the presence of the third dimension, depth.

The old stereoscope of childhood was a practical application of this theory. The right eye saw the right picture, and only the right picture. The left eye saw the left picture and that alone. As the pictures were the same scene photographed by lenses about as far apart as human eyes a stereoscopic effect was attained.

In obtaining a stereoscopic effect on the screen it is necessary to have two pictures, and have each eye see its own picture and only its own picture. Porter and Waddell have accomplished this by projecting simultaneously a green and a red picture, the pictures having been photographed at the same time through two lenses. Then, that each eye may only see its own picture, the green and red colored glasses are used. The green lens kills off one picture for one eye, and the red lens kills off the other picture for the other eye. So each eye sees its own picture, and only its own

EDWIN S. PORTER

picture, at the same differing angles as the human eyes behold any object, and the result is a stereoscopic effect.

Naturally the stereoscopic effect, with three dimensions, is more true to life than the usual effect with two dimensions. So there is a great possibility in stereoscopic motion photography, which the invention of Porter and Waddell realizes.

Mr. Porter himself expressed his ideas on the subject by saying: "Before I am satisfied it will be possible to have the true perspective of objects and persons as they appear in life on the screen without any artificial aid to the naked eye."

The subjects shown at the private exhibition were scenic views, some of them showing Niagara Falls, and scenes from some Famous Players productions, such as "Jim the Penman" and "The Morals of Marcus."

Figure 23.2. *Motion Picture News*, June 1915.

a true stage play live, not "shadowy figures." That reporter, too, found that the tree branches appeared to float in the theater. The body's relation with three-dimensional films can be seen in the need to believe in the three dimensions our brains re-create. Denig was quite aware of this when he wrote, "These pictures will appeal first for reason of their novelty, then because of the wonderful effects obtained, and after that, when they had become familiar, there would be the same old demand for an interesting story.... There must be no break to spoil the illusion."[41]

Conclusion

Unlike Jonathan Crary, whose conclusion refers the observer's experience back to Foucault's panoptic vision, I do not think that the solicitation of the body in the devices examined throughout this study could possibly lead to a totalitarian world.[42] It all depends on the technique.[43] The spectator's body was not necessarily constrained. It expressed itself. It moved. Until about 1915, viewers' bodies had a large role to play in film screenings. There is no "passive body" watching the screen. Elsewhere, I have discussed the audience's verbal and physical participation in the screening.[44] People stood up, cried, drank, and ate while films were being shown. Moreover, the voice of the film lecturer, sound effects, opera singing, and music produced emotional reactions and set the viewer's body in motion.

Porter's stereoscopic screening of 1915 demonstrated that the body was even more involved with three-dimensional films. The virtual 3-D space stimulated viewers' movements and reactions, or at least their body consciousness. Less than seven years after this initial large-screen projection, stereoscopic films were being shown in substantial numbers, with the first great wave of stereoscopic films dating from 1922 to 1926, with pop-out effects making the viewers bend down or turn their heads. Nevertheless, we must be careful not to draw a direct teleological line from the 1915 screenings to those of 1922. 3-D is one of the film industry's phenomena that has resurfaced most often.[45] But each time, either by seeing something pop out or by feeling absorbed in the picture, or even by other phenomena such as the tunnel effect, the viewers' bodies and senses were engaged.

All these elements, from the nineteenth century to 1915, can be viewed alongside contemporary techniques that continue to incite reaction from the body in a soundscape in three dimensions. Stereoscopy machines, existing since the mid-nineteenth century, enabled viewers to leave the outside world behind. Leaning over the film viewer, eyes focused on the stereoscopic cards, still or in movement, the body was suffused with sensations caused by the illusion the brain transmitted. The very contemporary Oculus Rift continues where the Kinematoscope of 1861 left off (even if there is no direct link between the two techniques). The three most widely used systems today already existed back in 1915: anaglyphic images (still used in graphic novels[46] and YouTube videos); intermittent projection (used by every system that requires active glasses, which are more effective and used in French art cinemas); and polarizing filters (the passive glasses used today in major commercial cinemas). Since the onset of the 3-D Fusion Camera System in 2005, in order to attract people who might otherwise watch a screen at home, motion pictures offer to "revive" the viewers' bodies, enveloping them in a world of sounds and images in which they can move virtually. The three-dimensional film relies on effects of depth, protrusion from the screen, and the sound environment. These are part of a tradition stretching back at least to the magic lantern show and to any spectacular cultural series that attempted to immerse the body in order to move it—in all senses of the term.

MARTIN BARNIER is Professor of Cinema Studies and Film History at the University Lumière Lyon 2. His recent books include *Bruits, cris, musiques de films. Les projections avant 1914*, *Le Cinéma 3-D: Histoire, économie, technique, esthétique* (with Kira Kitsopanodou), and *Une brève histoire du cinema (1895-2015)* (with Laurent Jullier).

TIMOTHY BARNARD is a translator, author, and book publisher. He has translated and published volumes by André Bazin and Jean-Luc Godard and is author of the short volume *Découpage*.

Notes

1. Martin Barnier, *Bruits, cris, musiques de films: Les projections avant 1914* (Rennes, France: Presses Universitaires de Rennes, 2010).
2. Michel de Certeau (interview with Georges Vigarello), "Histoire de corps," *Esprit* 1667 (February 1982): 179.
3. See, for example, Alain Corbin, Jean-Jacques Courtine, and Georges Vigarello, eds., *Histoire du corps* (Paris: Seuil, 2005/2006); and Dominique Memmi, Dominique Guillo, and Olivier Martin, eds., *La tentation du corps: Corporéité et sciences sociales* (Paris: EHESS, 2009).
4. Ray Zone, *Stereoscopic Cinema and the Origins of 3-D Film (1838–1952)* (Lexington: University Press of Kentucky, 2007), 13.
5. Such as Alexander Becker's stereo peep show cabinet or the stereorama (ibid., 15, 20). See also William Darrah, *The World of Stereographs* (Gettysburg, PA: Darrah, 1977).
6. Generally speaking, it was mostly genre paintings that came to take on hitherto unseen dimensions, but some historical paintings also adopted immense formats.
7. See Laurent Guido and Valentine Robert, "Jean-Léon Gérôme: un peintre d'histoire présumé 'cinéaste,'" *1895* 63 (2011): 8–23, http://1895.revues.org/4322.
8. Laurent Mannoni, *Le Grand art de la lumière et de l'ombre: Archéologie du cinéma* (Paris: Nathan, 1994), 157.

9. Joseph Charles d'Almeida, "Nouvel appareil stéréoscopique," *Les Comptes rendus de l'académie des sciences* 47 (July 12, 1858): 61–63.

10. This show occurred on June 8, 1890, in Paris, and was undoubtedly the first anaglyphic screening for a group of people with a dual-lens lantern projecting vertically.

11. Letter from Molteni to Marey on December 5, 1890, in Thierry Lefebvre, Jacques Malthête, and Laurent Mannoni, eds., *Lettres d'Étienne-Jules Marey à Georges Demenÿ 1880-1894* (Paris: AFRHC/BIFI, 2000), 495–96.

12. Zone, *Stereoscopic Cinema*, 28–32.

13. Hervé Lauwick, "Louis Lumière va présenter ce jour même à l'Académie des Sciences son invention nouvelle," *Le Jour*, February 25, 1935; "Optique: Ecrans colorés pour projections stéréoscopiques: Notes de M. Louis Lumière (lundi 25 février 1935)," in *Comptes rendus hebdomadaires des séances de l'Académie des Sciences* 200 (January–June 1935): 701–4.

14. Jean-Pierre Sirois-Trahan, "Mythes et limites du train-qui-fonce-sur-les-spectateurs," in Veronica Innocenti and Valentina Re, eds., *Limina: Le Soglie del Film/Film's Thresholds* (Udine, Italy: Forum, 2004), 203–21.

15. Maxim Gorki, "Review of the Lumière Programme," first published in the journal *Nijegorodskilistok* on July 4, 1896, reedited and translated in Jay Leyda, *Kino: A History of Russian and Soviet Film*, 3rd ed. (London: Allen and Unwin, 1983), 408.

16. Quoted by Sirois-Trahan, "Mythes et limites," 207.

17. Ibid.

18. H. de Parville, *Le Journal des débats*, July 17, 1895, quoted by Sirois-Trahan, "Mythes et limites," 207.

19. Sirois-Trahan, "Mythes et limites," 207.

20. Ibid., 203–21.

21. Quoted by Robert C. Allen in "Contra the Chaser Theory," *Film before Griffith*, ed. John L. Fell (Berkeley: University of California Press, 1983), 110.

22. Martin Barnier and Kira Kitsopanidou, *Le Cinéma 3-D: Histoire, économie, technique, esthétique* (Paris: Armand Colin, 2015).

23. Lauren Rabinovitz, "From *Hale's Tours* to *Star Tours*: Virtual Voyages, Travel Ride Films, and the Delirium of the Hyper-Real," in *Virtual Voyages: Cinema and Travel*, ed. Jeffrey Ruoff (Durham, NC: Duke University Press, 2006), 42–60.

24. Alison Griffiths, *Shivers down Your Spine: Cinema, Museums, and the Immersive View* (New York: Columbia University Press, 2013).

25. Errki Huthamo, *Illusions in Motion. Media Archaeology of the Moving Panorama and Related Spectacles* (Cambridge, MA: MIT Press, 2013), 315–16.

26. "The Maréorama at the Paris Exposition," *Scientific American*, September 29, 1900, 198.

27. See Erkki Huhtamo, "Encapsulated Bodies in Motion: Simulators and the Quest for Total Immersion," in *Critical Issues in Electronic Media*, ed. Simon Penny (Albany: State University of New York Press, 1995), 159–86.

28. J. Cher, "A Glimpse of Vienna and the Kinoplastikon," *The Bioscope*, March 20, 1913, 82–83.

29. Gerrick D. Kennedy, "Coachella 2012: Tupac 'Responds' to His Reincarnation," *Los Angeles Times*, April 16, 2012.

30. *The Times* (London), April 28, 1913.

31. Zone, *Stereoscopic Cinema*, 69.

32. Barnier and Kitsopanidou, *Le Cinéma 3-D*, 163. The Pepper's Ghost technique continues to be used today to create virtual characters in three dimensions, such as drawings of Japanese singers who draw crowds in stadiums (the Vocaloids Hatsune Miku, Meiko, Rin and Len, etc.)

33. Lynde Denig, "Stereoscopic Pictures Screened. Edwin S. Porter and W. E. Waddell Show Remarkable Three-Dimension Photography to the Audience at the Astor Theater," *Moving Picture World*, June 26, 1915, 2072.

34. Denig, "Stereoscopic Pictures." See also the documentary film *Before the Nickelodeon: The Early Cinema of Edwin S. Porter* (Charles Musser, 1982).

35. Denig, "Stereoscopic Pictures."

36. Ibid.

37. "Stereoscopic Pictures Give Sense of Depth to Images," *Motion Picture News*, July 3, 1915, 62.

38. C.R.C., "Stereoscopic Pictures Shown," *Motography*, June 26, 1915, 1040.

39. "Stereoscopic Films Shown," *New York Dramatic Mirror*, June 16, 1915, 21.

40. Denig, "Stereoscopic Pictures."

41. Ibid. For a comment by the producer, Adolph Zukor, looking back at Porter's stereoscopic films as "ahead of their time," see Adolph Zukor and Dale Kramer, *The Public Is Never Wrong: The Autobiography of Adolph Zukor* (New York: Putnam, 1953), 121.

42. Jonathan Crary, *Techniques of the Observer: On Visions and Modernity in the Nineteenth Century* (Cambridge, MA: MIT Press, 1990).

43. Martine Bubb, "La *camera obscura*, au-delà du "dispositif foucaldien" proposé par Jonathan Crary dans *L'art de l'observateur*," *Appareil*, June 20, 2008, http://appareil.revues.org/461.

44. Barnier, *Bruits, cris*.

45. Barnier and Kitsopanidou, *Le Cinéma 3-D*.

46. Matthias Picard, *Jim Curious: Voyage au coeur de l'océan* (Strasbourg, France: Éditions 2024), 2012.

24 Moving the Spectator, Dancing with the Screen

Early Dance Instruction Films and Reconfigurations of Film Spectatorship in the 1910s

Kristina Köhler

Embodied/Disembodied: Historiographies of Film Spectatorship

The history of cinema spectatorship has often been told as a story of physical discipline, closely linked to cinema's institutionalization. With the construction of movie theaters in the 1910s, as one prevalent story goes, the "crowd" learned how to "behave as spectators" in cinema spaces that would be increasingly regulated.[1] This narrative implies a significant shift in concepts of spectatorship: While early cinema has often been described as physically stimulating the spectator's body (conceived as excitable and impulsive), conceptions of later forms of spectatorship have highlighted cinema's imaginary, immersive, and psychological effects.[2] Tom Gunning, Miriam Hansen, Scott Curtis, and others have shown, however, that these developments were not linear; instead, they were accompanied by struggles and crises, by countermodels and alternative practices.[3] In this sense, we can look on the early 1910s as a time of controversial debates, in which different concepts of spectatorship coexisted. Within this field, the spectator's body formed a highly symbolic site of negotiation that could be summoned as an argument either *for* or *against* the cinema. While representatives of the church, state, or educational institutions often criticized the stimulation of the spectators' bodies as a threat to public order, film advertisement used the promise of physical excitement as a selling point. Managing the spectators' bodies was also a central concern for cinema owners and showmen: How should the audience be situated in the cinema space? How many people could enter at once?[4]

It is perhaps no coincidence that at the same time, a number of film practices emerged that similarly negotiated the question of the spectator's body and his or her position and movement in cinema space. As an example for the broader field of body discourses, I consider a little-studied phenomenon from the early 1910s: dance instruction films. Although these films and their practices were not exactly at the forefront of the early-twentieth-century cinema debate, they nevertheless shared some of its central concerns: the concept of film spectatorship as a mobilizing, corporeal, and participatory experience. Here, I take a closer look at how and where these films were screened. The spatial settings and performative strategies form a compelling starting point to (re-)consider the role of the spectator's body within the cinematic *dispositif* and to discuss interactions between screen bodies and audience response.[5]

Early Dance Instruction Films

Around 1913, several film companies—especially, but not exclusively in the United States—began to produce dance instruction films.[6] These films were less indebted to the tradition of stage dancing or early cinema's dance scenes than one might imagine, arising instead from a cultural context that was highly marked by social and ballroom dancing. Around 1900, social dancing constituted an established cultural practice and mass entertainment; these forms of dancing were embedded in the attraction culture of fairgrounds and amusement parks.[7] They emerged from and responded to a similar fascination with movement, sensory excitement, and kinesthetic pleasures. As thousands danced in enormous ballrooms like the ones on Coney Island, film companies discovered that dance instruction was a lucrative business and began to produce films for dance education.

One of the first movies of this kind was *Motion Picture Dancing Lessons*, a three-reeler made in 1913 by the Kalem Company. The film provided dancing lessons for the tango, the turkey trot, and the Viennese hesitation waltz; Kalem advertised that it would give "three lessons *complete* for the price of an admission."[8] The film became an international success; it was screened—even during the war years—in the United States, Germany, France, Great Britain, and probably other countries. Although no copies of this or other early dance instructions films seem to survive, the advertising texts and pictures, catalog descriptions, and reviews give a pretty detailed account of what these films looked like. *Motion Picture Dancing Lessons*, for example, already employed all the film techniques that would become characteristic of the genre: intertitles explained the steps and exercises—sometimes explicitly imitating or quoting a dance teacher; close-ups of the feet allowed viewers to study the footwork in detail; repetitions of individual steps helped viewers memorize them and study the male and female parts separately before dancing the complete choreography as a couple. Obviously, these films borrowed from established techniques of dance teaching; the editing, for example, reproduced the structure of a dance lesson through filmic means. The demonstrative mode of address also made it quite clear that these films were more than a recording of a dance number; they were specifically designed to

Moving the Spectator, Dancing with the Screen | 277

Figure 24.1a–b. Advertisements for the film *Motion Picture Dancing Lessons* from *Motion Picture World*, November 1913.

"teach" the audience how to dance. At the same time, they modeled cinema as a place of corporeal education—a place where "techniques of the body" (to quote Marcel Mauss) could be learned and transmitted.[9]

Indeed, none of the advertisements missed the opportunity to emphasize the effectiveness of these cinematic dance instructions. *Motion Picture Dancing Lessons*, the Kalem Company promised, "will help even the most awkward to become perfect dancers."[10] Likewise, a German distributor boasted, "The theater audience will be able to dance after having watched this movie."[11] These promotional discourses were blatantly optimistic; they concealed the often lengthy and laborious process of learning new dance techniques. Nevertheless, they conceptualized cinema as a medium in which the visual and the corporeal were intrinsically connected. According to their logic, *seeing* the steps and *dancing* would be more or less the same thing.

If these films were designed to stimulate direct interaction between screen bodies and audience response, we may ask: How were the films screened, in which contexts and settings? There were at least three different scenarios. First and foremost, films such as *Motion Picture Dancing Lessons* were shown in regular cinemas and vaudeville theaters as part of larger programs. We can suppose that spectators had to watch and memorize the dance steps in order to practice them *afterward*—at home, or in a café or ballroom. In some cases, "leaflets" and "printed details" with step diagrams and explanations were distributed (or sold) to the audience.[12] They would serve as a memory aid to bridge the temporal gap between the film projection and the actual dance practice. Still, some questions remain. How would a seated cinema audience deal with the films' appellative character? Wouldn't they feel encouraged to try some of the steps during the film projection—shuffling their feet under the seat? Or, on the contrary, would the direct instructions make them even more aware of their seated position? Of course, there are no definite answers to these questions. And yet it is impossible to overlook how the films' purpose, to engage the spectators physically, was at odds with the spectators' position in the movie theater—with its seating rows, limited space, and dimmed auditorium.

In a second scenario, the dance instruction films were screened with home-cinema devices. An ad for the Pathéscope from 1914 suggests that home projectors would allow individuals to project the instruction films in the private space of a living room so that they could dance the steps *at the same time*.[13] In this case, the dancing couples on screen and in front of the screen would be perfectly synchronized—even so perfectly, the pictures suggest, that neither the man nor the woman would actually have to *look at* the screen. The simultaneity of watching and dancing was also the main feature of a third scenario. Starting in the 1910s, it was not uncommon—either in the United States or Europe—to show these films in specific ballroom settings that would merge the architectural sites

Figure 24.2. Advertisement for the Pathéscope from *Talking Machine World*, August 1914.

of cinema and ballroom. The case of the Tanz-Kinema, which opened its doors in Berlin in 1921, presents a compelling example. Although from a slightly later period, it gives detailed insights into how these cinematic ballroom settings were arranged and how they should facilitate the spectators' mobility, participation, and corporeal interaction with the screen.

Making Space for the Spectators to Dance:
The Tanz-Kinema Alexanderplatz

The brief and turbulent story of the Tanz-Kinema begins in December 1920 with the official launch of the company. The enterprise combined three different fields of activity: "the production and distribution of films, especially dance instruction

Figure 24.3a–b. *The Tango Waltz* (Selsior 1914). Courtesy of Swedish Film Institute.

films, and the organization of film screenings, especially of dance instruction films for the purpose of dancing lessons."[14] The company was founded and managed by Oskar John Peterton-Rausch, an Austro-Hungarian immigrant born in the 1880s. For Rausch, film production was not an entirely new business. In the years preceding World War I, he had worked in London and developed the Selsior dancing films—a system for presenting dance films in sync with a live orchestra.[15] The technique consisted of integrating an image of the conductor who would give directions for the live musicians. This procedure guaranteed synchronization between the dance and the music.

With the Tanz-Kinema, Rausch extended this concept to the film spectator. What he had in mind was to screen dance films in a setting where people could watch them *and* dance at the same time. After initial difficulties, he found suitable premises in a former café on the first floor of a shopping arcade in the animated nightlife district of the Alexanderplatz. The café neighbored a restaurant, cinema, billiard hall, and variety theater. Walter Benjamin would probably have enjoyed this location, highly symptomatic of the modern, mobile subject who fluently navigated between different spaces and attractions—a concept that was not unlike the "dancing spectator" that Rausch had in mind.

Before Rausch got the official license to organize "cinematographical dance instructions," he had to complete extensive renovations.[16] The building plans give an impression of how the spatial setting of the café was transformed into a cinematic ballroom. A projection room was installed in a former wine bar; the projection light would cross the room, slightly diagonally, and appear on a screen on the opposite wall. The dance floor—on some plans also called the "auditorium"—was directly in front of the screen, surrounded by tables and chairs where the clients could rest, have drinks and refreshments between dances, watch the dancing couples, or join them if they wished to. A stage provided enough space for a band, which would accompany the dances and the film projections. Altogether, the room could accommodate 250 people—a capacity that was never even close to being exploited. The café was illuminated by large windows; Rausch used (or planned to use) a daylight projector to screen the films.[17] On a practical level, this lighting arrangement would allow the spectators to dance and move within the space without too much risk of getting hurt; on a more symbolic level, the fact that the room was "brightly lit" was also a promise of social control—one that should underline the respectability of the project and distinguish it from the darkness of a cinema. Altogether, the layout shows how Tanz-Kinema merged the spatial setting of the ballroom with that of the cinema. Unlike the latter, the spectators were not assigned a fixed place; the whole setup would facilitate a free circulation of dancers and spectators (and probably waiters) within the space, encouraging fluent transitions between the activities of watching and dancing, and allowing the spectators to position themselves toward the screen.

282 | *Corporeality in Early Cinema*

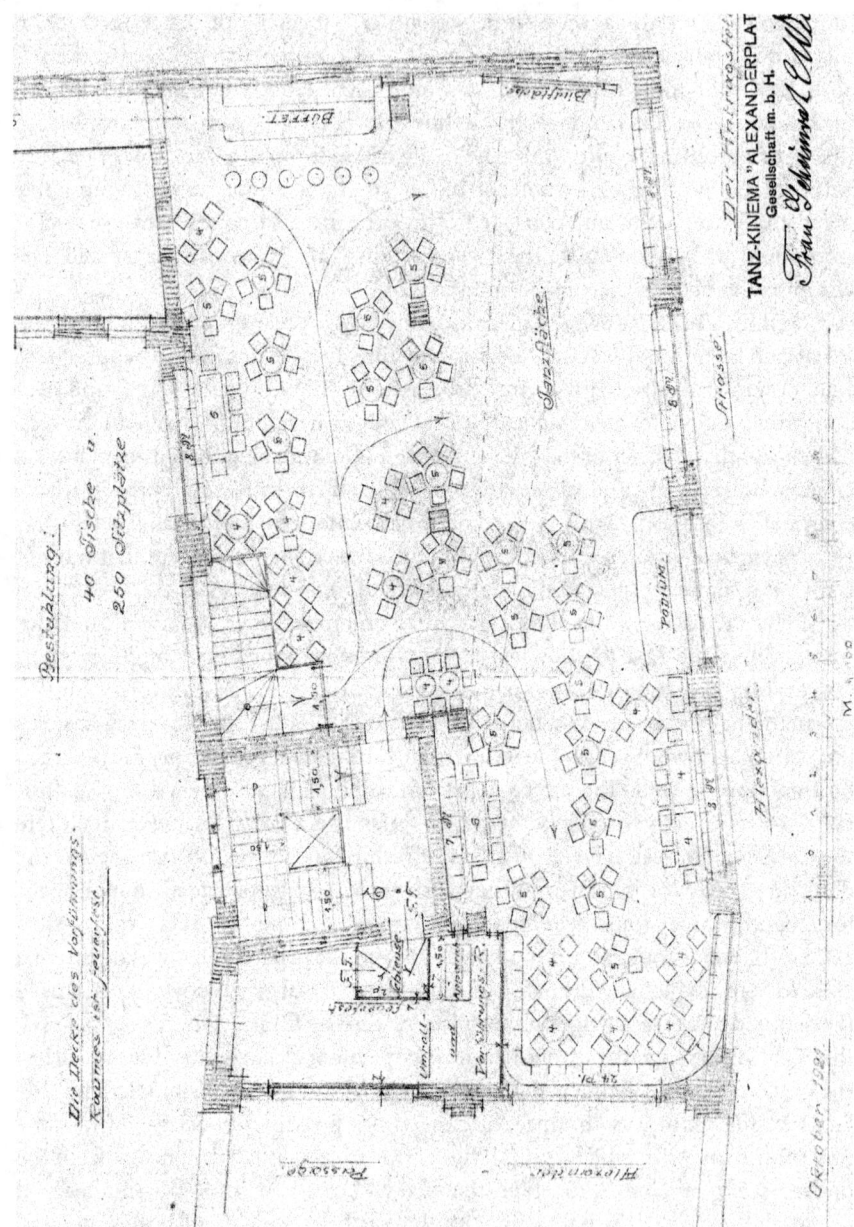

Figure 24.4. Building plans for the Tanz-Kinema Alexanderplatz, 1921. Landesarchiv Berlin, A Pr. Br. Rep. 030-05, Nr. 1275, Pl. 99.

If the building plans give us one perspective of how screen-spectator relations were organized, we might then ask what exactly happened here during the dance events. What do we know about the interactions between the screen and the bodies? In September 1921, the Tanz-Kinema was officially inaugurated. Numerous posters were hung up in the surroundings of the Alexanderplatz to attract customers; a huge one fixed on the façade of the arcade promoted the Tanz-Kinema with the slogan "Film as dancing teacher." The same slogan was used in an advertisement published in the daily evening paper with the claim "Anybody can dance after this film."[18] This sentence is highly characteristic of the whole enterprise of the Tanz-Kinema; the promising and inclusive "*anybody* can dance" firmly points to the participatory design that characterized the project— although ambiguously—on all levels.

Thanks to numerous police reports, which were delivered with monthly frequency, we have detailed information about the place, its clientele, and the events. One of these reports states, "The Tanz-Kinema is located in a large and light room on the first floor, furnished as a café. A band composed of 5 men plays dance music, so that the guests have the opportunity to dance on a huge dance floor occupying a space of approximately 25 to 30 square meters."[19] Several reports allude to the mostly "well-to-do, or upper-class customers."[20] Visitors received a "certificate of participation"—a necessary measure to legitimate the *educational* purpose of the events (and to distinguish it from mere "dance amusements"). And yet the status of the events in the Tanz-Kinema remained vague—only a thin line separated dance instruction and amusement. This hybrid status also applied to the film screenings: "Approximately every hour, a dance instruction film is screened, demonstrating the foot positions and postures of the dances. Each film runs for about five minutes." The reports mention two film titles, *Wladimira Foxtrott* and *Boston*, both produced in 1921 by the Tanz-Kinema. Censorship cards and police reports make it clear that these films employed strategies similar to the dance instruction films mentioned earlier. By means of editing and close-ups, the dance was divided into segments, then shown as a whole.

The Tanz-Kinema's films also integrated "step diagrams"—a visual strategy meant to accentuate the film's didactic and instructional nature. Intertitles explained the steps and stimulated the spectators' activity by addressing them with rather prosaic instructions such as, "Gentleman: Embrace the lady delicately with your right arm"; "Lady: Put your left hand on the gentleman's shoulder. Lady and Gentleman: Keep the upper body smooth and loosely clung to each other, otherwise supple movements will be impossible." Most significantly, both films ended with an invitation to the audience: "Ladies and Gentlemen! May I ask you to join the dance?"[21] With these forms of direct address, the Tanz-Kinema films borrow from early attractions cinema; not unlike the film lecturer of previous decades, the intertitles addressed the audience. If the films' temporality was closely tied to what Tom Gunning has conceptualized as early cinema's "nowness," the spatial and performative strategies of the Tanz-Kinema would have reinforced this "liveness."[22] After the film projections, a report states, "a dancing master would demonstrate the presented dances with his partner, requesting the audience to immediately follow on these steps."[23]

There is some evidence that the dancing couples who gave the live demonstration after the film projection were the same as those who appeared on screen. Some programs show that the famous exhibition dancers Janos and Olivia, who presented the dance instruction in the films, performed regularly in the Tanz-Kinema. These live performances, in conjunction with the presentation of the dance instruction, would thus create a smooth transition between the film projections and the dancing exercises for the audience.

In a similar way, the live music accompaniment would strengthen the relationship between screen and audience. Each film had a special musical score. An article from the journal *Der Artist* stressed the importance of the live music in this setting. According to this observer, the music was crucial for "establishing the necessary contact between the dancers and the films."[24] These remarks form an interesting starting point to contextualize the Tanz-Kinema within a history of early sound synchronizations. In the case of the Tanz-Kinema, however, synchronization not only referred to the coupling of image and sound but also included the spectator and his or her body.

Even though the Tanz-Kinema would allow the spectators to move more freely than in a conventional cinema, its participatory character remained highly ambiguous: while the films and the ballroom setting encouraged the spectators to dance, they provided a stimulus-response model that would "prescribe" or "control" the spectators' movements on the dance floor. However, spectator-dancers would not necessarily follow the filmic instructions on screen. One police officer noted indeed that dances were performed "too competently, too comfortably, and too briskly." Apparently, hardly anyone would come to the Tanz-Kinema to actually "learn" to dance.

Soon after the inauguration, the hybrid status of the Tanz-Kinema as education *and* amusement became a major problem for the whole enterprise—particularly when Rausch started organizing other events that he did not have the necessary license for: performances by vocal artists and ballet dancers, as well as screenings of "other" regular films. One of these events is especially interesting in characterizing the Tanz-Kinema as a place where the audience was activated and playfully involved in the performances. In April 1922, an ad announced a "Da-pu-fi"—a humoristic abbreviation for "Das Publikum filmt!" (The audience shoots a movie!). At this comedic event, the audience could participate in the live staging of a film production that would be shot "in the middle of the auditorium" and "with the collaboration of the audience. . . . Anybody can participate!"[25]

These and other activities clearly exceeded the Tanz-Kinema's license, which caused increasing troubles with the police. This, together with the seemingly low attendance figures, led to it closing only eight months after its inauguration.

Media Archaeologies of the Dance Instruction Film

The Tanz-Kinema in Berlin was not a long-lasting success story, and it did not revolutionize Berlin's nightlife and amusement culture. Yet it provides a compelling example that allows us to address a number of questions on spectatorship and embodiment. The Tanz-Kinema's "dancing spectator" constitutes a highly ambivalent figure within the broader negotiations of film spectatorship in the 1910s. If, on the one hand, these practices negotiate the possibilities of a mobilized and physically involved spectatorship, on the other they display cinema's potential to exert discipline on the spectator—to synchronize bodies and modern technologies. In this sense, the integration of film projections into the ballroom served a double purpose: it supplied the dance hall with a "modern" attraction, while at the same time transforming it into a site of "education" where people would learn to control their bodies.

This ambivalence not only reflects the tensions and debates of the 1910s but also anticipates a number of later screen practices that would recur on a mass scale, one century later, under the conditions of digital culture: Today, dance instruction videos on YouTube and interactive video games such as Nintendo Wii's "Just Dance" synchronize the spectators' bodies to the dance moves on-screen—in a similar but even more meticulous way as the Tanz-Kinema Alexanderplatz. With Nintendo's Wii, the motion-capturing technology allows the players to continuously supervise their movements and adapt them to the screen—so that, as Nintendo promises, "anyone can dance regardless of talent."[26] Although early-twentieth-century dance instruction films and their *dispositifs* did not integrate *technologies* of live feedback yet, they foregrounded similar forms of a participatory spectatorship based on interaction and bodily response.

On the other side, we can also use the example of the dance instruction films—as peculiar and remote as they may seem—to *broaden* our understanding of early-twentieth-century film culture. As a matter of fact, the genre flourished in the 1920s, revitalized by the emergence of new dances like the foxtrot or the Charleston. Some of these later films propelled experiments with filmic techniques. Close-ups demonstrated the do's and don'ts (for example, how to place the hands); slow motion was added so that the footwork could be literally "studied." Some films experimented with extreme camera angles that showed footwork from below, through a glass plate as in *The New Waltz Made Easy* (British Pathé, 1927), or with a moving camera from the dancer's perspective, as in *The New Fox Trot Made Easy* (British Pathé, 1927). Experiments like these were not too far off from Abel Gance's "unleashed cameras" or the avant-garde's physiological aesthetics, which similarly shaped forms of spectatorship based on sensation and bodily reactions.[27]

These questions were even more prominently negotiated in the short film *1000 Schritte Charleston* (*A Thousand Steps of Charleston*, Deutsche Vereins-Film AG, 1926), screened in German cinemas in 1926. The film presented a dance instruction that was shot entirely in close-ups of feet; the intertitles encouraged the spectators to try the steps: "You cannot dance the Charleston? That's a shame! For the first hour, all you need is a comfortable chair and good spirits!"[28]

While the Tanz-Kinema reinvented cinema from inside the ballroom, *A Thousand Steps of Charleston* adapted the Charleston for the movie theater, thus explicitly taking into account the cinema audience, seated in the limited space of a dimmed auditorium. With the hybrid image of a film audience, seated yet dancing, this film is highly symbolic of the heterogeneous concepts of spectatorship that coexisted at that time—as if to remind us that, in cinema, watching and participating, resting and moving, are *not* mutually exclusive.

Practices like these challenge our historical understanding of the spectator as seated and immobile; they force us to think outside dichotomies like *active* and *passive* and to reconsider the all-too-linear historiography from early cinema's *embodied* spectator to classical cinema's *disembodied* one. In this sense, we should perhaps no longer describe the transitional period of the 1910s as the moment in which cinema spectators "*lost* their bodies," but rather as a phase in which various practices and spaces allowed them to reassert, renegotiate, and playfully experiment with forms of embodied spectatorship.

KRISTINA KÖHLER is Assistant Professor at the Institute for Film, Drama, and Empirical Cultural Studies at the Johannes Gutenberg University Mainz. She is author of *Der tänzerische Film: Frühe Filmkultur und moderner Tanz* (Marburg, Germany: Schüren, 2017).

Notes

1. This narrative underlies many early and traditional cinema historiographies; see, for example, Oskar Kalbus, *Vom Werden deutscher Bildkunst* (Altona-Bahrenfeld, Germany: Cigaretten-Bilderdienst, 1935): 12–13. More importantly perhaps, the rhetoric of a discipline (exerted on the spectator) is also highly characteristic of the cinema discourses in the 1910s and was articulated (more or less explicitly) by various groups: Cinema reformers and academics publicly debated how to "educate" the audience; cinema owners sought to upvalue their sites as "sanitarily" and morally controlled spaces. During the same period, film censorship was institutionalized in most Western film cultures—and with it the debates on cinema's effects on the spectators.

2. On concepts of the excitable and nervous spectator around 1900, see Rae Beth Gordon, *Why the French Love Jerry Lewis: From Cabaret to Early Cinema* (Stanford, CA: Stanford University Press, 2001); Mireille Berton, *Le corps nerveux des spectateurs. Cinéma et sciences du psychisme autour de 1900* (Lausanne: L'Âge d'Homme, 2015).

3. Tom Gunning, "The Cinema of Attractions: Early Film, Its Spectator and the Avant-Garde, " in *Early Cinema: Space, Frame, Narrative*, ed. Thomas Elsaesser (London: British Film Institute, 1991), 56–62; Miriam Hansen, *Babel and Babylon: Spectatorship in American Silent Film* (Cambridge, MA: Harvard University Press, 1994); Scott Curtis: *The Shape of Spectatorship: Art, Science and Early Cinema in Germany* (New York: Columbia University Press, 2015).

4. See, for example, Arthur Mellini, "The Education of Moviegoers into a Theater Public" [1910], reprinted in *The Promise of Cinema: German Film Theory 1907–1933*, ed. Anton Kaes, Nicholas W. Baer, and Michael Cowan (Oakland: University of California Press, 2016), 151–53.

5. With the term "dispositif," I refer to the French traditions of the apparatus theory and their emphasis on the ideological and spatial configurations of the (conventional) cinema setting. For a more detailed discussion of the concept and its theoretical frameworks, see Frank Kessler, "Notes on *dispositif*," paper presented at the Utrecht Media Research Seminar in June 2004, http://www.hum.uu.nl/medewerkers/f.e.kessler/Dispositif%20 Notes11-2007.pdf.

6. For a more comprehensive account of the history of dance instruction films in the early 1910s, see Kristina Köhler, "Tango Mad and Affected by Cinematographitis. Rhythmic 'Contagions' between Screens and Audiences in the 1910s," in *Performing New Media, 1890–1915*, ed. Kaveh Askari et al. (New Barnet, UK: John Libbey, 2014): 203–13.

7. Julie Malnig, *Dancing till Dawn: A Century of Exhibition Ballroom Dance* (New York: NYU Press, 1992).

8. From an advertisement for *Motion Picture Dancing Lessons* in *Moving Picture World* 18, no. 3 (October 18, 1913): 331.

9. Marcel Mauss, "Techniques of the Body," *Economy and Society* 2, no. 1 (1973): 70–88.

10. "News Items of the Kalem Company," *Evening News*, November 1913, 7.

11. Advertisement for *Motion Picture Dancing Lessons* in *Lichtbildbühne* 2 (January 1914): 2–3 [my translation].

12. As Jenny Hammerton has highlighted in her study on British Pathé newsreels, the distribution of leaflets with "Ballroom Hints" was a common feature for dance instruction films throughout the 1920s; see Jenny Hammerton, *For Ladies Only? Eve's Film Review. Pathé Cinemagazine, 1921–33* (Hastings, UK: Projection Box 2001): 117–18.

13. Ad for the Pathéscope in *Talking Machine World* 10, no. 8 (August 15, 1914): 23.

14. From the company documents at the commercial register, in *Generalakten betreffend Tanz-Kinema "Mozartsaal" Gesellschaft mit beschränkter Haftung*, Amtsgericht Berlin Mitte Abt. 122, Landesarchiv Berlin, A Rep. 342-02, Nr. 5859, 1920–1928 [my translation].

15. Stephen Bottomore, "Selsior Dancing Films, 1912–1917," in *The Sounds of the Silents in Britain*, ed. Julie Brown and Annette Davidson (Oxford, UK: Oxford University Press, 2013): 163–82.

16. See *Akten des Polizei-Präsidiums zu Berlin, Versammlungsräume, No. 704, betreffend Alexanderstrasse 39/40 (1916–1930)*, Landesarchiv Berlin, A Pr. Br. Rep. 030-05, Nr. 1275 Th [my translation].

17. An ad announces that the Tanz-Kinema was to present the dance instruction films "in the illuminated hall" ("im erleuchteten Saal"); see ad for the Tanz-Kinema, in *8-Uhr-Abendblatt Berlin*, September and October 1921 [my translation].

18. Advertising for the Tanz-Kinema, in *8-Uhr-Abendblatt Berlin*, September and October 1921 [my translation].

19. For this and the following quotes, see *Akten des Polizei-Präsidiums zu Berlin, Versammlungsräume, No. 704, betreffend Alexanderstrasse 39/40 (1916-1930)*, Landesarchiv Berlin, A Pr. Br. Rep. 030-05, Nr. 1275 Th [my translation].

20. This was explained by the fact that the bar served rather exclusive drinks (such as wine and liqueur), and that clients had to pay an elevated entrance fee of 5 Marks.

21. As indicated on the censorship cards, which are held at the Bundesarchiv-Filmarchiv Berlin (dated 1/09/1921, No. B.04297 and B.04296) [my translation].

22. Tom Gunning, "'Now You See It, Now You Don't': The Temporality of the Cinema of Attractions," in *Silent Film*, ed. Richard Abel (New Brunswick, NJ: Rutgers University Press, 1996): 71–84.

23. *Akten des Polizei-Präsidiums zu Berlin, Versammlungsräume, No. 704, betreffend Alexanderstrasse 39/40 (1916–1930)*, Landesarchiv Berlin, A Pr. Br. Rep. 030-05, Nr. 1275 Th [my translation].

24. "Eine gute Kapelle vermittelt den Tanzenden und jenen, die sich der Tanzkunst lernend hingeben, den zwischen ihnen und dem Filmbild nötigen Kontakt." Anonymous, "Kinomusik. Kinomusikalische Streifzüge [Tanzkino]," in *Der Artist. Central-Organ der Circus, Varieté-Bühnen, reisenden Kapellen und Ensembles* 39, no. 1909 (1921): n. p. [my translation].

25. Tanz-Kinema, *Das Extrablatt*, program flyer preserved within *Akten des Polizei-Präsidiums zu Berlin, Versammlungsräume, No. 704, betreffend Alexanderstrasse 39/40 (1916–1930)*, Landesarchiv Berlin, A Pr. Br. Rep. 030-05, Nr. 1275 Th [my translation].

26. Kiri Miller, *Playable Bodies: Dance Games and Intimate Media* (Oxford, UK: Oxford University Press, 2017): 200.

27. Dance, as a model for new forms of sensory-bodily experience, recurred more widely as a prominent trope throughout early-twentieth-century film culture; see also Kristina Köhler, *Der tänzerische Film. Frühe Filmkultur und moderner Tanz* (Marburg, Germany: Schüren, 2017).

28. From the censorship cards held at the Bundesarchiv-Filmarchiv (No. 14379-14382, Microfiche B 492) [my translation].

25 A Rational and Entertaining Species of Amusement to Bipeds of All Ages
The Splendid Camera Obscura

Alison Reiko Loader

IMAGINE YOURSELF IN a room so dark that you see nothing but a single beam of external light. Your pupils dilate, your eyes adjust, and there you are spying, sharing (perhaps even touching) a virtual, vivid, and full-color moving picture of outside activity, as it happens. Photography has not been invented, so there is no CCTV, no web camera or any kind of filmic, electronic, or digital device—only a mirror and a lens that project sunlight into darkness, and cast onto the tabular surface at your fingertips a live and living image of the exterior world. The traffic and unwitting denizens of the town below go about their affairs unaware that they appear on the screen before you, like miniature figures on an animated map. You are huddled around this luminous view when, using the controls that hang from the ceiling, your guide spins it into a new picture that is upside down and facing the opposite way. As she takes you on a virtual tour of the outside surroundings and you double your gaze to accommodate the swivels of an image askew, you wonder: What is this thing? How does it work? Who built it? When and why?

You are inside a nineteenth-century *splendid camera obscura*, a term I adopt after old advertisements to distinguish the configuration from earlier and related devices designed for mobile and personal use.[1] Long after its wondrous applications by natural magicians and before its photographic chemical inscription, early-nineteenth-century instrument makers transformed the long-observed optical principle into room-size architectural apparatuses for sightseeing. Improvements to lens grinding enabled larger and brighter projections, and periscopic arrangements mobilized mechanical eyes to scan all around and shift their outlooks from near to far. For over a century, numerous splendid cameras obscura operated at seaside resorts, pleasure grounds, and popular observatories, only to be lost and largely forgotten. Consequently, media histories generally overlook these overlooking devices.

Figure 25.1. "The Camera Obscura at Central Park." *Frank Leslie's Popular Monthly*, 1877.

Existing accounts of the camera obscura tend to ignore its application as a nineteenth-century spectacle, despite its overtly panoptic and voyeuristic qualities, and the historiographic attention paid to related contrivances. The device may be another "cinema machine" that anticipated cinema's "formal invention," and enduring past its early years, also a form of astonishment that paralleled the cinema of attractions.[2] Histories of optical media, however, generally abstract and conflate the many sizes and configurations of the camera obscura into a singular notion that they tend to treat in one of two ways. One discusses the camera obscura almost exclusively as a technological forerunner or aid in histories of other media (such as painting and photography) that position their development in a continuous march toward realistic representation. The other, chronicling its discursive history, explores the camera obscura as a model of ideology, ontology, knowledge, and sight. Jonathan Crary disrupts the teleology of the former approach through an application of the latter. In *Techniques of the Observer*, he argues that a rupture occurred in the 1820s and 1830s when a newly dominant focus on the body replaced an earlier paradigm of decorporealized vision that had positioned the camera obscura as the governing model for sight.

With the revelation of corporeal interactions between bodies, screens, and controls inside the splendid camera obscura, I wonder: How does that problematize or reinforce Crary's notion of a shift that abandoned the interiorized and individuated observer, whose "physical and sensory experience is supplanted by the relation between a mechanical apparatus and a pregiven world of objective truth"[3]? In exploring the tactile and sensual qualities of an apparatus long associated with disembodiment, I suggest that the camera obscura itself transformed with the posited rupture that replaced its oversimplified, discursive model. Contrary to the imagined object equated with seventeenth- and eighteenth-century understandings of bodiless vision, the camera obscura in its splendid, tangible, and re-created format participated in nineteenth-century discourses of the body, differentially and corporeally constructing and engaging its subjects captured on, captivated by, and controlling its screen.

Splendid cameras obscura, which include extant and recent installations, are attractions best experienced firsthand. Some have self-operated or static devices, but the Edinburgh Camera Obscura and a nearby installation in Dumfries have guides that further animate their live, and therefore already animated, pictures by framing and reframing their projections through narrative and technical manipulations. Drawing attention to various features, recounting local histories and anecdotes, and explaining the apparatuses themselves, the mechanics of the cameras obscura are made as central to their experience as the sights they show. The Dumfries museum boasts an extant device that retains its original 1835 parts, and to adjust its focus, operators gently lift and lower its counterweighted screen. Tight quarters require that its table be smaller than its projection, but what otherwise might seem a restriction becomes an asset when viewers use white paddles to *catch* the parts of the image that extend beyond the screen. In Edinburgh, guides offer paper to viewers at the end of their presentations to *lift* bits of the projection—often images of unwitting pedestrians—that sometimes they encourage to handle gently, and at other times, they incite to shake and slap violently down. Touching the screen was a violation resulting in disaster for *Uncle Josh at the Moving Picture Show* (Edison, 1902), yet visitors at the splendid camera obscura are encouraged to contravene the prohibition that was implicitly in place by the early-cinema era. Instead of laughing at the ignorance of the unsophisticated spectator confounded by the technology of projection, laughter comes from being the rube and disrupting illusion for tactile pleasure.[4]

A version of the Edinburgh interaction dates to the 1947 replacement of its nineteenth-century device, which entailed lowering its table to a more secure floor to accommodate the swell of postwar tourism. The new optics, having a longer focal distance and range, eased operation and kept its projection in focus well above the screen.[5] A newspaper reviewing the renovation explained, "The commentator in charge was a pleasantly discursive young man, who did something that the previous operators had omitted. Pointing to a motor car on the screen he would catch its image on his wrist and lift it up the Royal Mile. This pleasing sleight of hand sent our associate into raptures, and bitter was her disappointment when, on descending the firm earth, she found that she could not scoop a Corporation motor bus up—not even with both hands."⁶ The writer highlighted other embodied aspects of their visit, including the arduous five-story climb up the tower stairs and how two of them boosted their little rube-like companion as they "moved slowly round the screen."⁷ Recalling earlier exhibitions, they commented that the view was "as stirring as ever" and that "the same old washing flutters on the same old line and was pointed out with even more than the same old candour."⁸ In short, they reported a dynamic, intimate, and physically engaging performance that remained in the midtwentieth century, despite its long history, "one of the most fascinating screen shows in town."⁹

Founded as the second location of Short's Observatory, the origins of the Edinburgh Camera Obscura date to 1834, when Maria Theresa Short obtained permission from municipal officials to build her first popular observatory on Calton Hill.¹⁰ As her promotional materials suggest, alongside the splendid device with its then unquestionably touchable early touchscreen, Maria's visitors could see and interact with telescopes, microscopes, and the various other optical and scientific instruments on display.¹¹ This tactile accessibility and appeal to hands-on learning might identify her exhibitions with early museums that, before later no-touch policies, saw curators acting more like "gracious hosts" displaying private cabinets, and their visitors handling proffered objects with the reverence of "polite guests."¹²

However, with Short's Observatory presenting the wonders of science to *anyone* for a single shilling, Scotland's solicitor general, Lord Cockburn, assumed its attraction to the impolite and even the unruly. Perhaps he dreaded the "gapers and gawkers," who, going to "see a show," spurned educational uplift and museum-appropriate behavior, because he targeted mostly its camera obscura and the subsequent spectacles he thought it would herald.¹³ A year before the opening of Short's Observatory and a full two years before the installation of its splendid device, the future judge protested: "I need not explain to any person of intelligence, the effect of this profanation of that sacred ground. The proposed structure in itself will be abominable. It is intended for a Camera Obscura, and for other such exhibitions. . . . A building of this sort, once sanctioned on the Calton Hill, will be speedily followed by the erection of Panoramas, Dioramas, the migratory mansions of Travelling Giants, Wonderful Dwarfs, wild beasts, etc, etc."¹⁴

Was Cockburn right in doubting Short's pedagogical appeals? In his 1981 study, John Hammond attributes the nineteenth-century peak in camera obscura popularity as due, at least in part, to the application of its room-size version as an "entertaining diversion."¹⁵ As they grew in popularity, the most common locations for splendid cameras obscura shifted from displays of scientific optical instruments and popular observatories, as in Edinburgh and Dumfries, to holiday spots near the sea. Brighton, the Isle of Man, Margate, Portobello,

Figure 25.2. "At the Beach," *Puck*, August 30, 1890.

and Swansea are among the numerous resorts in the United Kingdom alone that hosted seaside cameras, situations that Lord Cockburn would have doubly abhorred. Unable to endure "maritime indecency," Cockburn had dubbed Portobello, the seaside suburb of Edinburgh, "Porto Nudo," calling it "the most immodest place in Scotland."¹⁶ He had long passed away when Portobello Pier opened its camera obscura in 1878, which was "said to be the largest and finest in the kingdom."¹⁷ Nevertheless, let us imagine Lord Cockburn as an indignant spectator at the splendid camera obscura in the illustration "At the Beach" that appeared in an issue of *Puck* magazine in 1890. Though no bathers can be seen, the lurid allure of the seaside attraction is evident in the capture of a private indiscretion. Spectators look on as a man prepares to embrace his companion. Unaware of their appearance on the screen of a nearby camera obscura, he exclaims, "Ah Alicia, at last we are by ourselves, away from unsympathetic and prying eyes!"

There is no mistaking the voyeuristic qualities of a splendid camera obscura: the elevated eye, its panoramic view, and its unseen watchers. Although they often overlooked picturesque sites and emerged in the Romantic era, contemporary descriptions link the apparatus to surveillance, not aesthetics—neither beauty nor the sublime ever merit mention. Seemingly more interested in monitoring bodies and behavior than viewing landscape or weather, some even imagined them as crime-stopping instruments. After the 1824 Glaswegian Fair Week, the *Glasgow Mechanic Magazine* advocated the placement of cameras obscura in "all public places of amusement and exhibition," impressed that a pickpocket was arrested after being caught by a device's screen. Years later, describing a visit to Short's Observatory on Castlehill, memorialist George Scott-Montcrieff recalled his childhood fantasy of seeing "some horrible crime enacted on a roof-top, the perpetrator presuming himself safe from all eyes, but forgetting the Camera Obscura!"[18] And while talk of using the devices to police criminality was rare, the policing of sexuality became an increasingly common trope.[19] Conflating two threats to Victorian morality and extending vision to action, the author of an 1898 newspaper article titled "That Camera Obscura" recounts being inside watching like "an invisible ghost" as a "bold-faced thing, with pink bonnet ribbons" flirted with her fiancé, and then later, after seeing that other woman lift his wallet, rushing outside to alert the police.[20]

Alongside anecdotes that seem more fiction than fact, illustrations of splendid cameras obscura depict fantasies of spectatorship and sexuality that privilege physical interaction between bodies both outside *and* in. Whereas Crary's discursive camera obscura of the previous prerupture era constructed an isolated observer cut off from the exterior world, depictions of its splendid version show groups of viewers in close quarters together peering intently at the screen. Some watch projections of fellow sightseers engaged in outdoor activities that seem relatively benign, but others witness scenes of courtship or coercion. Reactions of insiders range from dismay to curiosity to titillation. While such images might serve as disciplinary warnings to would-be paramours, potential predators, and their targets, they also suggest the pleasure of catching moments of privacy between unwitting pairs. In depictions of the interior of a splendid device, Freud's primal scene (the unseen observation of parental coition) and its arousal are enacted and doubled when an intercourse of spectator bodies is also put on display. Though they should be invisible ghosts shrouded in the dark, we watch *them*, as they perform intimate and tactile engagements with each other and with the screen. As if attempting to enter a scene of seduction, voyeurs lean forward, sometimes touching the image before them. Young women appear provocatively vulnerable—outside in the clutches of aggressive lovers, or inside bent over the screen, bustles prominent but forgotten in their owners' enchantment.

Some imagined the erotic potential of the splendid camera obscura early in its history. In a fictitious letter written in 1802, the protagonist of humorist Josef Richter mused, "Since they haven't quite finished painting Vienna yet at the Panorama hut, they're going to show a camera obscura. (That way they'll have a little money coming in at least.) A few days ago I heard one of our young men-about-town ask a friend, 'What on earth is that?' And when he learned it means 'dark room,' the young gent leered and said, 'Well, if they've got pretty girls in their dark room, I suppose I'll go too.'"[21]

If a splendid camera obscura does not guarantee the bodies of fellow onlookers to touch or even ones outside to ogle, it might tempt its visitors with other bodies to desire. Unlike the arrangement of modern cinemas, viewers stand at the edge of the screen, with the picture, controls, and its operator well within reach. Self-operated devices, such as the Clifton Observatory in Bristol, oblige viewers to make their own virtual tour. Hanging from a ceiling track above the screen, the handle that rotates the camera must be passed from one viewer to another or moved by someone circumnavigating the table—its wooden frame and unplastered surface being precautions against wear from the contact and caresses of unsupervised visitors. In the time I spent haunting the Bristol device, I observed more interaction than at Edinburgh or at Dumfries. Perhaps emboldened by the absence of staff, visitors openly conversed, took pictures of themselves and the screen, pointed to sites of interest, and walked around, taking turns at the controls and sometimes manipulating them to follow the people outside and below. Perhaps they thought, like me, how much it was like an interactive installation, a surveillance drone, a digital touchscreen.

Yet guides at other sites do more than guard and operate the device. Not only might they actively encourage certain types of engagement, they themselves perform. In playing a key role in the exhibition—determining what is seen and said—isn't a spectacular guide another part of a spectacle's allure? Consider the 1823 notice for the Holroyd camera obscura displayed on Edinburgh's Mound, which advertised a "rational and entertaining species of amusement to bipeds of all ages," and alongside it, the owners "Honest Ben and his *Vrow* [wife], Dolly." The enticement concludes, "It may be regarded as a moot point, whether the instruments or the *proprietors* be most curious or most attractive."[22] Three decades later, the camera at Nelson's Monument in Edinburgh may have also engaged the physical assets of its operator. In a local newspaper item from 1856, the "Calton Hill Victim!!!" complained of being accosted while walking on the hill, taken to the monument, and forced to pay admission. Using the camera obscura *secretly* installed there seven years before, its "young leddy" commented on women drying clothes, a strolling couple ("twa lubers a-walking") and finished "by displaying her own precious limbs and her dog Toby on a particular stone."[23]

The Nelson Monument exhibition was the last of the *three* splendid cameras obscura that opened and closed in overlapping succession on Edinburgh's Calton Hill. Agnes MacArthur was keeper of the first, installed around 1815 in the Old Observatory House, a place first occupied by the family of Maria Short. Agnes worked for the Astronomical Institution, the private association that founded what would become the Royal Observatory of Edinburgh, and until the removal of the device in 1839, she exhibited the splendid camera obscura for the exclusive pleasure of members and their guests.[24] Maria Short introduced her camera obscura in 1836 as the proprietor of a popular observatory that, to the dismay of Lord Cockburn and the Astronomical Institution, addressed an audience "no longer confined to the wealthy and the learned."[25] And in 1849, the tenant of the Nelson Monument punched a hole through the roof of city property to install a third device.[26] Competitive and unregulated behavior nevertheless resulted in the eviction of Short's Observatory a year later. Its irrepressible founder rebuilt at the present site on Castlehill and installed a splendid camera obscura that could view Calton Hill from the top of its tower.

A place to see, see from, and be seen, Calton Hill enjoys a long history as both a viewing platform and as a stage for Edinburgh.[27] Robert Barker devised his first panorama, "The View of the City of Edinburgh and the Surrounding Country from the Calton Hill," by adapting sketches made from the roof of the Old Observatory House in 1788, when only the Short family occupied the hill.[28] Under the approving eye of gentlemen like Cockburn, subsequent decades saw the summit constructed, concretely and figuratively, as the Acropolis of Edinburgh as Modern Athens—its neoclassical and castellated architecture celebrating Scottish participation in both enlightenment and military conflict. Though it welcomed respectable lady sightseers, and working women continued to bleach their linens on the hill, the building of the scientific Royal Observatory and its numerous monuments to heroic men masculinized the site.

And yet, in nineteenth-century Edinburgh, all three of the splendid cameras obscura on Calton Hill hosted gazes controlled by women: Agnes, Maria, and the nameless young lady with the precious limbs. I wonder: How did those women picture that prospect? Did they, as contemporary discourses and visual culture imagine, make spectacles of themselves and other women—the sightseers and the washerwomen—occupying the hill? Or did they watch other bodies and use their controls to manipulate the pictures on screen in different ways?

That the panorama and the splendid cameras obscura should represent and sometimes occupy the same places is no coincidence. Both attract sightseers in search of lofty views, and both, being forms of virtual travel, shelter their visitors from the discomforts of inclement weather as well as the ability of the view itself to look back. Moreover, each presents its visitor the possibility of two forms of seeing: one denoting mastery, and another provoking confusion. As Denise Oleksijczuk notes, "Three of the Panorama's distinguishing features—its enhanced realism, multiperspectivalism and elevated, central vantage point—had a tendency to produce cognitive uncertainty and disorientation as much as a sense of domination and control."[29]

Hovering above a miniaturized and uncanny tableau, a viewer in the splendid camera obscura occupies a position that is likewise open to a dominant or vertiginous sensation. Should the latter invoke what Alison Griffiths refers to as "shivers down your spine," touching its screen could offer stability and reassurance.[30]

Its solid surface might steady any dizziness that the projection it catches induces. A dramatic downward tilt of its periscopic camera and the sky appears to open beneath you, and instead of an expected lateral motion, a pan across the horizon translates to a swirl. By creating reeling moments that disorder vision through the madness or ecstasy of a moving picture that spins and swings, the operator of the splendid camera obscura—be she an Agnes, a Maria, or an anonymous young lady—could subvert the scene and engender another form of bodily disruption.[31]

Attention to bodies and physical interactions inside splendid cameras obscura and their representations enriches and problematizes existing accounts that ignore the operation of early optical media by women; it associates the device with a "motionless, bodiless, vacant gaze cited by Metz" that scholars of cinema long ago discounted as "oversimplified and ahistorical."[32] While feminist and postmodern scholars describe early and proto-cinematic spectatorship as multiple, mobile, and embodied—doing much to undo apparatus and gaze theories that posit the spectator as a disembodied ideological (and male) subject—little has challenged the association of the observer *inside* the camera obscura with notions of decorporealized and passive vision derived from the limitations of sensorial stimulation and embodied interaction.[33] Yet my examination reveals corporeal engagements and differential bodies pursuing tactile, as well as visual—surveillant and voyeuristic—pleasures. I consider the apparatus a participant in what Linda Williams calls the "frenzy of the visible," the co-constitutive precinema and prehardcore logic of "maximum visibility" that articulated knowledge of bodies with power and pleasure.[34] But I like to imagine that the women I found in charge of splendid cameras obscura resisted such notions of truth or domination. I hope they applied their own imaginations, told their own tales, and manipulated their periscopic eyes into baroque visions—disrupting and destabilizing projections of class, race, sex, and gender that might circulate on and about their touchable screens.

ALISON REIKO LOADER is a part-time faculty member at the Concordia University Faculty of Fine Arts and a lapsed National Film Board of Canada filmmaker. She holds a PhD in Communication Studies and specializes in digital animation, old optical media, and media installation.

Notes

1. For examples, see *The Scotsman*, July 16, 1836; May 19, 1852; and October 8, 1863. Also see C. B. Tait and T. Nisbet, "Catalogue of Valuable Philosophical and Astronomical Instruments belonging to the Royal Observatory, Edinburgh," June 19, 1848, in Papers of George Airy, Cambridge University Library (RGO 159 item 42).

2. See Jean-Louis Comolli, "Machines of the Invisible," in *The Cinematic Apparatus*, ed. Teresa De Lauretis and Stephen Heath (New York: St. Martin's Press, 1980), 121–42; and Wanda Strauven, ed., *The Cinema of Attractions Reloaded* (Amsterdam: Amsterdam University Press, 2006).

3. See Jonathan Crary, *Techniques of the Observer* (Cambridge, MA: MIT Press, 1993), 39.

4. See Wanda Strauven, "Early Cinema's Touch(able) Screens: From Uncle Josh to Ali Barbouyou," *NECSUS European Journal of Media Studies* (Autumn 2012), https://necsus-ejms.org/early-cinemas-touchable-screens-from-uncle-josh-to-ali-barbouyou/

5. A postwar increase in attendance and safety concerns was related to me in an interview conducted at the Dumfries Museum on July 9, 2015, with the architect who oversaw the 1947 renovation, the late Anthony Wolfe, who had his first office in the Edinburgh Camera Obscura building when it was known as Outlook Tower.

6. *The Scotsman*, May 19, 1947, 4.

7. Ibid.

8. Ibid.

9. Ibid.

10. For a concise history of Maria Short, see Veronica Wallace, "Maria Obscura," *Edinburgh Review* 88 (1992): 101–9.

11. Ibid. Printed ephemera for Short's Observatory is also kept in the pamphlet collection at the University of Edinburgh library, at the National Archives of Scotland, and in the Bill Douglas Collection at the University of Exeter. On the "early touchscreen" as a pre-cinematic "screen that can be touched," see Strauven, "Early Cinema's Touch(able) Screens."

12. On touch in the museum, see Constance Classen, *The Deepest Sense: A Cultural History of Touch* (Urbana: University of Illinois Press, 2012), 138–39.

13. On immersion, interaction, hands-on learning, and spectacle at nineteenth-century science museums, see Alison Griffiths, "Back to the (Interactive) Future," in *Shivers down Your Spine* (New York: Columbia University Press, 2008), 159–94.

14. "Calton Hill," *The Scotsman*, June 23, 1834, 3.

15. J. H. Hammond, *The Camera Obscura: A Chronicle* (Bristol, UK: Hilger, 1981).

16. H. A. Cockburn, *Some Letters of Lord Cockburn* (Edinburgh: Grant and Murray, 1932), 66; Lord [Henry] Cockburn, *Circuit Journeys* (Roxburghshire, UK: Byways, 1983), 175–76.

17. "Portobello Pier Opening of the Season," *The Scotsman*, June 11, 1880, 1.

18. George Scott-Montcrieff, *Edinburgh* (London: Batsford, 1947).

19. In the late 1940s, police arrested Kenneth Anger, the future avant-garde filmmaker and author of *Hollywood Babylon*, for having sex at the Santa Monica camera obscura in a sting operation targeting gay men. The device is now housed in a seniors' recreational center. See Bill Landis, *Anger: The Unauthorized Biography of Kenneth Anger* (New York: HarperCollins, 1995). (Thank you to Tom Gunning for making the association.)

20. "That Camera Obscura," *Blackburn Standard*, April 30, 1898, 7.

21. Quoted in Stephan Oetterman, *Panorama: History of a Mass Medium* (New York: Zone, 1997), 288.

22. "Ycleped Royal," *The Scotsman*, July 9, 1823, 4.

23. "Correspondence," *Caledonian Mercury*, October 23, 1856, 3.

24. Information on Agnes MacArthur and the camera obscura appears in the Minute Books of the Astronomical Institution kept at the Royal Observatory of Edinburgh.

25. See Wallace, "Maria Obscura."

26. The town council forgave their tenants (Mr. and Mrs. Ker) for the unauthorized installation of the camera obscura at Nelson Monument. It occupied a ground-floor room

until at least 1863, when papers reported fire damage caused by lightning in the roof above the camera. See *The Scotsman*, July 4, 1849, and February 5, 1863.

27. On the history of Calton Hill and visual culture, see Sara Stevenson, "The Hill View: 'the eye unsatisfied and dim with gazing,'" *History of Photography* 30, no. 3 (September 1, 2006): 213–33.

28. On Robert Barker's Calton Hill panorama, see Denise Oleksijczuk, *The First Panoramas: Visions of British Imperialism* (Minneapolis: University of Minnesota Press, 2011). Note that Maria Short's family lived there until 1788. After the death of Thomas Short, newborn Maria, her mother, and sisters were evicted in favor of a male heir from a previous marriage. See Wallace, "Maria Obscura."

29. Ibid., 11.

30. See Griffiths, *Shivers down Your Spine*.

31. See Martin Jay, "Scopic Regimes of Modernity," in *Vision and Visuality*, ed. Hal Foster (Seattle: Bay Press, 1988), 3–28.

32. Linda Williams, ed., *Viewing Positions: Ways of Seeing Film* (New Brunswick, NJ: Rutgers University Press, 1994), 3.

33. Media historical explorations of embodied spectatorship that inspired this research include Giuliano Bruno, *Atlas of Emotion: Journeys in Art, Architecture and Film* (New York: Verso, 2002), and Anne Friedberg, *Window Shopping: Cinema and the Postmodern* (Berkeley: University of California Press, 1993), in addition to already cited texts by Constance Classen, Alison Griffiths, Wanda Strauven, and Linda Williams,

34. See Linda Williams, *Hard Core: Power, Pleasure, and the "Frenzy of the Visible"* (Berkeley: University of California Press, 1999).

Appendix
Original French Texts

26 Le corps sous le scalpel de la presse illustrée et du cinéma

Jérémy Houillère

DANS LA DEUXIÈME moitié du XIXe siècle, l'homme a cherché à se réapproprier son corps. La pratique des sports et la mode vestimentaire sont des manières très populaires, à cette période, de modifier son apparence physique. Des gravures et des dessins de divers sportifs (lutteurs, jockeys, boxeurs) commencent à circuler abondamment dans la presse populaire. La publicité regorge également de toutes sortes de soins corporels visant tout autant à améliorer son apparence qu'à se soigner contre des maladies improbables (une pilule développera notre poitrine, une lotion fera repousser nos cheveux, un sirop guérira tous nos maux). Dans la sphère privée, l'usage du bain se diversifie ; on l'utilise désormais pour nettoyer et soigner son corps. Ce mouvement hygiéniste, principalement européen, exacerbe l'image d'un corps sain, en bonne santé et jeune[1]. Les progrès scientifiques vont participer de cet élan, notamment dans le domaine de la médecine et de l'anatomie. La santé devient un enjeu de société majeur, en même temps que se développent les connaissances sur le corps humain. La microbiologie, et surtout la découverte des rayons X en 1895, vont radicalement changer notre perception du corps, qui semble ne plus avoir aucun secret à livrer[2]. Pour la première fois, avec les rayons X, l'homme peut contempler de son vivant son propre squelette ; il prend connaissance de son « portrait intérieur ». Toutefois, comme le signale David Le Breton, ce passage ne s'est pas fait sans un bouleversement des mentalités. L'expérience des rayons X ne laisse pas indemne et la confrontation à l'image « satanique » de son propre squelette est particulièrement traumatisante[3]. La revue *Life* caricature le procédé par un crâne ricanant, légendé « Un sourire s'il vous plaît »[4].

À la fois cynique et morbide, cette illustration renvoie à la tradition caricaturale du médecin. Il est courant en effet que des crânes ou plus largement des squelettes humains jonchent les cabinets de médecins dans la presse satirique du XIXe siècle. Plutôt qu'une leçon d'anatomie, la présence de ces carcasses suggère au lecteur que le médecin provoque plus souvent la mort de ses patients qu'il ne parvient à les soigner. Sans cesse raillé par les dessinateurs pour son manque d'empathie envers les malades ou pour l'inefficacité patente des ses interventions, le médecin (ou chirurgien : les deux termes sont utilisés pour désigner le même fléau) est régulièrement comparé à un boucher, un marchand de viande. Malgré les progrès dans de nombreux domaines scientifiques, cette méfiance qui s'est installée dans la culture populaire traduit bien les réticences à confier son corps aux sciences médicales. Le cas de l'anesthésie, en plein développement à partir de la moitié du XIXe siècle, illustre bien cette ambivalence. Si elle permet d'éviter des douleurs atroces au malade, elle est surtout vue comme un moyen machiavélique de le déposséder de la maîtrise de son corps, et de donner au chirurgien, démiurge omnipotent, tout pouvoir sur le corps du patient.

Le cinéma, dont l'invention participe du bouillonnement scientifique de cette fin de siècle, s'est tout de suite emparé de la figure satirique du médecin. De la presse illustrée au premier cinéma, on voit ainsi circuler plusieurs récits qui mettent en scène le médecin et son patient. C'est par exemple le chirurgien qui, après l'opération, se rend compte qu'il a oublié nombre de ses effets personnels dans le corps du patient. Méliès a reproduit le motif en 1902 avec *Une indigestion*. Puis Gaumont s'en est emparé en 1909 dans *Le Chirurgien distrait*. Dans ce film, le patient s'apprête à partir après avoir subi son opération mais le chirurgien se rend compte qu'il a perdu son lorgnon. Il le retrouve ... dans le ventre du malade ! Il rouvre donc son patient, récupère son lorgnon, recoud le ventre et se rend compte qu'il y a également laissé son journal ; puis son cure-dent, son chapeau et son portefeuille ... Dans le journal *Le Rire*, le gag est décliné sous la forme d'un court texte, paru également en 1909 sous le titre « Une opération » : trois chirurgiens opèrent et chacun d'eux égare un objet quelque part dans le corps du patient : une tabatière dans le ventre, une pince dans l'intestin grêle, des lunettes dans le rectum[5].

Le corps du patient est au cœur de ce récit-type. La négligence du médecin conduit à pratiquer sur le malade de multiples incisions, lesquelles dans un autre contexte pourraient s'apparenter à de la torture (nous verrons d'ailleurs plus loin à quel point la figure du médecin est proche de celle du bourreau). Le corps maltraité, malmené, abusé, peut ainsi être envisagé sous l'angle de l'intermédialité. La figure satirisée du médecin, au croisement de la presse illustrée et du premier cinéma, entretient un rapport constant avec le corps, que cet article souhaite interroger. Nous commencerons par nous intéresser au médecin lui-même et aux différentes caricatures qui circulent d'un média à l'autre. Puis nous étudierons plus en détails le corps du malade et particulièrement la manière dont le cinéma s'en est emparé pour en faire un corps à toute épreuve, invulnérable, bien loin du corps souffrant et meurtri des journaux illustrés.

Figures de chirurgiens

À la fin du XIXe siècle, la tradition satirique du médecin est bien installée dans la presse illustrée[6]. Chirurgiens et médecins sont dépeints comme des parangons d'indifférence vis-à-vis de leurs patients. Alors que les gravures du XVIIIe siècle montraient de prestigieux chirurgiens, opérant en manche de dentelles, avec des gestes élégants[7], la mauvaise réputation dont jouissent les médecins au cours du XIXe siècle a largement transformé ce type de représentation[8]. Il est courant, dans les caricatures des journaux pour rire, que le chirurgien, distrait, se trompe dans le membre à amputer. Le patient, allongé et maintenu fixement lorsqu'il n'est pas endormi, n'a pas souvent son mot à dire sur l'opération qui se déroule. Il fait la plupart du temps office de figurant. Dans un dessin paru en 1901 dans le journal *Le Pêle-Mêle*, deux chirurgiens « marchandent » les jambes de leur patient[9]. L'un pense qu'il est nécessaire de couper une jambe, l'autre deux. Finalement, ils se mettent d'accord sur une jambe et demie. Ce compromis se fait bien entendu au détriment de la santé du malade. Ce dernier regarde la scène d'un œil mauvais confiné dans son lit, au second plan de l'image. On ne lui voit que la tête. Son corps est censé être l'enjeu principal de ce débat mais il est quasiment absent de l'image, alors que les médecins, souriants, posent au premier plan. Même le titre du dessin – « Entre chirurgiens » – souligne l'effacement du patient...

Dans la relation entre le médecin et son patient, le dialogue a très peu de place. Et quand dialogue il y a, les répliques sont bien souvent empreintes de cynisme. Dans un autre dessin du *Pêle-Mêle* (figure 3.1), le chirurgien dit à son patient, amputé d'une jambe, que ses chaussettes lui dureront désormais un an au lieu de six mois[10]. Dans le coin supérieur droit de l'image, l'interne étouffe un rire d'une main, avec son couteau dans l'autre. Cette attitude pourrait être mise sur le compte de la légendaire « irrévérence » des carabins – ces apprentis médecins qui avaient la réputation de reproduire ou développer certains comportements de leurs prédécesseurs : « vocabulaire déshumanisé, humour noir, utilisation grotesque ou comique de morceaux cadavériques, projection de débris lors de "batailles de bidoche" »[11]. Il n'est dès lors pas étonnant de voir plusieurs dessins flirter avec une certaine forme de cruauté, que les auteurs dépeignent ironiquement, comme si le chirurgien prenait plaisir à découper son patient. D'ailleurs, les cas sont nombreux dans le dessin de presse où un malade qui ne nécessite pas forcément d'une amputation se voit retirer un membre dans le seul but de satisfaire le zèle de son praticien.

Ces dessins prennent avant tout pour cible une profession dans son ensemble, faisant peu la distinction entre le petit médecin de campagne et le praticien hospitalier. Il arrive cependant, dans les publications les plus « politisées », que des personnalités publiques soient directement visées par les caricaturistes, comme le docteur Doyen. Un numéro spécial de *L'Assiette au beurre*, intitulé « Les Écorcheurs », fait ainsi figurer sur sa couverture un portrait en pied de Doyen, dont le nom est d'ailleurs inscrit sur le pupitre derrière lequel il se tient[12]. Dans *Chanteclair*, il s'apprête à anesthésier une momie putréfiée[13] ; à sa ceinture, plusieurs couteaux et une tenaille ensanglantés font écho au titre de *L'Assiette*. La figure symbolique de la mort, sous les traits d'un squelette ailé, surplombe la scène d'un

Figure 26.1. « Consolation » de chirurgien, dessin paru dans *Le Pêle-Mêle*, 8 juillet 1900, p. 12 (Bibliothèque nationale de France, Gallica).

air horrifié, une faux à la main. Même la mort semble craindre le docteur Doyen, c'est tout dire.

Le cinéma n'est pas en reste de ce type de caricatures. Thierry Lefebvre évoque à ce propos le film de Méliès mentionné plus tôt, *Une indigestion* (1902) ou encore *le Malade hydrophobe* (1900) dans lequel le médecin utilise les mêmes instruments qui ont fait la notoriété de Doyen : une pince emporte-pièce, des mortaiseuses, un maillet et un ciseau à épaulement[14]. Mais le film le plus célèbre – et le plus cité – est très certainement *Opération chirurgicale*, produit par Pathé en 1905. Selon Lefebvre, ce film aurait été réalisé pour se venger de Doyen à la suite d'un procès qu'il a intenté contre Pathé quelques mois auparavant[15]. Dans le film, un chirurgien (interprété par Alphonse Émile Dieudonné) assisté de ses internes opère un patient duquel il extrait toutes sortes d'objets improbables : une pipe, un chapeau, une corde, un éventail, etc. Le chirurgien pratique l'opération avec une légèreté déconcertante. Il fouille le ventre de son patient comme s'il s'agissait d'un coffre à jouet. À côté de lui, les internes sont hilares et s'amusent avec les objets au fur et à mesure qu'ils sont extraits du ventre. Le dernier objet sorti est une montre à gousset, que le patient s'empresse de récupérer. La présence de cette montre, qui constitue le seul objet de valeur prélevé par le chirurgien et que le patient ne veut pas lui laisser, est très certainement une allusion à l'avidité dont sont régulièrement accusés les médecins.

Doyen ne fait donc pas exception. Tout comme ses confrères, il est caractérisé par sa cupidité. Une large majorité des dessins satiriques montrent en effet des médecins très concernés par leurs honoraires, quitte à faire passer la santé du patient après leur argent. Dans certains cas, le dessinateur va même jusqu'à comparer explicitement le chirurgien à un commerçant, voire à un banquier. Dans un dessin du *Pêle-Mêle*, on suggère par exemple de pratiquer les opérations, à titre d'essai, sur des mannequins vivants[16]. Le chirurgien, à la manière d'un couturier, fait la démonstration d'un échantillon de son savoir-faire à un potentiel client – au détriment bien sûr du patient-mannequin qui est, pour le coup, véritablement opéré. Chaque opération a un prix, souvent très élevé. Elle se mérite. On comprend bien dans un autre dessin du *Pêle-Mêle* prophétisant un cabinet de chirurgie des années 1920 que la chirurgie n'est pas accessible à tout le monde[17]. Au rez-de-chaussée, les malades sont imaginés répartis selon leur classe sociale. Pour les moins fortunés (fonctionnaires, militaires et membres du clergé), l'accès aux soins est difficile : ils doivent faire un détour par un autre guichet. Lorsqu'on est ouvrier, on passe tout simplement son chemin . . . Dans la salle de traitement, les opérations se déroulent à la chaîne, selon un modèle appliqué notamment dans l'industrie automobile. Tout est mis en place pour rationaliser le travail et améliorer la cadence de traitement, dans le but bien sûr d'augmenter les profits. Ce système, qui fait primer la performance sur la qualité, assimile le corps à une vulgaire marchandise, un bien de consommation.

Le corps morcelé

Ce mépris affiché pour le corps malade est un motif récurrent de la presse illustrée et va jusqu'à prendre une tournure morbide. À l'instar du dessin sur Doyen, la mort est presque toujours présente, que ce soit de manière explicite et brutale, ou de manière plus diffuse, en filigrane. Dans un dessin du *Pêle-Mêle* (figure 3.2), le chirurgien s'adresse en ces termes au lecteur : « J'avais à peine commencé que

Figure 26.2. Un chirurgien « consciencieux », strip paru dans *Le Pêle-Mêle*, 26 mai 1907, p. 12 (Bibliothèque nationale de France, Gallica).

je m'aperçus que le patient était mort. Je n'en continuai pas moins l'opération avec tout le soin et le zèle qui me sont coutumiers »[18]. Certains dessinateurs semblent même en faire un jeu, comme des clins d'œil adressés au lecteur. Par exemple, dans un dessin pour *Le Rire*, Manfredini place un révolver parmi les instruments du médecin, au second plan de l'image[19].

Il faut croire que cet attrait pour le macabre est spécifique à la presse illustrée car de son côté, le cinéma offre un regard un peu plus optimiste sur le sort des patients. Si le chirurgien est zélé, il parvient néanmoins – dans des circonstances souvent rocambolesques – à soigner ses malades. Le film d'Alice Guy, *Chirurgie fin de siècle* (Gaumont, 1900), décrit de bout en bout le déroulement d'une opération chirurgicale. La première moitié du film est entièrement consacrée au choix des outils par le chirurgien. Il hésite tout d'abord longuement, sur le bord gauche du cadre, pendant que les internes pratiquent l'anesthésie sur le patient. Il commence par sélectionner une scie égoïne, puis se rabat rapidement sur une scie à cadre, celle utilisée habituellement pour les amputations, avant de se saisir d'une large paire de ciseaux. Les outils chirurgicaux font l'objet d'un traitement particulier dans les films et les dessins de cette période. Ils sont la plupart du temps disproportionnés, et parfois même maculés de sang. Ils ne sont pas là pour rassurer le patient, le lecteur ou le spectateur, au contraire. Ils témoignent, par métonymie, de la sauvagerie avec laquelle le chirurgien pratique son opération. Et justement, notre chirurgien se met ensuite à opérer en alternant plusieurs fois entre ses trois instruments avant d'arriver, enfin ! à amputer le bras et la jambe de son patient.

C'est toute la barbarie associée à l'imaginaire de la chirurgie qui se cristallise dans ce début de film. Le chirurgien, caricatural au possible, s'y reprend une dizaine de fois avant de parvenir à amputer le malade. Ce film semble vouloir nous rappeler que la chirurgie était pratiquée originellement par des bourreaux, dans les chambres de torture. Durant les interrogatoires, les bourreaux posaient leur question, puis soignaient la victime en réduisant les luxations et les fractures ou en amputant les membres meurtris[20]. Ce n'est pas un hasard si l'on trouve dans notre corpus certaines représentations qui comparent explicitement le chirurgien au bourreau[21]. L'image du chirurgien serait ainsi restée associée à celle du tortionnaire et ses outils assimilés à des outils de torture.

Dans la deuxième partie du film, le chirurgien quitte la pièce et laisse agir ses internes. Ces derniers ont pour tâche de greffer au patient de nouveaux membres. Ils apportent un lot de « pièces de rechange » qu'ils fixent sur le patient amputé à l'aide de colle animale, couramment utilisée pour recoller les os entre eux. Après un court délai de séchage, le patient se relève et s'agite comme si de rien n'était : il est guéri. Les membres meurtris ont été remplacés par de nouveaux, en bon état.

Au moment où Alice Guy réalise son film, en 1900, la greffe humaine n'est pas encore à l'ordre du jour. Il s'agit toujours d'un fantasme. Les premiers essais de greffes réalisés par des chirurgiens en France ont eu lieu à partir de 1906, et sur des animaux. Il est d'ailleurs très peu question de ce type de reconstitution miraculeuse dans la presse illustrée. Les patients amputés sont nombreux mais semblent voués à le demeurer. L'amputation est irrémédiable et participe de la cruauté dont se rend coupable le médecin. Cependant, sur les scènes de théâtre, de cirque et de music-hall, les pantomimes et spectacles de magie regorgent de corps démembrés et remembrés. Dans son théâtre Robert-Houdin, avant de le faire devant une caméra, Méliès a longtemps découpé des corps pour les reconstituer dans la foulée. Les recherches de Patrick Désile ont bien montré l'importance du motif de la décapitation comique dans les spectacles de la Belle Époque et sa circulation dans le premier cinéma[22]. Les têtes se mettent à rouler et le reste du corps court après, dans l'espoir de la remettre en place. C'est davantage dans ce contexte, à mon avis, qu'il faut envisager des films tels que *Chirurgie fin de siècle* ou encore *Chirurgie esthétique* ([Lux], 1907[?]). Dans ce dernier, un chirurgien farfelu retire la tête de sa patiente afin de lui en apposer une nouvelle, qui convient certainement mieux aux canons de beauté de l'époque. La tête détachée continue de s'agiter sur son présentoir, les traits du visage se tirent, se crispent pour former toutes sortes de grimaces, exactement à la manière de l'astrologue décapité dans *Zazezizozu* (1835) dont la tête intervient tout au long de la pièce[23].

Le spectacle de la machine

Le corps morcelé et reconstitué du premier cinéma serait donc avant tout un corps de spectacle, une attraction. Élaborée sur scène, cette attraction s'est vue saisie par le cinéma qui s'est empressé de la « mettre en machine ». De la même manière que le premier cinéma a « machiné le monde », selon le mot de François Albera[24], on pourrait dire qu'il s'est mis à « machiner le corps ». Le corps se déconstruit et se reconstruit à l'envi. Dans le film Lumière *Chirurgie mécanique* (1903), le chirurgien, à la manière d'un forgeron, se sert d'une enclume et d'un marteau pour redresser la jambe d'un patient boiteux. Une fois la jambe réparée, il la refixe sur le malade qui se remet instantanément à marcher. Il réitère l'opération sur un bossu en frappant son dos à grands coups de masse, le redressant miraculeusement.

Ce modèle *mécanique*, qu'on peut faire remonter à Descartes et La Mettrie[25], s'inscrit dans ce que François Albera et Maria Tortajada nomment « l'épistémè *horlogère* ». La dissociation, l'assemblage, l'articulation, l'automatisme, sont des formes récurrentes de cette épistémè que le premier cinéma a abondamment explorées[26]. Dans le contexte de la « médecine fin de siècle », cette conception mécaniste du corps humain trouve des applications étonnantes. C'est par exemple un « estomac mécanique », mis au point par le docteur Lesuc-Gastrique (figure 3.3), dont l'avantage est de pouvoir remplacer de manière infaillible un estomac défectueux[27]. Le corps mécanique est censé être inusable, capable de pallier toutes les défaillances du corps biologique. Chaque membre est interchangeable : le membre défaillant est remplacé par une « pièce de rechange », à l'instar du patient sauvagement découpé dans le film d'Alice Guy. L'aboutissement de ce modèle est bien sûr l'automate, un corps-machine entièrement mécanisé, très populaire au tournant du siècle. Dans le *Pêle-Mêle*, on se demande justement « Où s'arrêteront les progrès de l'automatisme ? ». L'article évoque la création, en Hollande, d'un « médecin automate »:

> L'appareil offre l'aspect d'un vieux médecin à perruque, dans le corps duquel sont pratiquées une foule de petites ouvertures portant chacune le nom d'une maladie. Si vous souffrez d'une affection quelconque, que ce soit un rhume de cerveau ou le ver solitaire, vous n'avez qu'à insinuer une pièce de dix centimes dans la case « rhume de cerveau » ou « ver solitaire », vous recevrez aussitôt le remède approprié.[28]

Le cinéma comique regorge de ce genre de personnages agissant à la manière d'automates. On pense par exemple au film *Calino a mangé du cheval* (Pathé, 1908) où le personnage-titre est soudainement saisi d'une frénésie qui le propulse en ville à toute vitesse, avec une vélocité sans pareille. Le corps de Calino est emporté dans une course que rien ne semble pouvoir interrompre. Ses jambes le portent malgré lui ; il ne peut que « boire l'obstacle », tel le pneu Michelin. Saisissant une charrette à bras, il renverse tout ce qui se trouve sur son passage. Le procédé de l'accéléré donne encore plus de vitesse à ses mouvements. Son corps est infatigable, comme délesté de ses contraintes biologiques. Des agents parviennent finalement à le stopper et le conduisent de force chez un médecin. Ce dernier, au terme d'une opération sommaire, extrait du ventre de Calino un cheval (de bois) qui s'était logé là. Une fois cette pièce retirée, le corps retrouve son état d'origine. Littéralement, ce « cheval-vapeur » qu'il avait dans l'estomac lui donnait les capacités phénoménales d'une automobile ou mieux : d'une locomotive, symboles par excellence de la modernité lancée à toute allure. La seule solution pour arrêter cette machine infernale a été de lui retirer son moteur, ni plus ni moins.

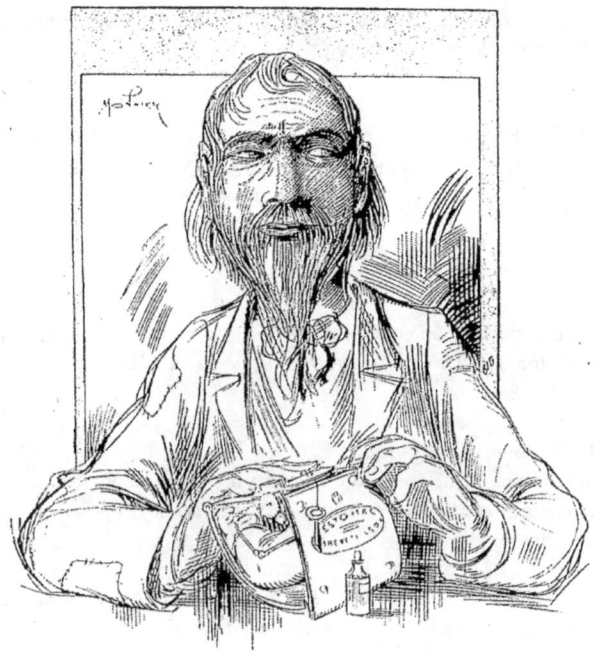

UNE TROUVAILLE

Le docteur Lesne-Gastrique, inventeur d'un estomac mécanique à réglage variable, échappement à ancre, broyeur, concasseur, tritureur automatiques. Cet instrument remplace avantageusement les vieux estomacs délabrés et hors d'usage.

Figure 26.3. « Trouvaille » d'un chirurgien doué en mécanique, dessin paru dans *Le Pêle-Mêle*, 10 mars 1901, p. 3 (Bibliothèque nationale de France, Gallica).

Le cinéma ne reconnaît aucune limite au corps-machine. Alors que la presse illustrée, à travers la figure du chirurgien, décrit des corps souffrants, morcelés, des corps aliénés, muselés, soumis aux caprices de guérisseurs incompétents et avides, le cinéma montre qu'il est capable de transformer et de réparer les corps, de les rendre plus forts, plus rapides. Les procédés qu'il utilise sont bien connus et lui sont propres : l'usage de l'accéléré, notamment, pour augmenter la vitesse des corps ; ou les trucages du type « arrêt de caméra » pour décomposer et recomposer les corps. La mécanique du cinéma met le corps en mouvement, en action. Contrairement au dessin de presse qui ne peut représenter que des corps figés, des corps sans vie, le corps cinématographique – ou corps cinétique – semble voué à l'agitation perpétuelle – à l'instar de Calino et son « cheval-vapeur ». Comme ces personnages de jouets optiques dont parlent André Gaudreault et Nicolas Dulac :

> Les sujets y sont envisagés comme des Sisyphe condamnés, *ad infinitum*, à tournoyer, à sauter, à danser . . . Ce sont en quelque sorte des hommes-machines, infatigables, inaltérables, des "sujets agités" plutôt que des "sujets

agissants". [. . .] Seraient-ce des machines éternelles, incassables, dignes des rêves les plus fous de la modernité ?[29]

JÉRÉMY HOUILLÈRE est doctorant et chargé de cours en histoire du cinéma à l'Université Rennes 2 et à l'Université de Montréal.

Notes

1. Jean Poirier, *Histoire des mœurs I*, vol. 1, Paris, Gallimard, 1990, p.642-645.
2. David Le Breton, *La Chair à vif. Usages médicaux et mondains du corps humain*, Paris, Métailié, 1993, p.107-108.
3. *Ibid.*, p.108.
4. *Life*, 27 février 1896, cité dans *Ibid.*
5. Gabriel de Lautrec, « Une opération », *Le Rire*, n°353, 6 novembre 1909.
6. Elisabeth Dixmier et Michel Dixmier, « *L'Assiette au beurre* » : *revue satirique illustrée. 1901-1912*, Paris, F. Maspero, 1974, p.135.
7. Jean Poirier, *op. cit.*, p.789-790.
8. Sandra Menenteau, « Le corps autopsié à l'épreuve du XIXe siècle », dans Frédéric Chauvaud, *Corps saccagés : une histoire des violences corporelles du siècle des Lumières à nos jours*, Rennes, Presses Universitaires de Rennes, 2009, p.33.
9. *Le Pêle-Mêle*, 15 décembre 1901, p.5.
10. *Le Pêle-Mêle*, 8 juillet 1900, p.12.
11. Sandra Menenteau, *op. cit.*, p.35.
12. *L'Assiette au beurre*, n°187, 29 octobre 1904, première de couverture.
13. *Chanteclair*, n°92, 1er décembre 1911, p.3.
14. Thierry Lefebvre, *Cinéma et discours hygiéniste (1890-1930)*, thèse de doctorat, Paris III, 1996, p.42.
15. Thierry Lefebvre, « *Les Joyeux Microbes* : un film sous influence ? », *1895*, n°53, décembre 2007, p.178.
16. *Le Pêle-Mêle*, 25 mars 1906, p.8.
17. *Le Pêle-Mêle*, 22 janvier 1905, p.8.
18. *Le Pêle-Mêle*, 26 mai 1907, p.12.
19. *Le Rire*, 25 avril 1914, n.p.
20. Jean Poirier, *op. cit.*, p.794-795.
21. *Le Pêle-Mêle*, 23 septembre 1906, p.8.
22. Voir notamment Patrick Désile, « Une "atmosphère de nursery du diable". Pantomime de cirque et premier cinéma comique », *1895*, n°61, septembre 2010, p.115-127.
23. Théodore Baudouin d'Aubigny *et al.*, *Zazezizozu*, féerie-vaudeville en cinq actes, Paris, Marchant, 1835. Merci à Patrick Désile pour cette référence.
24. François Albera, « 'L'école comique française', une avant-garde posthume ? » *1895*, n°61, septembre 2010, p.81.
25. Bruno Jacomy, « Automates et hommes-machines, de la Renaissance à nos jours », dans Jean-Pierre Changeux (dir.), *L'homme artificiel*, Colloque annuel du Collège de France, Paris, Odile Jacob, 2007, p.32.

26. François Albera et Maria Tortajada, « L'Epistémé 1900 », dans André Gaudreault, Catherine Russel et Pierre Véronneau, *Le Cinématographe, nouvelle technologie du XXe siècle*, Lausanne, Payot, 2004, p.45.
27. *Le Pêle-Mêle*, 10 mars 1901, p.3.
28. Robert Trinquet, « L'automatisme », *Le Pêle-Mêle*, 11 janvier 1903, p.11.
29. André Gaudreault et Nicolas Dulac, « La circularité et la répétitivité au cœur de l'attraction : les jouets optiques et l'émergence d'une nouvelle série culturelle », *1895*, n°50, décembre 2006, p.37.

27 Corps mis en scène, corps mis en cage

Le cinématographe au temps des zoos humains

Rodolphe Gahéry

Corporalité et imageries de l'altérité

Au sein du catalogue Lumière, deux séries semblent cristalliser la problématique du corps, plus particulièrement du corps de l'Autre, le corps noir. Il s'agit de vues captant un dispositif de « zoo humain », les « villages noirs » du tournant du siècle en France : *Le Village noir au jardin d'acclimatation de Paris* (deux films, sans doute tournés entre juin et juillet 1896)[1], et *Le Village Achantis à Lyon* (14 films, tournés entre avril et mai 1897)[2]. Au moins deux raisons justifient la pertinence de ces films pour un questionnement de l'altérité par la corporalité.

D'abord, ramené à sa définition la plus étroite, le zoo comme dispositif correspond à la rencontre entre deux désirs, voire deux pulsions : exhibitrice d'une part, et voyeuriste de l'autre. Or, dans notre cas, l'objet de désir et de pulsion principal est bien sûr le corps, le corps noir, qui est à la fois le centre de gravité de ces mises en scènes tout en étant son origine, son fondement. L'on montre *surtout* des corps ; mais l'on a aussi montré *d'abord* des corps. Une approche par la corporalité permet donc à la fois une analyse des phénomènes d'exhibition humaine ainsi que de leur histoire, de leurs évolutions comme dispositif.

Une approche par la corporalité permet ensuite, et c'est sans doute encore plus important ici, d'analyser les images produites par ce dispositif. Autrement dit, d'appréhender la délicate question de la représentation. Car les « zoos humains » sont bien sûr d'abord affaires de représentations, représentations d'un Occident qui, au XIXe siècle, construit et affirme de manière inédite son rapport à l'altérité, qu'elle soit coloniale ou non, en construisant et affirmant par corollaire une « identité » occidentale. Or, cette figuration de l'altérité passe nécessairement par sa corporalité : représenter l'Autre, c'est avant tout mettre son corps en images, puis le mettre en scène pour l'investir progressivement des attributs de son altérité, de ses altérités, car celles-ci sont plurielles, évolutives, et souvent contradictoires. Les corps sont les vecteurs privilégiés des représentations de l'Autre tout en étant eux-mêmes à la fois *des* représentations et, dans le cadre des exhibitions, systématiquement *en* représentation. Les corps sont ainsi les objets d'une *imagerie de l'altérité*.

Par cette expression, l'on désignera donc la production et la réception, à une échelle civilisationnelle ou au moins « collective », de supports visuels médiatisant une représentation de l'Autre. Ce qui inclut les images des exhibitions et les exhibitions elles-mêmes, en ce qu'elles sont déjà en soi un spectacle, une représentation. On se livrera d'abord à un exercice d'archéologie de ces imageries, en tâchant d'en distinguer trois qui sont apparues, sur un temps parfois très long, comme déterminantes dans l'avènement d'une imagerie fin de siècle d'un corps noir « zoologique ». Exercice qui trouvera son aboutissement dans l'examen des images cinématographiques et de leur place au sein de ces imageries entre 1890 et 1910.

Trois imageries des corps noirs

Cette archéologie s'appuie sur une compilation des travaux menés depuis plus de vingt ans par le groupe de recherche nommé ACHAC (Association pour la connaissance de l'histoire de l'Afrique contemporaine), autour du concept de « zoo humain » ainsi que de son histoire et de son historiographie, si l'on résume très rapidement[3]. L'on s'appuiera plus précisément sur la dernière grande synthèse scientifique de ces travaux, parue en 2011[4]. C'est principalement cet ouvrage qui a permis de dresser une typologie déclinée en trois imageries déterminantes du corps noir, étant entendu qu'il ne s'agit en rien de prétendre ici à l'exhaustivité.

Objet d'exploitation : le corps noir exhibé

Sur un temps long, voire très long, il semble d'abord nécessaire de prendre en compte une pratique séculaire de l'exhibition du corps de l'Autre, une pratique au sein de laquelle le corps noir n'est qu'un corps parmi d'autres, un corps de l'altérité exhibée qui devient à l'époque moderne un corps exotique. Ainsi, « déjà, dans l'Égypte Ancienne, on exhibait des nains noirs provenant des contrées soudanaises »[5]. Autrement dit, dès ses origines, la pratique exhibitrice est synonyme de domination, et c'est bien sûr par un rapport de domination que passe la construction d'une altérité. À l'échelle de l'Occident, cette histoire de l'Autre est inséparable d'une histoire de la découverte progressive du monde et des modalités de sa domination.

C'est pourquoi l'époque moderne et les « Grandes Découvertes » entamées à la fin du XVe siècle constituent une étape importante. Pascal Blanchard et ses confrères soulignent également l'importance cruciale, surtout à partir du XVIIIe siècle, de l'essor de pratiques aristocratiques comme les cabinets de curiosité ou les ménageries d'animaux⁶. L'on distinguera trois aspects. D'abord, l'époque moderne européenne réinvente son rapport à l'altérité avec l'exotisme⁷. Ensuite, cette fascination pour le merveilleux et le curieux n'est l'apanage que des élites, en particulier aristocratiques⁸. Enfin, dans ce cadre, l'exhibition d'individus noirs est semblable à celle d'autres populations, à l'instar de ce Tahitien « ramené » par Bougainville en 1769, ou encore de cette « troupe d'Africains » installée à Francfort en 1784 par le duc Frédéric II de Hesse-Cassel⁹. Avec néanmoins une spécificité notable, peu prise en compte par les historiens de l'ACHAC : ces corps noirs exhibés sont également des corps noirs exploités. Si l'on ne peut développer ici cet aspect, on conviendra que les traites négrières ont joué un rôle considérable dans l'histoire de la construction d'un imaginaire occidental du corps noir, et qu'elles sont certainement l'un des points de départ de la projection sur ces corps de bien des fantasmes, entre « sauvagerie » et « domesticité », force physique et paresse, etc.¹⁰ Sans oublier que l'exhibition elle-même s'apparente, dès ses origines, à une forme d'exploitation.

Pour en revenir à la chronologie du corps exhibé, il faut noter ensuite que le XIXᵉ siècle apparaît comme un tournant majeur en ce qu'il démocratise des pratiques jusqu'ici réservées aux seuls aristocrates et à quelques savants. Après la Révolution française, l'observation d'êtres vivants « exotiques » (animaux ou êtres humains, parfois peu, voire non différenciés) est désormais considérée comme une sorte de droit à l'instruction auquel les masses peuvent et doivent prétendre, au titre d'une éducation que l'on souhaite « populaire ». D'où l'essor, un peu partout en Europe, de jardins zoologiques gratuits ou très peu chers, par exemple¹¹.

Objet scientifique : le corps noir racialisé

Seconde imagerie à prendre en compte, le corps en tant qu'objet scientifique. Là encore, le XVIIIᵉ siècle des naturalistes est déterminant, avec des figures telles que Georges Louis-Leclerc de Buffon et son *Histoire naturelle* (36 volumes parus entre 1749 et 1789), mais le XIXᵉ siècle positiviste et raciste demeure le véritable tournant. Le premier savant à classifier le genre humain par « races » est Johann Friedrich Blumenbach, en 1795, ouvrant la voie à une série de travaux traversant le siècle, qui reposent tous sur le postulat d'un lien entre certains aspects physiques ou physiologiques, donc corporels, et certaines aptitudes morales, intellectuelles ou culturelles¹².

Le corps, objet scientifique racialisé, est ainsi étudié, observé, classé, mesuré, disséqué par des savants pour qui les exhibitions s'avèrent être souvent des opportunités pour travailler sur des sujets vivants, même si certains d'entre eux (peu nombreux avant la fin du siècle), sont plus critiques¹³. Au sein de ces nombreux articles produits par la « science » raciste (Pascal Blanchard et ses confrères ont dénombré plus de 80 articles pour les seules revues françaises traitant des exhibitions au Jardin d'acclimatation jusqu'en 1909)[14], le corps racialisé est représenté, souvent sous la forme de gravures ; il est aussi très tôt photographié, l'on y reviendra.

Au sein de cette vision raciste, le corps noir est peut-être celui qui est le plus défavorisé, eu égard aux critères de la physiognomonie et la taxonomie en vigueur, tels que l'échelle colorimétrique de la peau (de moins en moins « favorable » plus elle est foncée), la mesure de certains angles faciaux ou la forme de certains nez . . . Autant d'élucubrations qui sont alors considérées comme des « tares », faisant du corps noir racialisé un corps « taré », renvoyé dans les bas-fonds de l'« échelle civilisationnelle » mondiale, qui se trouve, elle, légitimée en retour par l'autorité du discours scientifique.

Objet politique : le corps noir colonisé

La troisième et dernière « imagerie » du corps noir a trait au politique. En effet, selon l'ACHAC, il y aurait un lien entre les conquêtes et politiques coloniales des métropoles et leurs modalités de représentation et d'exhibition des populations colonisées. Cela se concrétiserait notamment en une évolution de la présentation du corps noir dans les « zoos humains ».

> « Le statut de l'Autre, au sein de ces exhibitions, se transforme [au gré des changements politiques]. Dans un premier temps réifié en "sauvage", l'"exotique" est progressivement "apprivoisé" alors que les conquêtes coloniales s'achèvent, puis "civilisé" afin d'expliciter la progression de la "mission civilisatrice" coloniale. »[15]

Cette transformation passe fondamentalement par la corporalité. Le corps « sauvage » n'est pas semblable au corps « exotique » puis au corps « civilisé ». Très schématiquement, l'on pourrait presque dire qu'il implique un renversement de la perception du côté des colons, de la répulsion à l'attraction, tant au plan « physique » que « moral », même si le couple répulsion/attraction reste inhérent au dispositif zoologique. Là où le corps « sauvage » inspire la peur et une certaine animalité, le corps « civilisé » peut être vecteur d'une certaine sympathie, voire d'une fascination, quand il ne s'agit pas d'une érotisation[16].

Les principales conquêtes coloniales menées par la France en Afrique noire se déroulent durant les années 1870 et 1880 — elles débouchent, en 1895, sur la création de l'AOF (Fédération d'Afrique occidentale française). Or, les premiers « villages noirs » exhibés en métropole apparaissent au début des années 1880, soit, si l'on se fie à l'ACHAC, simultanément à cette phase dite « d'apprivoisement » de l'Autre.

Ces trois imageries en s'amalgamant sans pour autant s'annuler l'une l'autre, semblent avoir permis l'essor, à partir des années 1870, d'une imagerie d'un corps noir que l'on peut qualifier de « zoologique ».

Des imageries aux images, des « villages » aux écrans

L'essor des « villages noirs »

Dans le large éventail de dispositifs pouvant être considérés comme des « zoos humains », le « village » paraît s'inscrire au sein d'une généalogie dont, au XIXᵉ siècle, il constituerait une troisième étape, précédée par l'exhibition et le destin de la tristement célèbre « Vénus Hottentote », à Londres puis à Paris, entre 1810 et 1815[17], puis par l'essor d'exhibitions dites « ethnographiques » ou « (zoo-)anthropologiques », à partir des années 1870 un peu partout en Europe[18].

Avec ces deux premiers dispositifs d'exhibition, le spectateur est bien souvent cantonné à son rôle de « voyeur », car la frontière qui le sépare des exhibés est forte, parfois matérialisée par des grilles, et c'est en cela que les « villages reconstitués » correspondraient à une nouvelle et troisième étape. Apparus essentiellement dans le cadre d'expositions officielles et impériales[19], ils se distinguent par la promesse d'une « rencontre » avec l'Autre. Si la barrière entre exhibés et spectateurs reste bien réelle, et leur rencontre bien factice, les grilles, elles, disparaissent, au profit de décors folkloriques d'un ailleurs fantasmé ; les corps, quant à eux, se parent de costumes du même gabarit et sont intégrés dans des mises en scène censées illustrer une vie quotidienne immuable (repas, toilette, école...) ou des savoir-faire artisanaux et artistiques (musique, danse, combat...). En une décennie, le phénomène essaime un peu partout en Europe (en particulier en Allemagne, en France et en Suisse), ainsi qu'outre-Atlantique[20] ; et s'il règne un manque apparent d'homogénéité des pratiques, on estime que plus de la moitié des troupes ou individus exhibés dans ces « villages reconstitués » sont des Noirs[21]. Les années 1890-1900 apparaissent donc comme une phase très propice à ce dispositif d'exhibition des corps noirs, au moment même où se développent les premières images animées et projetées.

Les images des « villages noirs »

Les images de ces « villages noirs » se caractérisent avant tout par leur très grand nombre, la pluralité de leurs supports et des modalités de leur production et de leur réception. À nouveau, impossible de prétendre ici à l'exhaustivité ; l'on isolera simplement quelques catégories significatives :

- Les gravures scientifiques, déjà évoquées, s'inscrivent directement dans ce que l'on a appelé une « imagerie scientifique des corps noirs », qui se caractérise par une racialisation des corps, obsédée d'un côté par la taxonomie, donc le classement, la catégorisation de toute l'humanité, et d'un autre côté par la valorisation de « tares », de difformités et autres « aberrations » physiologiques venant soi-disant nuancer le grand schéma universel positiviste.

- Les affiches et illustrations de presse sont toutes deux très proches, tant dans leurs modalités de figuration que dans leur fonction, à la fois informative et éminemment commerciale, publicitaire. D'où une propension marquée au sensationnalisme, directement issu de la vulgarisation du prétendu savoir scientifique. Ce sont ces images qui véhiculent de la manière la plus explicite des corps « extrêmes », tant du côté de la répulsion (liée à l'animalité, la sauvagerie, la violence, la barbarie, l'étrangeté) que de l'attraction (liée à la valorisation des « us et coutumes », l'exotisme, la sensualité, voire à l'érotisme,). Les affiches et dessins de presse apparaissent à ce titre comme les plus purs produits de cette imagerie de l'exhibition populaire outrancière, bien qu'ils deviennent moins caricaturaux avec le temps.

- Les cartes postales sont le support visuel le plus répandu, et attestent de l'ampleur et du succès de ces exhibitions[22]. On y distingue au moins deux sous-catégories : dessins et illustrations d'un côté, très proches des affiches et de la presse, et photographies, telles que l'on va les décrire plus bas. Si la carte postale est intéressante comme cas d'étude, ce n'est pas tant comme support que du point de vue des fonctions dont elle est investie, en générant pour le spectateur un souvenir, une trace, une mémoire. Avant l'image animée, et selon des modalités certes différentes, les cartes postales inscrivent dans la durée la vision de ces corps noirs auprès des spectateurs. Notons enfin une spécificité des « villages reconstitués » : la confection, par les peuples exhibés eux-mêmes, de cartes postales[23] vendues auprès d'un public qui, dès lors, peut se fantasmer en anthropologue en herbe — et à domicile . . .

- Les photographies : si la carte postale est certainement le support le plus répandu, la photographie est la technique la plus utilisée, déclinée à peu près sur tous les supports et dans tous les registres. L'on trouve dès lors des photographies des « villages noirs » à visée scientifique, journalistique, touristique, publicitaire, etc. Cette inclination pour la technique photographique s'explique non seulement par la nouveauté visuelle qu'elle incarne mais aussi par l'authenticité supposée de sa représentation, propice à fasciner aussi bien les spectateurs anonymes que les « savants » tels Roland Bonaparte cherchant à construire « scientifiquement » une imagerie de l'autre[24].

L'équivoque cinématographique

Si l'image cinématographique partage alors prétendument la même « vérité » que l'image photographique, une première singularité s'impose : le nombre réduit de films. Contrairement aux autres médias, et même s'il faut prendre en compte les aléas du temps et de la conservation archivistique, parmi les images de « villages noirs » tournées en France entre les années 1890 et 1900, il semble difficile de trouver d'autres vues que celles correspondant aux deux séries Lumière, évoquées en introduction. On peut citer quelques vues de « Ouoloves » tournées par Félix-Louis Régnault en 1895 au Jardin d'acclimatation (très proches de la photographie scientifique)[25], ainsi qu'une vue attribuée à Eugène Pirou, *Les Plongeurs soudanais*, tournée en 1896 à Paris[26].

Quant aux seize vues Lumière, elles forment un ensemble de scènes de baignades, de danse, de combats, de repas, d'école et même d'allaitement et de toilette des enfants. Et, contrairement aux images évoquées précédemment qui, fixes et contemplées isolément, avaient en commun une grande simplicité et une grande clarté, autrement dit une univocité, les films Lumière présentent un caractère fondamentalement équivoque. Cette « équivoque cinématographique » passe au moins par deux éléments.

D'abord, il y a des indices explicites de mise en scène. Par exemple, dans la vue *Baignade de nègres*[27], la présence d'un homme blanc, au bord du bassin, donnant des ordres aux jeunes noirs pour qu'ils plongent. Est-ce vraiment un accès d'autorité improvisé, un exercice de domination usuel d'un simple visiteur, ou s'agit-il d'un acte de mise en scène réalisé de concert avec l'opérateur afin de mener à bien la prise de vue ? Dans le même registre, que penser de certains regards, notamment dans les scènes intitulées *Toilette d'un négrillon, I et II*[28], où des mères allaitent et lavent leurs enfants, regards interrogateurs dirigés *a priori* vers l'opérateur, comme si elles attendaient ses instructions ? Ou encore de ces enfants, dans la vue *Repas des négrillons, I*[29] qui, si l'on y prête suffisamment attention, ne mangent pas vraiment ? Plus largement, une mise en scène qui se donne ainsi à voir reste-t-elle vraiment une mise en scène ? Certes, le « zoo humain », et plus encore le « village reconstitué », est déjà en soi une représentation, un spectacle. Mais tout se passe comme si le cinématographe, en découvrant ses « trucs », en dévoilant une partie de son propre dispositif, faisait en même temps obstacle au spectacle, le recouvrant d'un voile qui en occulterait une partie des contenus aux spectateurs qui, dès lors, doivent composer avec une certaine ambiguïté.

Le deuxième facteur de l'équivoque que l'on peut isoler tient dans le statut même des films. À l'époque, les contemporains les considèrent parfois comme des « actualités », du moins est-ce le cas de la presse locale : le journal *Le Lyon républicain* du 2 mai 1897 évoque un « nouveau programme » qui comprend « toute une série d'actualités prises chez les Aschantis »[30]. Émerge alors, si ce n'est un paradoxe, du moins une tension, entre un ancrage dans un présent plus ou moins proche propre aux « actualités », et un ancrage dans un passé immémorial, presque hors du temps, qui est l'apanage des mises en scène de ces « villages reconstitués ». Cette équivoque se manifeste également à travers la pratique consistant à projeter aux exhibés leurs propres images — en l'occurrence, une séance est organisée dans un hôtel de Lyon, relatée par *Le Progrès*, le 25 mai 1897, en présence d'une trentaine de noirs exhibés, dont de nombreux enfants[31]. L'ambiguïté cette fois vient s'immiscer entre la fonction *spectaculaire* et la fonction *spéculaire* de ces films.

Des « corps-objet » au « corps-sujet » ?

Les éléments caractérisant cette équivoque cinématographique sont nombreux, et mériteraient certainement d'être un peu développés. Faute de place, l'on se contentera de formuler quelques hypothèses conclusives. Cette équivoque des vues Lumière par rapport aux autres images émanant des « villages noirs » — mais aussi par rapport aux autres images cinématographiques des Noirs[32] — n'est peut-être que le fruit d'une subjectivité propre, hypothèse qui serait évidemment la moins intéressante ...

S'il semble prudent de ne jamais éluder sa propre subjectivité, une autre explication pourrait tenir davantage à la question des corps, justement, et en particulier à la spécificité du « corps cinématographié ». En effet, l'un des grands points communs des images non cinématographiques est de parvenir assez systématiquement à réduire le corps noir au rang de pur objet (objet scientifique, d'amusement ou de divertissement, de curiosité ou de fantasme, etc.), d'où leur clarté, leur univocité. À l'inverse, les vues Lumière n'y parviennent pas, un peu comme si l'acte filmique en soi ne pouvait totalement réduire un corps, fût-il aussi dominé que celui des exhibés, à un pur objet. Ce qui ne signifie pas que la volonté pour le faire soit moindre ou absente, ni que le cinéma des premiers temps soit moins raciste que la presse ou la science ... N'en émerge pas moins une vaste, une ultime question : un corps peut-il être autre chose qu'un sujet dès lors qu'on le filme, et, par corollaire, jusqu'où l'acte filmique peut-il le réduire à l'état d'objet ?

RODOLPHE GAHÉRY est doctorant à l'université Paris Nanterre. La thèse de doctorat qu'il est actuellement en train de rédiger s'intitule *Les premières actualités filmées (1895–1914): des Cinématographes au Cinéma ?*

Notes

1. Vues n°12, 66 (Lumière) ; n°517-518 (Aubert & Seguin). Pour référencer les vues Lumière, on distinguera ici la numérotation issue des catalogues d'époque (« Lumière ») de celle issue du travail de Michelle Aubert et Jean-Claude Seguin (dir.), *La production cinématographique des Frères Lumière*, Paris, Mémoire du Cinéma, 1996 (« Aubert & Seguin »).
2. Vues n°441-452 et 464-465 (Lumière) ; n°520-533 (Aubert & Seguin).
3. Pour plus de détails, on consultera le site Internet de l'association, à cette adresse : http://achac.com/zoos-humains/.
4. Pascal Blanchard, Nicolas Bancel, Gilles Boëtsch, Éric Deroo et Sandrine Lemaire (dir.), *Zoos humains et exhibitions coloniales : 150 ans d'inventions de l'Autre*, Paris, La Découverte, 2011.
5. *Ibid.*, p.12.
6. *Ibid.*, p.10.
7. *Ibid.*, p.40.
8. *Ibid.*, p.10.
9. *Ibid.*, p.13.
10. À ce sujet, on pourra se reporter à cet ouvrage de référence : Olivier Pétré-Grenouilleau, *Les Traites négrières, essai d'histoire globale*, Paris, Gallimard, 2004.
11. Pascal Blanchard *et al.*, *op. cit.*, p.10-11.

12. Pour une approche plus fine des naturalistes et de la racialisation, voir Jacqueline Duvernay-Bolens, « L'Homme zoologique : race et racisme chez les naturalistes de la première moitié du XIXe siècle », *L'Homme*, vol.35, n°133, 1995, p.9-32.
13. Pascal Blanchard *et al.*, *op. cit.*, p.23.
14. *Ibid.*, p. 29, note 1.
15. *Ibid.*, p.28.
16. *Ibid.*, p.35.
17. *Vénus noire* (Abdellatif Kechiche, 2010) est l'un des derniers symptômes de ce « phénomène » (pour reprendre les termes de Pascal Blanchard et Gilles Boëtsch, « La Vénus hottentote ou la naissance d'un "phénomène" », dans Pascal Blanchard *et al.*, *op. cit.*, p.95-105), et prouve la persistance de l'attraction du cinéma pour ces exhibitions historiques du corps noir, exploré désormais *via* un discours filmique critique et dénonciateur.
18. Notamment sous l'impulsion de deux individus, l'Allemand Carl Hagenbeck et le Français Geoffroy de Saint-Hilaire, directeur du Jardin d'acclimatation de Paris. Voir entre autres William H. Schneider, « Les expositions ethnographiques du Jardin zoologique d'acclimatation », dans Pascal Blanchard *et al.*, *op. cit.*, p.132-141.
19. Celles d'Amsterdam dès 1883, de Londres en 1886 ou de Paris en 1889 : cf. Pascal Blanchard *et al.*, *op. cit.*, p.48
20. *Ibid.*, p.48.
21. *Ibid.*, p.42-43.
22. *Ibid.*, p.23.
23. On trouvera quelques exemples dans le catalogue d'exposition de Pascal Blanchard, Gilles Boëtsch et Jacomijn Snoep Nanette (dir.), *Exhibitions. L'invention du sauvage*, Paris, Acte Sud/Musée du Quai Branly, 2011.
24. Sur Roland Bonaparte, voir notamment Elizabeth Edwards, « La photographie ou la construction de l'image de l'Autre », in Pascal Blanchard *et al.*, *op. cit.*, p.484-485, et Gérard Joly, « Bonaparte (Prince Roland) », dans le *Dictionnaire biographique des géographes français du XXe siècle, aujourd'hui disparus*, Paris, PRODIG, 2013, p.39.
25. Voir Marc-Henri Piault, *Anthropologie et cinéma. Passage à l'image, passage par l'image*, Paris, Nathan, 2000, p.13.
26. Voir Camille Blot-Wellens, « Les plongeurs soudanais », dans *El cinematógrafo Joly-Normandin (1896-1897). Dos colecciones: João Anacleto Rodrigues y Antonino Sagarmínaga*, Madrid, Ministerio de Educación, Cultura y Deporte/ICAA/Filmoteca Española, 2014, p.163-165. Merci à l'auteure d'avoir porté cette vue à ma connaissance.
27. Vue n°12 (Lumière) ; n°517 (Aubert & Seguin).
28. Vues n°449-450 (Lumière) ; n°529-530 (Aubert & Seguin).
29. Vue n°447 (Lumière) ; n°532 (Aubert & Seguin).
30. Dans un article reproduit dans Michelle Aubert et Jean-Claude Seguin (dir.), *op.cit.*, p.174 *sqq*.
31. *Ibid.*
32. Par exemple, la vue Lumière *Nègres dansant dans la rue*, 1896 (n°252 du catalogue d'époque), ou, chez Pathé Frères, le *Nègre gourmand* (1905).

28 Paul Capellani

Le corps à l'épreuve du cinéma

Sébastien Dupont-Bloch

« Comment un comédien utilise le cinématographe pour faire de la sculpture » : sous cet intitulé paraît le 3 juillet 1909 dans l'hebdomadaire *l'Illustration* un article consacré à *L'Enlisé*[1]. Non pas le film Pathé *L'Enlisé du Mont Saint-Michel* sorti début 1908 – son titre n'est même jamais évoqué –, mais *L'Enlisé*, une sculpture réalisée par Paul (frère d'Albert) Capellani, exposée au Salon des Artistes Français de 1909. Toutefois, l'article prétend que cette sculpture a bel et bien été façonnée *d'après* le film, plus précisément d'après ce que l'on pourrait appeler une *étude de corps filmée*.

D'après l'article, repris par le quotidien *L'Ouest-Eclair* le 12 juillet suivant[2], Paul Capellani voulait expérimenter et filmer son propre enlisement « désireux de synthétiser le mouvement de la figure projetée » afin de connaître et mieux transcrire l'expression de ces moments proches de la mort pour réaliser une sculpture.

Des photographies par Charles Gerschel agrémentent l'article, montrant, sur le tournage, l'acteur qui s'enlise réellement, et en miroir la sculpture à peine achevée. Elles prouvent que *L'Enlizé*[3] incarne un surprenant acte d'intermédialité. L'artiste a en effet transformé un plan cinématographique, objet dynamique sans coordonnées de profondeur en une sculpture, objet statique sans coordonnées de temps. Il a transformé des images planes mais animées (dont les informations ont des coordonnées horizontale, verticale et temporelle) en un objet tridimensionnel statique (dont les éléments constitutifs ont des coordonnées horizontale, verticale et de profondeur). Un corps a été ainsi projeté d'un espace d'expression à l'autre par la substitution de paramètres quantifiables qui ne peuvent pas être confondus avec la part de l'interprétation artistique.

Cette sculpture est présentée comme étant le produit désiré du drame que l'artiste a réellement vécu, Paul Capellani ne voulant pas d'une simulation par un modèle ou par le comédien qu'il était par ailleurs. L'article précise que le tournage cinématographique a bien failli coûter la vie à l'artiste et à l'équipe. L'enlisement réel de l'acteur puis du matériel aurait nécessité une équipe de secours arrivée « juste à temps ».

Figure 28.1. Paul Capellani jouant dans le film de son frère Albert Capellani *L'Enlisé du Mont Saint-Michel* (1908) - photographie de Gerschel parue dans *L'Illustration*, n°3462, 3 juillet 1908, p. 12.

Le film

Le film est actuellement considéré comme perdu. On peut toutefois en retrouver des traces. Le 26 janvier 1908, par exemple, le rédacteur du journal *Le Sémaphore algérien* cite, parmi des vues ayant remporté « tous les suffrages » au Kursaal Omnia d'Alger, « *L'Enlizé du Mont Saint-Michel*, grand drame du plus poignant effet »[4]. Sorti quelques jours plus tôt au théâtre Pathé-Grolée à Lyon, son exploitation dans le réseau durera au moins une année puisqu'il est encore projeté à l'Omnia de Rouen en octobre 1908. Ce film de 150 mètres[5] a été produit et édité par Pathé Frères et, bien que non crédité, il est peut-être réalisé par Albert Capellani qui débute sa carrière de réalisateur chez Pathé en 1906 avec une fiction, *Le Chemineau*, interprété par Paul Capellani et inspiré de *Fantine*, première partie des *Misérables*[6]. Une seule certitude puisqu'il est physiquement reconnaissable, le rôle du personnage qui s'enlise a bien été interprété par Paul Capellani (1877-1960), frère cadet d'Albert. Certes, le film ne consiste pas tout entier en une scène d'enlisement. Le résumé du catalogue réinscrit la scène dans tout un déroulement dramatique[7]. Néanmoins, l'acmé du film, comme le laisse entendre ce résumé qui l'inscrit en scène finale et comme le confirme l'affiche, se situe bien dans cette vision de Paul Capellani s'enlisant dans les sables mouvants.

Original French Texts | 325

Figure 28.2. E. Marche, Affiche de *L'Enlisé du Mont Saint-Michel*, 1908 - lithographie éditée par Pathé, 160 x 120 cm, reproduite avec la permission de la BNF.

L'affiche est signée « E. Marche », qui ne fait pas partie des professionnels œuvrant à cette époque pour la maison Pathé tels que Candido de Faria ou Adrien Barrère. Le choix et l'utilisation des couleurs, la composition savante du dessin révèlent la facture d'un artiste confirmé doublé d'un illustrateur capable de réaliser une synthèse entre attraction spectaculaire, dramaturgie et narration[8]. La représentation de l'effroi dans la posture et les traits de Paul Capellani a singulièrement traversé le temps. Après avoir été détourné par le journal *Le Rire* dans sa couverture du 31 juillet 1909[9], l'affiche est réapparue plagiée en 1994 sur la couverture d'un roman n'ayant aucun rapport avec l'histoire, ni avec le film de 1908.

La sculpture

Enlisé est exposé depuis 1909 dans un recoin du musée du Mont Saint-Michel avec pour seule indication muséologique : « *Enlisé dans les sables mouvants* – Cette

Figure 28.3. Paul Capellani, *L'Enlisé*, 1909 - plâtre conservé au Musée historique du Mont Saint Michel, photographié par les frères Neurdein (collection privée, image reproduite avec la permission de l'agence Roger-Viollet).

sculpture, réalisée en 1909 par Paul Capellani, rappelle les dangers de la baie du Mont Saint-Michel qui fut pendant longtemps surnommée 'Le Mont Saint-Michel au péril de la mer' ». D'expression académique, l'œuvre est en plâtre [Fig.28.3]. Le visage et les yeux expriment clairement la terreur, les dernières parties émergentes du corps évoquent sa puissance musculaire autant que son impuissance.

La comparaison des images sculpturales et filmiques tend toutefois à nous faire considérer la démarche artistique annoncée dans l'article avec quelque suspicion. Contrairement aux photographies, le modèle sculpté ne porte ni moustache ni barbe. Il ne ressemble ni à l'acteur photographié, ni au personnage de l'affiche. L'acteur portait-il une fausse barbe ? Le sculpteur l'aurait-il rasé, changé, épuré ?

En tant que possible extériorisation d'un traumatisme, cette sculpture représente un acte d'intermédialité. Elle est une forme particulière de *sculpturation* telle qu'elle est définie par Michel Delage, à savoir comme un « outil de psychologie clinique cadrant l'expression d'émotions par le seul corps »[10]. Cette fois, la projection d'un espace modal à l'autre n'est pas seulement dimensionnelle : elle donne forme à une représentation mentale par le truchement du corps. Le personnage est représenté seul, et l'on ne peut savoir ni à qui s'adresse son cri, ni si quelqu'un peut seulement l'entendre. L'essentiel est exprimé par le visage, la partie du corps la plus proche des sens et de la conscience. En regardant ce visage, on est au plus près de la perception de la mort à venir. La chemise est ici le seul vêtement, collé au corps, ne se distinguant vraiment de la peau que par des plis évoquant des veines saillantes sous l'effort. Une main actionne une forte poussée, rejetant la matière assassine que l'on sent résistante comme de la pierre, l'autre main glisse inutilement sur cette même matière qui se dérobe lorsqu'on cherche, au contraire, à exploiter cette résistance. Le corps est ici inutile, acteur de sa propre mort à venir, machine impuissante à se sauver elle-même.

L'incarnation

L'Enlisé du Mont Saint-Michel, qu'il soit image, film ou sculpture, peut aussi être lu comme la fatale impuissance des miséreux face à un acharnement aveugle d'injustices sociales ou naturelles. Un programme que n'aurait pas renié André Antoine, père fondateur du théâtre naturaliste et de la mise en scène moderne, pour lequel Paul Capellani joue justement à l'Odéon pendant l'année du tournage de *L'Enlisé* en 1907[11]. Et selon Jacques Richard, plus qu'un « interprète », Paul Capellani serait même le « disciple » d'Antoine, en gardant « l'empreinte de son maître » dans les films réalisés par Albert Capellani[12].

Engageant son corps dans les sables mouvants devant la caméra à la recherche d'une représentation vraie et naturelle, Paul Capellani outrepasse les préceptes[13] d'Antoine pour qui « c'est le milieu qui détermine les mouvements des personnages, et non les mouvements des personnages qui déterminent le milieu »[14]. Et si le naturalisme peut être défini comme « une représentation authentique et expressive de la nature et des corps »[15], c'est précisément ce qu'a modélisé l'acteur/sculpteur Paul Capellani dans sa performance.

Il est possible que la sculpture n'ait été qu'un résultat secondaire du film. Que le tournage ait eu sa propre autonomie, que la sculpture fût elle-même le résultat non prémédité, mais improvisé et thérapeutique visant à concrétiser l'expression d'un événement traumatisant. Le film est sorti en janvier 1908 et la sculpture a été présentée au Salon des artistes français en mai 1909. Il s'est donc écoulé plus d'une année entre le tournage du film et l'exposition. Capellani a pu trouver dans cet intervalle une catharsis à un événement qui a réellement failli lui coûter la vie.

Intentionnelle ou non, thérapeutique ou non, cette sculpture – tout comme le film – représente l'agonie enregistrée d'un corps. Le changement de coordonnées du corps, migrant du cinématographe à la sculpture, est une cristallisation temporelle, mais aussi une amplification des détails anatomiques.

Et si l'on admet que Paul Capellani a réellement risqué la mort pendant le tournage et que sa sculpture ultérieure est un témoignage de première main exprimé sans équivoque, on peut la considérer comme l'illustration de la plus grave épreuve qu'un corps puisse subir au nom de l'art cinématographique.

SÉBASTIEN DUPONT-BLOCH est doctorant à l'Université Paris 1 Panthéon-Sorbonne et chargé de cours à l'Université Caen-Normandie.

Notes

1. *L'Illustration*, n°3462, 3 juillet 1908, p.12.
2. « Un sculpteur consciencieux s'est enlisé lui-même pour donner à son œuvre plus de réalisme et de vie », *L'Ouest-Eclair*, n°3833, 12 juillet 1908, p.1.
3. L'orthographe varie au gré des rédacteurs des différents journaux annonçant la projection du film. En 1908, l'orthographe évoluant, la forme « enlisé » apparait comme moderne et remplace progressivement « enlizé » qui garde un temps la spécificité des sables mouvants (sans doute grâce à Victor Hugo dans *Les Misérables*). Nous respecterons ici l'orthographe de chaque rédacteur.
4. *Le Sémaphore Algérien, organe de la marine, du commerce, de l'industrie, de l'agriculture et des travaux publics*, n°508, 26 janvier 1908, p.3. Il y est précisé que le film est projeté entre *Le premier cigare d'un collégien* (Pathé, 1908) et *Le gendarme a bon œil* (Pathé, 1908).
5. Henri Bousquet, *Catalogue Pathé des années 1896 à 1914*, Bures-sur-Yvette, Editions Henri Bousquet, 1994, p.68.
6. Lucien Logette, « De l'écrit à l'écran: Les Misérables », *1895*, n°68, décembre 2013, p.57.
7. « Un homme misérablement vêtu demande la charité dans les rues du Mont St Michel. Il ne recueille rien. Cependant, une famille l'accueille, le fait entrer dans sa misérable maison et lui donne à manger. L'aîné des enfants lui fait fête mais il fait malencontreusement une chute et se fait une grave blessure à la tête. Le père fait un mot pour le docteur. Le chemineau décide d'aller la porter. Il doit traverser le bras de mer qui sépare le Mont de la terre ferme. Mais il se trompe, se trouve pris dans des sables mouvants et meurt. (Scénario d'après vision) » Henri Bousquet, *op. cit.*, p.68.
8. Il pourrait s'agir du peintre Ernest Gaston Marché (1864-1932), formé à Paris à l'Ecole Nationale des Arts Décoratifs. Tout comme Paul Capellani, Ernest Marché a fréquenté et exposé au Salon des Artistes Français à la même période.
9. Merci à Jérémy Houillère pour cette référence.
10. Michel Delage, *La résilience familiale*, Paris, Odile Jacob, 2008, p. 203.
11. Édouard Noël et Edmond Stoullig, *Les Annales du théâtre et de la musique*, Paris, Librairie P. Ollendorff, 1907, p. 179, 194, 198.
12. Jacques Richard, « Des acteurs qui échappent au théâtre », *1895*, n°68, décembre 2013, p.121.
13. Dès le premier plan de son premier film, *Le Chemineau* en 1905, Paul Capellani engage tous son corps au cinéma comme il le ferait au théâtre. N'hésitant pas à transgresser les codes cinématographiques pour incarner la postérité du Théâtre Libre d'Antoine au cinématographe, le chemineau Paul Capellani apparaît dans une démarche fragile et, sans jamais quitter la caméra du regard, s'approche pour provoquer littéralement un gros plan de son visage habité par le rôle.
14. A[ndré] Antoine, « Causerie sur la mise en scène », *La Revue de Paris*, vol.2, mars-avril 1903, p.603.
15. Aurélie Gendrat, *Zola, l'œuvre*, Paris, Bréal, 1999, p.16.

29 Poils et pilosités dans le cinéma des origines

Jean-Claude Seguin

Les poils et les pilosités occupent une place de choix dans l'histoire des différentes cultures. Marqueurs de genre, symboles religieux, indicateurs sociaux... ils ne cessent de parcourir discrètement les cultures et les arts depuis des temps immémoriaux[1]. S'attacher par conséquent à leur présence et leur rôle dans le cinéma des origines, c'est s'interroger d'une part sur leur intégration dans de brefs récits entre 1896 et 1906 et, d'autre part, sur leurs fonctions dans la société du tournant du XIXe siècle, en particulier sur la manière dont ils construisent (et peuvent dès lors menacer ou déconstruire) le genre (*gender*), l'identité, voire même l'humanité du corps filmé. Le destin du poil dans les vues dites « générales » ou « de genre » (au sens cette fois du statut familier et anecdotique du thème représenté) permettraient de composer un portrait assez juste de ce qui définit « l'homme » de la Belle Époque et de mettre au jour une caractéristique importante de la représentation du corps dans le cinéma des premiers temps.

Le barbier

Nous allons entamer notre voyage pilaire par celui qui, depuis des temps lointains, a pour office de s'occuper de nos cheveux et de nos pilosités faciales, à savoir le barbier. C'est dans la Black Maria, à la fin de 1893, que William Heise produit pour W.K.L. Dickson, *The Barber Shop*. Dans la filmographie Edison établie par Charles Musser, il occupe la 18e place[2]. Cela est loin d'être anodin. Faire du barbier l'une des premiers métiers représentés (avec le forgeron et le maréchal ferrant) montre l'importance sociale que revêtait alors cette profession. La brièveté du métrage n'en offre pas moins une scène de genre, comme celle que nous pouvons trouver dans la gravure ou la peinture du XVIIIe siècle.

L'espace restreint de la scène de la Black Maria constitue une contrainte, compensée dans le cas présent par la structure de l'image en trois plans: le décor, le barbier et son client et les deux clients plus près de nous. C'est donc sur la profondeur de champ que joue exclusivement l'opérateur. Mais que nous donne à voir cette saynète ? S'il s'était agi, simplement, de représenter un client qui vient se faire raser, l'intérêt aurait été moindre. Ce qui fait tout le charme de *Barber Shop*, c'est, à n'en pas douter, les deux clients au premier plan. Ils nous en disent bien plus sur l'espace social que constitue le salon du barbier. Avant tout, nous sommes dans l'espace masculin, totalement et absolument masculin. On aurait du mal à imaginer dans ce lieu surgir une silhouette féminine sans risquer le trouble et l'émeute. Mais le salon du barbier est aussi un espace de sociabilité, où l'attente et son comblement sont essentiels. On n'y façonne pas seulement le corps, le comportement aussi est soumis à des codes. L'identité masculine s'y dessine non seulement dans ses caractéristiques physiques mais aussi sociales. Le succès de ce premier film conduit Edison à en proposer un *remake* dès janvier 1895, légèrement plus élaboré et plus complexe où trois actions se superposent : un barbier et son client, un cireur de chaussures et le sien, ainsi que deux autres personnes[3]. Le catalogue proclame que « c'est l'un des films les plus populaires jamais produits »[4].

La popularité de ces films qui matérialisent spatialement et physiquement l'ordre social est révélatrice de leur caractère conventionnel. Et cet « ordre établi » sera précisément mis en péril par l'apparition de jambes féminines dans une autre production Edison, datée de 1898 (puis connaissant un remake en 1901), *What demoralized the barber shop*[5]. Le comique se fonde ici, sur l'irruption du « féminin » dans le monde « masculin », un désordre dont on voudra bien penser qu'il est clairement érotisé – nul doute que les jambes appartiennent à des demoiselles de petite vertu qui arpentent le trottoir – et qui suscite non seulement l'agitation extrême des clients, mais aussi celle du barbier qui semble à deux doigts de trancher le cou du pauvre client particulièrement malmené. On observera en l'occurrence que les femmes occupent, dans cet ordre masculin « renversé », une position dominante.

Si le salon du barbier peut être représenté comme un lieu social structuré et structurant où l'intrusion féminine vient semer le trouble, il existe d'autres vues dont le sujet tend à se concentrer sur la relation barbier-client à des fins purement comiques, avec ou sans l'utilisation de trucages. Si le cinéma des origines porte une attention particulière à la figure du barbier, c'est aussi parce que l'espace de son salon est celui où se produit un déséquilibre entre le barbier – figure dominante – et le client – figure dominée et soumise. C'est au fond de cette situation inégale que naît le gag. C'est ainsi le cas du célèbre film *Le Barbier fin de siècle* (Pathé, [1896]). La vue combine deux genres des origines : la scène de trucage et la vue comique.

Ce trucage – un homme qui perd la tête, au sens propre – est un classique dans le monde de la prestidigitation et, bien entendu, chez Georges Méliès. Ce qui pourrait nous interroger davantage est le choix d'un arrière-plan de boutique de barbier. Il s'agit, en filigrane, de jouer sur les peurs éventuelles que pourraient faire naître les instruments du barbier : couteau, lame, ciseaux ... Autant d'objets qui peuvent se changer en armes et menacer les corps qui leur sont soumis non seulement dans leurs attributs masculins, mais dans leur vie même. Le trucage vient ainsi jouer sur cet arrière-fond à la fois comique et inquiétant.

Il ne s'agit là que d'un exemple parmi tant d'autres qui nous invite à de multiples variations sur des thèmes voisins, mais qui se fondent sur le principe du « dérèglement » d'un ordre spatial et social établi qui deviendra, comme l'a montré Petr Král, la forme de « désordre » du *slapstick*[6]. Le client à moitié rasé parce qu'il est arrivé en retard dans *Le Barbier facétieux* (Pathé, 1903) ou le client blessé dans *El Barbero* (1898), un superbe flip-book espagnol de Pablo Audouard, sont ainsi des variantes qui pourraient presque se décliner à l'infini et qui esquissent les contours de ce que l'on pourrait considérer comme un « genre ».

Le salon du barbier, lieu clos et dont le décor n'évolue guère, ne laisse pourtant pas les pilosités s'exprimer pour elles-mêmes, elles apparaissent, au bout du compte, comme un accessoire de plus qui légitime le rapport dominant/dominé entre le barbier et son client. La maîtrise des poils y devient le symbole d'un pouvoir social sur la masculinité des corps. Cependant, le cinéma des premiers temps a bel et bien fait de la barbe, et accessoirement de la moustache, l'élément essentiel de certaines vues animées.

La Barbe

La barbe est un marqueur de virilité que le cinéma des origines va mettre à contribution dans de nombreuses productions. Il va de soi que nous ne prétendons pas répertorier les films dans lesquels un personnage masculin est affublé d'une barbe, mais de nous en tenir à quelques exemples où elle tient un rôle emblématique.

En focalisant l'attention du spectateur sur un élément pileux caractéristique du « masculin », les films jouent, peu ou prou, sur le rapport que l'homme établit avec sa virilité, ou au moins, sa masculinité. Ainsi, toute attaque – coupure, rasage, etc. – peut se lire symboliquement comme un jeu sur la castration – conformément au registre allégorique qui rendait la figure du barbier si « puissante ». Qu'aujourd'hui, les barbes soient devenues « tendance », que le salon de barbier – et non plus de coiffeur – fasse florès, sont autant de signes qui marquent le retour d'une affirmation physique de la masculinité. Au tournant du XIXe-XXe siècles, la barbe était plus « naturelle » et toute atteinte à son intégrité prenait du sens. Prenons le cas du film *Ah ! La barbe* (Pathé, 1905) attribué à l'Espagnol Segundo de Chomón. Ce curieux film met au centre du récit le rasage, ou plutôt, l'auto-rasage. Cela est d'autant plus souligné que le personnage se trouve placé devant un grand miroir.

Le rasage tel qu'il était pratiqué autrefois était par ailleurs une opération complexe qui demandait de la dextérité, du savoir-faire et de la patience. Des traités entiers étaient consacrés à cet « art du rasage »[7], l'associant à une certaine notion de plaisir. Notre personnage, face à la glace, prend un évident plaisir à étendre sur son visage le savon, plaisir qui le conduit même à goûter goulument la mousse, comme s'il s'agissait d'une glace ou d'une friandise. Quelques secondes plus tard, il passe son rasoir avec délectation sur le cuir ... Cette délectation et cette érotisation tendent à assimiler cet art du rasage à une pratique onaniste, ou peu s'en faut. Tout est prêt pour que le brave homme s'adonne à ce plaisir solitaire. Et dans ce dispositif, la glace occupe une place de choix : elle est le témoin du rasage. Certes elle est d'abord fonctionnelle – il est préférable de se raser devant un miroir pour éviter des accidents –, mais on ne peut oublier que le personnage fait, en quelque sorte, son autoportrait, une sorte de *selfie*. Or, tandis que l'homme, tout à son image, commence à user de son coupe-chou, des figures apparaissent dans la glace comme autant de visages « alternatifs ».

Ces trois têtes renvoient toutes au monstrueux, au sens latin du terme : *monstrum* (« avertissement des dieux, présage », « chose bizarre, monstre, prodige »). Le premier a l'air plutôt clownesque, le second, d'un vieux savant et le troisième, d'un enfant stupide qui lui tire la langue. Si nous laissons de côté le trucage, dans l'art duquel Segundo de Chomón était passé maître, ces trois portraits semblent surgir comme autant d'alternatives que proposerait le miroir au personnage, construisant ainsi un avant et un après rasage. C'est bien une question d'identité qui est alors au centre de l'acte de rasage à laquelle mettra un terme le jeune homme en brisant le miroir. Cette saynète d'à peine quarante mètres avait certes pour objet de faire rire le public grâce à des trucages, déjà classiques à l'époque, mais elle en appelait également à cet art et cette vanité du rasage, ce fantasme de sculpter son propre visage et d'en changer, en défiant l'ordre de la nature.

Les cheveux et les postiches

Les cheveux ou leur substitut constituent la matière première de nombreux films dont nous ne retiendrons ici que quelques cas exemplaires. Dans la grande majorité de ces films centrés sur les cheveux, l'essentiel de leur récit concerne la question de la repousse des cheveux ou leur remplacement. À la différence de la barbe – dont nous avons souligné la dimension « virile » ou « masculine » –, les cheveux sont utilisés comme attributs *humains* dont on retient surtout la valeur esthétique.

La calvitie est alors considérée comme un handicap, voire un drame, qui aiguise l'appétit des marchands de produits miracles de tout « poil », à l'instar de celui qu'utilise le personnage dans *Lotion miraculeuse* (Pathé, 1903), remake de *L'Eau merveilleuse* (Pathé, 1901). La pousse incontrôlée et anarchique des cheveux est l'argument sur lequel se construit le *gag*, et le remède est pire que le mal. Alors que la « barbe » regardait du côté du masculin/féminin, on peut admettre que dans le cas présent, c'est le rapport être humain/animal qui est au centre du film. Le double dérèglement – absence ou abus de cheveux – participe d'une remise en cause de l'intégrité de la personne.

Le corps est menacé d'hirsutisme, ou plus précisément d'hypertrichose, une peur ancestrale dont rendent compte les traités naturalistes comme le plus célèbre d'entre eux, la *Monstrorum Historia* d'Ulisse Aldrovandi, publiée au XVIIe siècle. Les personnes atteintes d'hypertrichose – particularité génétique de la célèbre famille González, qui fit les beaux jours des cours européennes au XVIe siècle -, étaient assimilées à des monstres, mi-hommes, mi-animaux. Le XIXe siècle envoyait l'essentiel de ces personnages vers le monde du cirque, où ils s'exhibaient parmi les créatures hybrides (telles que Julia Pastrana, la mexicaine femme-singe, Fedor Jeftichew, l'enfant à tête de chien ou Stephan Bibrowski, l'homme à tête de lion), juste à côté des femmes à barbe – figures emblématiques par leur pilosité qui les situait précisément entre-deux genres et à la frontière de l'animalité. Dans les films des premiers temps, la pousse soudaine et truquée des cheveux, et dans certains cas des poils sur le corps, apparaît comme une variante cinématographique du mythe du loup-garou.

Derrière l'effet comique, on ne peut s'empêcher de voir une forme de « morale ». Même chauve, l'être humain devrait se contenter de son sort, invité à se méfier des charlatans et autres savants fous qui abusent de ses faiblesses pour se livrer à leurs expériences diaboliques. Morale sans doute conservatrice ... s'il n'était « l'expérience cinématographique », qui triomphe.

Les films des premiers temps se sont par ailleurs souvent amusés à « scalper » leurs personnages, en prenant pour cible les postiches. *La Perruque* (Pathé, 1905) est un classique qui, sur le mode comique, dénonce les faux-semblants et les maquillages de tout type. Le bellâtre du film tente de combattre les outrages du temps afin de séduire sa belle. Le vieux beau, figure classique de Molière à Max Ophüls, cherche des subterfuges pour échapper à sa décrépitude. La figure la plus intéressante est, sans nul doute, celle du petit diablotin qui, sous couvert de plaisanterie, se faufile parmi les adultes et, révélant leur calvitie, dénonce leur vanité. *La Course à la perruque* (Georges Hatot, Pathé, 1906) reprend la figure de l'enfant espiègle, qui, par jeu, bouleverse le bon ordre des choses. Profitant de l'assoupissement simultané d'une vieille dame et d'un vendeur de ballons, les deux garnements accrochent ces derniers à la perruque de la femme. En détournant les ballons de leur fonction première, ils deviennent des objets aériens important avec eux la perruque. Après cet introït, nous allons assister à une classique course-poursuite qui occupe la quasi-totalité du film. Pourtant, la calvitie féminine n'est pas présente, à notre connaissance, dans le cinéma des origines, ou de façon purement marginale. C'est qu'en effet, contrairement, à celle de l'homme, elle est moins propice aux rires et aux plaisanteries. Le cinéaste a donc résolu la question en utilisant un homme travesti pour jouer le rôle de la vieille femme – là aussi un classique de la comédie depuis Shakespeare jusqu'à Buñuel. Le ressort comique du travestissement est efficace pour autant qu'il soit « homme vers femme » et non pas « femme vers homme »[8]. Dès lors, notre « vieille femme » peut multiplier les cabrioles, les sauts et les culbutes et déclencher assurément les rires des spectateurs, ceux de l'époque en tout cas. *La Course à la perruque* renoue ainsi avec la question du genre dans nos sociétés contemporaines, celle des territoires respectifs du masculin et du féminin et des « sorties du territoire ».

Bilan

Les films interrogés, essentiellement comiques dans une démarche qui sera reprise par le burlesque de la décennie suivante, portent en eux, de façon implicite, une réflexion sur l'attachement de la société de la Belle Époque à des formes extérieures d'appartenance au sexe social et en particulier aux pilosités fonctionnant comme des « caractères sexuels secondaires », pour reprendre une expression propre au champ d'étude anthropologique où les poils et cheveux ont acquis une incontestable importance au cours de ces dernières années[9]. S'il existe aujourd'hui une ample littérature théorique sur la question de la pilosité ou de son rejet[10], il n'existe pas d'ouvrage qui fasse le point sur cette question au cinéma et moins encore sur le cinéma des origines[11]. Le corps chevelu ou barbu représente néanmoins un ressort narratif récurrent des films comiques des premiers temps, et ce corpus – dont nous n'avons proposé ici qu'un échantillon[12] – se révèle souvent un lieu d'ébranlement ou de parodie de certaines normes genrées, de certains clivages homme/femme. Avec la complicité tacite du spectateur impliquée par les codes de ces premiers films comiques (et la force de normativité qu'engage le rire collectif), les stéréotypes de genre et les attributs de la « virilité » de l'époque en sortent parfois réaffirmés, mais parfois aussi – ainsi que nous espérons l'avoir démontré – bousculés.

JEAN-CLAUDE SEGUIN est professeur émérite à l'Université Lumière Lyon 2. Il est l'auteur de *Histoire du cinéma espagnol*, *Pedro Almodóvar o la deriva de los cuerpos* et *Alexandre Promio*. Il est l'éditeur avec Michelle Aubert de *La Production cinématographique des Frères Lumière*.

Notes

1. Voir Marie-France Auzépy et Joël Cornette (dir.), *Histoire du poil*, Paris, Belin, 2011 ; Yve Le Fur (dir.), *Cheveux chéris, frivolités et trophées*, Paris, Actes Sud/Musée du Quai Branly, 2012 ; Christian Bromberger, *Trichologiques*, Paris, Bayard, 2010.
2. Charles Musser, *Edison Motion Pictures 1890-1900, An Annnotated Filmography*, Washington, Smithsonian Institution Press, 1997, p.18.
3. D'après Charles Musser, cette description pourrait d'ailleurs correspondre à une troisième version, car le cireur de chaussure est blanc. *Ibid*, p.168.
4. Ohio Phonograph Co., *The Edison Kinetoscope*, Price-List, Août 1895, p.9 ("Barber Shop").

5. Ce film sera encore plagié, quatre ans plus tard, par l'American Mutoscope and Biograph Company, sous le titre *The Barber's Dee-light* (1905).
6. Petr Král, *Le Burlesque ou Morale de la tarte à la crème*, Paris, Stock, 1984 et *Les Burlesques ou Parade des somnambules*, Paris, Stock, 1986.
7. Georges Malet, *Théorie de la barbe ou comment il faut se raser*, Paris, Les Éditions Orah, 1928.
8. Sur le travestissement des femmes en hommes, voir Laura Horak, *Cross-Dressed Women, Lesbians, and American Cinema, 1908-1934*, New Brunswick (NJ), Rutgers University Press, 2016.
9. Voir notamment Christian Bromberger, *op. cit.* ; Yves Le Fur (dir.), *op. cit.* ; Lucinda Hawksley, *Moustaches, Whiskers & Beards*, Londres, National Portrait Gallery, 2014.
10. Sur la « dictature du lisse », on pourra consulter: Jean Da Silva, *Du velu au lisse, histoire et esthétique de l'épilation intime*, Paris, Complexe, 2009, et Stéphane Rose, *Défense du poil, contre la dictature de l'épilation intime*, Paris, La Musardine, 2010.
11. Le terrain a cependant été défriché avec de grandes promesses par le chapitre « Projections ; la virilité à l'écran » d'Antoine de Baecque, dans Alain Corbin, Jean-Jacques Courtine et Georges Vigarello (dir.), *Histoire de la virilité*, tome 3, Paris, Seuil, 2011, p.431-460.
12. La mise en ligne des catalogues de production cinématographique des premiers temps (actuellement in progress, voir « Los orígenes del Cine » sur le site https://www.grimh.org) permettra d'établir un corpus bien plus vaste et complet. Notons que nous n'avons pas abordé, dans le cadre restreint de cet article, la pilosité intime – ou son absence –, qui nous aurait conduit à sortir de la comédie.

30 Le corps du spectateur en mouvement
Effets réels et virtuels des spectacles tridimensionnels

Martin Barnier

L<small>E CORPS DANS</small> l'espace de la salle de spectacle n'est pas seulement un regard face à un écran plat. Nous savons que de nombreuses séances de projections (fixes ou en mouvement) du cinéma des premiers temps étaient accompagnées de voix, de bruits, de musiques[1], éléments qui font vibrer les corps. Et même s'il y avait aussi des projections dans le silence, chacun pouvait déceler la présence corporelle de ses voisins ne serait-ce que par la respiration. En outre, dès le milieu du XIXe siècle, différents dispositifs émergent qui présentent des images tridimensionnelles pouvant impliquer le corps de celui qui regarde dans l'espace de représentation. Cette immersion pouvait être amplifiée par l'impression de réalité développée grâce à des dispositifs techniques élaborés pour mettre le corps du public en mouvement. Face à cette importance et cette variété de « présences », nous devons nous poser la question de l'implication du spectateur en fonction des sens sollicités, et de ce qui « fait corps » dans le cinéma des premiers temps.

Nous allons mettre ici en perspective les corps face aux spectacles de projections, et aux images, avant 1914, dans les pays occidentaux. Quelle était la place du corps du spectateur dans l'espace de la salle ? Michel De Certeau, interrogé par George Vigarello, dans *Esprit* en 1982, définit le corps comme un système de gestes et de perceptions. Selon lui, « chaque 'corps' serait la combinaison d[e] déterminations » touchant essentiellement à ses « limites » (où s'arrête ce corps ?) et au développement de ses « sens (l'audition, l'odorat, la vue ?) »[2]. L'histoire sociale du corps spectatoriel commence à se développer depuis une dizaine d'année en France, dans la suite des travaux sur l'histoire des corps[3].

Le corps s'arrête à la place assignée dans la salle ... mais la perception de l'image en trois dimensions peut le faire basculer dans un espace virtuel. Au XIXe siècle les dispositifs permettant aux corps des spectateurs de s'immerger dans un environnement tridimensionnel fictif se multiplient. Nous retracerons ici suivant un parcours chronologique la manière dont ces divers procédés ont essayé de placer les corps des spectateurs dans l'espace, concret et virtuel.

Les spectateurs absorbés

Regarder des images avec une profondeur accentuée donne l'impression d'entrer dans cet espace, de le visiter. Le cerveau « projette » le corps dans ces images, et ce processus est renforcé par l'observation avec visionneuse, qui exclut le spectateur du « monde réel ». Le procédé d'images en relief le plus simple qui s'est répandu le plus rapidement est celui de la photographie stéréoscopique. Sa popularité commence au milieu du XIXᵉ siècle. En 1851 David Brewster offre un stéréoscope à la reine Victoria. Jusqu'à la Première Guerre mondiale, des millions d'images stéréoscopiques sont vendues. Au cours de la seule année 1862, la London Stereoscopic Company vend un million de vues en relief[4]. Le public est fasciné par la vision d'images et de photos en relief, par cette sensation d'avoir son corps « aspiré » par cet espace en profondeur, trompé par le cerveau qui détecte un espace en trois dimensions lorsqu'on propose une image légèrement décalée à chaque œil.

Tandis que de nombreux autres procédés se développent en permettant au public de la seconde moitié du XIXᵉ siècle de voir des images en relief et de s'imaginer dans un espace tridimensionnel[5], les conventions picturales elles-mêmes semblent répercuter ces enjeux. En effet, les grands tableaux classiques de l'époque, dits « pompiers » en France, représentent des scènes, presque grandeur nature, et ultra-réalistes. Les spectateurs dans les musées et galeries de peintures peuvent se projeter dans ces lieux historiques devant les immenses toiles peintes[6]. Ils imaginent leur corps face aux gladiateurs de Jean-Léon Gérôme dans *Pollice Verso* de 1872. La sensation physique de proximité avec l'espace représenté permet aux contemporains de comprendre l'exploit artistique. Comme en bordure de la fenêtre stéréoscopique du cinéma en relief, le corps de l'observateur du tableau géant ultra-réaliste semble pouvoir basculer dans un paysage immense. Les peintures académiques ont eu une influence sur l'iconographie cinématographique[7]. Elles sont à mettre en lien avec tous les espaces représentés qui cherchent l'immersion pour les corps des observateurs, dont les panoramas sont les exemples parmi les plus spectaculaires.

La multiplication des panoramas, durant la même période, permet au corps spectatoriel d'entrer dans un univers virtuel avec la sensation d'être sur les toits d'une grande ville, ou devant un champ de bataille. La construction d'une profondeur virtuelle donne la sensation au corps de pouvoir avancer dans un paysage. La création de la fenêtre stéréoscopique, dans les projections cinématographiques, continue ce principe.

Les spectateurs happés

Placé dans une salle sombre face à des images immenses, changeantes et mouvantes, le spectateur expérimente un autre type d'immersion. Les lanternes magiques se perfectionnent durant le XIXᵉ siècle et certains spectacles sont spécialement illusionnistes, à l'instar du Fantascope de Robertson. Robertson projette notamment des images de fantômes sur des fumées en créant un saisissant effet de relief. Dans la salle le public peut voir une forme spectrale tridimensionnelle flotter dans les airs, avancer dans le noir. Le spectateur éprouve avec la peur un réflexe de recul. Il prend conscience de son corps car c'est une mise en mouvement musculaire concrète que peut provoquer le Fantascope: se lever, se baisser, fuir pour éviter la fumée lumineuse. De plus, le public des spectacles de Robertson est soumis à des effets kinesthésiques et multisensoriels : un orgue de verre accompagne les projections de spectres ; en plus de la musique, des senteurs d'herbes qui se consument donnent une atmosphère particulière ; pour certaines séances des assistants habillés de noir se glissent parmi les spectateurs en tenant un masque éclairé de l'intérieur comme un spectre qui approche[8]. Tous les sens sont convoqués pour faire réagir, physiquement, le public.

Une considération particulière du corps et des sens du spectateur sont impliqués dans ces spectacles. Ainsi Charles D'Almeida, lanterniste qui fait des projections stéréoscopiques anaglyphiques en 1858, écrit que ses « images en trois dimensions pouvaient être vues de différents points dans la pièce »[9]. Il conçoit donc les corps de ses spectateurs dans leur pluralité, et même dans leur mouvement : l'observateur peut se déplacer face à l'image en relief. Une trentaine d'années plus tard, alors que les articles scientifiques et les brevets se multiplient concernant la projection en relief, Alfred Molteni propose une séance de projection stéréoscopique anaglyphique qui reprend le principe des anaglyphes de D'Almeida. Avec une seule lanterne munie de deux objectifs sur lesquels se trouvent des filtres verts et rouges, le spectacle fait date par la fiabilité de son matériel[10]. Les spectateurs sont munis de lunettes avec verres rouges et verts afin de voir chaque image en relief. En d'autres termes, le dispositif de Molteni, de la même manière que celui de D'Almeida, transforme la vision des spectateurs, contrôle leurs sens eux-mêmes. Une lettre d'Alfred Molteni à Etienne-Jules Marey donne un peu plus de détails sur le ressenti suscité : « la sensation des trois dimensions est créée immédiatement et est très prononcée pour certaines images »[11]. Le public dans la salle peut donc se « projeter » dans la scène en profondeur de champ. Les spectateurs peuvent imaginer une interaction entre les vues en relief qui se développent sur un grand écran et leur propre corps. Le paysage reproduit en taille réelle donne envie d'avancer vers ce monde « virtuel ».

Le corps d'une seule personne peut aussi être ému par des vues stéréoscopiques animées. De très nombreux appareils proposent des vues en relief et en mouvement, pour un seul observateur happé par des paysages ou attiré par des personnages, à partir d'une série d'images fixes : par exemple le Stéréofantascope de Jules Duboscq en 1852, le Kinematoscope de Coleman Sellers en 1861 ou encore, en 1907, le Stéréo-Cinéma d'Emile Reynaud[12]. Il s'agit de se pencher sur

Figure 30.1. *La Nature*, issued December 27, 1890.

un appareil, non de voir une projection sur un écran. Le corps est sollicité en ce que le spectateur doit avancer ses yeux vers le double oculaire et, la plupart du temps, tourner une manivelle. En outre, certaines vues stéréoscopiques sollicitent fortement ses sens... On sait que de nombreuses visionneuses d'images en relief proposaient des photographies « osées ». Le corps d'un spectateur masculin (une partie du moins) pouvait se mettre en mouvement grâce à l'attrait érotique des images proposées.

Les projections d'images en mouvements, sans stéréoscopie, qui se développent à partir de 1896, font réagir violemment les corps du public. Dans la longue lignée du « réalisme par la perspective », la sensation du corps spectatoriel qui s'engouffre et se déplace dans un espace très vaste, un paysage avec des lignes de fuite, s'accentue avec les *travelogues et phantom rides*. De manière corollaire, *L'arrivée du train en gare* (1896) proposée par Louis Lumière et les nombreuses autres arrivées de train sont souvent décrites comme donnant un effet de réel ou un effet de relief. Il est ainsi significatif que Louis Lumière, 40 ans plus tard, en 1935, ait reposé sa caméra au même emplacement, dans la gare de La Ciotat, pour faire un remake de son film *en relief anaglyphique*[13]. Les films non stéréoscopiques des premiers temps font néanmoins déjà une très forte impression. Jean-Pierre Sirois-Trahan a recensé des réactions de spectateurs qui bougent face à l'image de la locomotive en mouvement et face à d'autres avancées spectaculaires (de véhicules, de cavaliers) vers la caméra[14]. Gorki, décrivant sa première projection, est très précis en ce qui concerne la façon dont son corps semble être « touché » par l'image :

> Tout à coup on entend cliqueter quelque chose ; tout disparaît et un train occupe l'écran. Il fonce sur nous – attention ! On dirait qu'il veut se précipiter dans l'obscurité où nous sommes, faire de nous un infâme amas de chairs déchirées et d'os en miettes.[15]

Sirois-Trahan a trouvé bien d'autres exemples d'articles semblant témoigner d'un mouvement des corps des spectateurs face à l'image, comme lorsque les cavaliers chargent dans la vue Lumière n°883 : « On a presque peur. On veut leur faire de la place », « vous allez être écrasés »[16]. Sirois-Trahan souligne que « les réactions *haptiques* (recul, sursaut physique, effroi, cris des spectateurs) sont nombreuses à l'époque »[17]. Et les exemples de mouvements dans la salle se multiplient en effet : « une tapissière [voiture à cheval] vient droit sur les spectateurs. Ma voisine est si bien sous le charme qu'elle se leva d'un bond ... et ne se rassit que lorsque la voiture tourna et disparut »[18] ; « je m'agite sur mon siège », « des dames [. . .] se reculent d'horreur », etc.[19] Si le débat continue pour savoir si les spectateurs du premier film de « train arrivant en gare » ont crié ou non, il est donc avéré que les projections « grandeur nature » d'une machine en mouvement dans un espace en profondeur de champ fait réagir le corps du spectateur, au moins par un léger mouvement pour contrebalancer l'effet de perspective et de jaillissement[20].

A la suite du succès « sensationnaliste » (au sens de sensation forte qui implique le corps) des arrivées de train, et d'autres véhicules, les *phantom rides*, qui désignent tous les trajets filmés à partir de l'avant d'une locomotive ou d'un métro, se multiplient. « On retient son souffle » dit un article du *New York Mail and Express* du 25 septembre 1897 à propos du film *Haverstraw Tunnel*, de Billy Bitzer[21]. Le spectateur prend donc conscience de son corps et a l'impression de s'engouffrer dans un tunnel. On a là un des effets très recherché dans les films stéréoscopiques et que j'ai dénommé "effet tunnel" et "effet vortex"[22]. Dans les travelogues filmés à partir du pare-bœufs de la locomotive, l'effet kinesthésique de réel donne au spectateur la sensation de vitesse. Ces films sont à la fois description de paysage que le spectateur ne connaît pas et immersion dans le réel. L'attraction perceptive est encore décuplée quand ces films sont projetés dans les Hale's tours (1905-c. 1915), une attraction foraine dans laquelle les spectateurs sont assis dans un véritable wagon qui bouge concrètement, avec de l'air envoyé sur le spectateur[23] ...

On pouvait mettre en mouvement encore plus nettement les corps du public, en combinant les procédés repris à toute une tradition de l'immersion[24]. Un cas particulier combine de nombreux éléments : mouvements sur vérins hydrauliques pour que le public bouge avec un faux bateau, musique, bruitage avec coups de sifflet, effets de vent, d'embruns et de variation lumineuse. Il s'agit du Maréorama[25]. La reconstitution virtuelle d'un voyage a sans doute atteint un niveau maximum avec cet immense dispositif pour l'Exposition Universelle de Paris en 1900. Le Maréorama, avec ses toiles déroulantes peintes par Hugo d'Alesi, recrée une traversée en bateau, mais sans utiliser de films[26]. On peut dire que les concepteurs de cette attraction sont allés plus loin que les panoramas habituels dans la recherche de réalisme. Il s'agissait de faire vivre une réalité physique en montant sur le pont d'un faux bateau. Le corps du passager était sollicité assez fortement par le tangage et roulis, et autres effets. Le processus de l'immersion obtenu par l'utilisation des dernières technologies est régulièrement retrouvé par différentes attractions et le Maréorama est symptomatique de cette recherche d'un corps « bougé » pour obtenir un plaisir des sens[27].

Les spectateurs ébranlés

Si le Maréorama peut éventuellement provoquer le mal de mer, d'autres reconstitutions de relief peuvent créer un léger malaise. Le Pepper's Ghost existait depuis 1862. Il servait surtout à intégrer des spectres dans des pièces de théâtre. Le Pepper's Ghost est réutilisé avec des films dans les années 1910. Un spectacle a du succès à Londres sous le nom de Kinoplastikon en 1913. Il allie les corps réels sur scène avec des corps filmés et projetés en 3-D sur une vitre. Un journaliste en rend compte ainsi: « Never before had I witnessed such a moving picture spectacle. It was practically the illusion of life, remarkable and astonishing, almost *uncanny* in its realness »[28]. Cette expression d'un malaise dû à une trop grande impression de réalité reviendra devant les projections « en relief ». Citons par exemple un article récent sur un procédé identique, basé sur le Pepper's Ghost (et improprement appelé « hologramme »). Quand Tupac, le rappeur assassiné, est « revenu » chanter sur scène en 2012, un journaliste réutilisa le terme « uncanny »[29]. Le corps tridimensionnel et animé a ainsi été exploré dans ses aspects les plus inquiétants, défiant la réalité, la physicalité, et la vie même.

L'intérêt essentiel du Kinoplastikon tient à l'absence d'écran visible. Les personnages projetés semblent flotter comme des spectres directement dans l'espace scénique. Le *Times* de Londres explique en 1913: « Visitors of the Scala Theater last week were able to see the latest development of the cinematographic art – living stereoscopic pictures shown without a screen »[30]. L'absence d'écran transforme la perception cinématographique habituelle, renforçant l'aspect haptique des images. Celles-ci sont en outre accompagnées de façon synchrone par le Vivaphone (un des appareils de reproduction du son sur disque). La publicité devant la salle proclame : « Singing, Talking, Moving Picture Figures in Solid Stereoscopic Relief, Without a Screen »[31]. Images et sons participent donc à créer cette « étrange » impression de réel, dans un espace qui confond les corps réels et immatériels, voix performées et enregistrées. La vue et l'ouïe du spectateur sont autant stimulées que trompées[32].

Cette tromperie des sens du spectateur est un ressort fondamentalement ludique. La vision d'un film en relief peut pousser l'observateur à vouloir « toucher » les objets qui « dépassent dans la salle ». Les enfants ne sont pas les seuls à vouloir attraper les bonbons Haribo que la publicité 3-D fait jaillir dans les cinémas des années 2010. Déjà un siècle auparavant, les journalistes expliquent être tentés d'agripper les feuillages qui semblent surgir de l'écran lors d'une projection de films stéréoscopiques d'Edwin S. Porter que certains reçoivent comme « précurseurs d'une nouvelle ère dans le réalisme cinématographique »[33] – c'est encore l'abusif « effet de réalité » qui est mis en avant.

Connu pour avoir filmé des trains et un gangster menaçant le public (ne s'est-on pas baissé pour éviter le pistolet face caméra dans *The Great Train Robbery* [Edwin S. Porter, 1903] ?), Porter est aussi l'un des premiers à mettre au point une stéréoscopie anaglyphique sur un projecteur standard, présenté à l'Astor Theater de New York le 10 juin 1915. Il explique que c'est l'aboutissement de dix ans de recherche, mais ne donne que des éléments généraux et ne précise pas les détails techniques[34]. Nous savons qu'il y avait des lunettes en carton, qui gênaient le chroniqueur du *Moving Picture World* et le faisait espérer que dans une étape suivante la projection en relief se verrait à l'œil nu. Cet élément gêne son visage, mais son corps se prend au jeu :

> Holding these glasses before the eyes, one gains a truly stereoscopic effect that is nothing short of startling in lifelikeness. The screen seems to be brought to within a few feet on the onlooker and the objects animate and inanimate stand out in correct perspective, quiet as though the vision were centered on an actual room, a landscape or whatever the subject may be.[35]

La perspective recréée permet de se sentir comme dans une « véritable pièce », ou un vrai « paysage naturel », nous dit le journaliste. L'impression est donc que le corps est dans un espace virtuel. Si l'image contemplée sans lunettes est décrite comme distordue à cause de la superposition des images rouges et vertes, avec les lunettes « the reds and greens are neutralized into an even tone and out of the chaos, a duplicate life emerges »[36]. Cette « vie dupliquée » est constituée

MOTION PICTURE NEWS   Vol. 11. No. 26.

Stereoscopic Pictures Give Sense of Depth to Images

Invention of Porter, of Famous Players, and Waddell, Late of Edison, Recently Shown at Private Exhibition in New York, Promises Revolutionary Improvement in Screen Vision

STEREOSCOPIC motion pictures, an invention on which Edwin S. Porter, of the Famous Players Film Company, has been working for about eight years, the last two of which have been in collaboration with William E. Waddell, formerly of the Edison company, have advanced so far that they were shown recently at a private exhibition.

The pictures really achieve the third dimension on the screen. That is to say, the figures have the apppearance of depth, or perspective, as well as breadth and height. They were viewed through colored lenses, green for the right eye and red for the left. The lenses may be made from glass celluloid or any transparent matter. Thus viewed the pictures have color value, but not full tones. Also, due to the eyes superimposing two images, as they do constantly in every day life, it is hard to portray action quickly crossing the lens by this stereoscopic photography. For instance, a horseman could ride at full speed straight toward the camera and be distinct, but he could not ride across the field of vision and be distinct.

From this it follows that many times, when the stereoscopic pictures portray action, the registration is indistinct. The figures seem to have three dimensions, but, through some illusion, they seem very close to the eye but small. Also the eyes feel the strain of viewing the pictures through differently colored lenses.

The stereoscopic process, according to Mr. Porter, is entirely in the film by the time it reaches the exhibitor, and may be projected on any projection machine or on any size screen.

But, because of the need for colored lenses and the sometimes imperfect registration, it is fair to say that stereoscopic pictures are not yet ready to be a commercial success. But those shown by Messrs. Porter and Waddell are far ahead of any others yet seen; so far ahead that it seems likely that the hardest obstacles have been overcome, and that perfecting the process for commercial use may be only a matter of a few months.

A stereoscopic effect can only be seen with two eyes. The reason for this lies in the fact that the distance between the eyes causes the two optics to see any article, a chair leg for instance, at slightly differing angles. The right eye sees the chair leg, and the left eye sees it. But the brain only gets one impression. So, to some extent, two eyes see around behind the chair leg, and so demonstrate, ocularly, the presence of the third dimension, depth.

The old stereoscope of childhood was a practical application of this theory. The right eye saw the right picture, and only the right picture. The left eye saw the left picture and that alone. As the pictures were the same scene photographed by lenses about as far apart as human eyes a stereoscopic effect was attained.

In obtaining a stereoscopic effect on the screen it is necessary to have two pictures, and have each eye see its own picture and only its own picture. Porter and Waddell have accomplished this by projecting simultaneously a green and a red picture, the pictures having been photographed at the same time through two lenses. Then, that each eye may only see its own picture, the green and red colored glasses are used. The green lens kills off one picture for one eye, and the red lens kills off the other picture for the other eye. So each eye sees its own picture, and only its own.

EDWIN S. PORTER

picture, at the same differing angles as the human eyes behold any object, and the result is a stereoscopic effect.

Naturally the stereoscopic effect, with three dimensions, is more true to life than the usual effect with two dimensions. So there is a great possibility in stereoscopic motion photography, which the invention of Porter and Waddell realizes.

Mr. Porter himself expressed his ideas on the subject by saying: "Before I am satisfied it will be possible to have the true perspective of objects and persons as they appear in life on the screen without any artificial aid to the naked eye."

The subjects shown at the private exhibition were scenic views, some of them showing Niagara Falls, and scenes from some Famous Players productions, such as "Jim the Penman" and "The Morals of Marcus."

Figure 30.2. *Motion Picture News*, June 1915.

essentiellement de paysages comme le rédacteur du *Moving Picture World* l'explique. La série de trois bobines, montage de petits films en relief, produite par Zukor, se compose de travelogues et d'extraits de films de fiction. Le spectateur peut donc croire son corps au contact de vastes espaces en relief, ou face à des phénomènes naturels spectaculaires (les chutes du Niagara).

Le rédacteur du *Motion Picture News* est trop gêné par les lunettes pour être conquis[37], mais celui de *Motography* admire le nouvel appareillage, en particulier lorsque des arbres sont vus au premier plan et que les branches semblent s'étendre au-dessus de la scène (« the branches of the trees appeared to extend right out over the stage »). Cela donne l'impression que l'observateur au premier rang pourrait attraper ces arbres (« grabbed one of the branches »)[38]. Il y a donc surgissement et effet haptique avec l'impression de proximité entre les objets filmés et le corps dans la salle.

La part de subjectivité de chaque personne est à prendre en compte. Les trois comptes rendus de cette séance montre des réactions corporelles différentes. Dans le *New York Dramatic Mirror*, comme dans le *Moving Picture World*, on trouve que les actions rapides ne ressortent pas clairement[39]. Lynde Denig, rédacteur du *Moving Picture World*, observe que le plus mauvais passage (et donc celui qui le fait « sortir » du film) est une danse orientale « in which the performers were blurred [flou] and the film in its entirety shimmered [scintillait], something like a reflection on a lake. Then there were other instances in which quick moments failed to register »[40]. Au contraire, le rédacteur anonyme du *Mirror* a eu l'impression de voir une véritable pièce de théâtre sur la scène et non pas des silhouettes fantomatiques (*shadowy figures*). Lui aussi trouve que les branches d'arbres semblent flotter dans la salle. Le rapport du corps au film en relief s'exprime dans le besoin de croire à ces trois dimensions recréées par notre cerveau. Denig s'en rend bien compte quand il explique :

> These pictures will appeal first for reason of their novelty, then because of the wonderful effects obtained, and after that, when they had become familiar, there would be the same old demand for an interesting story [. . .]. There must be no break to spoil the illusion.[41]

Conclusion

Contrairement à Jonathan Crary, qui dans sa conclusion, renvoie les expériences de l'observateur à la vision panoptique de Foucault, nous ne pensons pas que la sollicitation du corps au sein des dispositifs envisagés dans cette étude puisse pousser vers un monde totalitaire[42]. Tout dépend de la façon dont la technique est utilisée[43]. Le corps du spectateur n'est pas forcément contraint. Il s'exprime. Il bouge. Jusque vers 1915 le corps du spectateur est très libre dans les salles où des films sont projetés. On ne peut pas trouver de « corps passif » face à un écran. J'ai expliqué ailleurs la participation orale et physique du public[44]. Les gens se lèvent, crient, boivent, mangent, pendant que des films sont projetés. De plus, bruitages, voix du bonimenteur-conférencier, chants d'opéra, musique jouée dans la salle font vibrer les corps, provoquent des émotions. La projection en relief de Porter en 1915, montre que le corps est encore plus sollicité par le film en relief. L'espace virtuel en 3-D favorise les mouvements et réactions corporelles du spectateur, ou au moins la prise en compte de son propre corps. Moins de sept années après cette première projection sur grand écran, des films stéréoscopiques sont montrés en nombre, puisque la première grande vague de films stéréoscopiques s'étend de 1922 à 1926, avec des effets de jaillissement qui incitent le spectateur à se baisser ou à tourner la tête. Il est néanmoins nécessaire de se méfier de la présentation en filiation directe, dans une vision téléologique, des projections de 1915 et celles de 1922. La stéréoscopie est un des phénomènes de l'industrie cinématographique qui a connu le plus de résurgences[45]. Mais à chaque fois, que ce soit par jaillissement, immersion, ou par d'autres phénomènes comme l'effet-tunnel, le corps spectatoriel est impliqué.

Tous ces éléments des années 1800 à 1915 peuvent être mis en parallèle avec les procédés actuels qui continuent de faire réagir les corps dans un espace sonore en 3-D. Les machines de vision stéréoscopiques existant depuis le milieu du XIXe siècle permettaient de s'abstraire du monde extérieur. Penché sur la visionneuse, les yeux concentrés sur les cartes stéréoscopiques fixes ou en mouvement, le corps est traversé de sensations dues à l'illusion transmise par le cerveau. Le très contemporain Oculus Rift continue le Kinematoscope de 1861 (même s'il n'y a pas de lien direct entre les deux procédés). Les trois systèmes les plus utilisés en stéréoscopie aujourd'hui existaient déjà en 1915 : l'anaglyphique (toujours utilisé pour des BD[46] ou des vidéos sur Youtube), la projection à éclipses (tous les système de lunettes actives, plus efficace et surtout utilisés en France dans les salles d'arts et d'essai) et les filtres polarisant (les lunettes passives utilisées aujourd'hui dans tous les grands circuits commerciaux). Depuis l'apparition du Fusion Camera System en 2005, pour attirer au cinéma ceux qui pourraient rester devant un écran chez eux, les cinémas proposent de « réanimer » le corps et de l'immerger dans un espace de sons et d'images où le spectateur peut virtuellement se déplacer. Le film en relief repose sur des effets de profondeur, de surgissement et d'environnement sonore, dont la tradition remonte au moins aux spectacles de lanterne magique et à toute la série culturelle spectaculaire qui essaie d'immerger le corps pour le mouvoir, ou l'émouvoir.

MARTIN BARNIER est professeur en études cinématographiques à l'université Lumière Lyon 2. Il est l'auteur de *Bruits, cris, musiques de films. Les projections avant 1914*, *Le Cinéma 3-D: Histoire, économie, technique, esthétique* (avec Kira Kitsopanodou), et *Une brève histoire du cinema (1895-2015)* (avec Laurent Jullier).

Notes

1. Martin Barnier, *Bruits, cris, musiques de films. Les projections avant 1914*, Rennes, Presses Universitaires de Rennes, 2010.
2. Michel de Certeau (entretien avec Georges Vigarello), « Histoire de corps », *Esprit*, n°1667, février 1982, p.179.
3. Voir par exemple Alain Corbin, Jean-Jacques Courtine, Georges Vigarello (dir.), *Histoire du corps*, Paris, Seuil, 2005/2006; Dominique Memmi, Dominique Guillo et Olivier Martin (dir.), *La tentation du corps. Corporéité et sciences sociales*, Paris, EHESS, 2009.
4. Ray Zone, *Stereoscopic Cinema and The Origins of 3-D Film (1838-1952)*, Lexington, University Press of Kentucky, 2007, p.13.
5. A l'instar du cabinet stéréoscopique d'Alexander Becker ou du stéréorama (*Ibid.*, p. 15, 20). Voir aussi William Darrah, *The World of Stereographs* (Gettysburg, PA: Darrah, 1977).
6. De manière générale, c'est surtout la peinture de genre qui trouve des dimensions jusqu'alors inédites, mais certaines peintures d'histoire adoptent aussi des immenses formats.
7. Voir Laurent Guido et Valentine Robert, « Jean-Léon Gérôme : un peintre d'histoire présumé « cinéaste », *1895*, n°63, avril 2011, 8-23, URL : http://1895.revues.org/4322.
8. Laurent Mannoni, *Le Grand art de la lumière et de l'ombre: Archéologie du cinéma*, Paris, Nathan, 1994, p.157.
9. Joseph Charles d'Almeida, « Nouvel appareil stéréoscopique », *Les Comptes rendus de l'académie des sciences*, n°47, 12 juillet 1858, p.61-63.
10. Cet événement qui a lieu à Paris le 8 juin 1890 est sans doute la première projection anaglyphique devant un groupe de personnes avec une lanterne à double lentille de projection verticale.
11. Lettre de Molteni à Marey du 5 décembre 1890, dans Thierry Lefebvre, Jacques Malthête et Laurent Mannoni (dir.), *Lettres d'Étienne-Jules Marey à Georges Demenÿ 1880-1894*, Paris, AFRHC/BIFI, 2000, p.495-496.
12. Ray Zone, *op. cit.*, p.28-32.
13. Hervé Lauwick, « Louis Lumière va présenter ce jour même à l'Académie des Sciences son invention nouvelle », *Le Jour*, 25 février 1935, et « Optique. Ecrans colorés pour projections stéréoscopiques: Notes de M. Louis Lumière (lundi 25 février 1935) », dans *Comptes rendus hebdomadaires des séances de l'Académie des Sciences*, n°200, janvier-juin 1935, p.701-704.
14. Jean-Pierre Sirois-Trahan, « Mythes et limites du train-qui-fonce-sur-les-spectateurs », dans Veronica Innocenti et Valentina Re (dir.), *Limina. Le Soglie del Film/Film's Thresholds*, Udine, Forum, 2004, p.203-221.
15. Maxime Gorki, article paru dans le journal *Nijegorodskilistok*, 4 juillet 1896 traduit par Claude-Henri Rochat dans Jay Leyda, *Kino. Histoire du cinéma russe et soviétique*, Lausanne, L'Âge d'Homme, 1976, p.472-473.
16. Cité par Jean-Pierre Sirois-Trahan, *op. cit.* p.207.
17. *Ibid.*
18. H. de Parville, *Le Journal des débats*, 17 juillet 1895. Cité par Jean-Pierre Sirois-Trahan, *op. cit.*, p.207.
19. *Ibid.*
20. *Ibid.*, p.203-221.
21. Cité par Robert C. Allen, « Contra the Chaser Theory », dans John L. Fell (dir.), *Film Before Griffith*, Berkeley, University of California Press, 1983, p.110.
22. Martin Barnier et Kira Kitsopanidou, *Le Cinéma 3-D. Histoire, économie, technique, esthétique*, Paris, Armand Colin, 2015.

23. Lauren Rabinovitz, « From *Hale's Tours* to *Star Tours*: virtual voyages, travel ride films, and the delirium of the hyper-real », dans Jeffrey Ruoff (dir.), *Virtual Voyages: Cinema and Travel*, Durham (NC), Duke University Press, 2006, p.42-60.
24. Alison Griffiths, *Shivers down Your Spine: Cinema, Museums, and the Immersive View*, New York, Columbia University Press, 2013.
25. Errki Huthamo, *Illusions in Motion. Media Archaeology of the Moving Panorama and Related Spectacles*, Cambridge (MA), MIT Press, 2013, p.315-316.
26. « The Mareorama at the Paris Exposition », *Scientific American*, 29 Septembre 1900, p.198.
27. Voir Erkki Huhtamo, « Encapsulated Bodies in Motion: Simulators and the Quest for Total Immersion », dans Simon Penny (dir.), *Critical Issues in Electronic Media*, Albany (NY), State University of New York Press, 1995, p.159-186.
28. J. Cher, « A Glimpse of Vienna and the Kinoplastikon », *The Bioscope*, 20 mars 1913, p.82-83. C'est nous qui soulignons.
29. Gerrick D. Kennedy, « Coachella 2012: Tupac 'Responds' to His Reincarnation », *Los Angeles Times*, 16 avril 2012.
30. *The Times* (Londres), 28 avril 1913.
31. Ray Zone, *op. cit.*, p.69.
32. Martin Barnier et Kira Kitsopanidou, *op. cit.*, p.163. Les *Pepper's Ghost* continuent aujourd'hui d'être utilisés pour créer des personnages virtuels en trois dimensions, comme des chanteuses japonaises dessinées qui rassemblent des foules dans des stades (les Vocaloïdes Hatsune Miku, Meiko, Rin & Len, etc.). Le public danse en suivant les chorégraphies indiquées par les chanteuses virtuelles. Le corps obéit à un « fantôme ».
33. Lynde Denig, « Stereoscopic Pictures Screened. Edwin S. Porter and W. E. Waddell Show Remarkable Three-Dimension Photography to the Audience at the Astor Theater », *Moving Picture World*, 2 juin 1915, p.2072.
34. *Ibid.* Voir aussi le film documentaire *Before the Nickelodeon : The Early Cinema of Edwin S. Porter* (Charles Musser, 1982).
35. *Ibid.*
36. *Ibid.*
37. « Stereoscopic Pictures Give Sense of Depth to Images », *Motion Picture*, 3 juillet 1915, p.62.
38. C.R.C., « Stereoscopic Pictures Shown », *Motography*, 26 juin 1915, p.1040.
39. « Stereoscopic films shown », *New York Dramatic Mirror*, 16 juin 1915, p.21.
40. Lynde Denig, *op. cit.*
41. *Ibid.* Pour un commentaire rétrospectif du producteur de ces films stéréoscopiques, Adolph Zukor, sur leur caractère quasi visionnaire, « en avance sur leur temps », voir Adolph Zukor et Dale Kramer, *The Public is never wrong. The Autobiography of Adolph Zukor*, New York, Putnam's Sons, 1953, p.121.
42. Jonathan Crary, *Techniques de l'observateur : Vision et modernité au XIXe siècle*, Frédéric Maurin (trad.), Bellevaux, Dehors, 2016.
43. Martine Bubb, « La *camera obscura*, au-delà du "dispositif foucaldien" proposé par Jonathan Crary dans *L'art de l'observateur* », *Appareil*, Article en ligne, 20 juin 2008, URL : http://appareil.revues.org/461.
44. Martin Barnier, *op. cit.*
45. Martin Barnier et Kira Kitsopanidou, *op. cit.*
46. Matthias Picard, *Jim Curious : Voyage au cœur de l'océan*, Strasbourg, Editions 2024, 2012.

Index

Page numbers in italics refer to figures.

Abbeville Courthouse (1913), 212
Abbey Theatre (Dublin), 249, 250–51, 252
Abel, Richard, 3
Abyss, The (1910), 135
acting: dangerous situations, 123, 167, 171; fantastical appeal, 125–26, 131, 133n14; physical demands, 119–20, 123, 167, 171; playing ugly characters, 209–12, *211*; studio life and, 128
adolescence, 219–20, 231–37, 238n11
Adriaensens, Vito, 11
advertisements, 85, 103, 268, 275; "black villages," 98–99; body-care products, 35; dance instruction films, 276, *277*, 278, *279*, 287n12; of nervous effects of cinema, 243–45, 246
After Death (1915), 193–95, *194*
Agamben, Giorgio, 115n1
agency, 114, 204n17
ag-gag laws, 82, 84n35
Ah! La barbe (1905), 177
Albera, François, 41
Albertini, Luciano, 152, 155n30
Aldini, Carlo, 152, 155n30
Alonso García, Luis, 59
Altenloh, Emilie, 222, 225
Americanitis, 233, 234
American Mutoscope and Biograph Company, 27, 86–88, 227
Anae, Nicole, 150
Anger, Kenneth, 298n19
animal bodies: cataloging, 74; and human hybrid bodies, 178; physiological experiments, 59, 74–78; vivisection films, 79–82, *80*
animated body, 261, 268
Antoine, André, 171, 172n13

anxiety, 219, 221, 225, 242; in youth, 232. *See also* nervousness
Arrivée du train en gare, L' (1897), 266
art and nature boundary, 30
artificial darkness, 16
Artists' Studio, The (Hyde), 163
Assiette au beurre, L', 37
assimilation, 106, 109, 111, 113
Association pour la connaissance de l'histoire de l'Afrique contemporaine (ACHAC), 95, 96, 97
Atleta fantasma, L' (1919), 152
Attack on the Mill, The (1910), 258
Aubert, François, 181–83, *184*, 185–86, 189n17
audiences: cinema space and, 275–76; educating, 276, 283, 286n1; emotional responses, 7, 81–82, 236; execution films and reactions of, 85–86, 88; imitation instinct, 2, 226; impressionability, 6, 219; nervous reactions, 220, 226, 240–46, 248n17; point of view, 15; screen bodies and, 276, 278, 283; sexual desires, 6–7, 223–25, 227–28, 258; stage performers and, 253; supernatural themes and, 54; women's behavior, 221–23, 226–27, 228n1; working-class, 128, 220, 252–54 , 257–58. *See also* spectatorship
Auerbach, Jonathan, 117, 118
Ausonia, Mario. *See* Guaita-Ausonia, Mario
automaton, 42–43
Avenging a Crime (1904), 90

Bachelard, Gaston, 197
Baignade de nègres (1896), 99–100
Balcerzak, Scott, 125
ballrooms, 276, 278, 285; Tanz-Kinema (Berlin), 279, 281, 282, 283–84, 286, 288n17

Barber Shop, The (1893), 175–76
Barbier facétieux, Le (1903), 176
Barbier fin de siècle, Le (1896), 176
Barker, Jennifer, 15–18, 22–23
Barnardo, Thomas, 107–8
Barnier, Martin, 261
Barthes, Roland, 200
Bauer, Evgenii, 173, 198, 203n11, 205n25; *After Death* (1915), 193–95, *194*; *The Dying Swan* (1916), 191, 204n20; *Happiness of the Eternal Night* (1915), 194; *Life for a Life* (1916), 199–200, *200*, *201*
Bazin, André, 74, 182–83, 186, 201
Bean, Jennifer, 120–21
before-and-after pictures: cinematic contributions, 103–4, 112–15; doctored, 108; of Indigenous children, 3, 60, 103, 105–110, *108*; of racialized photography, 6; space of the interval, 104–5, 110–12
Belle Époque, 41, 147
Benjamin, Walter, 231, 235, 237, 281
Bernard, Claude, 74–79, *76*, 81, 83n7, 83n14; wife of, 83n16
Bernard, Ferdinand Bon, 181–82, *183*
Bertillon, Alphonse, 59
Berton, Mireille, 219, 241
Big Swallow, The (1901), 12, 14–16, *17*, 20
Biograph, 160–61, *162*, 163, 165nn21–22
Bioskop films, 134
Birth of a Nation, The (1915), 3, 90
Birth of the Pearl (1901), 162
Birth of Venus (1899), 158, *162*
black bodies: executions and lynchings, 88–89, 90; exhibition and exploitation, 60, 94, 96, 97–99; otherness of, 95; reduced to objects, 100–101; staged for film, 99–100
Blanchard, Pascal, 95, 96, 97
Blom, Ivo, 118
Blumenbach, Johann Friedrich, 96
Blumenberg, Hans, 205n26
bodily transformation, 25–26
body builders, 147
body-coding, 3
body language, 117
Booth, Walter, 52, 54
Bosch, Hieronymus, 31

bourgeoisie, 241, 242, 245–46
boxing, 134, 140–44, *141*, 153n7
Braun, Marta, 75
breath and breathing, 199–200
Brewster, Eugene, 213
British Medical Journal, 80–81
Brooke, Michael, 15
Browning, Robert, 51, 55n4
Burns-Moir Fight (1907), 254

Cabiria (1914), 147–48
Calino a mangé du cheval (1908), 43
Call of the Wild (1908), 113, *114*
camera obscura: description and applications, 289–90; embodiments, 3–4; exhibitions, *290*, 291–94, *293*, 295–96; spectatorship and sexuality, 262, 294–95, 298n19; women operators, 296–97
cameras, 14–15
Capellani, Albert, 118, 168, 171
Capellani, Paul: *Le Chemineau* (1905), 168, 172n13; *L'Enlisé du Mont Saint-Michel* (1908), *168*, 168–69, *169*, 172n7; *L'Enlisé* (sculpture), 167, *170*
Career of Crime, No. 5: The Death Chair (1900), 88
Carlisle Indian Industrial School, 103, 105–9, *108*, 110–12, 114
Carr, William, 88
Carrière, Eugène, 196
Cartwright, Lisa, 75
cataloging bodies, 6, 59, 96, 98
Catlin, George, 105
censorship, 6, 85, 135, 283, 287n1; first known example, 163; rise of, 228; struggles with, 159, 165n18
Chaney, Lon, 212
Chaplin, Charlie, 125, 235
Charcot, Jean-Martin, 65
Chefranova, Oksana, 173–74
Cherepnin, Alexander, 192, 193, 201, 203n7
Chesters, Timothy, 53
Chinese Mystery, A (1902), 51
Ching Ling Foo, 54, 57n31
Chirurgie fn de siècle (1901), 40–41
Chirurgie mécanique (1903), 41

Chirurgien distrait, Un (1909), 36
Choate, J. N., 107
Chomón, Segundo de, 52, 177–78
Christie, Ian, 11
Christmas Carol, A (Dickens), 47–48, 54, 56n9
chronophotography, 103, 112; compared to before-and-after pictures, 105, 110; of Muybridge and Marey, 13, 25, 111
cinema of attractions, 2–3, 21, 290
Clark, Kenneth, 157
Cleveland Leader (newspaper), 88
Cœur fidèle (1923), 193
colonialism: conquest, 97; expropriation, 109; Indigenous elimination, 106, 108; timeline and rescue narrative, 60, 111–12, 115; visual politics of, 114
communication, 236
Conan Doyle, Arthur, 54, 58nn33–34
Condon, Denis, 220
consciousness, 16–17, 22, 92, 170, 271
control of bodies: of animals, 78–79; dance instruction and, 285; of patients, 36, 59, 62, 66, 70–71
Cordiglia, Adrián, 186
Course à la perruque, La (1906), 179
Crafton, Donald, 261
Craig, Gordon, 192
Crary, Jonathan, 3–4, 111, 262, 271, 290, 294
cross-dressing, 179
Cruelty to Animals Act (1876), 80
cultural traditions, 46, 49–50, 53–54
Curtis, Edward, 115n4
Curtis, Scott, 75, 242, 275
Czolgosz, Leon, 87

D'Almeida, Charles, 265
Daly, Ann, 139–40
dance: ballet, 191–93, 195, 204n20; cakewalk, 137, 137–38; Charleston, 286; foxtrot, 285; "gaucho dance" in *The Abyss* (1910), 135, 136; modern, 142; Norwegian cultural identity and, 142–44; sensory-bodily reactions, 286, 288n27; sequence in *The Demon* (1911), 135–37; sequences in *Under the Law of Change* (1911), 137–40; synchronization of music, 281, 284; tango, 200. See also dance-instruction films
dance instruction films: early films and advertisements, 276, 277, 278–79, 279, 280, 285–86; exhibition spaces, 261–62; spectator's body and, 275–76, 286; Tanz-Kinema screenings, 279, 281, 282, 283–84
danger: faced by actors, 123, 167, 171; of film industry, 7, 119–21; of studio life, 125, 128, 129, 130
Dans les mansardes de Paris (1924), 149
databases, 8
Daughter of the Revolution, The (1918), 134, 140–43, 141
Davenport, Ira and William, 55n4
death: embalmment, 173, 181–82, 184, 185, 188n12; eyes and, 173, 182; life and, 28, 32; mask, 197, 201–2; moment of, 59, 167, 170–71; technologies and, 181. See also executions; lynchings
decapitation, 41, 42, 85
de Certeau, Michel, 263
deCordova, Richard, 123, 132n8, 210
Delage, Michel, 170
Demon, The (1911), 135, 136, 137, 139, 141, 143, 144
Denig, Lynde, 269, 271
Derrida, Jacques, 77
Désile, Patrick, 41
Diable Géant ou le Miracle de la Madone, Le (1901), 31
Diary of a Nobody (Grossmith), 51, 57n18
Dietrichson, Hedvig, 139
Dippie, Brian, 107
disembodiment, 22, 245; camera obscura and, 3, 262
dismembered bodies, 20–21, 37, 39–41, 40
dispositifs, 5, 276, 285, 287n5
Doane, Mary Ann, 66
doctors: caricatures, 35–36; educational films, 64–66, 70–71; machines and, 41–43, 42; satirical images, 36–37, 38, 39, 40, 42; surgical films, 37–39, 40–41
Domitor, 3
Doyen, Dr., 37–39
Duel au pistolet (1896), 182–83, 183, 186, 187nn6–7

Dulac, Nicolas, 43
Duncan, Isadora, 139, 143
Dupont-Bloch, Sébastien, 118
Dying Swan, The (1916), 191–92, 204n20

Edinburgh Camera Obscura, 291–92, 298n5; Calton Hill, 292, 295–96; Nelson Monument, 295–96, 298n26
Edison, Thomas, 13
Edison Manufacturing Company, 13, 27; barbershop themes, 173, 175; execution films, 85, 87; filmography, 175; supernatural themes, 51–52, 54
educational films, 64–66, 70–71. *See also* dance instruction films
Elcott, Noam, 16
elemental media, 191, 202
engravings: of racialized bodies, 96, 98; *The Three Graces* (1848), 157
Enlisé, L' (Capellani), 167, *170*, 170–71, 172n3
Enlisé du Mont Saint-Michel, L' (1908), *168*, 168–69, *169*, 172n7
enslaved children, 107, 108–9, 116n12
epistemology, 3–4
Epstein, Jean, 174, 193
eroticism: of camera obscura, 294; of cinematic spaces, 221, 265; in dance, 135, 137; of *poses plastiques*, 150; shaving and, 177; of stereoscopic images, 265; women's legs, 176. *See also* nudity
evolution, human, 233–34
excess, bodily, 121, 253–54
Excursión Escolar con el Dr. Maestre al Manicomio de Ciempozuelos: description and purpose, 64; psychiatric patients' bodies, 59, 65–66, *67–69*, 70–71; technical qualities and improvisation, 61–62; title card and first frame, 63
Execution by Hanging, An (1898), 88–89
Execution of a Murderess (1905), 86–87, *87*
Execution of a Spy (1900), 87–88
Execution of Czolgosz (1901), 87, 93n11
Execution of Mary, Queen of Scots, The (1895), 85–87, 89, 92
executions: American-made films, 59, 85–89, *87*, 91; of Antonio Navarro, 181–82; of

Emperor Maximilian, 182–83, *184*, 185–86, 188n12
exhibitions: of black bodies, 95–96, 102n17; "black villages," 60, 94, 97–99, 100; camera obscura, *290*, 291–94, *293*, 295–96; nude bodies, 157–58, 163
exoticism, 95–96, 97, 98, 138
Extraordinary Chinese Magic (1902), 51, 56n11
eyes: deep-set, 210; dying person's, 173, 182; glass, 185, 188n10, 188n12; twinkling of, 197–98; unblinking, 193–94

face: ballerina's, 191–92, 193, 201; close-ups, 173–74, 193–95, *194*, 197; clouds and air and, 199–200, 205n31; as death mask, 201–2; expressions, 170, 193, 209, 213–15, *214*; history of, 202n1; sky-gazing, 195–96; transformations, 191, 206–7, 212; trick effects of, 177–78. *See also* eyes; makeup
fantascope, 264–65
fantasy, 11, 13, 119, 142, 294
fashion, 35
features, bodily, 2, 59, 173–75. *See also* eyes; face; hair
Fédération Internationale des Archives du Film (FIAF), 2
Felke, Naldo, 241, 242
female bodies: eroticized or sexualized, 6, 221, 223–25, 227–28; legs, 176; as living statues, 26, 29–30, 34n22; nude, 118, 157–61, 163; physicality of, 117, 120–21, *124*, 127. *See also* dance; femininity
femininity, 130, 179, 222; of dancers, 118, 137, 140, 142, 144; film viewing and, 226–27
Figaro, Le (newspaper), 185
fighting, 118, 140. *See also* boxing
film culture, 1, 3, 6, 288n27; Western, 286n1
Filmoteca Española, 61, 62
"film's body" concept: Sobchack and Barker, 4, 16–18, 22; technology and, 18–19; viewers and, 5, 22
flaneur, 251–52
form and formlessness, 174, 191, 202
forzuti (strongmen), 118, 146, 151–52, 154n28
Foucault, Michel, 16, 72n18, 271
Freud, Sigmund, 232

From Manger to Cross (1914), 212
Fullerton, John, 173

Gahéry, Rodolphe, 60
Garb, Tamar, 147, 149
Garbo, Greta, 205n31
Gaudreault, André, 43
Gaumont, 27, 71n2, 159
Gaupp, Robert, 240, 242
gaze, 166n37, 195–98, 202, 297; male, 157, 225, 228; middle-class, 251; woman's, 166n32, 296
gender norms: chivalry, 120; hair and, 173, 175, 179–80; makeup and, 206, 212; at movie theaters, 7, 219, 221; slapstick comedy, 117, 121, 130; spectatorship, 166n32; vivisection and, 78, 83n20
genres, body, 3, 5, 7, 119, 132n1; working-class, 254, 257
German Cinema Debate, 240–46
gesture, 235–36
ghostly bodies: cultural traditions of, 46, 49–50, 53; fin de siècle films, 51–53, 55n1; illusory techniques, 48–49, 57n23, 268; modernization and, 54–55; national variations of, 47–48, 53–54; supernatural figures, 49–50
Ginsburg, Faye, 114
gladiators: films, 146, 148–49; paintings of, 147, 154n25, 264; *poses plastiques*, 149–52, *151*
Gladtvet, Ottar, 134, 140, 142, 143
Goethe, 23, 25, 53
Gorki, Maxim, 266–67
Great Train Robbery, The (1903), 269
Greek culture, 26, 29, 31, 149
Grieveson, Lee, 142, 232
Griffith, D. W., 90, 113, 210
Griffiths, Alison, 296
Gross, Kenneth, 32
Guaita-Ausonia, Mario: retirement in Marseille, 154n29; *Spartaco* (1913), 146, *148*, 148–49; Trio Ausonia tour and later films, 149, 150–52, *151*, 154n26
Gundersen, Jens Christian, 135, 140, 143
Gunning, Tom, 3, 12, 110, 181, 284; on ghosts, 46, 55; on impossible bodies, 4–5; meaning of "flickering," 198

Guy, Alice, 40–41, 42
gymnastics, 154n30

Häfker, Hermann, 242
hair: baldness and hair pieces, 178–79; barbershops, 173, 175–77; beards and shaving, 177–78; cutting, 107; gender norms and, 179–80; woman's underarm, 30
Hall, G. Stanley, 219–20, 231–37, 239n23
Hamilton, Susan, 78
Hammerstein, Oscar, 26
Hammerton, Jenny, 287n12
Hammond, John, 292
Hanging of William Carr, The (1897), 88
Hansen, Miriam, 237, 275
haptic visuality, 4–5
Hardie, Philip, 30
Hatôt, Georges, 52
Haunted Castle, The (1897), 52
Hearne, Joanna, 60
Hecht, Ann, 56n9
Heidegger, Martin, 20, 23, 77
Heise, William, 85, 175
Hennefeld, Maggie, 125
historiographies, 1, 8, 286n1
Holloway, Joseph: cinemagoing experiences, 220, 252–58; criticism of his diary, 249–50; family and profession, 251–52; image, *250*; interactions with Joyce, 249, 255
Hollywood, 117, 131, 174; studio culture, 123, 128
Holme, Daniel, 51
Holmes, Sherlock, 54, 58n33
Hotely, Mae, 210, *211*
Houillère, Jérémy, 11
housemaids, 125–27, 132n11
Hugo, Victor, 160, 161
"human zoos," 60, 94, 96, 97
hygiene movement, 35, 243, 245
hypertrichosis, 178
hysteria, 70, 73n20, 226–27, 228

identity: bodily, 110; changing, 52; concealing, 208; fluid, 214, 215; male, 176, 178; Norwegian cultural, 118, 137, 142–44;

on-screen/off-screen, 131; Western, 94; working-class, 119
illusion: matte techniques, 26; Méliès's effects, 13, 30–31, 32; of Ovid's aesthetics, 30; of phantoms, 264–65; stage, 48–49, 198, 268. See also magic
imagery: acheiropoetic, 194, 204n17; of black bodies, 97, 98; fantastical, 13, 29; lynching, 91; mesmeric power of, 225; of otherness, 60, 94–95, 99; sequential, 103, 110; water, 193. See also before-and-after pictures
imagination, 23, 40, 200, 201–2
imitation. See mimetic behavior
impossible bodies, 2, 4; inside/outside exchange of, 22–23; on-screen portrayals, 11–12; technology and, 18; trick film and, 5, 13–16, 19, 22
Ince, Ralph, 212
Indigenous peoples: before-and-after pictures of, 3, 103, 105–8, *108*; colonizing practices of, 108–9; in frontier melodramas, 112–14
Indigestion, Une (1902), 36, 37–38
insane asylums: educational field trips to, *63*, 64–65; patients' bodies, 59, 65–66, *67–69*, 70–71
inside/outside exchange, 5, 16, 18–19, 22–23
Inslee, Charles, 113, *114*
inventories, bodily, 2, 60
Irish Animated Picture Company (IAPC), 252, 255
Italian strongmen. See *forzuti* (strongmen)
Iversen, Gunnar, 118

Jackson, Robert, 90
Joyce, James, 249, 252, 255

Kalem Company, 276, 278
Karalli, Vera, 191–95, *194*, 198, 203n4, 204n20
Keil, Charlie, 117, 127
Kett, Joseph, 238n11
Keystone Studios, 127–28, 130–31, *131*
Khanzhonkov, Alexander, 192, 203n4
Kholodnaya, Vera, 195, 199–200, *200*, 201, 205n31
Kilanyi, Edward, 26, 27

kinematograph, 11, 100, 167, 192
kinetoscope, 13, 85, 87, 90, 173
King, Rob, 128, 130
Kingston, Winifred, 125, *126*
Kinoplastikon, 261, 268
Köhler, Kristina, 261–62
Král, Petr, 176
Krohg, Per, 135

laboring body: female actors, 120–21, 123, 125–26; risks and danger of, 7, 119; studio life and, 127–28
La Milo (Pansy Montague), 26
Le Breton, David, 35
Leeder, Murray, 46, 54, 57n29
Lefebvre, Thierry, 37–38
Lesuc-Gastrique, Dr., 42
Lichtbild-Bühne (journal), 243–44, 248n21
Life for a Life (1916), 199, *200*, 201
Life magazine, 35
light, 197–98, 200, 205nn25–26
liminality, 4, 5
Lindsey, Shelley Stamp, 227
living pictures. See *poses plastiques*; *tableaux vivants*
living statues: in Bauer's repertoire, 198; comic potential of, 31; in Méliès films, 28–31, 32, 34n22; popularity and variations, 25; Pygmalion trope, 25–27, 152. See also *poses plastiques*; sculptures; *tableaux vivants*
Lloyd, Harold, 123
Loader, Alison Reiko, 3–4, 262
Lotion miraculeuse (1903), 178
Lumière: agents, 181–82, 188n7; catalog, 182; pictures of black bodies, 94, 99, 100–101; supernatural themes, 49, 52, 54, 56n15; train arrival films, 266–67
Lykke-Seest, Peter, 140, 142
lynchings, 59, 85–86, 89–92, *91*
Lynching Scene at Paris, Texas (1897), 89
Lyon républicain, Le (newspaper), 100

Mabel's Dramatic Career (1913), 126–28
MacArthur, Agnes, 295–97
machine-body, 41–43, *42*

Maciste (1915), 147–48
Maciste character. *See* Pagano, Bartolomeo
Maestre Pérez, Tomás ("Dr. Maestre"), 61, 64–66, 70–71
magic, 13, 52; Chinese, 53, 54, 57n31; of cinema, 11, 31; lanterns, 21, 194, 264–65, 272, 273n10; theater, 46, 53, 55n4
Magicien, Le (1898), 28–30
Magic Lantern, The (1903), 21–22
Magic Sword, The (1901), 47, 47–48, 52, 53, 54
makeup: actor denial of use, 208–9; actresses made "ugly," 209–12, *211*; character and straight, 206–7, *208*; facial expressions and, 213–15, *214*; importance of, 174, 206; skin tone and, 165n27; stage *vs.* camera, 207–8; for transformation of race, 212
Malade hydrophobe, Le (1900), 38
male body, 140–42, 146, 265. See also *forzuti* (strongmen); masculinity
Mallarmé, Stéphane, 195, 204n20
Maltby, Richard, 223, 225
mannequins, 29–30
Mar, Ksenia, 195–97, 198, 204n21
Marché, Ernest Gaston, 169, 172n8
Maréorama, 267–68
Marey, Étienne-Jules, 11, 13, 75, 110–11, 265
Marez, Curtis, 109
Marks, Laura U., 4, 237
Marvin, Arthur, 89
masculinity, 118, 147, 179, 180, 223, 228; of boxers and fighters, 140–42, 144; hair and, 176, 177, 178. See also *forzuti* (strongmen); male body
Maskelyne, J. N., 51, 52, 53, 55n4
masks, 197, 201–2, 209
materiality, 117
Maurice, Alice, 174
Maximilian I, Emperor: execution and embalmment, 173, 181–83, 185–86, 188n8, 189n13, 189n16; last words, 190n20; photographic details, *184*, 188n10, 188n12, 189n17
Mayo, Edna, 207, 209–10
"McGinty at the Living Pictures" (Flynn), 156–57
McKenna, Denise, 117

McKernan, Luke, 156–57
Medium Exposed, The (Paul), 52–53
mediums (psychics), 51, 52–53, 55, 55n4
Méliès, Georges, 5, 11; doctor-patient films, 20, 23, 36, 37–38; ghost and fantasy films, 47, *48*, 49, 51, 53–54, 56n14; living-statue films, 28–31, 32, 34n22; trick films, 13–14, 20–21, 29, 32. *See also specific film title*
melodrama, 49, 104; Danish erotic, 135, 142; frontier, 112–15; Irish stage, 252–54; Norwegian rural, 143; Russian, 191, 193; sensational, 128, 244, 245
Merleau-Ponty, Maurice, 18–19, 23
Mes p'tits (1923), 151–52
metaspectatorship, 251–52, 255–56, 258
Mexico, 181–82, 187n7, 188n8
Midgley, Sager, Jr., 207–8
mimetic behavior: of adolescents, 220, 231–33; Benjamin on, 237; of female viewers, 221–22; of film spectators, 2, 7, 235, 236–37, 261
Minguet, Joan, 72n2
Miss Jekyll and Madam Hyde (1915), 214–15
mixed-gendered bodies, 117, 121
mobility, 125, 128, 130; of the face, 197, 209, 213–14
Modèle honnête, Le (Baudoin), 159–60
model (*naturshchik*), 192, 203n11
modernity, 1, 4, 72n18, 115n4, 237; faces of, 193, 196; industrial, 220; nervousness and, 220, 241–42, 244, 245–46; the supernatural and, 54–55; tradition and, 110, 113, 140, 142, 143–44
Molteni, Alfred, 265
morality, 76, 78, 222–23, 227, 294
Morey, Ann, 132n2
Mosjoukine, Ivan, 195–98, *197*, 200, 204n21
motion, bodies in, 1, 43, 59; in before-and-after pictures, 105; in early Norwegian films, 134, 135, 143–44; masculinity of, 140–42; studies by Muybridge and Marey, 11, 13; of viewers, 263, 271, 272. *See also* boxing; dance; living statues
Motion Picture Dancing Lessons (1913), 276, *277*, 278

Motion Picture Magazine, 119, *120*, 123, *124*, 213, *214*
Motion Picture News, 269, *270*
motion studies, 105, 110–11
Moving Picture World (journal), 85, 86, 91–92, 210, 269
Müller, Klara, 240
multiple-exposure technique, 11, 48–49, 57n23
Mulvey, Laura, 46
Münsterberg, Hugo, 231, 232
Musser, Charles, 27, 175, 180n3
mutoscope, 163, 166n32
Muybridge, Eadweard, 11, 13, 25, 110–11

National Police Gazette, 86
Native Americans. *See* Indigenous peoples
naturalism, 171
Navarro, Antonio, 181–82
Neck-Tie Party Given by the Vigilants, A (1898), *91*
Negro, Camillo, 62, 70–71
Neri, Vincenzo, 62, 72n18
nervousness: of female film viewers, 221–22, 225–27; German cinema discourse on, 220, 240–46, 243, 248n21
neurasthenia, 232, 241–42, 247n2. *See also* nervousness
neurology, 64, 70, 72n18
Neuropatología, La (1906-1918), 70–71
New York Clipper (newspaper), 86, 90
New York Dramatic Mirror (newspaper), 269
New York Times (newspaper), 90
nickelodeon era, 6, 91, 251; female audiences, 219, 221, 222, 228. *See also* theaters
Nobel Roed, Halfdan, 134, 140, 143
nonfiction films, 3, 112, 153n7
Normand, Mabel, 121, 123; *Mabel's Dramatic Career*, 126–28
North, Dan, 53
Norwegian cinema: boxing and fighting films, 140–42, *141*; cultural identity and, 142–44; dancing films, 135–40; first films shown, 134
nudity: in Birth of Venus films, 158–59, 161, *162*, 163, 165n28; body coverings, 160; flesh tones, 165n27; male, 147; "naked" distinction, 157–58; paintings, 147, 150, *161*; photographs, 166n38; postcards, 147, *151*, 152; stag films, 3, 158; voyeurism, 163–64

objects: bodies reduced to, 100–101; patients' bodies as, 59, 62, 66, 70–71; scientific, 96
Oftalmología (1917), 65, 71n2
Oleksijczuk, Denise, 296
Olsson, Jan, 90, 251
Omegna, Roberto, 71
Opération chirurgicale (1905), 38–39
Oracle de Delphes, L' (1903), 31, 34n22
orphaned children, 107
otherness, 60, 94–95, 97–98, 99
Ovid, 30; *The Metamorphoses*, 26–27

Pagano, Bartolomeo, 146, 147–48, 152
paintings: academic (*pompier*), 264; the face in, 196; genre, 272n6; nudity in, 147, *161*; *tableaux vivants* of, 27–31, 150, 160, *161*
panoramas, 264, 267, 296
Paraskeva, Anthony, 117
Pates, Gwendolyn, 212
Pathé, 54, 168–69; nude films, 158–59, 161, *162*
Pathéscope, 278, *279*
patients' bodies: dismembered, 20–21, 39–41, *40*; psychiatric, 65–66, 67–69, 70–71; satire of doctors and, 35–39, *38*
Patrick, G. T. W., 239n23
Paul, Robert, 47–48, 51–53, 54, 57n23
Pêle-Mêle, Le (newspaper), 37, *38*, 39, *40*, 42, 42–43
People's Popular Picture Palace (PPPP) (Dublin), 252–54
peplum films, 26
Pepper's Ghost, 48–49, 56n13, 268, 274n32
perception, human, 18
perfect bodies: female, 26, 157; male, 118, 146, 152
performing bodies, 2, 117–18, 119. *See also* acting; boxing; dance
Perruque, La (1905), 179
Petersen, Christina, 219–20
Peterton-Rausch, Oskar John, 281, 284
Petrov, Evgenii, 198

phantom rides, 3, 261, 266–67
phonographs, 5, 81, 181
Phonoscope, The (magazine), 88, 89, 90
photography: of bodies in motion, 13; comparative, 103, 105–6, 110–12, 114; fast-motion, 43; of Maximilian's execution, 173, 181–83, *184*, 185–86, 188n12; mummy complex of, 182–83; nude, 147, 166n38; racialized, 6; snapping pictures, 14–15; spirit, 11, 46, 48–49, 55n4; stereographs, 91. See also before-and-after pictures; camera obscura; chronophotography
Photoplay (magazine), 125, *126*, *129*, *131*
physicality, 11, 104; of film labor, 117, 119–20, 130; grotesque, 25, 27; of slapstick comedy, 121, 127; working-class, 128
physiology: animal experiments of, 13, 74–78, 83n13; human, 14, 15, 19; importance of film and, 79–81
Pierrot et le fantôme (1898), 49, 50
plasticity, 2, 11, 232
play, theories, 231–37
popular culture, 36, 51, 70, 90, 146; art and, 147, 155
pornography, 5, 132n11, 150, 158
Porter, Edwin S., 54, 87; stereoscopic films, 261, 268–69, *270*, *271*
poses plastiques: compared to *tableaux vivants*, 149; eroticism of, 150; Guaita-Ausonia's performances, 118, 146, 149, 150–52, *151*
postcards: of black bodies, 99; of cinemas, 223, 224, 225, *226*; of Indigenous children, 107, 111; male nudity on, 147, *151*, 152
Pratt, Richard Henry, 106–9
precocity, 233
premature aging, 233
"Progress of Science: Cinematographs and Vivisectors: How Pain can be Saved" (*The Times*), 79–81, *80*
projectors, 195, 269, 278, *279*, 281
Prometheus myth, 19
Proust, Marcel, 204n22
Provincial Cinematograph Theatres, 252, 255
psychiatry, 71, 240, 241, 242. See also hysteria; insane asylums; nervousness

Puck (magazine), 293
Pygmalion et Galathée (1898), 28
Pygmalion myth: cinematic adaptations, 27–30, 32; popularity, 25–26

Queen's (Dublin), 252–55
quicksand, 118, 167–68, 170–72
Quo vadis? (1913), 146, 147

racial difference, 110, 125, 214
racialized body, 60, 96–97, 98
Raestad, Bertha, *137*, 137–38
Raheja, Michelle, 114
realism, 11, 225, 267, 296; makeup and, 206, 208, 209, 212; of paintings, 264; three-dimensional, 265–66, 268
recreation, 231, 233–35
reenactments: of "black villages," 99–100; of executions, 86, 87–89, 92, 182
reform movements, cinema, 223, 224, 227, 242, 286n1
Reid, Wallace, 123
religious myth, 31
Renaissance, 49
Repas des négrillons, I (1897), 100
residential schools, 105–6, 113. See also Carlisle Indian Industrial School
Rêve des marmitons, Le (1908), 4
Rhodes, Gary D., 59
Richard, Jacques, 171
Rickard, Jolene, 109
Rilke, Rainer Maria, 204n19
Rire, Le (newspaper), 36, 39, 169
risk, bodily, 2, 7, 119–21, 123, 125
Robert, Valentine, 118
Robertson, E. G., 264–65
Rodríguez Lafo, Gonzalo, 65
Rouclere, Harry, 86
Russian cinema, 173, 191, 192, 203n10

Sacchetto, Rita, 140, 143
Sackville Picture House (Dublin), 252, 255–57
Salambò (1914), 148, 152
Sánchez Salas, Daniel, 59
Sandow, Eugen, 7, 147

savagery and civilization, 96, 97, 111, 112
Scardon, Paul, 215
Schultz-Figueroa, Benjamin, 59
Schwartz, Hillel, 236
scientific filmmaking, 74–75, 80–82
Scranton, W. A., 224
Scrooge, or Marley's Ghost (1901), 47–48, 56n7
sculptures, 27–28, 118, 147, 150, 198; faces of, 191, 192, 196–97, 202, 204n19; *L'Enlisé* (Capellani), 167, *170*, 170–71. See also living statues
Segal, Charles, 27
Seguin, Jean-Claude, 173
Sekula, Allan, 107
self, performances of, 142–44
Selig Polyscope, 89
Sennett, Mack, 126, 130, 235
sexuality: body-coding, 3; camera obscura and, 294–95, 297, 298n19; desire in films, 227–28; encounters at cinemas, 6–7, 221–25, 224, 225, 226; policing of, 294
Shaw, George Bernard, 26
Short, Maria Theresa, 292, 295–97, 299n28
Sienkiewicz, Henryk, 147
silent cinema, 146, 236; research, 2–3
Simmel, Georg, 202, 245
Simondon, Gilbert, 19–20
Simonson, Mary, 139
Singer, Ben, 128
Sirois-Trahan, Jean-Pierre, 266–67
skin color, 3, 97, 107; makeup and, 174, 207
sky, the, 196–97
slapstick comedy: disorder of, 176; disreputable qualities, 128, 130; domestic space and working-class themes, 125–27; gendered norms, 121, 130, 179–80; involving statues, 31; physicality and bodily risk, 119–20, 123; spectators of, 235; studio life and, 128, *129*
Smith, G. A., 49, 52, 56n14
"smoking concert," 158, 166n32
Sobchack, Vivian, 237; film's body concept, 4, 16–17, 22
social-reform movements, 105, 107
Society for Psychical Research (SPR), 49, 50–51, 58n34

Solomon, Matthew, 31
Song of Love Triumphant, The (1915), 199, 201
Soot, Botten, *138*
Soto Vázquez, Begoña, 59
soul, the, 191–92, 197–98, 199
sound synchronization, 281, 284
space: of before-and-after pictures, 104–5, 109, 110, 111–12; body and three-dimensional, 20, 263–69, 271; cinematic, 12, 16, 275–76, 286n1; depth and, 194; domestic, 125, 127; exhibition, 219, 261–62; female, 222–23, 225; imaginary of fantasy, 142; social, 173, 175–77, 253
Spartaco (1913), 146, 148–49, 152
spectatorship: camera obscura, 4, 262, 291–97; Dublin theaters and, 253–58; embodied, 4, 5, 231, 237, 285, 286, 299n33; female, 6–7, 158, 166n32, 219, 221–23, 228n1; and film relationship, 16–18; history of, 275, 286; nervousness and, 220, 226, 240–46; physical reactions, 227, 235–36, 256–57, 261, 268, 275; play and, 234; ritual imperial, 109; three-dimensional space and, 263–69, 271; youth, 220, 231. See also audiences; voyeurism
Spiritualism, 46, 50, 52, 54, 58n34; performers, 51, 55n4; séances, 51, 57n18
sports, 234–35, 239n23
St. Denis, Ruth, 139, 143
staging. See reenactments
Statue Animée, La (1903), 30
statues. See living statues
Steimatsky, Noa, 194
stereoscopy: machines, 265, 266, 271–72; Porter films, 261, 268–69, *270*, 271; sales of 3-D images, 264; use without a screen, 268; viewers' bodies and, 263, 265, 267–68
Stiegler, Bernard, 19–20, 22
Stoichita, Victor, 28, 30
stop-camera technique, 28, 43, 57n23, 85
Story of a Boy, The (1919), 140
Story of the Kelly Gang, The (1906), 253–54
storytelling, 7, 131
Streible, Dan, 142, 166n32
strongmen. See *forzuti* (strongmen)
studio culture, 123, 127–28, *129*, 130–31

stunts, 119, 121
Styka, Jan, 147
supernatural figures, 49–50, 53–55. *See also* ghostly bodies
surgeons. *See* doctors
surveillance, 75, 293, 295
Sutherland, John, 47
swallowing themes, 14–16, 18, 20, 22–23, 125

tableaux vivants: audience reaction to, 156–57; bodysuits, 160; compared to *poses plastiques*, 149; early films, 27–28; nudity, 7, 150, 157–58, 160; of paintings, 159–60, 161, 163; Pygmalion myth adaptations, 25–27; review of, 164n7; settings, 150, 153n13; synonyms, 25. *See also* living statues; *poses plastiques*
Tanz-Kinema Alexanderplatz (Berlin): building plans, 281, *282*, 283, 288n20; closing, 285; dance instruction films, 283–84, 286, 288n17; events and activities, 284–85; launch, 279, 281
technology: connectivity and, 5; death and, 181; experimental medicine and, 75; human body and, 19–20, 22–23; of immersion, 267–68; modern, 21, 241, 285; motion-capturing, 285; as something to hide, 21
temporality, 59, 283; of before-and-after pictures, 103, 105, 110–12, 114–15
Tentation de Saint Antoine, La (1898), 31
theaters: dance instruction screenings, 261, 278, 286; Dublin venues, 220, 249, 251, 252–58; female behavior at, 7, 221, 222–23; sexual encounters at, 6–7, 223–25, *224*, *225*, *226*; vaudeville, 27, 150, 160, 278. *See also* nickelodeon era
Thieving Hand, The (1908), 4, 20
Thousand Steps of Charleston, A (1926), 286
three-dimensional (3-D) images: animated bodies, 268; colored glasses for, 269; fantascope, 264–65; film effects, 266–67; popular systems, 271–72; viewer's body and, 263–64, 271. *See also* Pepper's Ghost
Tiempo Ilustrado, El (magazine), 186
Tiempo Semanario, Il (magazine), 186, 189n16

Tortajada, Maria, 41
Tracked by Bloodhounds (1904), 89–90
traditional art discourses, 244–45
train films, 266–67
travelogues, 266–67, 269
trick films, 20, 215; hair effects in, 176, 177–78; impossible bodies and, 4–5, 13–16, 19, 22
Turner, Florence, 121, 210
Two Republics, The (newspaper), 181, 185

Ullman, Sharon R., 227–28
"Uncle Josh" films (Edison), 51–52, 291
Under the Law of Change (1911), 134, 136–40, 141, 144; images, *137*, *138*, *139*
Up-to-Date Surgery (1902), 20, 23

Väliaho, Pasi, 72n18
vaudeville, 26, 149, 165n22, 242; houses/theaters, 27, 150, 160, 278
Velle, Gaston, 52
Veyre, Gabriel, 181–82, *183*
Vignola, Robert, 212
violence: bodily, 125, 128; of Ovidian myth, 26–27, 30, 32; vivisection and, 82. *See also* executions; lynchings
Visit to the Spiritualist (1899), 51
visual sovereignty, 112, 114
Vitagraph, 210, 212, 214
vivisections: on animal bodies, 6, 76–78; film's role in debate on, 59, 74–75, 79–82, *80*
Voloshin, Maximilian, 193, 196
Volta (Dublin), 249, 252, 255–58
voyeurism, 117, 118; art connoisseur or, 26, 157–58, 163–64, 166nn37–38; camera obscura, 293–94, 297

Wagner, Kristen Anderson, 130
Waif and the Wizard, The (1901), 52
Warfield, David, 209
Washington Post (newspaper), 88
Werder, Stephanie, 219–20
West, William, 212
westerns, 104, 109, 111, 112
What Demoralized the Barber Shop (1898), 176
Williams, Linda, 3, 21–22, 132n1, 297
Williams, Raymond, 238n2

Williamson, James, 12, 14–16
wind machines, 199, 205n31
Wolfe, Patrick, 106
Wood, Amy Louise, 89
working-class culture, 119, 121, 125–30, 141–42; cinemagoers, 128, 252–54, 257–58
workplace conditions, 7, 121, 123, 127–28
Wundt, Wilhelm, 232

X-rays, 35

Young, James, 206–8, *208*, 211
youth, 166n32; Indigenous, 106, 115; play and, 233–34, 237; spectatorship, 220, 231, 253

Zazezizozu (1835), 41, 44n23
zoos. *See* "human zoos"

www.ingramcontent.com/pod-product-compliance
Lightning Source LLC
Chambersburg PA
CBHW061422300426
44114CB00014B/1504